THE EUROPEAN BANKING UNION AND CONSTITUTION

In 2012, at the height of the sovereign debt crisis, European decision makers pushed for developing an 'ever closer union' with the formation of a European Banking Union (BU). Although it provoked widespread debate, to date there has been no coherent discussion of the political and constitutional dimensions of the European Banking Union. This important new publication fills this gap. Drawing on the expertise of recognised experts in the field, it explores banking union from legal, economic and political perspectives. It takes a four-part approach. Firstly, it sets the scene by examining the constitutional foundations of banking union. Then in parts 2 and 3, it looks at the implications of banking union for European integration and for democracy. Finally it asks whether banking union might be more usefully regarded as a trade-off between integration and democracy. This is an important, timely and authoritative collection.

The European Banking Union and Constitution

Beacon for Advanced Integration
or Death-Knell for Democracy?

Edited by
Stefan Grundmann
and
Hans-W Micklitz

•HART•
OXFORD • LONDON • NEW YORK • NEW DELHI • SYDNEY

HART PUBLISHING

Bloomsbury Publishing Plc

Kemp House, Chawley Park, Cumnor Hill, Oxford, OX2 9PH, UK

HART PUBLISHING, the Hart/Stag logo, BLOOMSBURY and the Diana logo are
trademarks of Bloomsbury Publishing Plc

First published in Great Britain 2019

A catalogue record for this book is available from the British Library.

Library of Congress Cataloging-in-Publication data

Names: Grundmann, Stefan, 1958-, editor. | Micklitz, Hans-W., editor.

Title: The European banking union and constitution : beacon for advanced
integration or death-knell for democracy? / edited by Stefan Grundmann, Hans W. Micklitz.

Description: Portland, Oregon : Hart Publishing, 2019.

Identifiers: LCCN 2018044173 (print) | LCCN 2018045920 (ebook) |
ISBN 9781509907564 (Epub) | ISBN 9781509907540 (hardback)

Subjects: LCSH: Banks and banking—State supervision—European Union countries. |
Banking law—European Union countries. | European Central Bank.

Classification: LCC KJE2189 (ebook) | LCC KJE2189 .E97 2019 (print) |
DDC 346.24/082—dc23

LC record available at https://lccn.loc.gov/2018044173

ISBN: HB: 978-1-50990-754-0
ePDF: 978-1-50990-757-1
ePub: 978-1-50990-756-4

Typeset by Compuscript Ltd, Shannon

To find out more about our authors and books visit www.hartpublishing.co.uk.
Here you will find extracts, author information, details of forthcoming events
and the option to sign up for our newsletters.

CONTENTS

PART III
EUROPEAN BANKING UNION,
DEMOCRACY AND TECHNOCRACY

CONTRIBUTORS

Busca, Alessandro is a PhD doctorate from the European University Institute. He holds a law degree from the University of Bologna magna cum laude, and holds a master degree LL.M. from the University of Chicago Law School. He has worked in a number of international institutions and international law firms.

Fabbrini, Sergio is the Director of the School of Government and Professor of Political Science and International Relations at the LUISS Guido Carli University Rome, where he holds a Jean Monnet Chair. He was the editor of the Italian Journal of Political Science from 2003 to 2009. He is Recurring Visiting Professor of Comparative Politics at the Department of Political Science and Institute of Governmental Studies, University of California, Berkley.

Federico, Ferretti is an Associate Professor in Economic and Financial Markets Law, Department of Sociology and Business Law, University of Bologna (Italy). Qualified Lawyer of the High Courts of Italy. Formerly, Senior Lecturer in Law at Brunel University London (UK). Member of the Financial Services User Group (FSUG) of the European Commission, advising the Commission in the preparation of legislation or policy initiatives which affect the users of financial services, providing insight, opinion and advice concerning the practical implementation of such policies, proactively seeking to identify key financial services issues which affect users of financial services, and liaising with and providing information to financial services user representatives and representative bodies at the European Union and national level.

Grundmann, Stefan is a Professor of European and International Private and Economic Law at University of Humboldt and a Professor of Transnational Private Law at European University Institute. He has held chairs of German and International Business Law at the universities of Halle-Wittenberg (1995–2001) and Erlangen-Nürnberg (2001–2004) before he went to Humboldt-University in 2004. He is founding president and current president of the Society of European Contract Law (SECOLA), president of the Luso-German Lawyers Association, co-founder and president of the steering committee of the European Law School and director of several institutes in the universities where he holds or held chairs. He is a member of the board of the German Society of Comparative Law, head of the section 'Fundamental Theory', and as such also a member of the International Academy of Comparative Law (Académie Internationale de Droit Comparé). Moreover, he is member of the European Law Institute and was also member of its council.

Guidi, Mattia is assistant professor in political science at Scuola Normale Superiore (Florence). His research focuses on delegation and institutions, independent regulatory agencies, EU competition policy and EU macroeconomic governance. He has published articles on several international journals, including *JCMS: Journal of Common Market Studies, Regulation & Governance, European Union Politics, European Political Science Review, Acta Politica, Comparative European Politics*, and book chapters for the publishers Palgrave MacMillan and Routledge. His monograph *Competition policy enforcement in EU member states* (2016) is published by Palgrave MacMillan in the European Administrative Governance series.

Micklitz, Hans-W. is Professor for Economic Law at the European University Institute in Florence and Finland Distinguished professor at the University of Finland. He held a Jean Monnet Chair of Private Law and European Economic Law at the University of Bamberg and is Head of the Institute of European and Consumer Law in Bamberg/Berlin. He took Studies of Law and Sociology in Mainz, Lausanne, Geneva, Giessen and Hamburg. He has acted as a Consultant for ministries in Austria, Germany, the UK, the European Commission, OECD, UNEP Geneva/Nairobi, the Gesellschaft für Internationale Zusammenarbeit and national European and international non-governmental organizations. He was Visiting Scholar at the University of Michigan, Ann Arbor; Jean Monnet Fellow at the European University Institute Florence; Visiting Professor at the Somerville College at the University of Oxford and at Columbia University New York; he won an ERC Grant 2011–2016 on European Regulatory Private Law.

Möllers, Christoph Dr. jur. (Munich), LL.M. (Chicago) is a Professor of Public Law and Jurisprudence, Faculty of Law, Humboldt-University Berlin. He was a Fellow at NYU School of Law and at the Wissenschaftskolleg zu Berlin. He is a member of the Berlin-Brandenburg Academy of Sciences. Since January 2011 he has acted as a judge at the Superior Administrative Court in Berlin. From April 2012 he became a Permanent Fellow at the Institute for Advanced Study. His main interests include German, European and comparative constitutional law, regulated industries, democratic theory in public law, and the theory of normativity.

Moloney, Niamh is a Professor of Financial Markets Law, London School of Economics and Political Science. Her research areas include EU financial market regulation, consumer financial protection regulation, institutional governance of financial markets, particularly the EU's institutional arrangements including the European System of Financial Supervision and Banking Union. She is a fellow of the British Academy and sits on the Board of Appeal of the European Supervisory Authorities.

Schweitzer, Heike is the Chair for Private Law and European Economic Law, Competition Law and Regulatory Law at the Freie Universität Berlin; Director of the Institute for German and European Economic Law, Competition Law and Regulatory Law; Director of the Master Program for Business, Competition and Regulatory Law (MBL-FU). In 2017, she became the Special Advisor to EU Commissioner Vestager on Competition Policy.

Singh, Dalvinder is a Professor of Law at the University of Warwick, School of Law. He is an author and editor of several monographs and a number of research papers on banking supervision. Managing Editor of the *Journal of Banking Regulation*, since 2003 and Financial Regulation International, since 2006; he was invited in 2008 to be a member of the International Association of Deposit Insurers, Research and Guidance, Expert Advisory Panel. He has participated in numerous international academic conferences, workshops and high-level policy seminars in financial regulation and supervision. He has delivered training for central banks and regulatory staff for Central Bank Publishing Ltd, and in-house training on UK and US financial regulation at Bank of America – MBNA. He was Fernand Braudel Senior Fellow, EUI, 2016. He is currently working on a monograph titled, *European Cross-Border Banking and Supervision*, Oxford University Press, 2019.

Smoleńska, Agnieszka is a Research Associate with the Florence School of Banking and Finance and a PhD Researcher at the European University Institute. She coordinates the Young Researchers Group of the European Banking Institute. She has taught and published on EU financial regulation matters. She holds a BA in European Social and Political Studies (University College London), an MA in European Interdisciplinary Studies (College of Europe) and a Diploma in Economic Policy from SOAS. Professional experience includes the European Commission (2010–2011) and the European Parliament (2011–2014). Research interests: EU financial governance, cross-border banking, EU competition and company law.

Tridimas, Takis is Professor of European Law at the Dickson Poon School of Law of King's College London and Director of the Centre of European Law. He is also the Nancy A. Patterson Distinguished Faculty Scholar and Professor at Pennsylvania State University and a Visiting Professor at the College of Europe, Bruges. He has acted as advisor to many public and private organisations, including the European Central Bank, the European Parliament, the European Commission and the EU Court of Auditors. He was senior legal advisor to the EU Presidency (2003) and Chairman of the Committee set up by the EU Council of Ministers to draft the Treaty of Accession of 2003 by which ten new States joined the EU. He is a barrister of England and Wales and a qualified advocate in Greece.

LIST OF ABBREVIATIONS

ABSPP	Asset-Backed Securities Purchase Programme
ACCIS	Association of Consumer Credit Information Suppliers
BRRD	Bank Recovery and Resolution Directive
BTS	Binding Technical Standards
BU	Banking Union
BVerfG	Bundesverfassungsgericht (Germany's Federal Constitutional Court)
CBPP3	Covered Bond Purchase Programme
CEE	Central and Eastern Europe
CEN	Comité Européen de Normalisation / European Committee for Standardization
CENELEC	Comité Européen de Normalisation Électrotechnique / European Committee for Electrotechnical Standardization
CESR	Committee of European Securities Regulators
CJEU	Court of Justice of the European Union (also ECJ)
CRD IV	Capital Requirements Directive IV
CRR	Capital Requirements Regulation
DGS	Deposit Guarantee Scheme
DGSD	Deposit Guarantee Scheme Directive
EAPP	Expanded Asset Purchase Programme
EBA	European Banking Authority
ECB	European Central Bank
ECJ	Court of Justice of the European Union (also CJEU)
ECOFIN	Economic and Financial Affairs Council
EDIS	European Deposit Insurance Scheme
EDPS	European Data Protection Supervisor
EFSF	European Financial Stability Facility
EFSM	European Financial Stabilisation Mechanism
EIOPA	European Insurance and Occupational Pensions Authority
ELA	Emergency Liquidity Assistance

EMU	Economic and Monetary Union
EP	European Parliament
ESA	European Supervisory Authority
ESCB	European System of Central Banks
ESFS	European System of Financial Supervisors
ESM	European Stability Mechanism
ESMA	European Securities and Markets Authority
ESRB	European Systemic Risk Board
EU	European Union
FCA	Financial Conduct Authority
IGA	Intergovernmental Agreement
IMF	International Monetary Fund
ITS	Implementing Technical Standards
LOLR	Lender of last resort
LTRO	Longer-term refinancing operations
MoU	Memorandum of Understanding
MREL	Minimum eligible own funds and liabilities requirement
NCA	National Competent Authority
NCB	National Central Bank
NRA	National Resolution Authority
OMT	Outright Monetary Transactions
PRA	Prudential Regulation Authority
PSPP	Public Sector Purchase Programme
QE	Quantitative easing
RAS	Risk Assessment System
RCAP	Regulatory Consistency Assessment Programme
RTS	Regulatory Technical Standards
SB	Supervisory Board
SMEs	Small and medium-sized enterprises
SMP	Securities Market Programme
SRB	Single Resolution Board
SREP	Supervisory Review and Evaluation Process
SRF	Single Resolution Fund
SRM	Single Resolution Mechanism

SSB	Single Supervisory Board
SSM	Single Supervisory Mechanism
TEU	Treaty on European Union
TFEU	Treaty on the Functioning of the European Union
TSCG	Treaty on Stability, Coordination and Governance in the Economic and Monetary Union
US	United States

1

The European Banking Union and Constitution – The Overall Challenge

STEFAN GRUNDMANN AND HANS-W MICKLITZ

I. The Challenge

A. Three Puzzles Regarding the 'European Banking Union'

The European Banking Union is a strange beast. It is a strange beast for at least three reasons.

First, while it can be stated that the Banking Union is only the second or third area of full integration in 60 years of existence – after EEC/EC/EU competition law in the founding years of the Community/Union, and, completely diverse in nature, (Euro) monetary policy installed by the Maastricht Treaty –[1] and while it can certainly be stated that competition law was a foundational policy for the Union in the initial phase, and that with Euro monetary policy (again Treaty-based), a policy of differentiated integration was powerfully installed, the European Banking Union is 'merely' an EU secondary law construct, consisting of two regulations (on supervision and on recovery/resolution), and with a third pillar (on deposit guarantees) still outstanding.[2] Full integration in this respect is used as a term to

---

[1] In the following, for simplicity's sake, we speak only of the 'European Union', irrespective of when the development took place: under the regime of the three Treaties (among them the EEC), later on, under that of the European Community (EC) and finally of the European Union (EU). As we mainly speak about the EU Banking Union – sometimes comparing with the beginnings of (EEC) competition law – these phases do not really matter. The initial step of a fully integrated competition law took place under the regime of the three Treaties, most importantly the Treaty on the European Economic Community (EEC). See on these phases and namely the early phase of EEC/EU competition law, the contribution by Heike Schweitzer, Chapter 5 in this volume.

[2] On these measures and those surrounding, see summary below, section II (and more complete accounts in the contributions by T Tridimas and S Grundmann, Chapters 2 and 4 in this volume. This characterisation – two regulations only – is not meant to bely a view where the whole compound of surrounding and connected acts is seen as well and where, under such a perspective, one can indeed speak of a 'conceptual accordion with different layers'. See R Lastra and J-V Louis, 'European Economic and Monetary Union: History, Trends and Prospects' (2013) 32 *Yearbook of European Law* 1 at 149.

describe a regional (supranational) legal order both at the legislative and at the administrative level, with directly applicable and fully fledged, self-standing EU regulations, ie not requiring national law or only doing so to a very limited extent, and with an EU institution being responsible for implementation in particular cases, again self-standing and with no significant leeway for discretion by the national authorities which might be called to help. Takis Tridimas (in Chapter 2 of this volume) speaks of a 'post-internal market model of regulation [with] strong EU presence' for all financial services now.

Second, the vivid discussion of the European Banking Union obscures to some extent that the bulk of the substantive harmonisation is by no means confined to it (see Niamh Moloney, Chapter 6, and Agnieszka Smoleńska, Chapter 7) but, rather, applies to the EU as a whole. The CRD IV package and the Bank Recovery and Resolution Directive (BRRD) – the latter fundamentally novel, the former also a huge step in more robust banking regulation, with tremendously increased own funds and liquidity requirements and a completely new banking governance, planning for the worst case scenario of bankruptcy – form the true core of the new banking supervision regime. The European Banking Union 'only' adds centralisation of the supervision as such, as administrative implementation for particular cases, while in the case of resolution, intergovernmental co-operation may prevail over centralisation, but has still led to more centralisation in these issues than existed before. Even the name of a 'European Banking Union' to some extent is preposterous. This is only an increased 'Eurozone' integration of banking supervision, namely at the administrative level.

Third, it is often stressed that neither the European Central Bank (ECB) nor the Single Resolution Board (SRB) (see section I.B) are competent for the large majority of banks. Nnowadays they cover 118 so-called SIFIs (Systemically Important Financial Institutions). The SRB exercises oversight over these SIFIs, as well as another 13 particularly interwoven cross-border groups,[3] These financial institutions and groups nevertheless account for the bulk of the banking business and assets in the Union.[4] In other words, the centralised supervision regime(s) (both for current supervision and in limits for recovery and resolution) may have been restricted to a relatively low number of financial institutions. This was partly for reasons of subsidiarity, but mainly because it is only with respect to these institutions that a strong risk of contagion, and hence a danger that regulatory capture of (national) supervisory authorities will affect the whole European Union, can be shown.[5] The impact of the centralised supervision is nevertheless such that

---

[3] For the full list of entities supervised by the ECB (as of 1 January 2018), see https://www.banking-supervision.europa.eu/ecb/pub/pdf/ssm.list_of_supervised_entities_201802.en.pdf. For the full list of cross-border groups covered by the SRM – in addition to the entities already supervised by the ECB (as of 1 February 2018), see https://srb.europa.eu/sites/srbsite/files/5_for_publication_srb_website_list_of_other_cross_border_groups_1februar.pdf.

[4] Between 80 and 85 per cent. For concrete figures for this: K Lannoo (ed), *ECB Banking Supervision and Beyond*, Report of the CEPS Task Force (Brussels, CEPS, 2014) 27.

[5] See more in detail in S Grundmann, Chapter 4 in this volume.

it covers the bulk of the business, and sets the standards for the rest of banking supervision in the Eurozone (see Article 6(5) of the Single Supervisory Mechanism (SSM) Regulation for ECB competence with regard to significant credit institutions) and even for the non-Euro Member States, ie the whole of the European Union.

B. A Summary of the Acts Constituting the 'European Banking Union'

When we look at the three puzzles described above, the substantive basis for the remarks made are the following EU law measures.

The rules on banking supervision as of 2014 are contained in the Capital Requirements Directive (CRD) IV and Regulation (CRR)[6] – for all Member States, supplemented and in some respects (rather moderately) modified in substance by the Regulation on the SSM for the Eurozone Member States.[7] These three measures, two for all Member States, and only the latter for the Eurozone exclusively, form the basis of the first pillar of the European Banking Union. Hence only the last measure formally solely targets the European Banking Union. Therefore, the particular law on the European Banking Union is based on a body of law which is distinct from the normal (albeit particularly dense) harmonisation measure of banking supervision for all EU Member States in three ways: the substance is slightly modified; the EU measure is no longer an EU Directive (to be transposed into national law), but an EU Regulation which is directly applicable within the Member States; and, most importantly, a supranational institution, ie the ECB, is installed to carry out day-to-day supervision (albeit with the help of national competent authorities). One consequence of this structure is that the ECB (not only each national authority) has to apply (slightly) diverging national banking supervision regimes for the respective banks under its supervision.

[6] Directive 2013/36/EU of the European Parliament and of the Council of 26 June 2013 on access to the activity of credit institutions and the prudential supervision of credit institutions and investment firms, amending Directive 2002/87/EC and repealing Directives 2006/48/EC and 2006/49/EC (CRD IV), [2013] OJ L 176/338, and, implementing this directive: Regulation (EU) No 575/2013 of the European Parliament and of the Council of 26 June 2013 on prudential requirements for credit institutions and investment firms and amending Regulation (EU) No 648/2012 (CRR), [2013] OJ L 176/1. For implementing measures (namely on the collaboration with national competent authorities) and for examples of national acts transposing this (package of) EU law measure(s), see the more detailed account in the contribution by S Grundmann, Chapter 4 in this volume.

[7] Council Regulation (EU) No 1024/2013 of 15 October 2013 conferring specific tasks on the European Central Bank concerning policies relating to the prudential supervision of credit institutions, [2013] OJ L 287/63 (based on Art 127(6) TFEU). On the legal basis (in the authors' view not really very doubtful from a purely legal perspective), see the very convincing argument by J Ruthig, 'Die EZB in der europäischen Bankenunion', *Zeitschrift für das gesamte Handelsrecht (ZHR)* 178 (2014) 443, esp at 45060; similar, T Tridimas, Chapter 2 in this volume, at least for the SSM, but probably also for the SRM.

Similarly, the regime on crisis management for banks, ie the recovery and resolution regime, which was much more novel also in substance (indeed this part is
the only one not existing as a harmonisation measure before the financial crisis),
is based on two legs: the substantive harmonisation in the BRRD for all Member
States[8] and the Regulation on the Single Resolution Mechanism (SRM),[9] now only
for the Eurozone Member States. In this case, the new authority created at the EU
level is not the ECB – as an institution already installed by the Treaty – but the
SRB in Brussels (Agnieszka Smoleńska, Chapter 7). The SRM and the Regulation
installing it – in their relationship to the general BRRD regime – again have the
three features identified with respect to the SSM Regulation in its relationship to
CRD IV and CRR.

The third pillar, the deposit guarantee regime (EDIS), has not yet been arranged
in this way, even though it is certainly closely linked to recovery and resolution –
there is only the general harmonisation in this field.[10] While the Banking Union
still looks incomplete, it is far from being clear whether EDIS will ever be adopted,
not least due to the strong resistance from Germany.

---

[8] Directive 2014/59/EU of the European Parliament and of the Council of 15 May 2014 establishing
a framework for the recovery and resolution of credit institutions and investment firms and amending Council Directive 82/891/EEC, and Directives 2001/24/EC, 2002/47/EC, 2004/25/EC, 2005/56/EC,
2007/36/EC, 2011/35/EU, 2012/30/EU and 2013/36/EU, and Regulations (EU) No 1093/2010 and (EU)
No 648/2012, of the European Parliament and of the Council, [2014] OJ L 173/190 ('the BRRD'). Again,
for a more detailed account, see S Grundmann, Chapter 4 in this volume.

[9] Regulation (EU) No 806/2014 of the European Parliament and of the Council of 15 July 2014
establishing uniform rules and a uniform procedure for the resolution of credit institutions and certain
investment firms in the framework of a Single Resolution Mechanism and a Single Resolution Fund
and amending Regulation (EU) No 1093/2010, [2014] OJ L 225/1 (based on Art 114 TFEU) ('the SRM
Regulation'). Positive on the possibility to create new regulatory authorities (in the case of the European Banking Union: the Single Resolution Board in Brussels with the Single Resolution Fund) on the
basis of the internal market competence (Art 114 TFEU): Case C-270/12 *United Kingdom v European
Parliament and Council* ECLI:EU:C:2014:18 (on ESMA and its regulatory powers, namely with respect
to short selling). It is with respect to this part of the European Banking Union system in particular
that the legal basis is seen sceptically and that an amendment of the treaties is called for, because decisions on resolution of banks are likely to provoke more actual litigation in courts, see, for instance,
vice-president of the German Central Bank (*Bundesbank*) Sabine Lautenschläger in Bundesbank of
10.02.2014: *Europäische Bankenunion – ein Großprojekt*; rather affirmative in his forecast that the
Court of Justice of the European Union was also a legal basis for the SRM scheme (see S Grundmann,
Chapter 4 in this volume).

[10] The current EU law regime is contained in: Directive 2014/49/EU of the European Parliament
and of the Council of 16 April 2014 on deposit guarantee schemes, [2014] OJ L 173/149. For the step
proposed towards stronger integration (bringing the scheme within the 'European Banking Union'),
see Proposal for a Regulation of the European Parliament and of the Council amending Regulation
(EU) 806/2014 in order to establish a European Deposit Insurance Scheme, 24.11.2015, COM(2015)
586 final. Some authors name a fourth pillar, the so-called financial backstop, in case the funds of
the Single Resolution Fund (administered by the SRB) are exhausted. See for instance, T Tridimas,
Chapter 2 in this volume, section I. Others see the Single Rulebook as a fourth pillar. In this sense,
for instance, the Austrian Parliament which summarises the so-called Four Presidents' paper 2012
(EU / ECB / IMF / Eurogroup) with the following structure (http://www.parlament.gv.at/PERK/GL/
EU/B.shtml): the European Banking Union encompasses (i) the Single Supervisory Mechanism (SSM),
(ii) the Single Resolution Mechanism (SRM), (iii) the harmonised deposit guarantee scheme and
(iv) the 'Single Rulebook'.

C. The Constitutional Challenge – And How it is Discussed in this Book

All this implies that the questions of advanced integration and of a potential democratic deficit – and linked to the latter, but distinct from it – of the lack of a legal basis for the EU (lack of competence) relate much more to the administrative imposition of the standards (ie to their application in particular cases and to rule production via administration) than to legislation on the standards. This general statement requires, however, specification and modification insofar, as (i) the Supervisory Authority (ECB) has considerable discretion (with regard to many open-textured terms, such as 'public interest' etc) *and* as (ii) the Supervisory Authority (ECB) acts to a large extent also as a Regulator (on the basis of the named Regulations and Directives), albeit in conjunction with or even under the guidance of others, namely the European Banking Authority (EBA) (Niamh Moloney in Chapter 6 puts the emphasis on their relationship). Still, for the discussion of the concerns raised in this book, it is important to note that they are mainly related to centralisation of administration, resulting in a very powerful administration with a lot of leeway in implementation. After Brexit,[11] it might well be that the influence of the ECB on the Single Rulebook even increases beyond the formal backstage role (see Chapter 6).

The constitutional 'turn' that the installation of a European Banking Union brings about can hence be summarised as follows. The European Banking Union in its essence is 'only' about centralisation of the supervisory aspects ('administrative law', more strongly in the SSM mechanism than with respect to SRM, see Agnieszka Smoleńska, Chapter 7, but *inter alia* also centralising data collection on loans, see Federico Ferretti, Chapter 11). Also, it is not about the imposition of banking supervision standards – regulated by a normal harmonisation procedure – and only a relatively small number of banks fall under the scheme of centralised supervision through the ECB. However, the amount of the business covered and the discretion and gap-filling regulatory power of this centralised supervision is such that, combined with a relative shakiness of the legal basis, constitutional concerns are strong. On the one hand, this amount of integration ('full integration') seems plausible as a sound policy step (even if the choice of institutions at the central level leaves some questions open). On the other hand, a strong concentration of decision-making power in the hands of the ECB, weakly legitimised for this issue, raises strong concerns of democratic deficit. These concerns cannot be outweighed by the more intergovernmental design of the SRM. Just the contrary is true. If compared and considered in their interplay, the SSM and the SRM might reflect the divide between monetary policy and centralised supervision in the hands of the ECB, and the economic and fiscal policy in

---

[11] ie the withdrawal of the UK from the European Union.

the hands of the SRB (see Sergio Fabbrini and Mattia Guidi, Chapter 9). However, the regulatory thicket that has been created through competence constraints is far from being based on a clear political concept that documents a political vision for a democratic Europe (see Christoph Möllers, Chapter 8).

In this book (and also in this introduction), the discussion of this core question – perhaps even a dilemma – is arranged in the following three steps:

(1)   The building of a European Banking Union with empowering institutions and authorities at the central level with the administrative implementation raises many constitutional questions – on which a survey is needed (Takis Tridimas, Chapter 2), and among which lawyers might even see the question of legal basis of the EU as the outstanding one (see parts of Chapter 2 and see Alessandro Busca, Chapter 3, in particular, and below section II). Clearly, the exchange between constitutional courts, in this case in Germany and at the EU level (with the Court of Justice of the European Union (CJEU)), concentrates on this issue, but in the line of three to four cases so far, legal basis has not been found to be lacking.

(2)   However, the two lasting and most important constitutional questions from a broad political and from a legal and social sciences perspective may well be two other questions. The first one is whether the best level and good instruments of integration have been found, whether the balance between local (State) influence on supervision and centralisation at the EU level has been struck, and whether and to what extent this new area of full integration affects – and should affect – the overall architecture of the EU and its Member States. In other words, whether the European Banking Union should be seen as a boost for integration more generally, for a new economic constitution (see below section III and Part 2 of the book). This question is first discussed with respect to the European Banking Union itself (Stefan Grundmann, Chapter 4, and also Hans-W Micklitz, Chapter 11 with regard to the differences from the Internal Market project), then the so-called managerial approach is compared to the first paradigm of such a full integration, ie competition law with its reliance on a rule-based approach (Heike Schweitzer, Chapter 5, also Niamh Moloney, Chapter 6, with regard to the ECB steering a particular business model). On this basis, the European Banking Union and its centralised versus federal structure is further explored with respect to four issues mainly: the collaboration between different institutions, namely the ECB and EBA; the impact that Brexit may have (both in Niamh Moloney, Chapter 6); the novel regime of the SRM in particular (Agnieszka Smoleńska, Chapter 7) and the differences in the decision-making procedures within the newly established institutions (Sergio Fabbrini and Mattia Guidi, Chapter 9).

(3)   The second outstanding constitutional question raised by the building of a European Banking Union, is that of the relationship between technocratic expertise and democratic accountability – the balance between expertise and participation (Takis Tridimas, Chapter 2, Niamh Moloney, Chapter 6, Christoph Möllers, Chapter 8, Hans-W Micklitz, Chapter 11). There are

considerable cross-roads between the issue of further integration (and even legal basis) and of democratic legitimacy, still both core questions can potentially receive quite a divergent answer, an ambivalent outcome. Also the second question – like the first one – is discussed in a series of chapters (see below section IV and Part 3 of this book): the first two chapters coming to diverging results, inspired by political philosophy and political science, one analysing the subtleties of deviations from traditional models and coming to the result that indeed democratic legitimacy is too weak (Christoph Möllers, Chapter 8), the other emphasising the still rather strong influence of national institutions and parliaments in the process and hence, with quite some legitimacy, characterising the scheme as one of 'tempered supranationalism' (Sergio Fabbrini and Mattia Guidi, Chapter 9). A third interpretation would seem to stand in between and invokes deliberative supranationalism and 'through put' as a new form of legitimacy (Agnieszka Smoleńska, Chapter 7). These three more overarching chapters are followed by others on more specific topics that sharpen the overall argument on centralisation versus supranational governance and on the new economic constitution enshrined in the Banking Union: the analysis of the Bank Credit Data Registry (AnaCredit) and the legitimacy questions that result from centralising data collection on loans in the hands of the ECB thus potentially superseding established national institutions that already aimed at providing information on creditworthiness (Federico Ferretti, Chapter 10); an inquiry into the relationship between the particular regime of fully integrated European Banking Union in strong contrast to the internal market agenda that underpins the particularities of the Banking Union (Hans-W Micklitz, Chapter 11); and finally an inquiry into the question of how governance of banking supervision in the Eurozone and governance in the non-Eurozone interrelate (Dalvinder Singh, Chapter 12).

II. An Introduction to the Constitutional Panorama

This book is on the European Banking Union and Constitution, mainly the EU 'Constitution'. It does, however, not aim to exhaust the constitutional questions which the evolution of the European Banking Union raises, but rather only those two which still stand out and are arguably of long-term constitutional importance. These are: (1) the European Banking Union as a (potential) boost to integration (or even new blueprint for integration), and (2) the European Banking Union as a (potential) blow to democracy. As this leaves out the other 'constitutional' questions raised by the installation of the European Banking Union, the book starts out with a panorama of a several of them. Most important among these questions, according to many authors, is that issues of legal basis are not taken up in the main two parts – or are only dealt with incidentally. The question of legal basis is not seen as one of the two outstanding features, but rather as an important, yet rather 'preliminary' question – which Takis Tridimas discusses in parts of Chapter 2 and to which Alessandro Busca devotes the whole of Chapter 3. Larger constitutional and democratic implications result from the impact of the Banking Union on the institutional architecture and the political direction of the EU.

A. A Panorama

This panorama, as Takis Tridimas puts it in Chapter 2,[12] encompasses the following issues (in part taken up in the course of the discussion). First, in the aftermath of the Maastricht Treaty, an asymmetry between monetary policy (fully centralised) and economic and fiscal policy (still strongly decentralised) constitutes a clear new architectural design feature of the Union. This has repercussions for the question of legal basis for several measures triggered by the financial crisis and also, at least indirectly, for those installing the European Banking Union. The picture may, however, also be changing, with the European Banking Union (which arguably is a part of economic policy and touches upon fiscal policy) now being so heavily centralised at the EU level, but also with the 'Six-Pack' pushing into this direction as well.

Second, in the tension between monetary and economic policy, the role of the ECB gained momentum not only because it was given banking supervisory powers for SIFIs – which was of course a huge gain in power – but also, more indirectly, because the European Court of Justice did not see the ECB as being excluded from influencing economic policy as long as monetary policy still remained a core aim and was not merely indirectly affected (*Gauweiler/OMT* case,[13] see section II.B).

Third, the European Banking Union – with a special regime for the Eurozone regime – perpetuates (for some authors 'exacerbates') the trend towards differentiated integration, powerfully brought into the constitutional architecture of the EU with the installation of the Euro. However, while monetary policy with respect to the Euro does not contain many instruments imposing requirements and commands on economic actors – and is mainly based on open market instruments – banking supervision is highly coercive and directed towards individual regulatory actions against particular banks. Therefore, in this area, differentiated integration also raises much more concern regarding (un)equal treatment of the economic players affected – the banks within and those outside the Eurozone.

Fourth, the creation of authorities with supervisory powers at the centralised (EU) level – still formally tested against the *Meroni* doctrine[14] – blurs the

---

[12] See also, particularly influential in the analysis carried out by Tridimas in Chapter 2: K Tuori and K Tuori, *The Eurozone Crisis. A Constitutional Analysis* (Cambridge, Cambridge University Press, 2014), and P Leino-Sandberg, 'Further developments of the EMU – should legitimacy come first or last?', available at http://eulawanalysis.blogspot.be/2015/11/further-development-of-emu-should.html.

[13] Case C-62/14 *Peter Gauweiler and Others v Deutscher Bundestag*, EU:C:2015:7.

[14] On the erosion of *Meroni* even before the Banking Union, see T Tridimas, 'Community Agencies, Competition Law and ECSB Initiatives on Securities Clearing and Settlement' (2009) 28 *Yearbook of European Law* 215.

lines firmly established in the old architectural design where centralisation was reserved for legislative matters, ie harmonisation at the EU level, but administrative implementation was left to the Member States. The outcome in the *ESMA/SSR* case before the CJEU (see section II.B) strongly puts in doubt this border and distribution of powers.

Finally, Tridimas analyses in detail how the role of the ECB has changed, with the increased leeway for policy decisions both on the grounds of the *Gauweiler* case (Outright Monetary Transactions (OMT) measures) and with the advent of banking supervision in 'full independence', two powerful extensions in a very short time. All this has taken place against a background of strongly diverging national views on what monetary policy should strive for – divergences which have already traditionally been internalised into the ECB decision process, but are becoming more numerous and hence transforming the ECB into a broader political actor (not necessarily helping its independence and neutrality). Tridimas rightly stresses the shift from monetary to financial stability as today's leading paradigm in the arena of currencies and finance, which blurs the line with fiscal policy.

B. Legal Basis in Particular

Questions of legal basis have been prominent over the last years regarding the ECB and EU authorities having centralised supervision powers in the area of financial services. This area is the first to have really triggered a 'conversation' between the European Court of Justice and the German Constitutional Court, which early on claimed an ultimate power of control with respect to fundamental rights, and in recent years with respect to the foundations of democracy and national constitutional identity. Still, the three, soon four, cases relevant in this respect do not reflect directly upon the EU law measures on which the European Banking Union is based.

The cases analysed in Chapters 2 and 3 (Takis Tridimas and Alessandro Busca) revolve around other, yet related, issues from the areas of monetary policy and financial supervision more broadly speaking. The most relevant case for matters of legal basis for the European Banking Union may well be the pending reference from the German Constitutional Court, while the CJEU cases concerning OMT measures and *Pringle* are mainly of importance in their general thrust inasmuch as they upheld the political solution chosen. In one case, this was the solution chosen by the Member States (*Pringle/ESM* where the Stability Mechanism was installed via their competence, namely an international convention); in the other, an action was taken by the ECB (*Gauweiler/OMT*, where the announcement by the ECB to take OMT measures to stabilise Member States' finance and thereby the Euro as a currency was scrutinised by the CJEU). Both measures as they had been taken were upheld, strangely converging in their defence of the existing competence order, because in one case the legal basis was found to exist for the Member States ('economic policy'), in the other it was found for the ECB ('monetary policy'). While OMT measures have never been in place, the Public Sector Purchase

Programme (PSPP) measures have resulted in massive volumes being purchased already. Therefore, it is possible that the picture will change with the new case pending (although the monetary thrust of this programme, in the present authors' view, is clearly higher than that of the OMT measures).[15] From *Gauweiler/OMT* to *PSPP* – both preliminary references by the German Constitutional Court – the style of 'exchange' between the courts shifted from confrontation to collaboration, namely on the German Court's side.

These cases would nevertheless not seem to be as relevant as the *ESMA* case[16] – dealing with the installation of a new supervisory authority and conferral of supervisory powers upon it. Indeed, Alessandro Busca in Chapter 3 sees a thin 'red line' between both areas which he analyses. In the *ESMA* case both installation of a new supervisory authority and conferral of supervisory powers upon it were upheld (on the very general basis of Article 114 of the Treaty on the Functioning of the European Union (TFEU)). As these powers were considerable (total ban of short selling) and given to a recently established EU body (ESMA, an EU agency), the conferral of supervisory powers on the basis of Article 127(6) TFEU to an already existing institution, ie the ECB, and on a specific, yet limited legal basis would seem *a fortiori* warranted. This is the view of the authors of Chapters 2 and 3. It seems all the more warranted as supervision is not only limited in terms of the number of banks under the direct supervision of the ECB, but covers broader areas and criteria of scrutiny (stability concerns, but not consumer protection issues, see Stefan Grundmann, Chapter 4). Even conferral of such powers upon the newly created SRB (again on the basis of Article 114 TFEU) would not seem to go clearly beyond the *ESMA* findings. The authors of this chapter would agree with Tridimas when he summarises: 'The dice is heavily loaded in favour of EU intervention.' The one puzzle remaining might, however, be that a whole sector – banking supervision, recovery and resolution – still is of a different dimension to 'solely' one type of transaction such as short selling (despite its enormous volume and importance in the financial crisis).[17]

---

[15] For the three cases see: C-370/12 *Pringle v Ireland*, EU:C:2012:756; Case C-62/14 *Gauweiler*, EU:C:2015:4005; Case C-270/12, *United Kingdom v European Parliament and Council* (ESMA), EU:C:2014:18. For the fourth case, still pending before the ECJ, see preliminary reference by the German Constitutional Court, *Weiss et al*, not yet in the *official reports*, but *Wertpapier-Mitteilungen (WM)* 2017, 1694 = *Neue Juristische Wochenschrift (NJW)* 2017, 2894 (*PSPP*); not admitted to the accelerated procedure under Art 105 of the ECJ Procedural Regulations, Case C-493/17 *Weiss et al*, EU:C:2017:792, as well as T Tridimas, Chapter 2 in this volume.

[16] See n 14 above.

[17] On figures in this respect (very uncertain before the introduction of disclosure requirements by the EU Short Selling Regulation), see S Grünewald, A Wagner and R Weber, 'Short Selling Regulation after the Financial Crisis – First Principles Revisited' (2009) 7 *International Journal of Disclosure and Regulation* 108; G Mattarocci and G Sampagnaro, 'Financial Crisis and Short Selling: Do Regulatory Bans Really Work? Evidence from the Italian Market' (2011) 15 *Academy of Accounting and Financial Studies Journal* 115; J Payne, 'The Regulation of Short Selling and Its Reform in Europe' (2012) 13 *EBOR* 413 (415 et seqq); P Tritschler, *Die Regulierung von Leerverkäufen als Folge der Finanzkrise* (Bern, Peter Lang, 2015) 21–27; see also Commission Staff Working Document – Impact Assessment Accompanying Document to the Proposal for a Regulation of the European Parliament and of the Council on Short Selling and Certain Aspects of Credit Default Swaps, *COM*(2010) 482, pp 28–30.

III. The European Banking Union as a Boost to Integration?

A. European Banking Union – Its Prominence and its Parts

Supposing that there is a suitable legal basis for both the legislation of the SSM and that of the SRM – which would seem to be the majority view and, for the SSM case even almost an unanimous view (see section II.B) – the core question remaining to be discussed in Part II of the book (and in this section III) is how full integration – and also integration and centralisation with respect to administrative procedures albeit in different degrees – is arranged. Again, SSM and SRM offer quite divergent features, and both schemes are thoroughly discussed. The SSM is covered by Stefan Grundmann in Chapter 4 and Niamh Moloney in Chapter 6 and also in the comparison carried out with competition law by Heike Schweitzer in Chapter 5. The SRM, with its particularly complex institutional design, is then addressed as a separate topic by Agnieszka Smoleńska in Chapter 7, leaning towards intergovernmental co-operation. In carrying out this analysis, attention is paid to the fact that 'administrative procedures' also imply the setting of technical and regulatory standards and other types of guidelines which carry a considerable amount of rule setting – an exercise in which the interplay between ECB (competent for the Eurozone), the EU Commission (as the prime regulator for the whole of the EU) and EBA (as the specific banking supervision regulator, also for the whole of the EU) is of particular importance (see, in particular, section III of Chapter 6 by Niamh Moloney).

The focus on the 'administrative procedures' is due to the fact that centralisation of the administrative implementation constitutes the only feature where the Eurozone regime (the European Banking Union) is distinct from the non-Eurozone regime, while the underlying harmonisation in the CRD IV package and in the BRRD applies to the whole of the EU (with EBA as specific regulator and coordinator between Eurozone and non-Eurozone Member States, Chapter 6, section III, by Niamh Moloney, and see also Chapter 12 by Dalvinder Singh). This focus on administrative centralisation does not, however, imply that the underlying harmonisation does not also constitute an enormous step, and, in the case of the BRRD, even something completely new – arguably a step of equal (and perhaps even higher) importance as (than) the 'European Banking Union'. The latter owes its higher prominence probably not only to the novelty of its constitutional design (centralisation of administration, here conceived, rather, as intergovernmental collaboration), but also to the fact that it is seen in conjunction with these substantive law dimensions, ie that the latter are 'factored in' when considering the European Banking Union.[18]

---

[18] For (a considerable variety of) delimitations of what constitutes the 'European Banking Union', see n 10 above.

B. European Banking Union – Main Points of Consideration on its Integration Design (SSM and SRM)

For the European Banking Union in general and for the SSM in particular (see Stefan Grundmann, Chapter 4, and Niamh Moloney, Chapter 6, section II), the starting point is that it constitutes only the second area where an administrative imposition of coercive measures on single economic players has been entrusted to an institution at the EU level – the potentially still more incisive SRM, the other pillar of the European Banking Union, following only two years later (and the monetary policy being of a different kind, with rather marginal coercive powers). Therefore, a comparison with EU competition law – when the imposition of the law was still totally entrusted to the EU Commission – would seem to be helpful to shed light on the characteristics (see Heike Schweitzer, Chapter 5, and also Stefan Grundmann, Chapter 4, section IV).

Looking at the overall development concerning the issue of centralisation and decentralisation, the single most important theoretical development would seem to be the development of a more positive view of decentralisation, namely with the concept of regulatory competition, which in the EU is also seen as governmental experimentalism.[19] More precisely, the state of the art today is that neither centralisation nor decentralisation are to be preferred systematically, but that a case-by-case analysis of the advantages and the disadvantages of centralised legislation, and also administration, is required. Centralisation will be the preferable answer in some areas or respects, decentralisation in others, and a mixture will be preferable in yet other cases (and, indeed, in most cases)[20] – the EU's motto of an 'ever closer Union' somehow lagging behind this development.

The design of the SSM clearly shows such a nuanced approach, with a careful delineation (i) of banks covered and banks not covered (ie only those with a high

[19] Ch F Sabel and O Gerstenberg, 'Constitutionalising an Overlapping Consensus: The ECJ and the Emergence of a Coordinate Constitutional Order' (2010) 16 *European Law Journal* 511; Ch F Sabel and J Zeitlin, 'Learning from Difference. The New Architecture of Experimentalist Governance in the EU' (2008) 14 *European Law Journal* 271; Ch F Sabel and J Zeitlin 'Experimentalism in the EU: Common Ground and Persistent Differences' (2012) 6 *Regulation & Governance* 410.

[20] Foundational, R Romano, 'Law as a Product – Some Pieces of the Incorporation Puzzle' (1985) 1 *Journal of Law, Economics, and Organization* 225. For today's view on these issues and namely regulatory competition as being embedded in this broader – constitutional – analysis, see, for instance: W Kerber, 'European System of Private Laws: an Economic Perspective' in F Cafaggi and H Muir-Watt (eds), *Making European Private Law – Governance Design* (Cheltenham, Edward Elgar, 2008) 65–97 (probably the most systematic account summarising literature on the possible advantages and disadvantages, with beautiful table summarising the effects at p 76); moreover on regulatory competition nowadays, among the many and for different areas: O Bar-Gill, M Barzuza and L Bebchuk, 'The Market for Corporate Law' (2006) 162 *Journal of Institutional and Theoretical Economics (JITE)* 134; R Cooter, *The Strategic Constitution* (Princeton, University Press, 2000) 130–39; K Gatsios and P Holmes, 'Regulatory Competition' in P Newman (ed), *The New Palgrave Dictionary of Economics and the Law*, vol 1 (London, Macmillan, 2002) 271 at 273–75; F Gomez, 'The Harmonization of Contract Law through European Rules: a Law and Economics Perspective' (2008) 4 *ERCL* 89 at 95–103.

risk of contagion, and hence impact on the whole Eurozone and its currency), (ii) of aims and areas under the supervision of the ECB (only stability concerns, not market integrity and consumer concerns as long as they do not also affect stability), and (iii) the design of the decision-making process within the ECB, namely the joint supervisory colleges (combining input of local information with a voting power that avoids [national] home country bias and regulatory capture). Diversity at least in parts (such as for the supervision on codes of conduct) with respect to countries covered and in institutions, is combined with unity in a nuanced way. It is clear, however, that the elements of unification and centralisation are dominant overall, and that the history of the financial crisis, with a strong element of regulatory capture at the decentralised level (on the side of the national supervisory authorities)[21] and with a direct conduit of contagion into savings in Euro in all Eurozone Member States, would seem to constitute rather strong arguments pointing into this direction – namely the disastrous links between bank funds and State funds (budgets), with the former investing into bonds of the latter, and the latter bailing out the former.

From an integration perspective – with respect to the question of whether administration should be centralised – one can also quite consistently justify the need, although at first sight it is not obvious, to make a distinction between supervision within and outside the Eurozone. Even if, for instance, the Bank of England had been or was taken by regulatory capture in much the same way as the national supervisory authorities within the Eurozone, centralising administrative powers for the latter only would seem to be plausible under a 'federalist' perspective, because the negative external effects experienced between Member States of the Eurozone are much stronger than those between the UK and the Eurozone countries (and external effects indeed strongly speak in favour of centralisation). The reason is that inside one currency zone, budgetary deficits caused by bailouts affect the stability of the currency of the others as well. These links led to the situation where the financial crisis did not remain only a financial crisis, but turned into a Eurocrisis in addition. This, however, constitutes only a rough delineation,

---

[21] On the concept of 'capture' of public bodies by their constituencies, first discussed for rule setting rather than administration or adjudication, see ground breaking G Stigler, 'The Theory of Economic Regulation' (1971) 2 *Bell Journal of Economics and Management Science* 3; and earlier S Huntington, 'The Marasmus of the ICC: The Commission, the Railroads, and the Public Interest' (1952) 614 *Yale Law Journal* 467; and F Böhm, 'Privatrechtsgesellschaft und Marktwirtschaft' (1966) 17 *ORDO* 75; further developed by J Laffont and J Tirole, 'The Politics of Government Decision Making. a Theory of Regulatory Capture' (1991) 106 *Quarterly Journal of Economics* 1089; M Levine and J Forrence, 'Regulatory Capture, Public Interest, and the Public Agenda – Toward a Synthesis' (1990) 6 *Journal of Law Economics & Organization* 167. On this phenomenon as cause of the financial and also – linked to it – of the Euro crisis, see for instance: D Sahil, Ch Franz, C Gandrud and M Hallerberg, 'Preventing German Banks Failures: Federalism and Decisions to Save Troubled Banks' (2015) 2 *Politische Vierteljahresschrift*.

and within the scheme more nuances are needed, for instance when it comes to groups of banks. The consciously calibrated interplay between (dominant) features of unity and features of diversity constitutes probably the one characteristic which most strongly distinguishes 'full integration' in banking supervision (within the European Banking Union) and 'full integration' in competition law (for more differences between managerial versus rule-based styles, see Chapter 5 by Heike Schweitzer).

The departure of the dominant non-Eurozone Member State from the EU (Brexit) will clearly have repercussions on the development of institutional design and practice (see on this, Niamh Moloney, Chapter 6, section III). Fears that Brexit would adversely affect the ECB in the prompt development of its own supervisory approach do not seem to have come true or, only to a rather moderate extent. On the other hand, however, the equilibrium between the EBA – as the homestead for a balance between all EU Member States in banking supervision issues – and the ECB will certainly be affected when the largest and particularly prominent non-Eurozone Member State leaves. While EBA remains competent to draft the Single Rulebook, with final approval of the European Commission, the content may well be influenced mainly by the ECB – and this Rulebook will dominate day-to-day supervisory practice and potentially also influence questions related to client relationships.

The SRM (see Chapter 7 by Agnieszka Smoleńska) constitutes a world apart. Probably the most interesting feature of the SRM – which also strongly diverges from the SSM scheme – is to be seen in the involvement of multiple decision-makers at various levels; the SRB clearly does not have the same 'last say' in questions of recovery and resolution as the ECB in questions of current supervision. This may have its explanation in the question of the legal basis (SRB being created on the basis of the general rule in Article 114 TFEU, not constituting an institution under the Treaty itself; the ECB is such an institution and one which moreover is called upon to supervise, at least in principle, under Article 127(6) TFEU). This may also be motivated by the more incisive – and hence also political – nature of a recovery or a resolution as compared to 'mere' current supervision. Agnieszka Smoleńska and also Sergio Fabbrini and Mattia Guidi (Chapters 7 and 9) see as a consequence a higher degree of accountability, at least to the Member States, but potentially also to (primarily national) parliaments. This is all the more important as core concepts and prerequisites are highly open-textured, such as those of 'public interest' (leading to recovery proceedings rather than resolution) or of 'critical functions' to be maintained in recovery proceedings. One of the most fascinating areas of interplay between the two regimes – and hence also of approach to different modes of mixture of centralised and decentralised supervision – is that of the so-called 'living will' and 'recovery planning' where, still under the auspices of the ECB, a future recovery is planned – starting from a set of diverging scenarios of (adverse) developments.

C. European Banking Union – Blueprint and Boost More Generally for Future Integration?

Starting from the view that the interplay of integration and of upheld diversity is astonishingly well designed – after all, it was speedily created in a moment of crisis – the answer to the overall question asked might surprise. Even if the SSM and SRM to a large extent can be seen as rather successful pieces of full harmonisation, taking into account the need for mixed and nuanced solutions, and also being 'state of the art' in theoretical terms, they should nevertheless *not* serve as a blueprint for other areas. Rather, they would seem to be a very particular case where a boost of integration was helpful and probably needed. Already, in the adjoining areas of deposit scheme guarantees and financial backstop, the political will to find a similarly integrated scheme seems to be less strong. In capital market law, another adjoining area, the push towards such solutions seems even less strong – with not even a strong alliance in favour forming (but with no convincing opposition, as with respect to EDIS). In still other areas, while single solutions developed in the SSM or SRM – like, for instance, joint supervisory committees – might find useful applications in other areas of the law, the overall question on the interplay between centralised versus decentralised administrative enforcement needs to be answered on a different basis. In order to do so it is key to refer to normative standards such as those developed in the theory of federalism (weighing the advantages and disadvantages of centralisation and of decentralisation, leaving leeway for national and European experimentalism) and not imitating or taking up the dynamics triggered by the installation of the European Banking Union.

IV. The European Banking Union as a Blow to Democracy?

The impact of globalisation (as illustrated by Lehman Brothers) and the claimed neoliberal movement by the EU in the aftermath of the Euro crisis have triggered much concern in the discussion of law,[22] legal theory[23] and political science.[24]

---

[22] There is a large volume of literature eg D Kochenov, G de Búrca, A Williams (eds), *Europe's Justice Deficit?* (Oxford, Hart Publishing, 2015); D Chalmers, M Jachtenfuchs and Ch Joerges (eds), *The End of the Eurocrats' Dream. Adjusting to European Diversity* (Cambridge, Cambridge University Press, 2016).

[23] There is a large volume of literature focusing on the changing role of the nation State. A Somek, *The Cosmopolitan Constitution* (Oxford, OUP, 2014), St K Vogel *Marketcraft. How Governments Make Markets Work* (Oxford, OUP, 2018); and on the regulatory role of law, M Findley, *Law's Regulatory Relevance?* (Cheltenham, Elgar, 2017).

[24] Again there is an abundant literature on the role of the Monetary Union here: F Scharpf, 'Monetary Union, Fiscal Crisis and the Pre-Emption of Democracy' (2011) 9 *Zeitschrift für Staats- und Europawissenschaften / Journal for Comparative Government and European Policy* 163; W Streeck, 'Scenario for a

The overall critique from the 'left' and the 'right' puts the loss of national sover-eignty and the salient hollowing out of democracy through globalisation and the EU into the limelight. Neoliberalism plays a key role in that discourse although it usually remains undefined.[25]

This book has a much narrower focus: it looks at how the Banking Union is being defined through its two pillars (SSM and SRM) or three pillars (EDIS) and the way this affects the constitution and the democracy. So far, only the compe-tence of the EU has been challenged before courts, in the three cases concerning ESMA/SSR, Gauweiler and Quantitative Easing.[26] There has not (yet?) been such a challenge regarding the constitutional function of 'independence' of the ECB and of the European Supervisory Authorities, or the impact of the Banking Union on national sovereignty, national identity – whatever the meaning of this might be in light of Article 4(2) of the Treaty on European Union –[27] as well as on the role and function of national Parliaments or the European Parliament, or the even more straightforward question on the claim of supremacy of EU law over national law. The non-competence issues, however, dominate the academic discourse and to some extent the public political discourse in an increasing number of Member States, in particular Hungary, Poland, and now Italy and the Netherlands. This debate is likely to gain pace in the post-Brexit area.

Out of the variety of questions triggered, two to three are taken up in the book. The first is the concept of 'independence' and the potential influence of national Parliaments on the European institutions, the second is whether and to what extent the EU is able to generate legitimacy through new modes of inter- and trans-institutional governance which meet democratic standards.

A. The Democratic Implications of Independence

All contributions to this book are united in the overall emphasis they put on the key role of the ECB and its two-fold increase of power – first through its supervision responsibilities, directly with regard to the systemically relevant banks, indirectly through its influence on those banks which are supervised by the national authori-ties and, secondly, through the more indirect influence that the ECB unfolds on the EBA in elaborating the Single Rulebook (see Chapter 6 by Niamh Moloney).

Wonderful Tomorrow, Book review of *Europe's Orphan: The Future of the Euro and the Politics of Debt* by Martin Sandbu (Princeton: Princeton University Press 2015)', (2016) 38 *London Review of Books* 7; W Streeck, *How Will Capitalism End?* (London, Verso, 2016).

[25] For a deeper understanding, see C Crouch: *The Strange Non-Death of Neoliberalism* (Cambridge, Polity Press 2011); W Davies, *The Limits of Neoliberalism, Authority, Sovereignty and the Logic of Competition* (London, Sage, 2014).

[26] See references in n 14 above.

[27] On these issues, albeit with respect to the Six-Pack, see (not yet published) PhD dissertation by A Busca, *A Legal and Economic Assessment of the EMU's Common Principles and Alternatives of Budget-ary Restraints* (2018).

Equally, there is agreement on the view that putting the supervision in the hands of the ECB was not a deliberate political choice but a combination of lack of alternatives and path dependency. One core concern has always been that supervision powers (over the most extended part of finance in the EU) now came in addition to powers in monetary policy.

The concentration of power in rule making and rule enforcing in one single supranational institution might already be a democratic problem *in se*, in particular when no serious system of checks and balances is in place. The accountability towards the European Parliament is weak, not only in practice (Niamh Moloney, Chapter 6),[28] but in particular through its constitutional design as clear sanctions in case of infringements are missing (Christoph Möllers, Chapter 8). Its constitutionally guaranteed independence in combination with its plenitude of power, both in monetary policy and in supervision, turns the ECB into the main political actor in the Banking Union, but also well beyond that, ie in the whole of finance in the EU. Of course, formally the monetary policy and supervision are divided. However, Sergio Fabbrini and Mattia Guidi (Chapter 9, section III.B) have convincingly shown how the SSM rules are designed so as to allow the ECB to dominate the Single Supervisory Board (SSB). Still, there is a difference between the constitutionally granted independence in the monetary policy and the independence granted via secondary law against intrusion from the Commission, the European Parliament or the Council in the decision-making process.[29] Here the ECB benefits from the independent status granted to the national authorities under EU law.

However, there is more than the legally guaranteed independent status of the ECB, be it via primary or secondary EU law, to be considered. In the Banking Union, there is no second EU actor holding a stable political position like that of the ECB, not even the European Commission (Christoph Möllers, Chapter 8). The presidency of the European Council changes every six months and the European Parliament is merely bound to engage in a dialogue. The statement by the President of the ECB, Mario Draghi: 'Within our mandate, the ECB is ready to do whatever it takes to preserve the euro' (see Alessandro Busca, Chapter 3) has turned the ECB into the single most important European actor. Draghi's declaration, formally within the ECB competence as approved by the CJEU and by the German Constitutional Court, was in fact a political statement that prepared the ground for the European Banking Union (see Hans-W Micklitz, Chapter 11). A single statement, economic in nature, but political in effect, is claimed to have gained a quasi-constitutional character.[30] Ironically enough, the building of the

---

[28] Where she refers to W Buiter, 'Alice in Euroland' (1999) 37 *Journal of Common Market Studies* 181 and F Amtenbrink and K van Duin, 'The European Central Bank before the European Parliament: Theory and Practice after Ten Years of Monetary Dialogue' (2009) *European Law Review* 561.

[29] On the understanding and the problematic of 'independence': A Ottow, *Market and Competition Authorities, Good Agency Principles* (Oxford, OUP, 2015).

[30] W Streeck, 'Heller, Schmitt and the Euro' (2015) 21 *European Law Journal* 361.

Banking Union and the way that it was targeted towards the ECB weakened its independent status. The ECB, argues Christoph Möllers, has become much more dependent on all sorts of informal influences – from the left and from the right, from sovereignists and Europeanists. There are no constitutional principles which guide the choice between Scylla and Charybdis (see Chapter 8).

What is true for the SSM and for the role of the ECB is not at all true for the SRM and the SRB. Sergio Fabbrini and Mattia Guidi (Chapter 9) provide a sophisticated analysis of their legislative history. It shows how the Member States transformed the supranational centralised proposals of the Commission into a more decentralised intergovernmental mechanism where the national parliaments are involved. This is true for the composition of the SRB, the resolution procedure and the legal instrument used to transfer funds to the Single Resolution Fund, and the managing of the 'transitional period'. If EDIS is ever adopted, it does not take much imagination to assume that the Member States and their national parliaments will have to play a key role in the composition of the relevant institutions and the design of the decision-making procedure.

Still, on the other hand, it is in the area of recovery/resolution and of deposit guarantee schemes that one other core concern is primarily rooted. While before the global financial crisis, and before the legislative and administrative reactions to that crisis in the EU, the EU could still be seen as an arbiter – although lacking considerable funds – which adjudicated between Member States and which took legislative action, but which could not steer economic and fiscal policies via sheer input of money, and therefore still satisfied the ordo-liberal design image of split of tasks, these times have changed. It is now also outside monetary policy that the EU disposes or steers huge volumes of funds. These, however, primarily flow into recovery/resolution and – potentially in the future – into deposit guarantee schemes. In this respect, it is the SSM, ie the first pillar, that is more 'conservative', with the EU still mainly playing the role of an arbiter and supervisor, not of the administrator of funds. On the other hand, one should bear in mind that the largest amounts, ie Quantitative Easing, flow into areas that arguably are within the area that is based on the most solid constitutional ground, namely monetary policy.

B. The Democratic Legitimacy of the Institutional Architecture

Perspectives matter: the specialists in law of finance might have become acquainted over time with the complex architecture of the two (three) pillars, each following a different design in the making of the rules and the underlying decision procedures, and in administrative enforcement, not to mention the interaction between the pillars and the relationship with the national enforcement authorities of the Euro Member States and non-Euro Member States (see Dalvinder Singh, Chapter 12). Much of the complexity results from the competence order of the TFEU, which the

Member States could have changed only via an amendment of the Treaty which was politically unfeasible even during the times of crisis. It is reflected in the distribution of responsibilities along the dividing line of monetary policy and economic and fiscal policy. Looking from inside the European constitutional order, the institutional design of the Banking Union seems rational. The deeper one dives into the architecture, the more impressed one might be how the Member States managed to design the two pillars and their interplay, even with regard to their accountability towards the Member States and the European Parliament (in that direction see Niamh Moloney, Chapter 6; with regard to the SSM, see Agnieszka Smoleńska, Chapter 7; and with regard to the SRM see Sergio Fabbrini and Mattia Guidi, Chapter 9).

However there is also another perspective, ie the one from outside – the one taken by the non-experts, by the non-technocrats and non-bureaucrats, by the politicians, and by political theory and political philosophy. Seen through these lenses, the institutional architecture looks less promising. The jumble and jungle of rules, of procedures, of regulatory competences, of institutions, and of interconnectedness at the national and the European level, is hard to reconcile with ideas of democratic legitimacy. Of course, not each and every institution must be democratic but there must be a democratic pedigree (Christoph Möllers, Chapter 8). One may wonder whether the institutional architecture meets these standards. The fact that the picture does not look much better if limited to the national architecture does not offer much comfort.

The magic formula which guides the debate on transnational and/or European governance is *accountability*.[31] There seems to be some disagreement between the different authors of the chapters. Sergio Fabbrini and Mattia Guidi (Chapter 9) stress the role of the national Parliament in the SRM, whereas Agnieszka Smoleńska (Chapter 7) invokes Vivian Schmitt's 'through put legitimacy' in furtherance to Fritz Scharpf's 'input-output legitimacy'[32] and sympathises with Christian Joerges' and Jürgen Neyer's deliberative supranationalism.[33] Both concepts tie legitimacy to conditions. Raymond Breton[34] requires that each level of governance must be relevant to the individual. This implies that the different addressees can identify

---

[31] I Chiu, 'Power and Accountability in the EU Financial Regulatory Architecture: Examining Inter-Agency Relations, Agency Independence and Accountability' in M Andenas and G Deipenbrock (eds), *Regulating and Supervising European Financial Markets: More Risks than Achievements* (New York, Springer Berlin Heidelberg, 2016) 67.

[32] V Schmidt, 'Democracy and Legitimacy in the European Union Revisited: Input, Output and "Throughput"' (2013) 61 *Political Studies* 2.

[33] Ch Joerges, 'Deliberative Supranationalism' – Two Defences (2002) 8 *ELJ* 133 and after the financial crisis the contributions in Ch Joerges and C Glinski (eds), *The European Crisis and the Transformation of Transnational Governance, Authoritarian Managerialism versus Democratic Governance* (Oxford, Hart Publishing, 2017).

[34] R Breton, 'Identification in Transnational Political Communities' in K Knop, S Ostry, R Simeon and K Swinton (eds), *Rethinking Federalism. Citizens, Markets, and Governments in a Changing World* (Vancouver, University of British Columbia Press, 1995) 40 at 42; F de Witte, *Justice in the EU, The Emergence of Transnational Solidarity* (Oxford, OUP, 2015) 171.

the responsible actor. Joerges and Neyer[35] credit the exchange between technical experts, provided they focus on problem-solving, and enjoy a clear mandate
with voting procedures with few formal rules, thereby proving leeway for deliberation and bargaining. There are two caveats: first and foremost one may wonder
whether the institutional architecture in the current form meets the requirements
set out in legal and political science doctrine or whether it comes much closer to
what Ulrich Beck had termed 'organised irresponsibility' with regard to the risk
society.[36] The second caveat results from the distrust of trying to find a substitute
for democratic legitimacy in accountability or deliberative nationalism, instead
of engaging in a critical discourse (Christoph Möllers, Chapter 8). A third one
might stem from the mere size of this area. It might be that legitimacy concerns
increase – and for good and legitimate reasons – with the size of the economic
volume at stake. The rationale would be that decisions taken in this sphere impact
strongly on budgets, hence on the freedom of manoeuvre of parliaments in
other areas.

V. Conclusions: The European Banking Union as a Constitutional Challenge

Even if the European Banking Union cannot serve as a blueprint for further integration measures, it brings a crucial question into the limelight: where and how to
strike the right balance between justified and democratically legitimate centralisation in the hands of EU institutions and the equally justified and legitimate need
for decentralisation? Taking a step back and looking at the problem from outside
might help to overcome the anxieties that are typical for all new institutions which
are eager to centralise, when taking a more relaxed attitude may reduce concerns
over legitimacy to the benefit of regulatory competition and experimentalism.

The development in competition law and in the economic freedoms provide
for helpful insights. In Regulation 1/2003 the EU decentralised the supervision
competences, to the benefit of both the European Commission and the national
cartel offices. The CJEU loosened its grip on exercising control over national
statutory rules that restrict the freedom of trade, thereby granting more leeway
to national courts in ensuring compliance with EU law.[37] The European Banking

---

[35] Ch Joerges '"Deliberative Political Processes" Revisited: What Have We Learnt about the Legitimacy of Supranational Decision-Making' (2006) 4 *Journal of Common Market Studies* 779; Ch Joerges
and H-J Neyer, '"Deliberative Supranationalism" Revisited', *EUI Working Papers*, Law 2006/20 available
at http://cadmus.eui.eu/handle/1814/6251.

[36] U Beck, 'Gegengifte. Die Organisierte Unverantwortlichkeit' [Counterpoison – Organised
Irresponsibility] in German only edition (Frankfurt, Suhrkamp, 1988) 9 and in particular chapter III
'Der Industrielle Fatalismus: Die organisierte Unverantwortlichkeit' [Industrial Fatalism: Organised
Irresponsibility] 96.

[37] J Zglinski, *Europe's Passive Virtues: The Margin of Appreciation in EU Free Movement Law*,
PhD thesis, European University Institute (2016) (forthcoming, OUP, 2018).

Union has introduced a similar power divide in the distinction between SIFIs and non-SIFIs; however, this may not be enough. The European Banking Union might need to consider using the distinction between major and minor infringements, well established in competition law and to some extent also in environmental law, as a design that could promote decentralisation.[38] Both competition law and the four freedoms are established fields with a long history of litigation. They demonstrate that a certain degree of disharmony in law enforcement does not endanger the integrity of EU competition law or of the four freedoms.

Such encouraging perspectives should not, however, lead to one key finding of this introduction and of this book being overlooked: that three major constitutional concerns cannot be overcome through such rather smooth forms of decentralisation.

The first concern is about the legal status of the European Central Bank, which is set in stone and which could, in theory, only be changed through an amendment of the Treaty so as to enhance its democratic legitimacy.[39] The deep conflicts behind that decision and the distrust in particular between France and Germany in the light of German unification demonstrates the sensitive political dimension of such a prospective policy shift, if it ever occurs.[40]

The second concern stems from the theoretically and also, in practice, underdeveloped relationship of the non-Eurozone Member States with the Eurozone Member States. Dalvinder Singh highlights the complexity of the institutional design (Chapter 12). The EU and the Member States would be well advised to grant much more attention to the deep implications that this divide may have not only for the Banking Union, but for the European constitution as a whole.

The third concern is about rule production through standardisation taking place below formal legislation and largely outside or with very limited judicial review (see Hans-W Micklitz, Chapter 11). It seems as if the European Banking Union has established a kind of legal underworld, that imposes effects not only on supervisory authorities inside and outside the EU, but also more indirectly via the supervising authorities on private parties and banks, as well as on the contracting partners of the banks and beyond on third parties. This growing underworld does more than yield legal uncertainty, it also raises legitimacy concerns.

---

[38] H-W Micklitz, 'Administrative Enforcement of European Private Law' in R Brownsword, H-W Micklitz, L Niglia and S Weatherill (eds), *The Foundations of European Private Law* (Oxford, Hart Publishing, 2011) 563.

[39] M van der Sluis, *In Law We Trust: The Role of EU Constitutional Law in European Monetary Integration*, PhD EUI 2017, http://cadmus.eui.eu/handle/1814/7088/browse?value=VAN+DER+SLUIS%2C+Marijn&type=author, where he discusses the potential for change.

[40] H James, *Making the European Monetary Union* (Cambridge MA, Harvard University Press, 2012).

PART I

Some Constitutional Foundations of European Banking Union

2

The Constitutional Dimension of Banking Union

TAKIS TRIDIMAS

I. Banking Union and the Constitutional Integrity of EU Law

The Banking Union (BU) is essentially a system for the supervision, regulation and resolution of banks within the Eurozone. Original in its design, it is the most intricate and far reaching of the law reforms undertaken following the Eurozone crisis and, although it was introduced without Treaty amendment, it is a mutation of the European Union (EU) architectural blueprint. BU does not consist of a single institution or instrument but has been described as a 'conceptual accordion with different layers'[1] containing an array of measures, including intergovernmental arrangements, EU legislation, administrative measures, soft law and national acts. BU is structured around the pillars of the Single Supervisory Mechanism (SSM)[2] and the Single Resolution Mechanism (SRM)[3] and built upon a common corpus of substantive rules, the Single Rulebook. It focuses on executive and institutional reform rather than normative harmonisation and thus departs from the traditional harmonisation paradigm transitioning to a post-internal market governance model recognising an enhanced EU presence in the field of supervision.[4]

BU was conceived as a response to the Eurozone crisis. The fundamental objectives of BU are to safeguard financial stability within the EU and promote

---

[1] R Lastra and J-V Louis, 'European Economic and Monetary Union: History, Trends and Prospects' (2013) 32 *Yearbook of European Law* 1, at 149.

[2] Council Regulation (EU) No 1024/2013 conferring specific tasks on the European Central Bank concerning policies relating to the prudential supervision of credit institutions, [2013] OJ L 287/63 ('the SSM Regulation').

[3] Regulation (EU) No 806/2014 of the European Parliament and of the Council establishing uniform rules and a uniform procedure for the resolution of credit institutions and certain investment firms in the framework of a Single Resolution Mechanism and a Single Resolution Fund and amending Regulation (EU) No 1093/2010, [2014] OJ L 225/1 ('the SRM Regulation').

[4] N Moloney, 'European Banking Union: Assessing its Risks and Resilience' (2014) 51(6) CMLR 1609 at 1611.

the internal market. The underlying rationale of the SSM is to contribute to the soundness of credit institutions and safeguard financial stability by laying down a centralised supervisory system.[5] Supervision and resolution are seen as complementary and mutually dependent aspects of the establishment of the internal market for financial services.[6] Although, consistently with its legal basis, the SRM Regulation stresses its internal market credentials, its centre of gravity lies with the substantive aim of pursuing financial stability through the establishment of burden-sharing arrangements. The purpose of those arrangements is to break up 'the negative feedback loops between sovereigns, banks and the real economy [which] is crucial for a smooth functioning of the EMU'.[7]

The SSM came into operation on 4 November 2014[8] and the SRM came into force on 1 January 2016.[9] The Single Resolution Fund (SRF) is to be established gradually to a target level of €55 billion over a period of no more than eight years.[10] There are two missing elements, both of them connected to financing and thus politically highly sensitive. The first is the establishment of a single European Deposit Insurance Scheme (EDIS) which was originally envisaged as the third pillar of BU. Its establishment is crucial. The objective here is to provide the same level of protection to all depositors in the BU irrespective of their geographical location, thereby underpinning the stability of the banking sector. The second is the creation of a backstop for the SRF with a view to enhancing confidence in the single resolution framework. The idea is that such a backstop would be used in combination with other resolution tools, namely, bail-in and the availability of the SRF[11] and would include, for example, using common funding in combination with the ECB instruments to cover liquidity shortfalls and provide more time to look for the best buyer of a bank in a specific situation.[12] The BU framework, therefore, is still under construction, both in that necessary parts of it are yet to be put in place and in that its existing pillars have yet to develop and be tested in practice. In October 2017, the European Commission ('the Commission') assessed the progress of BU as having been satisfactory and put forward a number of concrete steps for its completion by 2019 stressing the need to provide for the establishment of EDIS and putting in place a financial backstop.[13]

From a legal perspective, BU gives rise to issues of constitutional design, administrative law and banking regulation. Even though it has been introduced

---

[5] SSM Regulation, Art 1, para 1.

[6] SRM Regulation, Preamble, recital 11.

[7] SRM Regulation, Preamble, recital 6.

[8] SSM Regulation, Art 33.

[9] SRM Regulation, Art 99.

[10] SRM Regulation, Arts 67–74, and Inter Governmental Agreement on the transfer and mutualisation of contributions to the SRF concluded on 21 May 2014 (below n 52).

[11] See European Commission, *Communication on Completing the Banking Union*, COM(2017) 592 final, Brussels, 11.10.2017.

[12] Ibid.

[13] European Commission (n 11).

without Treaty amendment, it is an important step in the evolution of the constitutional system of the EU and a force towards the federalisation of financial
regulation. Being the product of a political compromise, it is characterised by
tensions and incorporates legal contradictions. Three underlying tensions can be
identified. The first is between the Economic and Monetary Union (EMU) and
the internal market; the second is between the disciplines of EU law and intergovernmentalism; and the third is between technocracy and politicisation. The
first tension is distinct. Although EU actions often pursue multiple objectives and
areas of policy are closely interlinked, in the case of BU, the tension between the
EMU and the internal market is particularly pronounced. Here the BU construct
is characterised by a high degree of ambiguity, which is exposed in particular by its
dual legal bases. The second tension is between, on the one hand, the disciplines
of EU law – *la methode communautaire*, as it has evolved in the post-Lisbon era
with emphasis on effectiveness and autonomy – and, on the other hand, intergovernmentalism. The third tension is between technocracy and politicisation and
is illustrated primarily in the growth of agencies and the decision-making process
of the SRM.

In their influential study, Tuori and Tuori identify a number of economic
assumptions made by the Treaty of Maastricht which formed the underpinnings of
a European Economic Constitution upon the establishment of the EMU.[14] Those
principles have undergone a series of mutations as a result of the legal reforms
necessitated by the crisis, especially the fiscal governance measures adopted by
the EU, the European Stability Mechanism (ESM) and the Treaty on Stability,
Coordination and Governance in the Economic and Monetary Union (TSCG).[15]
In the light of the mutation narrative, BU can be viewed as part of the constitutional redesign which has evolved without Treaty amendment and challenges
a number of policy choices manifested in the Treaty on the Functioning of the
European Union (TFEU).[16] These include the asymmetric treatment between
economic and monetary policy, the role of the European Central Bank (ECB), the
no-bail-out clause of Article 125 TFEU, and the limits to agency power established
by the *Meroni* doctrine.[17]

A key issue is the blurring of lines between economic and monetary policy
which sits uneasily with the traditional EMU paradigm. The dividing line between
economic and monetary policy is elusive. A prominent aspect of *Pringle*[18] and

---

[14] K Tuori and K Tuori, *The Eurozone Crisis. A Constitutional Analysis* (Cambridge, Cambridge University Press, 2014) 34. For a rebuttal of the mutation thesis, see B de Witte, 'Euro Crisis Responses and the EU Legal Order: Increased Institutional Variation or Constitutional Mutation?' (2015) 11(3) *European Constitutional Law Review* 434.

[15] Tuori and Tuori (n 14) 181.

[16] See T Tridimas, 'General Report on Banking Union' in Gy Bándi, P Darák, K Debisso (eds), *European Banking Union, FIDE Congress Proceedings*, Vol 1, Kluwer, 2016, 41–148 at 87.

[17] Case C-9/56 *Meroni v High Authority*, ECLI:EU:C:1958:7.

[18] Case C-370/12 *Pringle v Government of Ireland*, ECLI:EU:C:2012:756.

Gauweiler[19] is that, in determining the distinction between economic and monetary policy, the Court of Justice of the European Union (CJEU) placed emphasis on objectives rather than effects.[20] In *Pringle*, the CJEU considered that an economic policy measure, in that case the ESM, cannot be treated as equivalent to a monetary policy measure solely on the ground that it may have indirect effects on the stability of the euro.[21] The same reasoning was followed in *Gauweiler*, only this time in reverse regarding a monetary policy measure. The CJEU took the view that any effects of the Outright Monetary Transactions (OMT) programme on economic policy, such as its capability to contribute to the stability of the euro area, cannot lead to it being regarded as an economic policy measure. Focusing on objectives rather than effects allows the same action to be considered either as part of economic policy or as part of monetary policy, depending on the entity that undertakes it and its objectives. This results in the fusion of the two policies and, as *Pringle* and *Gauweiler* indicate, grants immense discretion to the entity that undertakes the action. While allowing for institutional discretion, the interdependence between economic and monetary policy works mostly to the advantage of the ECB, whose broad powers to pursue monetary policy objectives may have substantial and widespread spill-over effects on economic policy.

A further feature of *Gauweiler* is that the CJEU attached importance not only to the primary but also to the secondary objective of monetary policy, ie to support the economic policies of the Member States. By doing so, it granted the ECB discretion to develop an active role in that area. Given that the concept of the 'general economic policies in the Union' is very vague, the ECB essentially becomes an important institutional actor in the wider spectrum of economic policy.[22]

The reforms effected in the aftermath of the Eurozone crisis evince a shift of emphasis from price stability to financial stability. The latter has been elevated to 'the overriding objective which European economic policies, including the monetary policy of the ECB, are expected to serve'.[23] The objectives of BU are closely linked to financial stability, further confirming the emphasis on financial stability as the guiding principle of EU reform and the role of the ECB in that area.

This chapter focuses on the following constitutional aspects of BU: differentiated integration and the principle of equal treatment; its legal bases; and the division of competences between the EU and the Member States in the context of SSM.

---

[19] Case C-62/14 *Gauweiler and Others v Deutscher Bundestag*, ECLI:EU:C:2015:400.
[20] T Tridimas and N Xanthoulis, 'A Legal Analysis of the OMT Case: Between Monetary Policy and Constitutional Conflict' (2016) 23 *Maastricht Journal of European Law* 17.
[21] *Pringle* (n 18), paras 56 and 97.
[22] *Gauweiler* (n 19), para 109.
[23] Tuori and Tuori (n 14) 183.

II. Differentiated Integration and the Principle
of Equal Treatment

One of the most prominent aspects of the post-crisis paradigm is the differentiation between Eurozone and non-Eurozone Member States. The sovereign debt crisis urged Eurozone countries towards further integration in order to complete the EMU, as its imperfect architecture was crumbling under the weight of market instability. The cumulative effect of post-crisis reforms, especially the ESM and the TSCG Treaties, has been to sharpen the distinction between Eurozone and non-Eurozone Member States. The result is an imperfect sketch of a *two-speed* Europe.[24] The introduction of BU further accentuates that distinction, by splitting the system of financial supervision between Eurozone and non-Eurozone Member States. There is a risk that the resulting fragmentation will have adverse economic and political repercussions for the outsiders. There are two main concerns: closer integration among Eurozone Member States may impede access to the internal market by non-Eurozone Member States; and the commonality of interests within the Eurozone may lead to caucusing.

BU pursues equality as a political objective and is also bound by it as a principle of law. However, in the context of primary law and macro-level of EU policy, equality is not understood as precluding differentiated integration or enhanced cooperation but as openness, inclusion and mutual respect. One of the avowed objectives of BU is to avoid the fragmentation of the internal market and ensure the equal treatment of credit institutions.[25] The SSM Regulation contains specific provisions seeking to ensure equality of treatment at various levels. Thus, for example, Article 1 states that no action, proposal or policy of the ECB may, directly or indirectly, discriminate against any Member State or group of Member States as a venue for the provision of banking or financial services in any currency.[26] More broadly, participating Member States must be treated equally[27] and, in carrying out its tasks, the ECB should duly take into account the principles of equality and non-discrimination.[28]

Despite the fact that the BU legal framework is underpinned by considerations of non-discrimination, it inevitably makes a series of distinctions and classifications leading to differential treatment both between Member States and between financial entities. Among the distinctions made, the following are of particular importance. First, there is an inherent distinction owing to the selective character of EMU. Second, there is a distinction between participating and

---

[24] See, *inter alia*, J-C Piris, *The Future of Europe – Towards a Two-Speed EU?* (Cambridge, CUP, 2012).

[25] See SSM Regulation, Art 1(1).

[26] SSM Regulation, Art 1(4).

[27] See eg SSM Regulation, Art 26(12) which states that the rules of procedure of the Supervisory Board shall ensure equal treatment of all participating Member States.

[28] See SSM Regulation, recital 30.

non-participating Member States. Third, the SSM draws a distinction between 'significant' and 'less significant' credit institutions.[29] Fourth, in relation to certain decisions taken by the SRM, distinctions are drawn between Member States on the basis of their contributions to the SRF.[30]

A. Difference in Treatment Between Member States

Differentiated integration has been a systemic feature of EMU since its creation. The Maastricht Treaty granted opt outs to the United Kingdom and Denmark.[31] The existence of Member States with a derogation *ex hypothesi* establishes the existence of multiple regimes on a transitional, albeit indefinite, basis. Further-more, the special status of Sweden, which lacks Treaty basis, contributes to integration asymmetry and illustrates that the EMU edifice has a degree of in-built flexibility which stretches the formal understanding of equal treatment.

A fundamental distinction drawn by the SSM is between participating and non-participating Member States. While all Eurozone Member States belong to the first category, a Member State whose currency is not the euro may become a participating Member State by establishing a close cooperation between the ECB and its national competent authority (NCA) under the terms of Article 7.[32] The principle of non-discrimination is here understood as a principle of inclusion and fair balance. There is equality of opportunity since non-Eurozone Member States have the choice to opt in. Once the conditions laid down in Article 7(2) are satisfied, the ECB must accept the Member State that wishes to participate. There is a carefully crafted system to facilitate symbiosis. Failure to respect the rules is subject to an enforcement mechanism and may lead to suspension of participation[33] but there are two countervailing provisions in line with the open-door nature of participation. A participating non-Eurozone Member State may leave, subject to certain conditions.[34] Also, under a safeguard clause, where a participating non-Eurozone Member State disagrees with a draft decision of the Supervisory Board, it may ultimately request the ECB to terminate the close cooperation with immediate effect and will not be bound by the ensuing decision.[35]

---

[29] SSM Regulation, Art 6(4).

[30] SRM Regulation, Arts 52(2) and (3).

[31] Protocol No 16 on certain provisions relating to Denmark and Protocol No 15 on certain Provisions Relating to the United Kingdom of Great Britain and Northern Ireland.

[32] SSM Regulation, Arts 2(1) and 7.

[33] SSM Regulation, Art 7(5).

[34] SSM Regulation, Art 7(6).

[35] SSM Regulation, Arts 7(8) and 26(8). A further procedure governs the situation where a participating Member State whose currency is not the euro disagrees with an objection of the Governing Council to a draft decision of the Supervisory Board: see Art 7(7). For a specific illustration of fair balance, see SSM Regulation, Art 17(3).

B. Equality Between Financial Institutions

BU also gives rise to differential treatment among financial institutions. The SSM draws a distinction between significant and non-significant institutions. While the distinction is based on objective criteria, it remains porous, as it combines legislative guidance with executive discretion granting a central role to the ECB. In the field of resolution, the Single Resolution Board (SRB) may apply different requirements to different categories of institutions.[36] In relation to the SRM, differences in treatment may arise depending on the authority responsible for resolution, since the SRM Regulation provides only for partial centralisation of the resolution function. The SRM is responsible for the resolution of institutions which are considered to be significant, those in relation to which the ECB has decided to exercise direct supervisory powers, and cross-border groups.[37] The resolution of other entities falls within the responsibility of national authorities. Inevitably, the in-built flexibility of the system gives rise to the possibility of unequal treatment.

III. The Division of Powers Between the EU and the Member States

BU has effected a wholesale transfer of powers from the Member States to the EU. In that respect, it fits in with an empire-building narrative of the post-crisis reform. The granting of extensive powers to the ECB and the establishment of new agencies raises numerous challenges regarding ECB independence, accountability, good governance and democracy.

Two general observations may be made in relation to the novel institutional arrangements of BU. First, BU marks the latest stage in the journey towards the federalisation of the regulation of financial institutions and, in that respect, signals a post-internal market model of regulation which recognises strong EU presence not only in establishing the normative framework but also in institutional structures and supervision. Second, BU has to be seen in the context of other post-Eurozone crisis developments. The trend towards more centralisation is also evident in the ESM and the Fiscal Compact Treaties as well as in the 'six pack' and the 'two pack'.[38] Paivi Leino argues that EU competence was enhanced in matters of economic and fiscal policy – despite the EU Treaties clearly specifying that

---

[36] See eg SRM Regulation, Arts 11 and 12.
[37] See SRM Regulation, Art 7(2).
[38] The 'six pack' and 'two pack' are EU legislative packages to strengthen the Stability and Growth Pact.

this is a Member State competence.[39] Those developments, along with BU, can be seen as an eminent example of the creeping expansion of EU competence and the malleable nature of the existing Treaty framework.

A. The Enhanced Role of the ECB

One of the most important consequences of the post-crisis law reform has been that the powers, remit and importance of the ECB have been considerably strengthened. This occurred as a result of many factors. First, it resulted from the ECB's own institutional posture. The ECB showed leadership and took decisive action at critical times which, in turn, increased its stature and influence. Second, the reorientation of monetary policy objectives and the subtle shift of emphasis from price stability to the stability of the financial system expanded the ECB's influence on matters of economic policy. Third, the ECB benefitted from the Court's support. *Gauweiler* is a judgment of institutional empowerment, with the ECB emerging as the big winner. Essentially, the tensions and instability arising from the separation of competences in monetary and economic policy gravitate to the advantage of the Union. Finally, the ECB has also been granted additional responsibilities as a result of BU. The greater the power of the ECB, the more delicate the balance of internalising political considerations in its decision-making process without compromising its independence. That independence is further threatened by the assumption of powers in the field of prudential supervision.

The allocation of responsibilities between the ECB and the NCAs in the field of supervision is complex and characterised by a high degree of hybridity. This is eminently illustrated by the key distinction between significant and non-significant banks. Under Article 6(4) of the SSM Regulation, the distinction is based on objective criteria taking into account size, inter-state presence and relative strength within a national market. The distinction however is relativised by the fact that, under Article 6, both the ECB and the NCAs have a role to play in the supervision of both categories and the ECB may assume the supervision of a financial institution directly.[40] This creates essentially a system of joint supervision. In relation to significant banks, the effectiveness of supervision will depend on the cooperation between the ECB and the NCAs. In relation to non-significant banks, it will be necessary to ensure that supervisory standards do not diverge from those applicable to significant ones more than necessary. In effect, it will be for the ECB to cultivate a common supervisory culture among national authorities. The close cooperation between the SRM and the national resolution authorities will also be a key requirement for the success of the resolution procedure.

---

[39] P Leino-Sandberg, 'Further Developments of the EMU – Should Legitimacy Come First or Last?' (EU Law Analysis, November 2015), available at http://eulawanalysis.blogspot.be/2015/11/further-development-of-emu-should.html.
[40] SSM Regulation, Art 6(5)(b).

B. Application of National Law by the ECB

An innovation of BU is that it entrusts the ECB with applying national law. Under Article 4(3) of the SSM Regulation, for the purpose of carrying out its supervisory tasks, the ECB is to apply all relevant Union law. This includes national legislation transposing directives and national choices permitted by EU regulations.[41] The ECB must thus apply national legislation implementing, among others, the Directive on credit institutions (CRD IV).[42] This novel arrangement raises some interesting issues.

The ECB will have to interpret national law in order to apply it. Is it bound by an interpretation provided by a national court? EU institutions cannot claim to have the final say over the interpretation of national law which remains within the national judicial province. What if, however, the ECB considers that the national measures fall short of the requirements of a regulation or, more generally, EU law? An obligation on the ECB to apply national law as it finds it, even if it infringes EU law, would not appear to be compatible with the principle of legality. Further problems could arise, for example, in relation to directives. A national authority may not rely on an unimplemented directive against a credit institution but does the prohibition of inverse direct effect also apply to ECB? Prima facie, the answer should be in the affirmative. The rationale for prohibiting the inverse effect of directives applies irrespective of which authority seeks to enforce them since, in all cases, they must transposed into national law. By contrast, the ECB could rely, within the somewhat uncertain contours of the *Marleasing* case law, on the principle of *interpretation conforme*. The above difficulties spill-over to the field of process and judicial protection. In some cases, for example where the ECB applies national law, it may be unclear whether its decision is imputable to ECB or the Member State. It could be tempting for a national court to claim jurisdiction. Can it do so? As a matter of EU law, the answer should lie in the negative since, even when applying national law, the ECB acts in its capacity as an EU institution. It is likely that the SSM structure will give rise to some delicate issues pertaining to the joint liability of EU and national agencies on which the case law remains unclear. It is also likely that it will lead to the CJEU interpreting national law. In the labyrinthine structures of the SSM, legal uncertainty reigns.

Since 2016, the ECB has gradually assumed the exercise of supervisory powers granted under national law by issuing clarifications to national banks.[43] The power

---

[41] See SSM Regulation, Art 4(3), sub-para 1.

[42] Directive 2013/36/EU of the European Parliament and of the Council of 26 June 2013 on access to the activity of credit institutions and the prudential supervision of credit institutions and investment firms, amending Directive 2002/87/EC and repealing Directives 2006/48/EC and 2006/49/EC, [2013] OJ L 176/338.

[43] In the summer of 2016, the ECB assumed powers relating to: (i) activities of significant institutions in countries outside the European Union, (ii) outsourcing of activities, (iii) powers vis-à-vis shareholders; (iv) requests for information to auditors, (v) licensing – ancillary conditions to licences;

of ECB to apply national law, including national options permitted under EU directives, can be expected to lead to a process of greater convergence of regulatory and technical requirements. Uncertainty may also arise as to the scope of ECB's powers to apply national law. Such power follows the ECB's supervisory remit. Thus the ECB takes the view that it can exercise supervisory powers granted under national law, even if they are not explicitly mentioned in EU law provided that they (i) fall within the scope of the ECB's tasks under Articles 4 and 5 of the SSM Regulation and (ii) underpin a supervisory function under Union law. The ECB is therefore the authority competent to exercise the above-mentioned supervisory powers granted under national law under the conditions and within the limits defined in national law.[44]

C. Relations Between the ECB and the EBA

The second issue identified is the relationship between the ECB and the European Banking Authority (EBA). Under Article 4(3), to carry out its supervisory functions, the ECB must adopt guidelines, recommendations and decisions.[45] Those acts must comply with EU law, including legislative, delegated and implementing acts and, in adopting them, the ECB is subject to binding regulatory and implementing technical standards developed by EBA and adopted by the Commission, and to EBA guidelines.[46]

The obligation of the ECB to apply national law and heed to the powers of EBA give to rise to a reversal in the normal flow of power among hierarchically positioned institutions, which may be problematic.[47] It is justified, however, by a model which is designed to separate supervisory from regulatory competences. The ECB is meant to intervene as a prudential supervisor not as a law maker, and its supervisory powers should not encroach on the law-making powers of the institutions,

---

and (vi) credits to related parties. More recently, in March 2017, the ECB assumed, in addition, the following powers: approval of acquisitions by significant institutions of holdings in a non-credit institution or a credit institution outside the EU; approval of mergers/de-mergers involving significant institutions; approval of asset transfers/divestments involving significant institutions; approval of a significant institution's statutes; approval of the appointment of key function holders in significant institutions; approval/objection to the appointment of external auditors (to the extent such powers are linked to ensuring compliance with prudential requirements) of significant institutions; approval of specific banking activities relating to licensing with the exception of the authorisation for the issuance of covered bonds; approval of strategic decisions of significant institutions. See ECB, 'Additional clarification regarding the ECB's competence to exercise supervisory powers granted under national law', Letter SSM/2017/0140, 31 March 2017.

[44] See ECB, ibid.

[45] See SSM Regulation, Art 4(3), sub-para 2.

[46] See SSM Regulation, Art 4(3), sub-para 2.

[47] See, among others, B Wolfers and T Voland, 'Level The Playing Field: The New Supervision of Credit Institutions by the European Central Bank' (2014) 51(5) *Common Market Law Review* 1463, at p 1493. LM Levi, 'The European Banking Authority Framework: Legal Frameworks, Operations and Challenges Ahead' (2013) 28(1) *Tulane European and Civil Law Forum* 51.

the regulatory powers of the Commission or the remit of European Supervisory Authorities (ESAs). The SSM Regulation provides for formal processes of communication by enabling the ECB to participate in the development of draft technical standards or draw the attention of EBA to a potential need to initiate the amendment of existing standards.[48] Still, a neat separation of powers may be difficult to achieve. The statutory framework and institutional dynamics may favour a federalist bias leading to ECB imperialism. The power of the ECB to adopt decisions in combination with the need to ensure 'high standards of supervision'[49] may point strongly to the prospect of top down harmonisation with the ECB taking the role of standard setter. The application of a tapestry of national regulations by a single supervisor gives rise to practical challenges but is likely to prove a potent force of convergence.

IV. The Legal Bases of BU: Novelties at the Outskirts of Constitutionality

The introduction of BU without Treaty amendment was the result of necessity rather than choice. A Treaty amendment was politically unfeasible. While Europe was struggling to mount an effective response to the Eurozone crisis, the prospect of embarking on a Treaty revision was unappealing and did not receive serious consideration. BU was thus established within the existing EU constitutional structure with strong elements of hybridity at different levels, namely hybridity as to its legal bases and its legal sources. It was introduced by means of legislation, albeit assisted by international law, displaying some novelty and continuing the trend towards regulatory innovation and experimentation that has characterised post-crisis measures.

The SSM Regulation[50] is based on Article 127(6) TFEU. The SRM Regulation[51] is based on the general internal market clause of Article 114 TFEU but the financing arrangements of the SRF established therein are provided in an Intergovernmental Agreement on the transfer and mutualisation of contributions

---

[48] SSM Regulation, Art 4(3), sub-para 4.

[49] See SSM Regulation, Art 4(3), sub-para 1.

[50] Council Regulation (EU) No 1024/2013 conferring specific tasks on the European Central Bank concerning policies relating to the prudential supervision of credit institutions, [2013] OJ L 287/63. Note the accompanying Regulation No 1022/2013 amending Regulation (EU) No 1093/2010 establishing the European Banking Authority as regards the conferral of specific tasks on the European Central Bank pursuant to Council Regulation (EU) No 1024/2013, [2013] OJ L 287/5. That amendment was adopted on the basis of Art 114 TFEU: this was to be expected as Regulation No 1093/2010 had also been adopted under that legal basis.

[51] Regulation (EU) No 806/2014 of the European Parliament and of the Council of 15 July 2014 establishing uniform rules and a uniform procedure for the resolution of credit institutions and certain investment firms in the framework of a Single Resolution Mechanism and a Single Resolution Fund and amending Regulation (EU) No 1093/2010, [2014] OJ L 225/1.

concluded between the Member States (IGA).[52] The legislation which provides the backbone of the Single Rulebook and contains substantive rules of banking law has been adopted on classical internal market legal bases, namely Articles 53(1) and Article 114 TFEU. From the point of view of constitutional law, the legal bases of BU appears to be one of the most problematic areas. A number of commentators have voiced scepticism regarding the suitability of Articles 127(6) and 114 TFEU as the correct legal bases of SSM and SRM respectively.[53]

A. The SSM

The establishment of the SSM on the basis of Article 127(6) TFEU has given rise to controversy. Article 127 TFEU belongs to Title VIII dealing with monetary policy, which, for Member States whose currency is the euro, is an exclusive Union competence.[54] Prudential supervision is closely linked to financial stability. It seeks to secure the safety of deposits and the ability of banks to provide liquidity and manage the payment system.[55] It cannot, however, be said to be part of monetary policy since it does not aim to achieve the objective of price stability.[56] While the TFEU envisages a role in prudential supervision for the ECB, its involvement in that area appears to be curtailed. It is not considered to be one of the primary tasks of the ECB listed in Article 127(2) TFEU. Instead, it is provided separately in more hesitant and qualified terms in Articles 127(5) and 127(6). Article 127(5) states that the ECB is to contribute to the smooth conduct of policies pursued by the competent authorities relating to the prudential supervision of credit institutions and the stability of the financial system.[57] The term 'contribute' might give the impression that primary responsibility in the field of prudential supervision lies with the national authorities. On the other hand, it does not qualify the extent, means or intensity of the ECB's contribution.

On the face of it, the empowering clause of Article 127(6) appears to limit the ECB's mandate in several respects. The ECB may only be conferred 'specific' tasks which concern 'policies relating to' prudential supervision.[58] The powers finally

---

[52] Intergovernmental Agreement on the Transfer and Mutualisation of Contributions to the Single Resolution Fund, available at http://register.consilium.europa.eu/doc/srv?l=EN&f=ST%208457%20 2014%20INIT. The Agreement was concluded on 21 May 2014 between the then 26 Member States. It was envisaged that Member States would ratify the Agreement by 1 January 2016: see Arts 11, 12 and Declaration No 2 accompanying the Agreement.

[53] See Tridimas, above (n 16), 74–85.

[54] Article 3(1)(c) TFEU.

[55] For a detailed discussion in the EU context, see R Smits, *The European Central Bank, Institutional Aspects* (Alphen aan den Rijn, Kluwer, 1997) 319.

[56] Alberto de Gregorio Merino, Institutional Report in FIDE, above (n 16) at 169.

[57] This is confirmed also by Art 3.3 of the Statute of the European System of Central Banks (ESCB) and the ECB (see Protocol No 4 accompanying the TEU and the TFEU).

[58] There is also a further limitation in that the ECB's powers may not pertain to the supervision of insurance undertakings.

conferred to the ECB by the authors of the Maastricht Treaty are more limited than those envisaged in an earlier draft which enabled secondary legislation to grant the ECB an extensive, self-standing, role in prudential supervision.[59]

A narrow reading of Article 127(6) has been advocated by substantial parts of the literature.[60] A challenge against the legal basis of the SSM Regulation is, in fact, currently pending before the *Bundesverfassungsgericht*.[61] The applicants essentially argue that Article 127(6) offers an inadequate legal basis because it only allows the conferral of 'specific' powers to the ECB and cannot found the elevation of ECB to the Eurozone's single supervisor. It may be argued that Article 127(6) only allows the ECB to develop policies rather than engage in direct supervision. Also, the ECB's power to 'contribute' may appear to be at odds with the SSM model, which grants the ECB exclusive power in relation to certain supervisory tasks. Furthermore, it has been argued that the conferral of general supervisory responsibilities to the ECB greatly expands its powers through secondary law and goes beyond the limiting clause of Article 13(2) of the Treaty on European Union (TEU).[62] On another view, there is nothing in the preparatory works of the Treaty of Maastricht to found the view that Article 127(6) excludes the attribution to the ECB of direct supervision powers,[63] and the caveat 'specific' used in that provision has little constraining force: it simply means that the supervisory powers attributed to the ECB cannot be generic or unlimited.[64]

The truth is that, prudential supervision not being an exclusive EU competence, the ECB was not the only conceivable body that could be entrusted with the task of banking supervision.[65] The choice of Article 127(6) as the legal basis for the SSM appears to have been determined by a number of considerations,[66] some

---

[59] Article 25(2) of the draft Statute of the ESCB provided as follows: 'The ECB may formulate, interpret and implement policies relating to the prudential supervision of credit and other financial institutions for which it is designated as a competent supervisory authority'. *Europe* Document No 1669/167, 8 December 1990, pp 25–26 reproduced in Smits (n 55) 335, n 76. Note also that a Report produced by a Working Group headed by Professor J-V Louis somewhat prophetically envisaged a substantial supervisory role for the ECB including the coordination of home country control supervision, the interpretation and implementation of EU rules, and even a direct supervisory role. See J-V Louis (ed.), *Vers un Système européen de banques centrales: projet des dispositions organiques* (Brussels, Etudes européennes, editions de l' Université de Bruxelles, 1989).

[60] Wolfers and Voland (n 47), B Krauskopf, J Langer and M Rötting, 'Some Critical Aspects of the European Banking Union' (2014) 29(2) *Banking & Finance Law Review* 241 at 255, C Waldhoff, 'Art. 127 TFEU' in Siekmann (ed), *Kommentar zur Europaisschen Wahrungsunion* (Tubingen, Mohr Siebeck, 2013), F Martucci, *L'ordre économique et monétaire de l'Union européenne* (Brussels, Bruylant, 2015) point 62, J-V Louis et al, *Le droit de la CEE, Union économique et monétaire, Cohésion économique et sociale, Politique industrielle et technologie européenne*, (Bruxelles, Ed. de l'ULB, 1995) 94.

[61] Az 2 Bvr 16 186/14. See http://www.lto.de/recht/nachrichten/n/verfassungsbeschwerde-europ-olis-bankenunion-bankenaufsicht/ (German) and http://openeuropeblog.blogspot.co.uk/2014/07/banking-union-challenged-at-german.html (English).

[62] V Belling, L Marek and M Vojta, Czech National Report in Gy Bándi, P Darák, K Debisso (eds), *European Banking Union, FIDE Congress Proceedings*, Vol 1, Kluwer, 2016, at 304 309.

[63] Merino, above (n 56) at 168.

[64] Ibid.

[65] Above (n 56) at 166.

[66] Above (n 56) at 166–167.

of them positively pointing in favour of the ECB and others relating to the disadvantages of alternative arrangements. Thus, on the positive side, it made sense to utilise Article 127(6) since this is a specific legal basis provided in the Treaties for prudential supervision. Also, granting supervisory powers to the ECB appeared appropriate given the key role it acquired during the euro crisis, and would be in line with the position of many Member States which charge their national central banks with prudential supervision. On the negative side, attributing prudential supervision powers to a new agency would have faced the limitations arising from the *Meroni* doctrine. Furthermore, granting powers to the ECB under Article 114 TFEU, which applies to the whole of the internal market, would have encountered political objections from the United Kingdom.[67] Still, none of these arguments is conclusive and the key question is whether founding the SSM on Article 127(6) is within the discretion of the EU legislature.

All in all, the tasks entrusted to the ECB under Articles 4 and 5 of the SSM Regulation may be considered to be sufficiently specific. The general tenor of the case law on competence suggests that it is unlikely that the CJEU will adopt a narrow reading of Article 127(6). Thus, in the event of a challenge, the question is perhaps not whether the CJEU would uphold the SSM Regulation but what safeguards and conditions it might attach to ECB involvement.

B. The SRM

At first sight, it might appear odd to found a measure which applies only to some Member States on the basis of Article 114 TFEU, the purpose of which is to avoid the fragmentation of the internal market. The preamble to the SRM Regulation justifies recourse to Article 114 TFEU by pointing out the link between, on the one hand, the setting up of a unified resolution regime and, on the other hand, the establishment of a better integrated internal market for banking services and the fostering of economic growth.[68] The reasoning goes as follows. Local divergences in the treatment of creditors under bank resolution or bail-out regimes impact on the perceived credit risk, financial soundness, and solvency of national banks, and thus create an uneven playing field. This undermines public confidence in the banking sector and obstructs the exercise of the freedom of establishment and the free provision of services because financing costs would be lower without such differences in practices of Member States.[69] Furthermore, divergences between national resolution regimes may lead banks and their customers to have higher borrowing costs solely because of their place of establishment and irrespective of their true creditworthiness.[70] Internal market competence thus hinges

---

[67] Above (n 56) at 168.
[68] SRM Regulation, recitals 1–2.
[69] SRM Regulation, recital 3.
[70] SRM Regulation, recital 4.

on the link between lack of confidence and market instability and the distortions in the conditions of competition brought about by financial fragmentation. The economic basis of this rationale is sound although it is not based on any quantifiable direct link with the internal market.

It will be recalled that the case law has interpreted the competence of the EU legislature under Article 114 TFEU and its predecessors[71] particularly broadly. According to established case law, the adoption of a measure under Article 114 is justified where the measure is capable of either (a) removing obstacles to trade which arise from disparities between national laws and which have a direct effect on the functioning of the internal market or (b) eliminating 'significant' distortions of competition which arise from disparities between national laws. The standard of judicial review is not strict, however, and in its intervention the Court is minded to facilitate rather than inhibit a broad understanding of EU powers. The Court has adopted a wide and teleological interpretation of Article 114 TFEU, upholding institutional choices in all cases but one.[72] The case law raises essentially three issues: first, whether the test on direct impact on trade is appropriate; second, what is the standard of evidence required; third, the significance of subsidiarity. While the test of direct impact is in itself appropriate, the absence of economic analysis, the low threshold of proof demanded of the EU legislature, and the virtual absence of subsidiarity control result in regulatory empowerment of the Union. The dice is heavily loaded in favour of EU intervention. The case law has essentially elevated the competence of the EU under Article 114 TFEU to an existentialism issue: either the EU is empowered to intervene or there is little point in carrying on with the integration project.

A key feature of the SSM Regulation is that, apart from effecting substantive harmonisation, it also establishes the SRB as an independent agency at Union level. Article 114 may be used not only to adopt a harmonisation instrument strictly understood, ie to achieve a result which can be attained by the simultaneous enactment of identical legislation in each Member State, but also to establish an EU agency provided that the tasks conferred on it are closely linked to the subject matter and the objectives of harmonisation legislation.[73] In *UK v Parliament and Council* (the *ESMA* case),[74] the Court went a step further. It sanctioned the use of Article 114 as a legal basis to grant an EU agency power to adopt decisions addressed to specific individuals on condition that such power is well-circumscribed and exceptional. *ESMA* thus establishes that Article 114 may serve

---

[71] Article 114 TFEU was Art 95 of the Treaty establishing the European Community (EC), and before the Treaty of Amsterdam, Art 100a EC.

[72] See C-376/98 *Germany v Parliament and Council*, EU:C:2000:544 ('the *First Tobacco Advertising Case*'), paras 86 and 109 and, in which the Court struck down the Directive because it was incorrectly classified as an internal market measure; for a more recent confirmation, Case C-58/08 *The Queen on the application of Vodafone Ltd v Secretary of State for Business*, EU:C:2010:321, para 32.

[73] Case C-217/04 *UK v Council and Parliament* (ENISA case), EU:C:2006:279, para 44.

[74] Case C-270/12 *United Kingdom v European Parliament and Council* (*ESMA*), EU:C:2014:18.

as the legal basis for mandating an EU body to adopt measures which are addressed to specific individuals and substitute the regulatory power of NCAs. Notably, Jääskinen AG took the view that ESMA may not be conferred power to prohibit short selling under Article 114 TFEU. In his view, it was not a power to develop more specific and detailed harmonisation rules but a power of intervention in a specific financial market which fell within the remit of national authorities. Such power could be conferred on the basis of the flexibility clause of Article 352 TFEU but not on the basis of Article 114.

Overall, it may be said that the case law presents two overriding features. First, there is no denying that the Court has sought to empower rather than constrain the EU institutions and has understood EU competence broadly in three separate but inter-related areas which are conflated in the field of BU: internal market harmonisation, agency power and financial crisis management. Second, as *Pringle*[75] and *Gauweiler*[76] suggest, in the field of financial crisis, the case law is characterised by pragmatism, the Court interpreting the ambiguity of the Treaty to facilitate the constitutional containment of the crisis. *Pringle*, in particular, contains a remarkable irony in that, faced with the dichotomy between economic and monetary policy, the CJEU, perhaps for the first time, interpreted EU competence narrowly to advance integration.

C. The Single Resolution Fund

As stated above, the SRF was established to provide financing to the SRM and is based on an IGA on the transfer and mutualisation of national contributions. By the IGA, the Contracting Parties agree to transfer to the SRF their contributions raised in accordance with the Bank Recovery and Resolution Directive (BRRD)[77] and the SRM Regulation.[78] The IGA applies only to Member States whose institutions are subject to the SSM and the SRM[79] but is open to accession by all Member States[80] since the SRM Regulation is based on Article 114 and therefore applies to the entirety of the EU.

Although Member States have resorted to international agreements as a means of countering the Eurozone crisis a number of times, the reasons for using international law have not been the same in each occasion. The Fiscal Compact

---

[75] Case C-2019/13 *Pringle v Ireland*, EU:C:2012:756.
[76] Case C-62/14 *Gauweiler*, EU:C:2015:400.
[77] Directive 2014/59/EU establishing a framework for the recovery and resolution of credit institutions and investment firms and amending Council Directive 82/891/EEC, and Directives 2001/24/EC, 2002/47/EC, 2004/25/EC, 2005/56/EC, 2007/36/EC, 2011/35/EU, 2012/30/EU and 2013/36/EU, and Regulations (EU) No 1093/2010 and (EU) No 648/2012, of the European Parliament and of the Council, [2014] OJ L 173/190.
[78] IGA, Art 1(1)(a). For transitional arrangements, see Art 1(1)(b).
[79] See IGA, Art 1(2) and the detailed provisions of Art 12.
[80] IGA, Art 12(1).

Treaty took the form of an international agreement as a result of the refusal of the British Government to consent to Treaty amendment.[81] The ESM Treaty, on the other hand, was seen as necessary in view of the express prohibition in the TFEU barring the EU from providing financial assistance to Member States.[82] From the point of view of Member States, the use of international agreements presents distinct advantages and is more suitable in areas of high political sensitivity.[83] They enable national governments to act beyond the competence of the EU and negotiate outside the process and institutional confines of EU law while retaining the power of veto. Nevertheless, recourse to international agreements is not unproblematic. It may give rise to treaty-specific problems and encounters broader constitutional objections since international treaties are liable to breach the unity and coherence of EU law, run counter to the distinct instrumentalities of EU integration, and may fall foul of the constitutional constraints of the EU Treaties. It is perhaps an irony that although the Lisbon Treaty did away with Article 293 EC, which provided for the conclusion of international agreements by Member States in certain areas, the use of such agreements to complement EU law has since intensified.

Member State treaty-making power is constrained by EU law. In particular, Member States may conclude international agreements in areas which fall outside EU competence or, where an area falls within the scope of shared competences, to the extent that the Union has not exercised its competence.[84] Furthermore, EU pre-emption in the external sphere takes place where the conclusion of an international agreement 'may affect common rules or alter their scope'.[85] By adopting the SRM Regulation, the EU exercised its shared competence in the field of the internal market. It is, however, doubtful that it has occupied the field in a way that would prevent Member States from concluding the IGA. Primary law appears to favour a narrow understanding of pre-emption. The Protocol on the exercise of shared competence[86] states that, when the Union has taken action in a certain area, 'the scope of this exercise of competence only covers those elements governed by the Union act in question and therefore does not cover the whole area'. The purpose of this, somewhat inelegant, formulation appears to be to limit the 'field pre-emption' effect of EU legislation.[87] It means that, where the Union legislates in a certain field, the adoption of legislation does not automatically result in the EU occupying

---

[81] R Dehousse, 'The "Fiscal Compact": Legal Uncertainty and Political Ambiguity' (2012) *Notre Europe Policy Brief* no 33, p 2.

[82] See Arts 123, 125 TFEU.

[83] With regard to international agreements in general, see eg Dehousse (n 81).

[84] See Art 2(2) TFEU.

[85] Art 3(2) TFEU.

[86] Protocol No 25 annexed to the TEU and the TFEU by the Treaty of Lisbon.

[87] Although the Protocol is intended to cast light on the interpretation of Art 2(2) TFEU it should be considered to be relevant also to the interpretation of Art 3(2) TFEU.

the whole field so that Member States are excluded from adopting any measure.[88] They remain in principle free to act in the same area, as long as they do not enact legislation that conflicts with EU law or principles.[89] The pre-emptive effect of an EU measure, however, will ultimately depend on its scope and is a matter of interpretation. The Protocol introduces a presumption against field pre-emption but does not preclude it.[90]

The IGA is closely linked to, and dependent on, EU measures in a way that fuses EU and intergovernmental norms and decision-making. As highlighted by the Czech report, the IGA explicitly assumes, as a prerequisite for its implementation, the stability of the regulatory framework.[91] That framework, however, is based on the SRM Regulation and BRRD, namely, EU acts which may be amended independently of the will of the Contracting Parties to the IGA. Article 9 of the IGA makes the use of the Resolution Fund on a mutual basis and the transfer of contributions to it subject to compliance on a permanent basis with the fundamental rules of the SRM Regulation. Departure from those rules enables a Contracting Party to invoke the *rebus sic stantibus* principle under international law, subject to supervision by the CJEU. Furthermore, the Contracting Parties have undertaken, through a declaration, to vote unanimously on amendments to the harmonisation rules provided in the BRRD.[92] Complementarity between EU and international law disciplines is thus strong, albeit not necessarily stable. It may well be that, as the BU evolves, the system will progressively transition to a more coherent normative structure founded on EU law. Recourse to international law in the form of the IGA also means that the role of other EU institutions is curtailed. This applies in particular to the European Parliament, which is marginalised. The jurisdiction of the CJEU is also limited since it cannot rule on the validity of the IGA.

V. The Role of the CJEU

In the last few years, a significant body of EU case law has begun to develop relating to Eurozone matters. The cases that have reached the Court of Justice so far pertain to the allocation of competences between the Member States and the EU, the limits to the authority of the EU institutions, and the rights of individuals in

---

[88] See T Tridimas, 'Competence After Lisbon: The Elusive Search for Bright Lines' in D Ashiagbor, N Countouris, and I Lianos (eds), *The European Union After the Treaty of Lisbon* (Cambridge, CUP, 2012) 47–76 at 65.

[89] See House of Lords EU Committee, *The Treaty of Lisbon: An Impact Assessment*, 10th Report of Session 2007–08, Vol 1, p 24.

[90] Tridimas (n 88) at 65.

[91] IGA, Art 9.

[92] Declaration No 1 to the IGA.

the context of austerity programmes adopted as part of bail-out or bail-in plans. Some of the cases have raised issues of fundamental constitutional importance. While *Gauweiler* suggests that the ECB is a winner, in matters relating to fundamental rights, overall the CJEU appears to have followed a restrictive approach favouring wide discretion on the part of the EU institutions and a narrow understanding of property rights.[93]

So far, the CJEU has had the opportunity to adjudicate on two cases involving BU. While *Trasta Komercbanka* involved mostly procedural issues,[94] *Landeskreditbank Baden-Württemberg – Förderbank*[95] raised some interesting questions pertaining to the distinction between significant and less significant banks. A regional credit bank governed by public law and wholly owned by the Land of Baden-Württemberg had been classified as a significant bank, and thus being subject to ECB supervision, as it fulfilled the criterion of size under the Basic Regulation. It argued that, given its particularly weak risk-profile, the prudential supervision conducted by the national authorities was sufficient and therefore particular circumstances existed within the meaning of Article 6(4) of the Regulation which justified its classification as a less significant bank. Its argument was essentially that the SSM Regulation did not effect a transfer of competence to the ECB with respect to all of the tasks referred to in Article 4(1) of the Basic Regulation but only with respect to 'significant' entities. The General Court rejected that interpretation. It held that, in adopting the Basic Regulation, the Council did not seek to distribute autonomous powers to the ECB and the NCAs but sought to confer exclusive competence to the ECB and facilitate the decentralised exercise of those powers by the national authorities in certain cases. This reading of the regulation is correct but led the General Court to make a further pronouncement. It held that in the case in issue, under the SSM, the national authorities acted within the scope of decentralised implementation of an exclusive competence of the Union, not the exercise of a national competence.[96] Strictly speaking that statement is incorrect as the exclusive or otherwise character of Union competence flows from the Treaties and not by the decision of the EU legislature to exercise their powers in a field of shared competence. The ECB's powers in the field of prudential supervision are not exclusive. Nonetheless, the General Court was correct both in ascertaining the function of subsidiarity and proportionality in the circumstances of the case and

---

[93] See Belling, Marek and Vojta, above (n 62) at 309 and IGA, Art 9.
[94] Case T-247/16 *Trasta Komercbanka v ECB*, EU:T:2017:623, where a Latvian bank and some of its shareholders sought the annulment of the ECB decision withdrawing its authorisation. The case raised mostly procedural points but illustrates the close inter-relationship between EU and national law and signals the development of EU federal administrative law adjudication in the field of banking regulation. The General Court held that the shareholders of a bank have direct and individual concern to bring proceedings for the annulment of the ECB decision withdrawing its authorisation since such withdrawal directly affects their legal position *qua* shareholders.
[95] Case T-122/15 *Landeskreditbank Baden-Württemberg – Förderbank v ECB*, EU:T:2017:337.
[96] See para 73 in *Landeskreditbank Baden-Württemberg – Förderbank* (n 95).

in the interpretation of Article 6(4) of the Basic Regulation and Article 70(1) of the Framework Regulation.[97]

The applicant argued, essentially, that Article 70 should be interpreted in the light of the principle of proportionality and subsidiarity to mean that direct prudential supervision by the ECB must be necessary. It follows that the ECB ought to have ascertained whether prudential supervision by the German authorities afforded achievement of the objectives of the Basic Regulation. Therefore, in so far as the applicant did demonstrate that its profile showed a low degree of risk, the objective of protection of financial stability pursued by the Basic Regulation would be sufficiently achieved by the German authorities' exercising their supervision. Although, in that light, there was justification for reclassifying the applicant as a less significant entity under Article 70(1) of the SSM Framework Regulation, this is too broad an interpretation of special circumstances. It begins from the premise that the ECB may directly supervise entities that fulfil the criteria listed in Article 6(4) only where that is necessary, namely where supervision at national level cannot sufficiently achieve the objective of financial stability. This is, however, not the scheme of the SSM as evidenced by the provisions of the regulations. By contrast, Article 70(1) must be understood as meaning that special circumstances exist only where direct prudential supervision by the ECB is less able to ensure achievement of the objectives of the Basic Regulation than direct prudential supervision of that entity by the national authorities. On the other hand, a literal interpretation of Article 70(1) of the SSM Framework Regulation does not suggest reclassification of a 'significant entity' as 'less significant' on the ground that direct supervision by the national authorities under the SSM is just as able to achieve the objectives of the Basic Regulation as supervision by the ECB alone.

VI. Conclusions

BU is the most intricate and far reaching of the law reforms undertaken following the Eurozone crisis. It is daring both in terms of its objectives and in terms of

---

[97] Under the SSM Regulation, Art 6(4) the ECB is exclusively responsible for the supervision of significant banks while the supervision of less significant ones falls within the joint purview of the ECB and the national supervisory authorities. Article 6(4) uses three criteria for the classification of a bank as significant, namely its size, its importance for the economy of the Union or any participating Member State, and the significance of cross-border activities. Article 6(4) states that a credit institution is not to be considered less significant, unless justified by particular circumstances, if any of a number of conditions are met. These include inter alia, the case where the total value of its assets exceeds EUR 30 billion. Article 70(1) of Regulation 468/2014 states that 'particular circumstances' justifying the declassification of a bank as significant exist where there are specific and factual circumstances that make the classification of a supervised entity as significant inappropriate, taking into account the objectives and principles of the SSM Regulation and, in particular, the need to ensure the consistent application of high supervisory standards.

its novelty as a legal construct. The wholesale transfer of supervisory powers to the ECB, the establishment of a common resolution framework for credit institutions, and the gradual mutualisation of burden sharing, reticent as it may be, open a new chapter of EU law and take a firm step towards the federalisation of banking law. BU signals a post-internal market model of regulation which recognises strong EU presence not only in establishing the normative framework but also in institutional structures and supervision. The BU model is characterised by ambivalence in respect of its EMU and internal market legal bases and built upon a mixed normative framework including EU hard and soft law and intergovernmental measures standing outside the strict EU law framework, thus exacerbating the general picture of differentiated integration in the post-crisis EU law.

The hybrid nature of BU is prominently illustrated by the duality of its legal bases. The legal bases of both the SSM and the SRM are precarious, and acceptance that they are constitutionally sound requires a leap of faith. The SSM Regulation grants the ECB more extensive prudential powers than the reticent wording of Article 127(2) TFEU appears to allow. The SRM Regulation uses Article 114 TFEU to found a normative framework which applies to a selected group of Member States and is thus liable to fragment rather than unify the internal market. In the case of the SSM, there is a risk of overreach in terms of institutional empowerment. In the case of the SRM, the use of Article 114 suggests that the internal market is so malleable that it is difficult to establish meaningful legal limits to the EU's harmonisation competence. Still, the preamble to the SRM Regulation provides a powerful economic rationale and a strong link with internal market objectives. Rather than judging the applicable arrangements vis-à-vis an abstract ideal, one has to bear in mind what is politically feasible and legally possible under the existing Treaty framework. There is an argument to be made that, fragmented as it is, the SRM regime is not a retrograde step and contributes to the attainment of internal market objectives.

One of the key features of BU is that it has accentuated the difference in treatment between Eurozone and non-Eurozone Member States. While the BU regime pursues equality as a political objective and is constrained by the legal principle of non-discrimination, the application of the latter is heavily conditioned. An inevitable consequence of asymmetric integration is that the normative content of non-discrimination becomes more difficult to pin down. Equality of Member States is understood as a principle of inclusion, mutual respect, and the freedom to enter and exit which is buttressed by process requirements governing decision-making on regulatory standards.[98] The recognition of equality as an overarching principle in the SSM and the SRM Regulation bears legal consequences but, inevitably, the application of different rules to subsets of Member States leads to an

---

[98] See the double majority voting system introduced for the decision-making of EBA: Regulation (EU) No 1093/2010 establishing a European Supervisory Authority (European Banking Authority), amending Decision No 716/2009/EC and repealing Commission Decision 2009/78/EC, Art 44; and Tridimas, above (n 16) at 98.

uneven playing field. While some may see the resulting supervisory and regulatory incongruence as inherently destabilising, others may view it as facilitating a meaningful framework of fair symbiosis.

The following points should here be borne in mind. First, despite its perceived flaws, the BU regime in fact reigns in centrifugal forces and reduces the risk of fragmentation which arose from the sovereign crisis. Second, it provides for mitigating mechanisms, although it remains to be seen how these will operate in practice. Third, judicial oversight is important to ensure that the application of different rules in the field of financial supervision and regulation disrupts as little as possible the internal market. The ECB location policy case[99] provides an example of judicial awareness of the risks of regulatory spill-over from the EMU to the internal market and attempted usurpation of power.

The differentiated integration brought about by BU primarily covers the field of supervision and pertains to institutional mechanisms rather than the selective application of substantive rules. In that respect, the risk of creating an uneven playing field is contained. Nonetheless, as discussed above, spill-over risks exist and BU has to be seen in the wider context of the closer integration among Eurozone States. The BU model is characterised by ambivalence in respect of its EMU and internal market legal bases and built upon a mixed normative framework including EU hard and soft law and intergovernmental measures standing outside the strict EU law framework thus exacerbating the general picture of differentiated integration in the post-crisis EU law. In terms of classification, BU is a form of flexible cooperation on an indefinite basis and fits into an inclusionary *avant-garde* flexibility paradigm. A sub-set of Member States leads the way but with safeguards and open doors for the rest.

Under Article 4(3) of the SSM Regulation, a distinct aspect of the SSM is that the ECB is charged with applying national law implementing EU directives. It is also subject to binding regulatory and implementing technical standards developed by the EBA and adopted by the Commission, and EBA guidelines. This system entails a reversal of hierarchy at two levels. First, the ECB is bound by national implementing measures and, to the extent that Member States may exercise discretion in implementation, by national choices. Second, it has, at least indirectly, to heed the authority of an EU agency. The shift from a rules-based approach towards executive and institutional reforms disrupts the normal direction of power flows. Ironically, the assumption of direct supervision by the ECB leads to institutional and normative subordination to sources of power which stand at a lower level within the EU pyramid making institutional cooperation the key to smooth functioning. It is likely that institutional interaction and supervisory coordination,

---

[99] Case T-496/11 *United Kingdom v ECB*, EU:T:2015:133. In that case, the General Court annulled the ECB's Eurosystem Oversight Policy Framework which required central counterparties to be located in the Eurozone on the grounds that it went beyond mere oversight and the ECB lacked power to regulate clearing systems.

together with the objective of ensuring high standards of supervision,[100] will lead to a high degree of normative harmonisation and supervisory convergence. It is more likely than not that the ECB will develop to being the dominant player.

The supervisory supremacy of the ECB is likely to lead eventually to regulatory supremacy. The system is based on a model of separation between regulation and supervision which may in practice prove unsustainable because its complexity, and the institutional weight of the ECB, are likely to lead to its dominance.

---

[100] SSM Regulation, Art 4(3), sub-para (1).

3

The Thin Red Line Between the OMT
Decision and the Banking Union

ALESSANDRO BUSCA

I. The OMT Decision

A. Background to the OMT Decision

2012 will not be remembered for its cataclysmic events according to the Mayan prophecy, but it will be certainly remembered as the turning point of the European financial and sovereign debt crisis. In particular, summer 2012 represented the most severe moment of the crisis and saw, at the same time, the adoption of the most relevant, and in certain cases controversial, measures to tackle the emergency:[1] the Outright Monetary Transactions (OMT) decision, on the one hand, and the Banking Union, on the other hand. Before analysing such measures, it is, however, essential to reconstruct the relevant facts leading to their adoption in order to better understand their nature and further analyse their interplay.

Between 2007 and 2009, the financial crisis had severely damaged financial stability as well as price stability worldwide, but more specifically in the Eurozone.[2] In this context, the ability of the European Central Bank (ECB) to effect price stability by interest rate decisions had been significantly limited by dysfunctional money and securities markets.[3] Ordinarily, in practice, the Eurosystem supplies liquidity in the form of short-term loans to banks through its refinancing operations. Short-term money market interest rates represent the interest rates charged to banks for such refinancing operations, and through these interest rates the

---

[1] 'This year will in my view be remembered as the year when the long-term vision for the euro and the euro area was re-launched' (Mario Draghi in L Barber and M Steen, 'Interview with M. Draghi', *Financial Times*, 13 December 2012, edited transcript available at https://www.ft.com/content/6a4dd882-4537-11e2-858f-00144feabdc0).

[2] See especially J Trichet, 'State of the Union: The Financial Crisis and the ECB's Response Between 2007 and 2009' (2010) 48 *Journal of Common Market Studies* 7.

[3] See ECB, 'The ECB's Monetary Policy Stance During the Financial Crisis' (January 2010) *Monthly Bulletin* 63.

policy interest rates of the ECB are transmitted to the overall economy.[4] Money markets and well-functioning securities markets are thus indispensable for monetary policy to be effective. The financial crisis mainly produced liquidity shortages for banks that relied on the money market for refinancing. As a result, in order to ensure that they had sufficient funding at short notice, banks preferred to loan funds for very short periods rather than for longer periods.[5] The money market was thus hampered by mistrust, liquidity problems and bank solvency problems and this, in turn, produced substantial obstacles in the regular transmission of monetary policy. In order to overcome such issues and restore liquidity in the banking sector, the ECB was forced to undertake a number of non-standard measures – so-called 'enhanced credit support' – through two types of programmes: the longer-term refinancing operations (LTRO) operations[6] and the covered bond purchase programme.[7] According to the ECB, both measures were able to partially restore liquidity in the banking sector, and a phasing-out of the programme began in late 2009.[8]

However, around the end of the phasing-out process, the liquidity crisis gradually began to hit the balance sheet of sovereign States. The cause of this link is widely credited to the costs of bailing out and recapitalisation of the banking sector.[9] As the financial crisis turned into a sovereign debt crisis in various Member States, price stability and financial stability began again to be at risk since a well-functioning market for government bonds is also considered indispensable for monetary policy.[10] As a result, the ECB was forced to intervene for a second time, with the adoption of the Securities Market Programme (SMP).[11] Through

---

[4] See especially J González-Páramo, 'The European Central Bank and the policy of enhanced credit support', speech at the conference organised by Cámara de Comercio de Málaga and University of Málaga, Málaga, 18 June 2010, available at www.ecb.europa.eu/press/key/date/2010/html/sp100618_2.en.html.

[5] See J Eisenschmidt and J Tapking, 'Liquidity Risk Premia in Unsecured Interbank Money Markets' (2009) *ECB Working Paper*, no 1025.

[6] These LTROs provided liquidity to the banking sector for longer periods than short-term refinancing operations. In particular, they extended the maximum maturity of refinancing operations to one year, thus reducing the short-term need for refinancing requirements by banks.

[7] These covered bonds are long-term debt securities issued by banks to refinance loans to the public and private sectors, often in relation to real estate transactions. This operation was quite important because, as underlined by the former President of the ECB: 'The covered bond market is the largest and most active segment of the fixed income market in the euro area – even exceeding the corporate bond market – with the exception of the public sector bond market … This market nearly collapsed when the financial crisis intensified' (Trichet, 'State of the Union' (n 2) 13).

[8] ECB, 'ECB announces details of refinancing operations up to 7 April 2010', press release, 3 December 2009, available at www.ecb.europa.eu/press/pr/date/2009/html/pr091203_1.en.html. For the implementation of monetary policy see generally P Mercier and F Papadia, *The concrete euro* (Oxford, Oxford University Press, 2011).

[9] An alternative explanation is based on the collapse of tax revenues in light of the economic depression, see M Reinhart and K Rogoff, 'The Aftermath of Financial Crises' (2009) 99 *American Economic Review* 466, 470.

[10] González-Páramo, 'The European Central Bank' (n 4).

[11] ECB Decision of 14 May 2010 on establishing a securities markets programme [2010] OJ L 124/8.

the SMP, Central Banks of the Eurosystem could purchase, on the secondary market, eligible marketable debt instruments issued by the central governments or public entities of the Eurozone in order to restore an appropriate monetary policy transmission mechanism.

The SMP is central for the analysis undertaken in this chapter because it can be considered to be the predecessor of the OMT programme, as their essential features are quite alike (see also section I.C). The SMP is, similarly to the OMT, part of the mandate of the ECB to pursue price stability through open market operations – buying and selling marketable instruments according to Article 18.1 of the ECB Statute. Both programmes allow the ECB to purchase and sell, in the secondary markets, marketable instruments in the form of government sovereign bonds. Such a characteristic stands out and makes both programmes questionable principally from a legal perspective given the explicit prohibition concerning monetary financing and government bailout, respectively under Articles 123 and 125 of the Treaty on the Functioning of the European Union (TFEU) (for a more detailed analysis see section II). However, there exists, among others, one key characteristic distinguishing the two programmes and making the OMT even more questionable: the *ex ante* limited amount of marketable instruments purchase according to the SMP, and conversely the *ex ante* unlimited amount of marketable instruments purchase according to the OMT. The SMP had in fact a fixed limited amount of bond purchase. This, according to many sources, was, however, the main weakness of the programme as it did not convince private investors of the ECB's unconditional support for government bonds under financial pressure.[12] In other words, private investors perceived the SMP as limited and temporary, which in turns raised concerns about the effectiveness of the programme. The SMP was, as the result of this, a major disappointment in its two years of application. By the end of April 2012, the risk premia for governmental bonds of various euro area States was very high despite the fact that the programme's holdings (mainly Greek, Irish, Spanish and Italian bonds) were quite significant, in the amount of €210 billion.[13]

In this context, where, on the one hand, the SMP proved to be unsuccessful in lowering high risk premia and restoring a well-functioning market for government bonds, and where, on the other hand, the lack of confidence in fiscal consolidation and mistrust in the European institutions to tackle the crisis was

---

[12] According to some major financial source: 'In the first weeks of the SMP2, there was a belief that the ECB may have been targeting a limit close to 5% on 10-year maturities. The failure to defend such a limit created doubts about the existence of such a limit, triggering a flight to safety from private investors. Without an explicit yield target, it was impossible to convince investors that Italian 10-year bonds at 7% were a great opportunity under the SMP' (L Pagani, 'OMT: Watchdog for Spreads That Barks but May Not Bite' (February 2013) *European Perspectives* 2, available at www.pimco.com/en/insights/pages/omt-watchdog-for-spreads-that-barks-but-may-not-bite.aspx).

[13] ECB, 'Details on securities holdings acquired under the Securities Markets Programme', press release, 21 February 2013, available at www.ecb.europa.eu/press/pr/date/2013/html/pr130221_1.en.html.

widespread in the financial markets,[14] three major events occurred between June and September 2012.

On 28–29 of June 2012, an important Euro summit took place in Brussels in order to address the crisis threatening the euro's very existence. After a long negotiation, the meeting of EU leaders laid down the framework for a significant strengthen in budgetary and banking integration. In particular, the meeting was introduced by the report 'Towards a genuine Economic and Monetary Union', presented by the four Presidents, Herman Van Rompuy, José Manuel Barroso, Jean-Claude Juncker and Mario Draghi, which set out a series of reforms for the future of the Economic and Monetary Union (EMU). The report outlined four pillars on which to pursue further European integration: financial market union, fiscal union, economic union and political union.[15] The first block, in particular, referred to an integrated financial framework to ensure financial stability in the euro area. Further, given the interdependences resulting from the single currency, the report underlined the need for an integrated financial framework built on the single rulebook and based on two central elements: a single European banking supervision and a common deposit insurance and resolution framework. This proposal was groundbreaking as it would have directly addressed one of the major weaknesses causing the financial crisis: the lack of a unified and independent supervisory institution over the largest European banks, in order to prevent future solvency and liquidity problems and, ultimately, to avoid future government bailouts.

The second important event was the establishment on September 2012 of the European Stability Mechanism (ESM).[16] This was a permanent lending facility meant to replace the previous temporary instruments, namely the European Financial Stability Facility (EFSF) and the European Financial Stabilisation Mechanism (EFSM). The ESM was established as an international organisation whose purpose was to 'mobilise funding and provide stability support under strict conditionality', in order 'to safeguard the financial stability of the euro area as a whole and of its Member States' (Article 3 of the ESM Treaty). For this purpose, the ESM was 'entitled to raise funds by issuing financial instruments or by entering into financial or other agreements or arrangements with ESM Members, financial institutions or other third parties'.[17] The establishment of a permanent

---

[14] 'At a dinner in early July, the ECB chief and his fellow governors were discussing the question of whether the ECB's loans to Ireland's government-owned "bad bank" were consistent with the bank's current bylaws. It was a debate among experts, like many before it, but then something unusual happened: Draghi raised his voice. Such questions, he snapped at his opponents, could not always be discussed in exclusively legal terms' (S Böll, M Sauga and A Seith, 'Draghi's Pledge: ECB Divided over Efforts to Save Euro', *Der Spiegel*, 30 July 2012, available at www.spiegel.de/international/business/mario-draghi-s-new-euro-rescue-plans-sow-strife-in-ecb-council-a-847129.html).

[15] H Van Rompuy, 'Towards a Genuine Economic and Monetary Union', Brussels, 26 June 2012 (Four Presidents' Report) available at www.consilium.europa.eu/media/21570/131201.pdf.

[16] See generally Treaty Establishing the European Stability Mechanism (ESM) [2011] OJ L 91/1.

[17] According to Article 8 of the ESM Treaty, the ESM is expected to have an authorised capital of €700 billion, of which €80 billion is paid-in capital and the remaining €620 billion – if needed – will be loaned through the issuance of special ESM obligations at the capital markets.

stability mechanism was therefore needed as an extreme *ratio* in order to preserve the financial integrity of the euro area and avoid possible default of individual countries. Under the ESM, Member States and banks could apply for a bailout in case of financial distress according to a complex procedure which significantly empowers the European Commission and the ECB (and where possible the International Monetary Fund (IMF)).[18] In this case, however, a number of key Treaty provisions aimed at avoiding unlimited fiscal transfers and debt monetisation seemed to be preclusive in that sense: the 'no-bailout' clause (Article 125 TFEU), the monetary financing prohibition (Article 123 TFEU) and Article 122 TFEU which allows economic measures only in case of 'severe difficulties'. As a result, in order to provide full legitimacy under EU law, Article 136 TFEU was amended[19] to expressly authorise the establishment of the ESM. Such authorisation was, however, made expressly dependent on the conditionality requirement. This requirement, which also characterises the OMT programme, was in fact enshrined in the Treaty amendment as it represented the trade-off between financial assistance and public reforms in terms of fiscal consolidation.

The third major event, and the one that will be analysed in the following paragraph, was the decision by the ECB to adopt the OMT programme (the 'OMT decision'). The decision was anticipated and somehow the result of a well-known speech made by the newly elected president of the ECB, Mario Draghi, in London.[20] On 26 July 2012, the president of the ECB was invited to give a speech at the Global Investment Conference in London. The conference was the first of a series of business meetings towards the Olympic Games. After underlining the

---

[18] In particular, the procedure rests on a preliminary analysis by the Commission and the ECB in order to assess any risks to the financial stability of the euro area, the sustainability of the public debt, and financing needs of the ESM Member concerned. On the basis of such evaluation the Board of Governors of the ESM may decide to grant financial stability support 'in principle'. In case of a positive decision, the Board of Governors 'entrust the European Commission – in liaison with the ECB and, wherever possible, together with the IMF – with the task of negotiating a memorandum of understanding (an "MoU") detailing the conditionality attached to the financial assistance facility'. The proposal for financial assistance is then drafted by the Managing Director of the ESM and then signed by the European Commission on behalf of the ESM, subject to prior compliance with the conditionality and approval by the Board of Governors. The European Commission is also – in liaison with the ECB and, wherever possible, together with the IMF – responsible for the monitoring of the conditionality attached to the financial assistance facility.

[19] Art 136 TFEU was amended by Decision 2011/199/EU adopted by the European Council on 25 March 2011. This one entered into force on 1 May 2013 following receipt by the Secretary General of the EU Council of the notification by the Czech authorities, the last Member States, of the completion of their ratification procedures.

[20] The content of the speech was to some extent anticipated by Draghi himself in a previous interview with Le Monde: 'We [the ECB] stand ready to do more, if our powers were to be strengthened. In the extraordinary conditions that we are experiencing, it is necessary to see the ECB take a stand beyond monetary policy for matters that cannot be addressed by monetary policy, such as high public deficits, a lack of competitiveness or unsustainable imbalances, especially where financial stability may be at risk. Safeguarding the euro is part of our mandate' (E Izraelewicz, C Gatinois and P Ricard, 'M. Draghi: interview with Le Monde' (21 July 2012), transcript available at www.ecb.europa.eu/press/key/date/2012/html/sp120721.en.html).

strength of the euro and the progress made in the previous six months, Draghi concluded:

> We think the euro is irreversible. And it's not an empty word now, because I preceded saying exactly what actions have been made, are being made to make it irreversible …
> Within our mandate, the ECB is ready to do whatever it takes to preserve the euro. And believe me, it will be enough … To the extent that the size of these sovereign premia hampers the functioning of the monetary policy transmission channel, they come within our mandate.[21]

The statement surprised the audience as well as financial markets, and it was initially praised by the German Government according to some insiders in Berlin.[22] Many immediately considered this speech, along with the Lehman Brothers collapse, as one of the key moments in the financial and sovereign crisis. The speech was in fact quite resolute in its terms ('whatever it takes')[23] and provided somehow the constitutional foundations and the content for the resulting OMT programme. Manifest, in this sense, is that the London speech had the immediate effect of driving the decline in sovereign bond risk premia.[24] This effect can be considered as underlining the importance of this speech. In our modern world where financial markets have become increasingly central for corporations and individuals as well as for States, a simple but nonetheless extremely resolute speech was able to achieve, in terms of reassuring the financial markets, what neither the Euro summit nor the establishment of the ESM were able to do.

B. The ECB Executive Board and Governing Council at the Time of the Decision

After the London speech, many questions were raised, particularly whether Draghi had reached or sought a consensus for those remarks among his colleagues

---

[21] M Draghi, 'Speech at the Global Investment Conference in London', London, 26 July 2012, available at www.ecb.europa.eu/press/key/date/2012/html/sp120726.en.html.

[22] 'According to government insiders in Berlin, Merkel and German Finance Minister Wolfgang Schäuble characterised the Italian economist's plan as "important and valuable" and felt that Draghi's announcement alone had already had an effect' (C Reiermann, M Sauga and A Seith, 'The Bundesbank against the World: German Central Bank Opposes Euro Strategy', *Der Spiegel*, 30 July 2012, available at www.spiegel.de/international/europe/german-bundesbank-opposes-euro-crisis-strategy-a-852237. html).

[23] Draghi later explained his wording by saying that: 'What I thought was that the markets should know what our stance was. This was the objective of this speech. It was meant to be absolutely clear about our determination. I also made the point that it was not only our determination but it was also our leaders' determination to carry out the June summit conclusions. I said that markets underestimated the leaders' determination and the amount of political capital they have invested in the euro. This is what I said first and then added that it's our intention to be firm and to do whatever it takes but within our mandate' (in Barber and Steen, 'Interview with Mario Draghi' (n 1)).

[24] Some economists for example, estimated that the announcement decreased the Italian and Spanish two-year government bond yields by about two percentage points as well as an increase in credit, up to three percentage points, and ultimately a significant decrease in bond market volatility. See C Altavilla,

at the ECB. Draghi tried in the following months to clarify a number of doubts regarding these issues. In particular, he explained that he had discussed those remarks with the other colleagues before the London speech[25] but, at the same time, he admitted that within official meetings of the Governing Council the discussion was not specific.[26] In an interview with the *Financial Times* in December 2012 he acknowledged that he had not cleared that speech with 'anybody outside in the capitals' and also that the central bank realised the need for some sort of strong intervention only in the second half of the year.[27]

However, it is clear that the statement made in London required a broad consensus in the Executive Board and in the Governing Council of the ECB given its resolute language and content ('whatever it takes'). Without such consensus, it would have been impossible to implement any significant measure. A strong consensus was certainly needed in the Executive Board of the ECB, the responsible body for the current business of the ECB, and, for the implementation of monetary policy in accordance with the decisions laid down by the Governing Council. More specifically to this case, the Executive Board is responsible for carrying out open market and credit operations, including the announcement of conditions under which it will enter into such transactions.[28]

It is interesting to notice that, at the time of the OMT decision (July – September 2012), the Executive Board of the ECB included five members, thus falling short of its six mandatory members as provided under Article 11.1 of the ECB Statute. Those members were Mario Draghi, the President; Vítor Constâncio, the Vice-President and responsible for Administration and Financial Stability; Jörg Asmussen, responsible for International and European Relations; Benoît Cœuré responsible for Market Operations and for Information Systems and Payments and Market Infrastructure; and Peter Praet responsible for Economics, Human

---

D Giannone and M Lenza, 'The Financial and Macroeconomic Effects of the OMT Announcements' (2014) *CSEF working paper* no 352.

[25] 'As far as my remarks in London are concerned, there is not one word of these remarks that had not been discussed in the previous Governing Council meetings. So there was not one word of these remarks that surprised my colleagues' (M Draghi, 'Introductory statement to the press conference', Frankfurt am Main, 2 August 2012, available at www.ecb.europa.eu/press/pressconf/2012/html/is120802.en.html).

[26] 'There was no specific instance that led to us having the discussion we had today. There was just a sense of worsening of the crisis and of the worsening consequences of the financial market fragmentation in the euro area' (ibid).

[27] 'Clear visible signs of fragmentation had been with us since the second half of last year, gradually leading to a euro area-wide credit crunch by year-end. Then the ECB conducted the two LTRO operations, which removed another type of risk, namely the possibility of a banking crisis caused by lack of liquidity. They had a very powerful effect of calming financial markets for some time. But then, by the end of April this year, we saw all types of spreads widening again, and the amount of short positions against the euro picking up. These signs made clear that fragmentation had reached points beyond which we would not be able to deliver price stability. There certainly was a deep reflection going on in the months before, both in the ECB and in the Governing Council, about how to cope with this fragmentation. The objective was and still is to restore a financially integrated monetary area. The OMT was the result of this reflection' (Barber and Steen, 'Interview with Mario Draghi' (n 1)).

[28] Articles 12.1, 12.2 and 18.3 of the ECB Statute.

Resources, Budget and Organisation and the Target2-Securities Programme. The sixth member, José M González-Páramo, responsible for Market Operations, had terminated his eight years' tenure in May 2012 and was only replaced by Yves Mersch in December 2012.[29] This was the first time in the ECB's (although rather short) history that such a long period of time was required before an Executive Member could be replaced on the board. This was due to an intense debate regarding the debt crisis, and in particular, a battle between northern and southern Member States over the person to place in the Executive Board.[30]

In any case, although it is possible to rely on the official minutes of the ECB Executive Board meetings given their classified nature, it can be confidently stated, on the basis of a series of interviews and speeches gave in the aftermath of the OMT decision, that a broad consensus among the Executive Board members was present. Jörg Asmussen, the German member of the ECB Executive Board, supported the programme in a number of occasions and, most notably, in front of the German Constitutional Court for the OMT case.[31] Asmussen had joined the bank board as a more 'moderate view', after his predecessor, Jürgen Stark, resigned because of his disappointment over central bank bond-buying, which he and other German economists regard as a violation of the prohibition against central bank financing of governments. The Vice-President, Vítor Constâncio from Portugal, and Peter Praet, the Belgian member, expressly supported the programme.[32] The French member, Benoît Cœuré, was one of the most vigorous supporters of the programme and, in many instances, used the same words that Draghi used in his London speech.[33]

---

[29] The appointment is made by the European Council on a qualified majority voting following a recommendation of the Council. It also needs the prior, but not binding, approval of the European Parliament's Economic and Monetary Affairs Committee, and then of the European Parliament's plenary.

[30] For a reconstruction of the facts see M Jones, 'Euro top jobs tussle to leave ECB Board seat empty' (Frankfurt, 24 May 2012) *Reuters*, available at www.reuters.com/article/2012/05/24/us-ecb-board-idUSBRE84N0UV20120524.

[31] 'The announcement of OMTs was and is the necessary and appropriate step to eliminate the disruption in the transmission of monetary policy caused by concerns that there would be an unwanted break-up of the euro. The risks of not acting would have been greater. The ECB and its decision-makers are aware of the limits of its monetary policy mandate. Our measures are aimed at maintaining monetary policy transmission and preventing an unwanted break-up of the euro. It is not allowed to, is not able to and does not want to replace the actions of democratically elected governments. Quite the opposite. The OMT programme is therefore aimed at protecting the market mechanism so as to urge the Member States to make the necessary reforms' (J Asmussen, 'Introductory statement in the proceedings before the Federal Constitutional Court' (Karlsruhe, 11 June 2013)).

[32] 'With regard to your question on bond purchases, I do not know where that rumor could have arisen from. I have never spoken about the issue outside our meetings, and I am not going to do it now. I will just point out that, as the president mentioned before, this was approved unanimously today with one exception and it was not me!' (V Constâncio, 'Introductory statement to the press conference' (Frankfurt am Main, 2 August 2012)). See also P Praet, 'Debt, deficits and unstable markets', speech at the Hyman P. Minsky Conference, Berlin, 26 November 2012, available at www.ecb.europa.eu/press/key/date/2012/html/sp121126_1.en.html.

[33] 'The OMTs will enable the ECB to address severe distortions in government bond markets which originate from, in particular, fears on the part of investors of the reversibility of the euro … Let me be

Draghi, however, needed the approval not only of the Executive Board but also, and more importantly, of the Governing Council. The power to take the most important and strategically significant decisions rests in the hands of the Governing Council, as it sets forth the monetary policy and guidelines for implementation.[34] In particular, when taking monetary policy decisions, as was the case with the OMT decision, the Governing Council normally acts by a simple majority of the participants, provided that a quorum of two-thirds of the members having a voting right is met. Each member has one vote, but in the event of a tie, the President has the casting vote.[35] The principle of 'one member, one vote' reflects the status of all the members of the Governing Council, who are appointed in their personal capacity and not as representatives of their Member States.[36] For certain decisions on sensitive financial matters, the votes of the Governing Council are proportional to the shares of the National Central Banks (NCBs) in the subscribed capital of the ECB and, on such occasions, the votes of the members of the Executive Board are zero-weighted.[37]

The Governing Council comprises the members of the Executive Board of the ECB and the Governors of the national central banks of the Member States whose currency is the euro. Therefore, at the time of the OMT decision, the Governing Council comprised the five Executive Board members, as outlined above, as well as the Governors of the NCBs of the Eurozone (17 in total as of 2012). It is also interesting to notice that the meeting of the Governing Council discussing the OMT decision was additionally attended by the European Commission Vice-President, Olli Rehn.[38] This is due to the fact that the OMT decision had some clear policies implications involving the Union as a whole.

It is not possible to know whether Draghi had a strong consensus in the Governing Council, as the official minutes of the ECB Governing Council meetings, accompanied by the votes and arguments of its members were also confidential.[39]

---

very clear: the Maastricht Treaty refers to the "irrevocable fixing of exchange rates" when a country enters monetary union. The euro is irrevocable ... The OMTs are an instrument in the ECB's toolbox to help it fulfil its mandate, maintaining price stability. They will be conducive to the monetary authority restoring its power to control credit conditions in the euro area and, through that channel, inflation in the medium term' (B Cœuré, 'Completing Europe's Economic and Monetary Union', speech at the Palestinian Public Finance Institute, Ramallah, 23 September 2012, available at www.ecb.europa.eu/press/key/date/2012/html/sp120923.en.html).

[34] According to Article 12.1 of the ECB Statute: 'The Governing Council shall adopt the guidelines and take the decisions necessary to ensure the performance of the tasks entrusted to the ESCB under these Treaties and this Statute. The Governing Council shall formulate the monetary policy of the Union including, as appropriate, decisions relating to intermediate monetary objectives, key interest rates and the supply of reserves in the ESCB, and shall establish the necessary guidelines for their implementation.'

[35] Article 10.2 of the ECB Statute.

[36] See J Louis, *Commentaire Megret, Le Droit de la CEE 6: Union Economique et Monetaire, Cohesion Economique et Sociale, Politique Industrielle et Technologique Europeenne* (Brussels, Editions de l'Université de Bruxelles, 1995) 66.

[37] Article 10.3 of the ECB Statute.

[38] Draghi, 'Introductory statement to the press conference' (n 25).

[39] Article 10.4 provides: 'The proceedings of the meetings shall be confidential. The Governing Council may decide to make the outcome of its deliberations public.' The problem of transparency

It is interesting to notice that this lack of transparency was supported on the basis that it avoids 'nationalistic' overtones in an institution that is to be supranational and that has no long-term track record in that regard.[40] Some economists have tried to overcome this lack of information by discovering the decision model through a statistical model, showing that most decisions made by the Governing Council suggests that they were the outcome of bargaining.[41] However, as was the case for the Executive Board, it is possible to understand the personal preference of the Governing Council's members through a number of interviews and speeches.[42] Accordingly, it is possible to group the members into four different categories.

NCB Governors who strongly supported the programme, principally in light of the financial markets' pressure over their respective Member States: Patrick Honohan (Ireland), George Provopoulos (Greece), Luis M Linde (Spain), Ignazio Visco (Italy), Panicos Demetriades (Cyprus) and Carlos da Silva Costa (Portugal). The overall opinion can be summarised using the words of the President of the Central Bank of Ireland:

> The ECB has made clear its determination to do what is necessary to preserve the euro and remove unfounded euro break-up premia in sovereign yields. The OMT, designed as a backstop to inhibit negative self-fulfilling market dynamics, provides the necessary tools to deliver on that commitment.[43]

A second group comprised NCB Governors from Member States not under specific pressure by financial markets but who, nevertheless, positively viewed the decision for many different reasons: Christian Noyer[44] (France), Yves Mersch (Luxembourg) and Josef Bonnici (Malta). In particular, Mersch, from Luxembourg,

was raised also by Draghi in a speech (22 April 2014) which underlined that unconventional measures require enhanced communication. On 3 July 2014 'the ECB announces its commitment to publish regular accounts of the Governing Council's monetary policy meetings, which is intended to start with the January 2015 meeting. The publication of the accounts will be timed so that the account of the previous meeting is published before the date of the next one.'

[40] E Apel, *Central Banking Systems Compared: The ECB, The Pre-Euro Bundesbank and the Federal Reserve System* (New York, Routledge, 2003) 57.

[41] In more detail, the research shows that the Governing Council members follow national objectives and bargain over interest-rate setting based on weights derived from their country's share in the euro area's GDP and that the decision that is accepted by all its members is reached under the threat of potentially tougher negotiation as the outside option. The finding also throws some doubt on the ECB's official position that all its decisions are based on consensus. See B Hayo and P Méon, 'Behind Closed Doors: Revealing the ECB's Decision Rule' (2013) 37 *Journal of International Money and Finance* 135.

[42] For a general and journalistic picture of the ECB Governing Council's voting preference see M Bird, 'Here's a ranking of the European Central Bank's hawks and doves' *Business Insider* (London, 10 February 2015), available at uk.businessinsider.com/ecb-dove-hawk-scale-2015-2/21/?r=US.

[43] P Honohan, 'Sovereign Risk: A World Without Risk-free Assets' (8 January 2013) *BIS Papers* no 72, available at www.bis.org/publ/bppdf/bispap72d.pdf.

[44] A Benoît and G Thesing, 'Interview with C. Noyer' *Bloomberg* (17 November 2012), available at www.bloomberg.com/news/articles/2012-11-17/ecb-s-noyer-says-rejecting-omt-is-stance-against-price-stability.

who was later appointed as a member of the ECB Executive Board, despite being initially considered an 'inflation hawk', eventually stated:

> So if 'fragmentation' is the one word characterizing the main threat to our stability-oriented monetary policy, one of our most successful answers to it can be summarized in only three letters: OMT. This stands for the programme of Outright Monetary Transactions ... The ECB has not run out of ammunition. We can employ more tools and measures whenever they will be needed.[45]

A third group comprised NCB Governors who showed moderate support, but emphasised at the same time the importance of structural policies reform and expressed scepticism about the abilities of monetary policy to fix fiscally related problems: Ardo Hansson (Estonia),[46] Ewald Nowotny (Austria), Jozef Makúch (Slovakia) and Marko Kranjec (Slovenia).

Ultimately, a fourth group was composed by NCB Governors who did not enthusiastically welcome the programme: Jens Weidmann (Germany), Klaas Knot (Netherlands), Luc Coene (Belgium) and Erkki Liikanen (Finland). In particular, the President of the Bundesbank and the President of the Nederlandsche Bank have been very outspoken against the OMT programme, while the Presidents of the Belgium and Finland Central Banks have been less openly critical but nevertheless not pleased with the activation of the programme. In this sense, Mr Liikanen commented: 'The OMT programme has so far fulfilled its purpose well, as it were: it has considerably calmed the markets, even though there has been no need to activate the programme.'[47] Overall, it is clear that the majority of the Governing Council was composed by members coming from States under financial distress and this greatly favoured an agreement concerning the OMT decision. This particular situation had been raised as a giving rise to a potential bias of the ECB by many commentators as well as in a number of interviews.[48]

C. The Announcement of the OMT Programme and the Technical Features

The OMT decision was adopted by the Governing Council at the meeting held on 2 August 2012. As outlined above, the official minutes of the meetings remain

[45] Y Mersch, 'Monetary policy in an environment of low growth and interest rates', speech at the Nordea 3rd Annual Nordic AAA Seminar, Copenhagen, 13 June 2013, available at www.ecb.europa.eu/press/key/date/2013/html/sp130613_1.en.html.
[46] 'For me this conditionality was fundamental and central. It is not a blank cheque and we decide independently' (M Zydra, 'Interview with A. Hansson', *Süddeutsche Zeitung*, 24 November 2012, available at www.eestipank.ee/en/press/articles-and-interviews/interview-ardo-hansson-governor-eesti-pank).
[47] E Liikanen, 'The economic crisis and the evolving role of central banks', speech to the Paasikivi Society, Helsinki, 25 November 2013, available at www.bis.org/review/r131128c.htm.
[48] In an interview with the *Frankfurter Allgemeine Zeitung* Draghi was asked: 'Many Germans are concerned about the majority composition of the ECB Governing Council, which in numerical terms

confidential, however, the ECB conventionally considers the President's introductory statements to be the equivalent of the minutes of the Governing Council meeting, since its draft is approved by the Governing Council prior to the press conference.[49] Moreover, statements and press conference are also considered sufficient to deliver the 'message', as maintained by the Advocate General Cruz Villalón in the *OMT case*.[50] According to the President's introductory statement, it appears that the decision was not unanimous. There was one dissenting (or reserved) view.[51] The announcement of the programme in August was immediately followed by the presentation of the technical details in the beginning of September. On 6 September 2012 during the traditional introductory statement after the meeting of the Governing Council, the President of the ECB outlined the details of the main features of the OMT programme.[52] President Draghi again explained that the voting was not unanimous ('Well, it was not unanimous. There was one dissenting view. We do not disclose the details of our work. It is up to you to guess'), but at the same time he stressed the importance of having the strongest consensus possible within the Governing Council.[53]

The legal basis of the OMT decision, as was the case for the previous SMP programme, is Article 18.1 of the ECB Statute, according to which the Eurosystem may conduct operations of 'buying and selling marketable instruments'.[54] In the present case, marketable instruments are sovereign bond purchased or sold in the secondary markets. The legal details of the programme were provided through a press release.[55] It first clarified the name of the programme (Outright Monetary

is dominated by central bankers from fiscally weak countries' (H Steltzner and S Ruhkamp, 'Interview with Mario Draghi', *Frankfurter Allgemeine Zeitung*, 24 February 2012, available at www.ecb.europa.eu/press/inter/date/2012/html/sp120224_1.en.html).

[49] Apel, *Central Banking Systems Compared* (n 40) 58.

[50] 'The conventional monetary policy instruments, announcements, opinions or statements by the representatives of central banks generally play a crucial role in the development of monetary policy today' (Case C-62/14 *Peter Gauweiler and Others v Deutscher Bundestag*, EU:C:2015:7, Opinion of AG Cruz Villalón).

[51] Draghi remarked: 'The voting was, as I said, unanimous with one reservation, with one position that reserved itself' (M Draghi, 'Introductory statement to the press conference'(n 25)).

[52] ECB, 'Technical features of Outright Monetary Transactions' 6 September 2012, press release, available at www.ecb.europa.eu/press/pr/date/2012/html/pr120906_1.en.html.

[53] 'I have been blessed by almost having unanimity on the very important and fundamental decisions that we have taken in the last few months. There is nothing I would wish more than to have total unanimity, of course. So I am looking forward to having that' (M Draghi in ECB, 'Technical features' (n 52)).

[54] Article 18.1 of the ECB Statute reads: 'In order to achieve the objectives of the ESCB and to carry out its tasks, the ECB and the national central banks may: – operate in the financial markets by buying and selling outright (spot and forward) or under repurchase agreement and by lending or borrowing claims and marketable instruments, whether in euro or other currencies, as well as precious metals; – conduct credit operations with credit institutions and other market participants, with lending being based on adequate collateral.'

[55] According to the introductory statement of the 6 September 2012, the Council approved the main parameters of the programme of OMT. The Council also approved a draft Decision on outright monetary transactions and repealing Decision ECB/2010/5, as well as a draft Guideline on the

Transactions (OMTs)), its aim ('safeguarding an appropriate monetary policy transmission and the singleness of the monetary policy') and its scope ('Eurosystem's outright transactions in secondary sovereign bond markets'). In particular, the press release outlined the details of the main features of the programme, divided into six pillars.

The last four technical features did not add anything new to the features of the existing SMP programme as they reflect similar provisions. In the third pillar, the ECB clarified that in the OMT process of purchasing, as was the case for SMP purchase, the Eurosystem will legally act as a normal creditor accepting the same (*pari passu*) treatment as private or other creditors in accordance with the terms of such bonds. The Eurosystem will not, in other words, possess any special rights to seniority in connection with the bond purchase. The fourth pillar concerned the 'sterilisation' of the OMT. Sterilisation means that the liquidity created through outright monetary transactions will be fully offset by the withdrawals by the ECB of liquidity from the open market, ie withdrawing from circulation an equivalent amount of money. This is to say that the OMT – as was the case with the previous SMP but in sharp contrast with the various programmes of quantitative easing – will not involve any money creation. The fifth pillar, named transparency, provides that the ECB will also publish the aggregate OMT holdings and their market values on a weekly basis and the breakdown by country on a monthly basis. Finally, with the last pillar, the ECB terminated the SMP, clarifying that it will hold the SMP portfolio to maturity.

What were really innovative, instead, were the first two pillars of the technical features. The first pillar, named conditionality, provides that OMT purchase is strictly and effectively conditional to an appropriate European Financial Stability Facility/European Stability Mechanism (EFSF/ESM) programme, both in the form of a full EFSF/ESM macro-economic adjustment programme or a precautionary programme (a so-called 'Enhanced Conditions Credit Line'), 'provided that they include the possibility of EFSF/ESM primary market purchases'. This requirement, which, as seen above, also characterises the ESM, represented the trade-off between financial assistance and public reforms of fiscal consolidation and was the cornerstone of the legal arguments of the Court of Justice of the European Union (ECJ) in favour of the legitimacy of the OMT programme (see section I.D below). Additionally, the technical features clarifies that the Governing Council will act 'in full discretion and acting in accordance with its monetary policy mandate' in the decision over the start, continuation, suspension and termination of the programme (ie if the objective is achieved or there is non-compliance with the macro-economic adjustment or precautionary programme of OMT). With this statement, the ECB, on the one hand underlined the link between the OMT activation and the performance of monetary policy, thus stressing again the strict necessity of this instrument for its regular operation; on the other hand, it also sent

---

implementation of outright monetary transactions. Both drafts were subsequently amended at the meetings of the Governing Council on 4 October and 7 and 8 November 2012.

a signal to the markets that it will closely monitor with 'full discretion' any possible detriment to the Eurozone financial stability resulting from sovereign bond high risk premia.

The second pillar clarified that OMT could also be activated for Member States currently under a macro-economic adjustment programme if they regain bond market access, with the transactions focused on the shorter part of the yield curve (maturity of between one and three years). These three features of the programme were all incorporated in order to highlight the conditional and limited nature of the programme. However, on the other hand, it also powerfully provides: 'No *ex ante* quantitative limits are set on the size of Outright Monetary Transaction.' The *ex ante* unlimited amount of purchase was laid down to convince financial markets of the ECB's unconditional support for government bonds under financial pressure. This was clearly pointed out by Draghi in a later interview concerning the OMT decision: 'There was a sense that we had to overcome the limitations of the SMP and make sure that the signal to the market would be proportionate to the gravity of the situation.'[56] This, as was outlined above, was the other innovative feature of the OMT, in contrast with the previous SMP, but it was also the main source of criticism concerning the programme.

In any case, based on such technical standards as well as further clarification provided in the aftermath, it appears that four conditions need to be satisfied, cumulatively, in order for a Member State to be eligible for assistance under the OMT programme:[57]

(1) The Governing Council of the ECB must assess whether, on the basis of a variety of indicators (the bid-ask spreads, liquidity, the shape of the yield curves, volatility and the interest rates charged for the government bonds), there exists an unwarranted spreads on the government bond markets which eventually lead to a broken monetary policy transmission.[58]
(2) The Member State needs to have received financial support from the ESM, either in the form of direct macro-economic support or precautionary conditioned credit lines. The signing of a Memorandum of Understanding in accordance with the ESM financial support is thus a precondition.
(3) The Member State must constantly comply with the conditionality attached and it must satisfactorily implement the programme, under the monitoring of the Governing Council of the ECB.
(4) The Member State must have access, or regain access, to the government bonds market, precisely because 'the OMT is not a replacement for a lack of primary market.'[59]

[56] Barber and Steen, 'Interview with Mario Draghi' (n 1).
[57] Explaining such four conditions see especially Y Mersch, 'Oral hearing of the Federal Constitutional Court in the OMT proceedings' (Karlsruhe, 16 February 2016).
[58] Barber and Steen, 'Interview with Mario Draghi' (n 1).
[59] ibid.

D. Criticism of the OMT Programme and Legal Challenge

It is relevant to notice that the OMT programme marks the first time that the ECB's Governing Council has openly acknowledged an internal disagreement. Before, it had officially always reached decisions by consensus. Draghi later clarified:

> The endorsement to do whatever it takes – again, to use the same words – whatever it takes to preserve the euro as a stable currency has been unanimous. But, it is clear and it is known that Mr Weidmann and the Bundesbank – although we are here in a personal capacity and we should never forget that – have their reservations about programmes that envisage buying bonds.

In the following interviews, Draghi explained that although the framework was 'endorsed by all Governing Council members with one exception', the Council incorporated the dissenting concerns into the decisions. In particular, he pointed out that: 'You can be assured that, in taking measures, we stick strictly to our mandate', and that the reasoning of former member Jürgen Stark 'is not shared by the Governing Council of the ECB'.[60] On the other hand, Bundesbank President J Weidmann explained his position very clearly:

> I was already critical of the sovereign bond purchases that have been made to date – and I was by no means alone in that respect. Such a policy is too close to state financing via the money press for me. The central bank cannot fundamentally solve the problems this way. It runs the risk of creating new problems.[61]

In particular, the main legal arguments against the OMT programme rests on the scope of the ECB's monetary policy mandate and the prohibition of monetary financing of the Member States under the Treaty. Based on these arguments, the OMT was notably challenged before the Germany's Federal Constitutional Court (Bundesverfassungsgericht or simply BVerfG) by a huge number of German professors and politicians. The claimants ultimately challenged, *inter alias*, the constitutionality of the participation of the German Bundesbank in the implementation of the OMT decision, and the omission by the German Government to bring an action for annulment before the ECJ concerning the OMT programme.[62]

The German Constitutional Court upheld some of the legal arguments, and as a result, questioned the legality of the OMT programme under both German and EU law. First, the BVerfG challenged the compatibility of the OMT with the

---

[60] M Sauga and A Seith, 'Interview with Mario Draghi', *Der Spiegel*, 29 October 2012, available at www.ecb.europa.eu/press/inter/date/2012/html/sp121029.en.html.

[61] G Mascolo, M Sauga and A Seith, 'Interview with Jens Weidmann: Too Close to State Financing Via the Money Press', *Der Spiegel*, 27 August 2012, available at www.spiegel.de/international/europe/spiegel-interview-with-bundesbank-president-jens-weidmann-a-852285-2.html.

[62] Bundesverfassungsgericht [BVerfG – Federal Constitutional Court], 2 BvR 2728/13 (Jan 24, 2014), available at www.bundesverfassungsgericht.de/SharedDocs/Entscheidungen/EN/2014/01/rs20140114_2bvr272813en.html.

scope of the mandate of the ECB under the Treaty (Articles 119 and 127(1) and (2) TFEU) as well as under the ECB Statute (Articles 17 to 24 of Protocol (No 4) on the Statute of the European System of Central Banks (ESCB) and of the ECB). According to the Court, the OMT could be considered to be an economic policy measure rather than a monetary policy measure. More specifically, based on four aspects of the programme (conditionality, selectivity, parallelism and circumvention), the Court maintained that the OMT could constitute an *ultra vires act* in breach of the powers attributed to the ECB. Second, according to the BVerfG, the OMT might have circumvented the prohibition of monetary financing under Article 123(1) TFEU. The Court pointed out various technical features of the programme, such as the *pari passu* treatment and the possible unlimited purchase, to show that high financial risks would be shared among the Member States, and, accordingly, this could constitute a substantial circumvention of the prohibition laid down in Article 123(1) TFEU. As a result, the Court, for the first time in its history, requested a preliminary ruling under Article 267 TFEU from the ECJ, concerning the compatibility of the OMT decision with the TFEU.[63] In particular, the two legal questions outlined above were raised before the ECJ. The first question concerned the possible infringement of the monetary policy mandate of the ECB through the OMT programme. The second question concerned the compatibility of the OMT programme with the prohibition of monetary financing enshrined in Article 123(1) of the TFEU.[64]

It is easy to recognise that this legal challenge was very similar to the other legal challenges brought against the ESM before the ECJ,[65] as well as before national constitutional courts.[66] As explained by the judges of the German Constitutional

---

[63] For different analysis of the case and of the decision see the articles of special issue of the *German Law Journal* ((2014) 15 *German Law Journal* 107) regarding the OMT decision of the German Federal Constitutional Court. In particular, see *inter alias* U Di Fabio, 'Karlsruhe Makes a Referral' (2014) 15 *German Law Journal* 107 and D Murswiek, 'ECB, ECJ, Democracy, and the Federal Constitutional Court: Notes on the Federal Constitutional Court's Referral Order from 14 January 2014' (2014) 15 *German Law Journal* 147. See also T Petch, 'The Compatibility of Outright Monetary Transactions with EU Law' (2013) 7 *Law and Financial Markets Review* 13.

[64] GFCC, Order of the Second Senate of 14 January 2014 – 2 BvR 2728/13 – paras (1–24). See more generally, M Wendel, 'Exceeding Judicial Competence in the Name of Democracy: The German Federal Constitutional Court' OMT Reference' (2014) 10 *EuConst* 263; Editorial Comments, 'An Unintended Side-Effect of Draghi's Bazooka: An Opportunity to Establish a More Balanced Relationship Between the ECJ and Member States' Highest Courts' (2014) 51 *Common Market Law Review* 375.

[65] Case C-370/12 *Pringle v Government of Ireland, Ireland and the Attorney General*, EU:C:2012:756. For a critical analysis see B De Witte, 'The Court of Justice Approves the Creation of the European Stability Mechanism Outside the EU Legal Order: Pringle' (2013) 50 *Common Market Law Review* 805; P Craig, 'Pringle and Use of EU Institutions outside the EU Legal Framework: Foundations, Procedure and Substance' (2013) 9 *European Constitutional Law Review* 263.

[66] The EU financial assistance mechanism and the ESM have also been challenged a number of times also by national constitutional courts, and most notably by the German Federal Constitutional Court. The most important case involved the constitutionality of the ESM treaty and the fiscal compact, and the new Art 136 TFEU, which modified the bailout prohibition of Art 125 TFEU. The claimant maintained that it was allegedly introducing unconstitutional liability obligations for Germany. More in particular, the crucial point was as to whether these instruments created an unlimited financial obligation for Germany. The Court held that the overall budgetary autonomy of the Bundestag was not

Court, the substance of the two programmes is in fact 'functionally equivalent'. On this point, some authors went further, arguing that the only difference between the two instruments would be that 'the volume of purchases of government bonds by the ESM is limited by the ESM's financial endowment, while the ECB can buy unlimitedly' and that 'the ESM funds have been approved by the parliaments of the Member States'.[67] Other authors have, in contrast, maintained that the two are not functionally equivalent. According to this view, the ESM is the only measure involving a wealth transfer precisely because 'ESM loans and other support available from the ESM are provided to Member States at rates and conditions that very clearly do not reflect the market view of an adequate risk premium, given the perceived default risk of the beneficiary countries'.[68] In addition, it is interesting to notice that the German Constitutional Court announcement did not have any negative effect on the financial markets as the sovereign risk premia of Eurozone crisis countries declined steadily throughout 2014. According to some authors, this is because the financial markets believed in a 'compromise interpretation' in the worst case scenario.[69]

On January 2015, Advocate General Cruz Villalón issued his Opinion.[70] With regards to the first question, the Advocate General maintained that the OMT was both suitable and necessary. On the one hand, the means of reducing the interest rates on the government bonds of the States through bond purchase on the shorter part of the yield curve could be considered to be coherent with the goal of restoring the regular transmission of monetary policy. On the other hand, they were also necessary given the emergency and in light of the limited alternative options available for the ECB. The OMT programme, in this sense, is defined as 'limited and restricted to specific cases' especially given its conditionality requirement.[71] The Advocate General then turned to the general proportionality test by examining all the components of the measure in relation to each other. Overall, he maintained that the benefit, ie 'intervene in an exceptional situation in order to restore monetary policy' outweighed the cost, ie the exposure of the ECB to financial risk,

---

prejudiced, but that the Bundestag and the Bundesrat would need to be sufficiently informed, and the Bundestag's approval would need to be required for 'every large-scale federal aid measure'. See also the decision 2 BvE 8/11, judgment of 28 February 2012. For an overview of these decisions see S Schmidt, 'Sense of Deja Vu: The FCC's Preliminary European Stability Mechanism Verdict' (2013) 14 *German Law Journal* 1, 11. For a critical analysis of the last decision see especially H Deters, 'National Constitutional Jurisprudence in a Post-National Europe: The ESM Ruling of the German Federal Constitutional Court and the Disavowal of Conflict' (2014) 20 *European Law Journal* 204.

[67] Murswiek, 'ECB, ECJ, Democracy' (n 63) 149.

[68] C Gerner-Beuerle, E Kucuk and E Schuster, 'Law Meets Economics in the German Federal Constitutional Court: Outright Monetary Transactions on Trial' (2014) 15 *German Law Journal* 281, 309.

[69] H Siekmann and V Wieland, 'The German Constitutional Court's Decision on OMT: Have Markets Misunderstood?' (2014) *Policy Insight* no 74, Institute for Monetary and Financial Stability, Goethe University of Frankfurt, available at www.voxeu.org/sites/default/files/Image/FromMay2014/PolicyInsight74.pdf.

[70] Case C-62/14 *Peter Gauweiler and Others v Deutscher Bundestag*, EU:C:2015:7, Opinion of AG Cruz Villalón.

[71] ibid, para 178.

together with 'the moral hazard arising from the artificial alteration of the value of the bonds of the State concerned'.[72] He also added that, 'the absence of any *ex ante* quantitative limit is not a factor which is sufficient in itself for the measure to be considered disproportionate' because of the inherent risks associated with financial markets and of the existence of objective quantitative limits which the ECB explicitly admits but 'cannot be disclosed for strategic reasons'.[73] The Advocate General concluded that the programme was compatible with the principle of proportionality and its mandate as long as the ECB is not involved in the financial assistance programmes, and strictly complies with the obligation to state reasons and the requirements deriving from the principle of proportionality. With regards to the second question, he preliminarily observed that the respect of the principle of proportionality by the ECB is also a precondition for the answer to the second question. Accordingly, he dismissed all the features (*pari passu* status, default risk, holding until maturity and the encouragement to purchase additional bonds) which, according to the BVerfG, might lead to a monetary financing interpretation of the measure, and ultimately concluded in favour of the compatibility of the OMT with Article 123(1) TFEU. However, one argument made by the BVerfG was partially upheld, concerning the timing of purchase, and in particular, that the large scale and the short time of the bond purchase in the secondary market might have a similar effect to that of a direct purchase in the primary market. As a result, the Advocate General specifically required, for the compatibility of the OMT with Article 123(1) TFEU, that any implementation of the programme allows the actual formation of a market price in respect of the government bonds so that 'there continues to be a real difference between a purchase of bonds on the primary market and their purchase on the secondary market'.[74]

The ECJ issued its final ruling in June 2015 which substantially upheld the arguments of the Advocate General.[75] Concerning the first question, the ECJ, similarly to the Advocate General, affirmed that any bond-buying measure needs to be proportional to the objectives of the monetary policy and, that, in this sense, the economic and monetary reasoning provided by the ECB for the adoption of the programme were sound. The emergency economic situation and the broken monetary transmission on the one hand and the fact that the programme is conditioned and limited on the other hand, were crucial in concluding that the OMT programme does not infringe upon the principle of proportionality and the mandate of the ECB under the Treaty and the Statute. With regards to the second question, the ECJ acknowledged that, according to Article 123(1) TFEU, not only purchase of government bonds on secondary markets but also other types of purchase having the same equivalent effect are prohibited. According to the Court, sufficient safeguards must be built into the implementation of the programme to

---

[72] ibid, para 186.
[73] ibid, para 191.
[74] ibid, para 252.
[75] Case C-62/14 *Peter Gauweiler and Others v Deutscher Bundestag*, EU:C:2015:400.

avoid the prohibition of such monetary financing. However, the Court observed that such safeguards are present in the draft decision and the guideline of the ECB whereby a minimum period is observed between the issue of a security on the primary market and its purchase on the secondary market, and that no prior announcement will be made concerning any decision to carry out government bond purchase. Ultimately, the ECJ interpreted Articles 119, 123(1) and 127(1) and (2) TFEU as well as Articles 17 to 24 of Protocol (No 4) on the Statute of the ESCB and of the ECB as permitting the ESCB to adopt a programme for the purchase of government bonds on secondary markets, such as the OMT programme.

The case went back to the BVerfG for a final decision on the constitutionality of the measure. Although the Court is essentially bound by the interpretation of EU law by the ECJ, there was also a minor possibility that the BVerfG would still declare the illegitimacy of the programme under German law, giving rise to constitutional tension with a European dimension. The Court, in its judgment on June 2016, substantially recognised both interpretations provided by the ECJ, and, as a result, rejected the constitutional claims.[76] The Court, however, particularly stressed the importance of the features adopted by the ECJ to support the legality of the programme, and expressly made any implementation of the programme by the German Bundesbank subject to six conditions: (i) the bond purchases must not be announced by the ECB; (ii) the volume of the purchases must be limited from the outset; (iii) there must be a minimum period between the issue of the government bonds and their purchase by the ESCB that is defined from the outset and prevents the issuing conditions from being distorted; (iv) the ESCB may purchase only government bonds of Member States that have bond market access enabling the funding of such bonds; (v) purchased bonds will only in exceptional cases be held until maturity; and (vi) purchases are restricted or ceased and purchased bonds are remarketed should continuing the intervention become unnecessary. It is important to notice that all these conditions were clearly present in the decision of the ECJ but they were mostly indirect 'conditions' for the legality of the programme. The BVerfG essentially made what were implicit conditions in the ECJ decision into express conditions.

The decision in *Gauweiler* is significant for many aspects of EU law. The connection between national courts and the ECJ under the preliminary reference procedure is one of them.[77] The decision is mostly significant in respect to the different interpretation of the power of the ECB between the ECJ and the German Constitutional Court. What is important to underline here is not the different interpretative standpoints of the two courts, where the ECJ, on the one hand, was more orientated towards the monetary aspects, considering the OMT to be strictly

---

[76] 2 BvR 2728/13, 2 BvR 2729/13, 2 BvR 2730/13, 2 BvR 2731/13, 2 BvE 13/13, Judgment of 21 June 2016. Press Release No 34/2016 of 21 June 2016.

[77] See especially P Craig and M Markakis, 'Gauweiler and the Legality of Outright Monetary Transactions' (2016) 41 *European Law Review* 1.

linked to the objective of monetary policy transmission, while the BVerfG was more economic oriented, in terms of the impact of OMT on interest rate spreads.[78]

What is more important is the underlying reasoning behind these different decisions. In particular, as pointed out by other authors, the difference is essentially based on two different perceptions of the independence of the ECB.[79] The two courts, in this sense, significantly differ where the BVerfG is less deferent to the judgment of the ECB and strictly applies its power of judicial review, particularly in case of reviewing non-standard measures; while the ECJ explicitly practices judicial restraint in reviewing actions and decisions of the ECB. There are multiple evidence of these different practices. In its final ruling, for instance, the BVerfG expressly observed how the ECJ provided no answer to the fact that the 'independence granted to the European Central Bank leads to a noticeable reduction in the level of democratic legitimation of its actions and should therefore give rise to restrictive interpretation and to particularly strict judicial review of the mandate of the European Central Bank'.[80] The Advocate General's opinion, as well as the ECJ, in contrast, preliminarily acknowledged 'the exclusive competence and technical expertise of the ECB' to carry out its tasks, and accordingly, pointed out that the ECB must enjoy a broad discretion in its policy, and that courts, lacking the same specific expertise and experience, 'should exercise a significant degree of caution when reviewing the ECB's activity'.[81] Ultimately, these two rulings reflect two different visions of the European economic constitution: a constitutional tension between a national and a supranational economic interests which is not yet settled.[82]

Ultimately, it is interesting to notice that, as of the end of 2016, no OMT programme has yet been activated by the ECB. The reason for this is that no Member State has met all the conditions to apply for OMT support. An additional reason is that the OMT programme has been somehow superseded by three important monetary programmes,[83] together called the Expanded Asset Purchase Programme (EAPP), which have been implemented between late 2014 and early 2015: the Covered Bond Purchase Programme (CBPP3),[84] the Asset-Backed

---

[78] ibid.

[79] V Borger, 'Outright Monetary Transactions and the Stability Mandate of the ECB: Gauweiler' (2016) 53 *Common Market Law Review* 139, 192; G Anagnostaras, 'In ECB we trust … the FCC we dare! The OMT preliminary ruling' (2015) 40 *European Law Review* 744, 754–55.

[80] 2 BvR 2728/13, 2 BvR 2729/13, 2 BvR 2730/13, 2 BvR 2731/13, 2 BvE 13/13, Judgment of 21 June 2016. Press Release No 34/2016 of 21 June 2016.

[81] Case C-62/14 *Peter Gauweiler and Others v Deutscher Bundestag*, Opinion of AG Cruz Villalón (n 70) para 111.

[82] See on this point, D Adamski, 'Economic Constitution of the Euro Area After the Gauweiler Preliminary Ruling' (2015) 52 *Common Market Law Review* 1451, 1485.

[83] ibid, 1488.

[84] The third Covered Bond Purchase Programme (CBPP3), concerns the outright purchase of certain eligible covered bonds in the primary and secondary markets for two years. Decision ECB/2014/40 of the European Central Bank of 15 October 2014 on the implementation of the third covered bond purchase programme [2014] OJ L 335/22.

Securities Purchase Programme (ABSPP)[85] and the Public Sector Purchase Programme (PSPP).[86] All these policies, commonly referred as quantitive easing, are not, however, directly aimed at achieving economic growth but rather monetary growth, and in particular reaching an inflation rate in accordance with the ECB standard (close to 2 per cent). The bulk of the programme is the PSPP, according to which the ECB may buy bonds issued by euro area central governments, agencies and European institutions in the secondary market against central bank money. The particularity of the programme is that only 20 per cent of the asset purchases are subject to a regime of risk-sharing. In other words, only those losses arising out of the 20 per cent purchase will be shared.[87] This represents one of the main significant difference between the OMT programme and these programmes. As clarified by Draghi:

> The OMT scheme was meant to address the tail risk to the Eurozone of redenomination risk, which was concentrated in some countries. Broader-based asset purchases are a purely monetary response to the risk of an excessively prolonged period of low inflation.[88]

II. The Banking Union: Background and Main Features

Financial integration has been among the cornerstones of the internal market, since mid-1970s. A number of Council Directives on the coordination of legal rules and administrative provisions governing credit institutions were approved during that period, to promote a deeper financial market integration. These initial provisions, based on the principle of coordination, paved the way to the following measures based on the principle of mutual recognition and minimum harmonisation standards at EU level.[89] In particular, a number of following directives and regulations in the financial sector were essentially based on minimum

---

[85] The Asset-Backed Securities Purchase Programme (ABSPP) concerns the outright purchase of certain eligible asset-backed securities in the primary and secondary markets for two years. It will help banks to diversify funding sources and stimulate the issuance of new securities, for instance, via securitising loans. Decision ECB/2014/45 of the European Central Bank of 19 November 2014 on the implementation of the asset-backed securities purchase programme [2015] OJ L 1/4.

[86] The PSPP complements the ABSPP and the CBPP3. Under the PSPP the ECB and the National Central Banks, in proportions reflecting their respective shares in the ECB's capital key, may purchase outright eligible marketable debt securities issued by, *inter alias*, central governments of a Member State whose currency is the euro, on the secondary markets. Decision ECB/2015/10 of the European Central Bank of 4 March 2015 on a secondary markets public sector asset purchase programme [2015] OJ L 121/20.

[87] ECB, 'ECB announces expanded asset purchase programme', press release, 22 January 2015, available at www.ecb.europa.cu/press/pr/date/2015/html/pr150122_1.en.html.

[88] M Draghi, 'Monetary policy in a prolonged period of low inflation', speech at the ECB Forum on Central Banking, Sintra, 26 May 2014, available at www.ecb.europa.eu/press/key/date/2014/html/sp140526.en.html.

[89] B Haar, 'Organizing Regional Systems: The EU Example' in E Ferran, N Moloney and J Payne (eds), *The Oxford Handbook of Financial Regulation* (Oxford, Oxford University Press, 2014).

harmonisation standards in the first stage of the process,[90] up to a maximum harmonisation in the later stage.[91]

However, it soon became clear that the regulation of cross-border institutions and capitals also required coordination or harmonisation at the supervisory level. In particular, with the financial crisis of 2007–09, the need for a more effective macro-prudential as well as micro-prudential financial supervision emerged. As a result, the European Commission proposed a set of reforms in terms of common European financial supervision in order to 'restore confidence, stability and sustainability in the financial markets'.[92] In particular, the Commission recommended, on the basis of the working group on financial supervision headed by De Larosière,[93] the creation of a supervisory institution, the European Systemic Risk Board (ESRB), and a framework for financial supervision, the European System of Financial Supervisors (ESFS), with the overall purpose of avoiding collective action problems in connection with capital markets oversight. The main function of the ESRB was to prevent 'systemic risks'[94] by monitoring and assessing potential threats to financial stability which arise from macro-economic concerns (so-called 'macro-prudential supervision'). On the basis of these assessments, the ESRB would provide, without legally binding powers, early warnings as well as recommendations, both for action in general and to specific Member States in particular. The ESFS, on the other side, was conceived as a framework consisting of national supervisory authorities, the ESRB, and the new European Supervisory Authorities (ESAs) which would safeguard the financial stability of individual firms (so-called 'micro-prudential oversight'). Within the ESFS, the ESRB would work in tandem with the ESAs, namely the European Banking Authority (EBA), the European Insurance and Occupational Pensions Authority (EIOPA) and the European Securities and Markets Authority (ESMA), and with the supervisory authorities of the Member States, with the overall aim of acquiring better and more reliable information on cross-border risks.[95] However, the competence limitations of the ESAs and the strictly macro-prudential focus of the ESRB and its 'soft law'

---

[90] Directive 93/22/EEC of 10 May 1993 on investment services in the securities field (Investment Services Directive) [1993] OJ L 141/27, repealed by Directive 2004/39/EC of the European Parliament and of the Council of 21 April 2004 on Markets in Financial Instruments [2004] OJ L 145/1.

[91] Directive 2004/39/EC of the European Parliament and of the Council of 21 April 2004 on Markets in Financial Instruments [2004] OJ L 145/1.

[92] Commission Communication on 'European financial supervision' 27 May 2009, COM (2009) 252.

[93] J De Larosière, 'The High Level Group on financial supervision in the EU' (the De Larosière Report), 25 February 2009.

[94] For a good survey on the legal and economic issues associated with systemic risks in capital markets see S Schwarcz, 'Systemic Risk' (2008) 97 *Georgetown Law Journal* 193.

[95] Commission Proposal on 'Regulation of the European Parliament and of The Council on Community macro-prudential oversight of the financial system and establishing a European Systemic Risk Board', 23 September, COM(2009) 499; Regulations no 1092/1093/1094/1095/1096 of 24 November 2010 [2010] OJ L 331/1. See also the so-called Omnibus Directive which amended the legislation in the matter of financial services to ensure effective operation of the European System of Financial Supervisors: Directive 2010/78/EU of 24 November 2010 [2010] OJ L 331/120.

status described above, required a stronger mechanism for supervision and crisis prevention on the micro-prudential level.[96]

As outlined above (see section I.A), a few months before the announcement of the OMT programme, on 28–29 June 2012, an important meeting between EU leaders laid down the framework for significant integration in the budgetary and banking areas. In particular, the Four Presidents' report[97] outlined the need for an integrated financial framework built based on a single European banking supervision system which would have the ultimate responsibility to supervise banks as well as pre-emptive intervention powers applicable to all banks in the EU Member States. This system would complement, on the micro-prudential level, what the De Larosière Report provided for the macro-prudential level. As a result of all these efforts, the European Banking Union was established as a complex framework of common institutions and rules meant to tackle the financial stability of European banks under multiple perspectives. The overall framework is based on three pillars: a common set of rules to prevent financial risks (the single rulebook), a common prudential supervision under the ECB (Single Supervisory Mechanism – SSM) and a common fund in case of bank failure (Single Resolution Mechanism – SRM).

The single rulebook comprises a number of legislative acts: the Capital Requirements Regulation (CRR)[98] on common prudential requirements for credit institutions and investment firms; the Capital Requirements Directive IV (CRD IV) which implements strict capital requirements for banks based on Basel III;[99] the Deposit Guarantee Scheme Directive (DGSD) which provides a common regulation of deposit insurance to protect European consumers in case of a bank's failure;[100] and the Bank Recovery and Resolution Directive (BRRD),[101] for the recovery and resolution of credit institutions and investment firms and a common framework to manage the process of winding down the banks. The single rulebook is additionally completed by a number of Binding Technical Standards (BTS) drafted by the EBA and adopted by the European Commission. Such technical standards are legally binding and directly applicable in all Member States and are aimed at implementing the CRD IV, the BRRD and the DGSD for uniform harmonisation.

In order to ensure that the single rulebook is applied consistently and coherently in the euro area a common prudential supervisor of financial institutions in the euro area was established, the SSM.[102] The SSM gives the ECB responsibility

---

[96] B Haar, 'Financial Regulation' (n 89) 33.

[97] Four Presidents' Report of 5 December 2012 'Towards a Genuine Economic and Monetary Union'.

[98] Regulation (EU) No 575/2013 of 26 June 2013 on prudential requirements for credit institutions and investment firms [2013] OJ L 176/1.

[99] See Directive 2013/36/EU of 26 June 2013 on access to the activity of credit institutions and the prudential supervision of credit institutions and investment firms [2013] OJ L 176/338.

[100] See Directive 2014/49/EU of 16 April 2014 on deposit guarantee schemes [2014] OJ L 173/149.

[101] See Directive 2014/59/EU of 15 May 2014 establishing a framework for the recovery and resolution of credit institutions and investment firms [2014] OJ L 173/190.

[102] Following the European Parliament Plenary vote on the legislative resolution for the European Banking Authority (EBA) Regulation and the Council agreement conferring specific supervision tasks

for supervision over banks in the euro area (and other SSM-participating Member States). In particular the ECB is directly responsible for supervising the approximately 123 largest banking groups,[103] while the national supervisors will continue to monitor the remaining banks. However, the ECB may at any moment decide to directly supervise one or more credit institutions to ensure consistent application of high supervisory standards. The ECB and the national supervisors, working closely together within an integrated system, are to check that banks comply with the EU banking rules and to tackle problems in advance. In order to properly perform its new role, the ECB carried out a comprehensive assessment of EU banks in the face of the adverse economic situation. The assessment was in order to assess bank exposures, including the adequacy of asset and collateral (so-called 'asset quality review'); and to test the resilience of banks' balance sheets, performed in close cooperation with the EBA (so-called 'stress test').

The single rulebook and the SSM were established to avoid, or at least to decrease the chance, of bank failures. However, in case of potential bank failure, a common European fund was set up – the Single Resolution Mechanism (SRM). The SSM, the third pillar of this complex framework, is comprised of a board (the Single Resolution Board (SRB)) and a fund (the Single Resolution Fund (SRF)). In the case of financial distress, the Board, duly informed by the ECB, would have the responsibility to take a decision accordingly and, potentially, to prepare for the resolution of the bank. The total amount of the Fund is equal to at least 1 per cent of the covered deposits of all banks in Member States participating in the Banking Union (estimated to be around €55 billion), and is financed by all the banks in the Banking Union countries, but if there is insufficient funding, may be additionally funded through banking borrowing. In any case, the banking sector of the euro area remain ultimately liable for repayment by means of levies, including *ex post*.

The Banking Union is therefore a unified complex framework of common rules and institutions, with the overall purpose of promoting and enhancing financial stability by ensuring uniform application of financial standards and ultimately by tackling the connection between the banking sector and Member States. More specifically, the financial crisis has shown that potential divergences in integrated financial markets, as the case of the EU single market, may generate significant risks for the overall financial stability. Minimum harmonisation standards led in the past to different interpretations of standards and legal uncertainty, which in

---

on the European Central Bank, the European Union formally adopted the creation of a bank single supervisory mechanism (SSM), led by the European Central Bank, with the objective to strengthen the Economic and Monetary Union. See Regulation (EU) No 1024/2013 of 15 October 2013 conferring specific tasks on the European Central Bank concerning policies relating to the prudential supervision of credit institutions [2012] OJ L 287/63.

[103] In particular, the ECB will have responsibility for direct supervision of banks having assets of more than €30 billion or constituting at least 20 per cent of their home country's GDP or which have requested or received direct public financial assistance from the European Stability Mechanism (ESM).

turn provided the ground for the financial crisis. A unified regulatory framework for the EU financial sector would potentially complete and contribute to a more effective functioning of the Single Market and ensure uniform application of high financial standards (ie Basel III) in all Member States. Ultimately, this could also result in more effective banking oversight and potentially make it possible to avoid another liquidity crisis in the banking sector hitting the balance sheet of sovereign states because of bailing out and recapitalisation. As the Commission pointed out, the ECB 'will ensure a truly European supervision mechanism that is not prone to the protection of national interests, will weaken the link between banks and national finances and will take into account risks to financial stability'.[104]

III. The Interplay between the OMT and the Banking Union

From a broad overview of the two measures, the OMT on the one hand, and the Banking Union on the other hand, it is evident that a number of interconnections exist and are quite significant. First, the objective of both measures is complementary as they are both part of the same general process towards the strengthening of financial stability and financial market integration. More specifically, this chapter has highlighted that the focus of the Banking Union proposal is to break the vicious circle between banking crises and sovereign crisis by tackling the issues related to banking mismanagement and insolvency; while the OMT's aim is to tackle the short-term banking liquidity problems so to restore the broken transmission of ECB monetary policies. Overall, banks are at the centrepiece of the architecture, since they play a central role in both context. Banks are in fact part of the money market mechanism, which allow the interest rates of the ECB to be transmitted to the economy. Money markets and thus well-functioning markets for government bonds are, as explained above, indispensable for monetary policy to be effective, and also because government bond yields are often used as a reference rate for the market overall.[105] Therefore the OMT and the Banking Union are natural complements to each other as they tackle financial stability under two intertwined standpoints. Financial market integration is a second closing link between the Banking Union and the OMT programme. As underlined above, the integration of financial markets represents another essential goal of the Banking Union and at the same time, it is a pre-requisite of the monetary policies of the central bank. Imperfect financial integration may significantly alter the transmission of monetary policy, especially in currency union, as it produces non-uniform

---

[104] EU Commission Memo, 'Banking Union: restoring financial stability in the Eurozone', Brussels, 24 November 2015, available at europa.eu/rapid/press-release_MEMO-15-6164_en.htm?locale=en.
[105] González-Páramo, 'The European Central Bank' (n 4).

levels of interest rates across Member States.[106] Additionally, to clarify this connection, Mario Draghi maintained in 2012 before the European Parliament:

> Our OMT announcements have helped to support financial market confidence. The ECB's actions can help to build a bridge. But the bridge must have a clear destination. Reaching that destination involves three processes: first, full implementation of fiscal consolidation and structural reforms to enhance competitiveness; second, full implementation of financial sector reform; and third, completion of a genuine economic and monetary union. The establishment of a Single Supervisory Mechanism (SSM) is a key step in these processes.[107]

There is an additional and important technical link between banking supervision and the implementation of monetary policies, and it has to do with the exchange of relevant information on the banking sector. Micro-prudential supervision (as well as macro-prudential supervision) of banks has in fact a clear implication on the eventual acquisition of government bonds by the ECB. The ECB, in its supervisory function, would accordingly have much better insight and information about the banking sector of euro countries. This would in turns, put the ECB in a better position to correctly price government bonds as well as to (internally) set *ex ante* quantities much more precisely. Ultimately, by better pricing these government bonds, the risk of incurring major losses would ideally decrease. This scenario is however, highly theoretical, because there exists a separation (a so-called 'Chinese wall') between the functions of monetary policies and banking supervision.[108] Nevertheless, this connection exists and makes a stronger case in favour of the arguments advanced by some economists,[109] according to which, accurate and timely information about banking sector performance are essential for the central bank to effectively exercise its monetary policy functions. Therefore, a strict separation of supervision and monetary policies would not be desirable, and a coordination between the two responsible bodies would be more effective, especially during financial crisis.[110]

However, it is important to stress that the interplay between the two is not only technical, from an economic and financial standpoint, but also political and constitutional. Monetary and economic affairs have increasingly become a topic of political significance as Draghi admitted in his London speech:

> The third point I want to make is in a sense more political. When people talk about the fragility of the euro and the increasing fragility of the euro, and perhaps the crisis of the

---

[106] V Constâncio, 'Towards a European Banking Union', Lecture held at the start of the academic year of the Duisenberg School of Finance, Amsterdam, 7 September 2012.

[107] M Draghi, 'Hearing at the Committee on Economic and Monetary Affairs of the European Parliament' (Brussels, 9 October 2012), available at www.ecb.europa.eu/press/key/date/2012/html/sp121009.en.html.

[108] See in particular, Art 25 of Council Regulation (EU) No 1024/2013 of 15 October 2013, laying down the rules concerning the separation between monetary policy functions and supervisory functions.

[109] J Peek, E Rosengren and G Tootell, 'Is Bank Supervision Central to Central Banking?' (1999) 114 *Quarterly Journal of Economics* 629.

[110] See T Beck and D Gros, 'Monetary Policy and Banking Supervision: Coordination instead of separation' (December 2012) *Ceps policy brief* no 286.

euro, very often non-euro area Member States or leaders, underestimate the amount of political capital that is being invested in the euro.[111]

In this sense, it is interesting to notice that a technical monetary programme such as the OMT has raised a number of concerns in terms of democratic legitimacy and accountability towards the European Parliament and national parliaments like no other ECB programme before. This is exemplified by the first preliminary reference made by the Germany's Federal Constitutional Court in its history to the ECJ (see section I.D). As also discussed above, among the many concerns, some deal with the fact that the decisions of the ECB are highly technical and opaque, thus it is difficult for them to be legally reviewed by courts or by democratic elected institutions. This is also due to the lack of real substantive legislative powers of the European Parliament towards the ECB, and in turn accountability of the ECB to the European Parliament,[112] notwithstanding the OMT *ex post* disclosure procedure,[113] and the formal hearing before the European Parliament and annual report provided under the Treaty and the ECB Internal Rules.[114] This is illustrated by the fact that President Draghi did not openly disclose the OMT intervention in the weeks before his London speech, and in particular on 9 July 2012 at the hearing at the Committee on Economic and Monetary Affairs of the European Parliament. This is quite striking given the fact that during such hearings he specifically acknowledged the fact that:

> we need to accompany deeper euro area integration with significant progress on democratic legitimacy and accountability. There is no doubt that you and your colleagues – the members of the European Parliament, the directly elected representatives of the citizens of Europe – will continue to play a central role in the steps towards political union.[115]

Nevertheless, the substance of these constitutional concerns are centred in the powers of the ECB to purchase euro area government bonds under financial distress. This explains also why the connection between the two measures is also significantly political. The OMT and the Banking Union complement each other,

---

[111] Draghi, 'Speech at the Global Investment Conference' (n 21).

[112] 'The ECB reports to the EP are not analogous to the FED reports submitted to Congress since Congress has oversight responsibilities combined with the legislative power over the Fed, while the EP has oversight responsibilities with no substantive legislative powers over the ECB. It is also clear that the ECB is accountable neither to national government not to national parliament. Neither the President of the ECB nor any other member of the Executive Board appears before any national parliament or its committees', Apel, *Central Banking Systems Compared* (n 40) 63.

[113] In particular, Draghi explained in front of the EP that: 'The ECB will be fully transparent on its OMTs. We will report weekly on total portfolio holdings, and monthly on the average duration of our holdings and the breakdown by country' (M Draghi, 'Introductory statement – Hearing at the Committee on Economic and Monetary Affairs of the European Parliament (Brussels, 9 October 2012), available at www.ecb.europa.eu/press/key/date/2012/html/sp121009.en.html).

[114] The Treaty requires the ECB to submit an annual report to the EP, the Council of Minister, the Commission and European Council. Also, the President of the ECB has to present every three months at the European Parliament.

[115] M Draghi, 'Introductory statement – Hearing' (n 113).

in that the single European supervision together with the ESM and its conditionality requirement[116] functioned as a form of legal and political legitimisation of the bond purchase programme. In other words, these two measures provide legal and political support to the OMT decision with respect to courts and national governments. The bond purchase would be a justified measure in light of the political decision to establish the Banking Union which would ultimately avoid future bailing out and recapitalising of the banking sector affecting the balance sheet of Member States. On this point, it is interesting to notice that in a later interview Draghi underlined the importance of the June summit for the financial stability of the Eurozone, but at the same time contested the idea that these reforms represented a pre-conditions for the OMT programme.[117] However, despite the semantic, the legal and political connection between the two events is clear and sound, as admitted in 2014 by the former European Council President Herman Van Rompuy:

> The Central Bank was only able to take this decision because of the preliminary political decision, by the EU's Heads of State and Government to build a banking union. This was the famous European Council of June 2012, so just weeks before Draghi's statement; he himself said to me, during that Council, that this was exactly the game-changer he needed.[118]

This interplay and connection between the two measures has European-wide constitutional implications. These two measures indeed share two fundamental principles, paving the way for a new European economic constitution: on the one hand, the full risk-sharing regime and, on the other hand, the principle of irreversibility of the euro. In particular, full sharing means, in connection with bond purchases, that NCBs of the Eurosystem would purchase governmental bonds proportional to their share in the capital of the ECB. Accordingly, each NCB would assume the risks associated in proportion to the capital share that they have in the ECB.[119] In other words, risks associated with possible defaults will be shared

---

[116] The Euro summit resolution of 29 June 2012 adopted this recommendation and stressed the need for the adoption 'as a matter of urgency' of the single supervisory mechanism involving the ECB, as well as transition to the ESM in order to ensure the financial stability of the euro area.

[117] 'The June summit was important because, for the first time in many years, it laid out a medium-term vision for a genuine economic and monetary union, made by four pillars: fiscal union, the so-called banking union, economic union and political union, endorsed by the leaders. That was an important milestone.' In particular, Draghi maintained that: 'The June summit was not a precondition for the OMT, the decision for OMT was meant to pursue, within our mandate, our objective to deliver price stability' (Mario Draghi in Barber and Steen, 'Interview with Mario Draghi' (n 1)).

[118] H Van Rompuy, Speech at the Brussels Economic Forum 2014 – 4th Annual Tommaso Padoa-Schioppa Lecture, Brussels, 10 June 2014, available at www.consilium.europa.eu/uedocs/cms_Data/docs/pressdata/en/ec/143160.pdf.

[119] 'Will the purchases continue to be conducted by the national central banks according to the capital key, and will they take the risks associated with these purchases according to the capital share that they have of the ECB? Draghi: Well, the answer to the first question is yes.' Draghi, 'Introductory statement to the press conference (with Q&A)', 6 September 2012, available at www.ecb.europa.eu/press/press-conf/2012/html/is120906.en.html.

among the Eurozone Member States. Under a no-risk-sharing regime, in contrast, the acquisitions are carried out by NCBs, at their own risk. In case of default, individual central banks would be responsible for the ultimate risks of the bond purchases, thus confining the risk to the country in question. The risk-sharing regime represents the default mode according to the statutes of the ECB and the Governing Council decision but in this case it is somehow different and special.[120] Draghi himself specifically pointed out the importance of the risk-sharing regime for the OMT programme:

> In OMT full risk-sharing is fundamental for the effectiveness of that monetary policy measure and you understand why; because it's selective, it addresses specific countries, the countries are under stress, the debt sustainability is an issue and there are tail risks that could make things precipitate for certain individual countries. In that case, risk-sharing is fundamental for the effectiveness of monetary policy, and by the way, to address these risks, OMT is there, ready to be acted, in case there were risks of that kind, of that nature, tail risks were to materialize, and that programme is under full risk-sharing.[121]

The key to understanding the nature of OMT lies here. The OMT was essentially meant, as Draghi explained, to address the tail risk to the Eurozone of redenomination risk, which was concentrated in some countries. The OMT thus addresses only specific countries – those countries that are under financial stress – and it does that by sharing the risks associated with a specific country. However, the crucial element is that a full risk-sharing regime is carried out along with an (*ex ante*) unlimited sovereign bond purchase.[122] This combination of full risk-sharing and (*ex ante*) unlimited purchase makes it different from both the previous and the subsequent programmes. On the one hand, it is different from the SMP because it is relatively large and *ex ante* unlimited.[123] On the other hand, it is

---

[120] 'So the question on how to allocate risks in the euro area has been with the Governing Council since the very beginning. There is a combined ruling coming from the statutes of the ECB and from a Governing Council decision that a default mode is a full risk-sharing mode. However, the Governing Council is also free to decide what it deems more appropriate according to the circumstances.' Draghi, 'Introductory statement to the press conference (with Q&A)', ibid.

[121] Press release published by the ECB on the same day (ECB, 'ECB announces expanded asset purchase programme', 22 January 2015, available at www.ecb.europa.eu/press/pr/date/2015/html/pr150122_1.en.html).

[122] The ECB and the Commission explained before the ECJ that setting an *ex ante* quantitative limit on purchases of government bonds would seriously undermine the effects which the intervention on the secondary market sought to achieve, with the risk of triggering speculation. The ECB additionally specified, however, that intervention in the secondary government bond market would be subject to quantitative limits, albeit limits that were not set in advance or previously determined by law. The ECB in other words would not publicly announce *ex ante* quantitative limits but it would set up such limits internally, the amount of which cannot be disclosed for strategic reasons, in order to ensure that the OMT programme is effective.

[123] The differences between the SMP and the OMT are essentially four: (i) the strict conditionality of OMT versus SMP; (ii) the short-end of yield curve (like monetary policy actions) of the OMT; (iii) transparency: publication of OMT interventions; (iv) OMT encompasses buying and selling an *ex ante* unlimited amount.

different from the EAPP (quantitative easing) programme because it is directed towards specific countries and under full risk-sharing.[124] It is then evident that this combination of full risk-sharing and (*ex ante*) unlimited purchase ultimately clarifies that the entire OMT programme is unique and is essentially a redistributional fiscal action aimed at ensuring that some Member States continue to have access to capital markets. In this new structure of the European and Monetary Union, risk-sharing represents a redistributional effect. It is a significant amendment to the original dual structure of the European economic constitution based on ordo-liberal economic thinking, according to which the national level carries out redistributive policies, while the supranational level mainly pursues economic efficiency and undistorted completion.[125] The principle of a full risk-sharing regime is also an essential part of both the ESM and of the Banking Union itself. In connection with the Banking Union, the SRF is in fact in charge with providing finance to banks under financial distress. It is true that the euro area banking sector will ultimately be liable for repayment by means of levies, but again the underlying principle of the fund is a full sharing regime, among private banks and ultimately among Member States. The ESM works under the same regime as it provides Member States and banks a bailout if they are in financial difficulty or their financial sector is a stability threat in need of recapitalisation.

The second principle is the irreversibility of the euro. This was also the message behind the London speech where Draghi, as mentioned earlier, stated: 'we think the euro is irreversible. And it's not an empty word now, because I preceded saying exactly what actions have been made, are being made to make it irreversible'. In the introductory statement of the Governing Council on 2 August 2012 he repeatedly stressed the irrevocability of the euro,[126] and clarified that

> irreversibility means that it cannot be reversed. There is no going back to the Lira or the Drachma or to any other currency. It is pointless to bet against the euro. It is pointless to go short on the euro. That was the message. It is pointless because the euro will stay and it is irreversible.

---

[124] The EAPP is not individually based and has been adopted under a mixed risk-sharing, in which only a certain share (20 per cent) of the total programme, and in case of default the risk, would be shared among national central banks depending on their capital share.

[125] C Joerges, 'What is Left of the European Economic Constitution?' (2004/13) *EUI LAW Working Paper* 17. This is somehow in line with what Bundesbank President affirmed: 'We shouldn't act according to the motto "necessity knows no laws." There are good reasons why we have clearly defined, separate areas of responsibility. The central bank is responsible for monetary stability, while national and European politicians decide on the composition of the monetary union. It wasn't the central banks that decided which countries are allowed to join the monetary union, but rather the governments' (Jens Weidmann in Mascolo, Sauga and Seith 'Interview with Jens Weidmann' (n 61)).

[126] 'The Governing Council extensively discussed the policy options to address the severe malfunctioning in the price formation process in the bond markets of euro area countries. Exceptionally high risk premia are observed in government bond prices in several countries and financial fragmentation hinders the effective working of monetary policy. Risk premia that are related to fears of the reversibility of the euro are unacceptable, and they need to be addressed in a fundamental manner. The euro is irreversible.' Draghi, 'Introductory statement to the press conference (with Q&A)' (n 119).

In the same way, the irreversibility of the euro is also a clear key characteristic of the Banking Union. As it was highlighted by the Commission is its original proposal, the approval of a SSM, built around the ECB, and the SRM send a political signal of credibility to financial markets: 'It will show once again the irreversibility of the euro.'[127]

From a legal standpoint the irrevocable adoption of the euro traces its origin back to the Delors report, which suggested the creation of a single currency to make the monetary union irreversible.[128] As a result, it was later incorporated in the Maastricht Treaty under Article 3a(2) which referred to the irrevocable fixing of exchange rates that leads to the introduction of a single currency and Article 123(4) which refers to the exchange rates to which the currencies will be irrevocably settled.[129] Ultimately, after the Lisbon Treaty, both Article 49 and Article 140 TFEU now make reference to the exchange rates to which the currencies are irrevocably settled. Before the Lisbon Treaty a number of commentators maintained the possibility of a right of withdrawal based on the fact that sovereign States are always able to freely withdraw from international commitments.[130] After the Lisbon Treaty, the vast majority of authors are now convinced that an exit from the euro is not legally possible under the current legal framework, and apparently withdrawal from the EU would be the only way to leave the euro.[131]

The irreversibility of the euro was, for a long time, a merely theoretical and legal concept. The sovereign debt crisis changed this perception, as it triggered the need to demonstrate to the financial markets the unconditional and irrevocable commitment by the Member States to the preservation of the monetary union through concrete actions. However, these concrete actions, most notably the OMT programme, challenged the same foundations on which the euro was built. The President of the Bundesbank in an interview affirmed: 'I totally agree with Jörg Asmussen that no doubt can be allowed to arise concerning the character of the euro as a stable currency and its continued existence' but at the same time 'If the central bank were obliged to guarantee that Member States remain in the euro zone at all costs, it could come into conflict with its key mission of maintaining price stability. I also don't see how it's possible to fundamentally rule out that a sovereign Member State might decide to leave the monetary union'. In this sense,

---

[127] EU Commission Memo, 'Towards a banking union', Brussels, 10 September 2012, available at europa.eu/rapid/press-release_MEMO-12-656_en.htm.

[128] Presentation by the expert committee chaired by Mr Jacques Delors of the 'Report on economic and monetary union in the European Community – Committee for the Study of Economic and Monetary Union' EC Publications Office 1989 (Delors Report) 15.

[129] See B Cœuré, 'Completing Europe's Economic and Monetary Union' quoted in n 33 above.

[130] J Zeh, 'Recht auf Austritt' (2004) 2 *Zeitschrift für Europarechtliche Studien* 209. On the opposite end, see J Herbst, 'Observations on the Right to Withdraw from the European Union: Who are the "Masters of the Treaties"?' (2005) 6 *German Law Journal* 1755.

[131] For a recent analysis see P Athanassiou, 'Withdrawal and Expulsion from the EU and EMU – Some Reflections' (December 2009) *ECB Legal Working Paper Series* No 10.

the irreversibility of the euro raised a number of issues in terms of democratic legitimacy which have been addressed in many occasions by Draghi.[132]

The real issue at stake here is that irreversibility, in its absolute form (Member States shall remain in the euro at all costs) provides the ground for the new role of the ECB as lender of last resort (LOLR). According to such concept, central banks should rescue solvent institutions by providing unlimited liquidity against good collateral, at a high rate of interest.[133] What is implicit in the principle of the irreversibility of the euro is that it provides the necessary conditions and legal justification for the ECB to act as LOLR in connection with sovereign bond purchase. This role would indeed constitute the only economic regime under which Member States under financial distress and pressure from financial markets could nevertheless always finance their public debt and ultimately remain part of the Eurozone.[134] A group of well-known economic scholars admitted and supported this resulting new role of the ECB under the OMT programme.[135] However, as the ECJ ruling has acknowledged, the purchase of 'unlimited' government bonds as required by the LOLR, even in the secondary market, is not possible under the current Treaty rules. What is legally possible, according to the ECJ and the German Constitutional Court, is to purchase an *ex ante* undisclosed amount of limited government bonds in the secondary market, under the condition that the actual formation of a market price for government bonds is respected. The new role of the ECB as LOLR is therefore a second significant amendment to the current economic regime in place. The Banking Union is similarly connected with this concept, as the new supervisory functions and resolution funds represent a condition for the

---

[132] This problem of legitimacy was in fact the main concern in many interviews and speeches and Draghi had to defend his argument in many occasions. In one interview on the specific question 'The euro is irreversible and what gives you the democratic legitimation, the authority to say that', Draghi replied: 'What I said exactly is that – and I repeat what I said in London the first time – we will do whatever it takes within our mandate – within our mandate – to have a single monetary policy in the euro area, to maintain price stability in the euro area and to preserve the euro. And we say that the euro is irreversible. So unfounded fears of reversibility are just what they are: unfounded fears. And we think this falls squarely within our mandate.' In another interview with the *Süddeutsche Zeitung* on the specific question as to whether 'he speaks like the Chancellor of Europe?' Draghi replied: 'I am communicating this message as the President of the ECB to all stakeholders, citizens, businesses and markets. Investors need a long-term vision because they undertake long-term commitments. For them, it is very important that our leaders and governments are determined to keep the euro irreversible. So, if I say this, I am saying what our political leaders are fundamentally saying' (in A Hagelüken and M Zydra, 'Interview with, Mario Draghi', *Süddeutsche Zeitung*, 14 September 2012, available at www. ecb.europa.eu/press/inter/date/2012/html/sp120914.en.html).

[133] For more details see T Humphrey, 'Lender of Last Resort: The Concept in History' (1989) 75 *Economic Review* 8.

[134] See generally P De Grauwe, *Economics of Monetary Union*, 9th edn (Oxford: Oxford University Press, 2012).

[135] P De Grauwe, 'The European Central Bank: Lender of Last Resort in the Government Bond Markets' (2013) 59 *CESifo Economic Studies* 520; M Fratzscher, F Giavazzi, R Portes, B Weder di Mauro and C Wyplosz, 'A Call for support for the European Central Bank's OMT Programme' 19 July 2013, available at berlinoeconomicus.diw.de/monetarypolicy/a-call-for-support-for-the-european-central-banks-omt-programme/.

central bank's function as LOLR. The Banking Union does enhance the integrated banking system and provide a more effective management of a potential financial crisis, which naturally complements the extraordinary response provided under the LOLR system.[136]

IV. Conclusion

The banking liquidity crisis severely hit the balance sheets of Member States, mainly due to the bailing out and recapitalisation of the banking sector, and produced an unprecedented number of financial reforms. These measures have tackled both monetary and financial instability spreading across Europe. In particular, on the one hand, the ECB was forced to intervene with the adoption of non-standard measures to restore liquidity and trust in the money and bond market, given their implication on monetary stability. In such context, the OMT programme has been developed as the ultimate tool at the disposal of the ECB to do 'whatever it takes' to save the Eurozone. On the other hand, European institutions and Member States approved, in a relatively short time, a number of measures to establish the Banking Union, in order to enhance financial market integration and break the vicious circle between banking crises and sovereign crisis.

Overall, these two, apparently different, measures are complementary. Banking supervision and non-standard monetary policies appear as two sides of the same coin in this new EU regime for enhancing financial market integration. The integration of financial markets represents in fact an essential goal of the Banking Union and at the same time, a pre-requisite of the monetary policies of the central bank, whereas the transmission of monetary policy is highly dependent on the degree of financial integration. Banks represent in this context the cornerstone of the entire architecture, for they play a crucial role in both the government bonds market and money markets. The two measures are complementary not only from a financial and economic standpoint, but also from a political and legal standpoint. The Banking Union, together with the ESM and its conditionality requirement represent a form of political legitimisation for the bond purchase programme, with respect to courts and national governments. The bond purchase is justified in this context as long as the chance of future bailing out and recapitalisation of the banking sector is avoided by a single resolution fund and by a single European supervisor, potentially not subject to being captured by national interests.

This interplay between the two measures has European-wide constitutional implication. These two measures indeed share two fundamental principles, paving the way for a new European economic constitution. These are, on the one hand, the

---

[136] P Praet, 'The ECB and its role as lender of last resort during the crisis', speech at the Committee on Capital Markets Regulation conference on The lender of last resort – an international perspective, Washington DC, 10 February 2016.

full risk-sharing regime, and on the other hand, the principle of irreversibility of the euro. In this new structure of the European and Monetary Union, risk-sharing represents a redistributional effect. It is a significant amendment to the original dual structure of the European economic constitution based on ordo-liberal economic thinking, according to which, the national level carries out redistributive policies, while the supranational level mainly pursues economic efficiency and undistorted completion. On the other hand, irreversibility, in its absolute form (Member States shall remain in the euro at all costs) provides the ground for the new role of the ECB as LOLR. It represents the only economic regime under which Member States under financial distress and pressure from financial markets could nevertheless always finance their public debt and ultimately remain part of the Eurozone. However, the purchase of 'unlimited' government bonds, as the LOLR requires, would be impossible under the current Treaty rules as the ECJ and the German Constitutional Court ruling have acknowledged. This new role of the ECB as LOLR is therefore a second significant amendment to the current economic regime.

Ultimately, it is important to notice how, in our modern world where financial markets have become more and more central, a simple but extremely resolute speech (the London speech) was a crucial turning point for the entire Eurozone. This speech was somehow able to achieve and provide the constitutional foundations of this new European economic regime, more than the Euro summit in 2012 or the ESM approval. The London speech had the immediate effect of reassuring the financial markets, significantly more than the Euro summit or the establishment of the ESM, and drove the decline in sovereign bond risk premia across Europe. Its importance is also supported by the heated debate in the Governing Council concerning the resulting OMT programme, and by the preliminary reference of the German Constitutional Court to the ECJ. Both events signify a constitutional tension between two different visions of the European economic system, which is not settled yet. Future events, such as the activation of the OMT programme, will reveal how this tension will play out, and particularly whether this new economic constitution is able to survive and overcome all these challenges.

PART II

European Banking Union
and Full Integration

4

The European Banking Union and Integration

STEFAN GRUNDMANN

I. What Role for the Banking Union in Integration Dynamics?

This chapter discusses the role of the European Banking Union in (European) integration – hence the two concepts and their relationship, both being far from clearly defined – and it has one underlying thesis on what banking really means for integration. To sketch out the topic by way of introduction, a few words are needed on how the two concepts are conceived, and the underlying thesis should be spelt out – which will then be tested in the remainder of the chapter.

The first concept – or area of the law – is the compound of rule-setting and institutional arrangements summarised under the term 'European Banking Union'. This term and concept may be conceived narrowly, in a technical sense, comprising only those rules which govern the ongoing centralised supervision of 118 Eurozone banks (or groups of banks) by the European Central Bank (ECB)[1] in Frankfurt (plus the overall responsibility for Eurozone banking supervision at large) and those rules which govern the recovery and resolution procedures of those banks plus an additional 13 cross-border groups under the guidance of the Single Resolution Board (SRB) in Brussels.[2] Then, the discussion would be mainly or even exclusively on the Single Supervisory Mechanism (SSM) based on the SSM Regulation and the Single (Recovery and) Resolution Mechanism (SRM) based on the SRM Regulation (recovery still being encompassed in the SSM). For the topic discussed, it is, however, better to conceive the European Banking Union more broadly: (i) with the legislative acts (namely European Union (EU) wide harmonisation) providing for the substantive law on banking supervision,

---

[1] For the full list of supervised entities (as of 1 April 2018), see: https://www.bankingsupervision.europa.eu/ecb/pub/pdf/ssm.list_of_supervised_entities_201806.en.pdf.

[2] For the full list of cross-border groups (as of 1 February 2018), see: https://srb.europa.eu/sites/srbsite/files/5_for_publication_srb_website_list_of_other_cross_border_groups_1februar.pdf.

regulation and resolution which is to be applied (also) in the SSM and the SRM, and (ii) even more generally, together with the broader harmonisation and unification of the financial sector, including through the Capital Markets Union project, which is related to the move towards a European Banking Union (with the SSM and the SRM as its centrepieces).[3] This implies that levels and depths of integration diverge and enter into interaction with each other at several levels of governance, but that the wider scope of all EU banking law is also to be taken into account when questions about the Banking Union are asked, that is, not only about banking supervision from a microprudential point of view or resolution in its most narrow sense, for the simple reason that 'stability' of (single) institution(s) and of the financial system – as the core aim of the Banking Union – may depend as well on rules regulating financial markets more broadly or individual transactions as well.

Similarly to what has been explained for the concept of a European Banking Union, the concept of integration also encompasses a whole range and continuum of phenomena and does not denote just one clearly defined status of 'Europeanisation' or (technically more correct) of 'supra-nationalisation'. In fact there is not only the well-established difference between harmonisation and unification which plays a major role here, because the substantive law to be applied in the Banking Union, in its level I regulation, is based predominantly on EU directives to be transposed into Member State law, not regulations.[4] At the same time, at all other levels, there is clearly a thrust towards transforming this 'mere' status of harmonisation into as much 'unification' (complete uniformity) as possible – namely with EU implementing regulations for the (much more detailed) level II legislation, but also with the endeavour to establish a (uniform and detailed) Single Rulebook for the practical application itself, including the supervisory practice. Thus harmonisation and unification is the first distinction to be taken into account, but it already denotes not just two distinct poles but a range of possibilities – the extent to which uniformity is far-reaching in outcome or not. Moreover, a second type of distinction is of similar importance here, relating to the question for which type of decision-making one speaks of integration and/or unification: does one speak of integration just of rule-setting (as in traditional measures of harmonisation, namely on the basis of Article 114 of the Treaty on the Functioning of the European Union (TFEU)) or also of the EU implementing regulations and guidelines for the practice (such as in the Single Rulebooks for Supervision and Resolution), or even also of the administrative acts in the single cases. To some extent, the Banking Union can even be seen as sharing characteristics of both: rule-setting on the one hand (providing 'guidelines') and administrative application in the individual cases on the other (with the discretion enjoyed by the Single

---

[3] On the compound of rules and arrangements which are thus included, see in more detail section II.
[4] With the exception of the Credit Requirements Regulation, which covers part of the new microprudential regulatory framework to be applied by the supervisor.

Supervisory Board (SSB)), thereby blurring the borderlines between the two.[5] Taking all this into account, 'integration' in the title of this chapter is meant to give a common denominator for all these different phenomena and, in its essence, describes one thing: more 'integration' is synonymous of more uniform application in the final outcome, ie in the *individual* cases, because more of the final decision (rules, their interpretation and individual application to the case) is made at a centralised EU level – as opposed to the decentralised Member State level. These two distinctions – between the scope and the level – or, rather, these two palettes of shades – still do not exhaust the question of how strongly 'supra-national' the regime is in its ultimate outcome. One important aspect with respect to 'measuring' integration is also that it may well be that an institution at the (centralised) EU level makes the decision, for instance the ECB rather than a national supervisory authority, but that, on the other hand, in such a situation of centralisation, the body deciding at the EU level (the ECB), in the individual case, acts via a body, such as Joint Supervisory Teams, composed of representatives both of the central and of the Member State level.[6]

Within this broad area including the many shades of a 'European Banking Union' and of 'EU Integration' (which, in the following discussion, should be taken into consideration as broadly as possible), there is still one underlying thesis for this chapter: that the real interest of the relationship between the European Banking Union and Integration would seem to reside in the huge step taken conceptually – namely in that it is no longer only legislation (rule-setting) which is being transferred to the central EU level, but also its application/administration in the individual cases. And it might very well be the latter which proves decisive in answering the question whether a level playing field (for credit institutions and for Member States) can really be established. In other words: there may be more of a level-playing field of this kind in the Banking Union than more generally in the EU. In the area of financial services and capital market law, the so-called Lamfalussy architecture of legislation had already started this move towards much deeper unity in the application of law down into the single cases – with level I legislation by the EU Parliament and Council (typically, although not exclusively, via directives) on the most important principles, but then also, based on this, with level II and III legislation implementing and refining the basic principles and doing so via EU *implementing regulations* (directly applicable!) and via

---

[5] This is a discussion omnipresent today in public governance and modern administrative law literature. See, for instance, O Lobel, 'The Renew Deal: The Fall of Regulation and the Rise of Governance' (2004) 89 *Contemporary Legal Thought. Minnesota Law Review* 342, at 391: '[Today's] Governance model does not insist that legislation, implementation, enforcement and adjudication be separate stages; but rather seeks to form dynamic interactions among these processes.'

[6] Where the Single Resolution Board remains constrained by the *Meroni* doctrine limiting the scope of delegation of powers to an EU agency, the SRB is operationally reliant on national resolution authorities to a substantial degree, see A Smoleńska, 'Single Resolution Board: Lost and Found in the Thicket of EU Bank Regulation', Chapter 7 in this volume.

a testing of the degree of uniformity reached in the single cases.[7] While it is true that more uniformity could also be brought about in many individual cases via preliminary reference to the Court of Justice of the European Union (CJEU), ie via adjudication, this does not occur systematically and in fact does not cover the whole area. Administrative integration reaches much further in fact, even though, from a norm hierarchy perspective, it may be 'inferior' (and subject to overruling by courts, namely by the CJEU). Thus uniform (administrative) application in the single cases constitutes a 'leap' towards much more intense 'real' uniformity in applied law – as compared to mere legislative harmonisation or even unification (even if combined with the possibility of preliminary reference). With reference to the key area of regulation in EU market law (since its very beginning), competition law (antitrust law, merger control, state aid law), one can state: banking law – and perhaps soon also capital market law rather generally – constitute(s) the second wave of 'full integration', both at the legislative and at the administrative level, in individual cases. The impact that this harmonisation of law and its administration has had on antitrust, state aid and even public procurement law, and moreover its broader impact on the development of instruments of integration more generally – like, for instance, the concept of supremacy of EU law – suggests that similarly important concepts might be developed in the practice and adjudication of banking supervision.

Thus the question really is whether banking law may bring about a similar dynamism for integration as antitrust law has done – a second wave of similar importance. From antitrust law to banking law – are we entering a new era of integration? This comparison is based both on a positive and on a normative assessment of the current developments leading to the European Banking Union. In analysing this question, Heike Schweitzer (Chapter 5 in this volume) focuses more on the antitrust law side of this comparison and this chapter focuses more on the banking law side. Still, it is impossible to assess this development without an intense look across to the other side of the fence. Comparison with the other area is always needed (not only because of the simple fact that EU competition law – as the law on state aid – remains highly pertinent in the case of banking recovery resolution). In the case of this chapter, the focus is, however, mainly on banking supervision with some reference to competition law.

The chapter is structured as follows. First, the compound of rules is briefly presented, with a focus on banking supervision, but also occasionally with a broader look on banking and financial services law (see below section II),

---

[7] On the Lamfalussy architecture of legislation (as seen today), see Final Report of the Committee of Wise Men on the Regulation of European Securities Markets of 15 February 2001, Annex 5, 12, 20 et seq ('Lamfalussy Report'); Th Möllers, 'Sources of Law in European Securities Regulation – Effective Regulation, Soft Law and Legal Taxonomy from Lamfalussy to de Larosière' (2010) 11 *EBOR* 379; short summary and further references in S Grundmann, *European Company Law – Organization, Finance, and Capital Markets* 2nd edn (Antwerp/Oxford, Intersentia, 2012) § 22 para 1. For capital market law more generally, as a core area already densely harmonised, but still to be developed into a European Capital Market Union, see also below section V.C.

followed by a short introduction to the assumptions on which a normative assessment should be based (advantages and disadvantages of legislation/administration at the centralised or at the decentralised level, see below section III). With these tools, the degree of Europeanisation/supra-nationalisation of banking law (in the narrow and in the broad sense) is assessed – how far does it go, what shades exist, and how far should it go or should it have gone? These questions are asked first for the core of banking supervision itself (see below section IV), then for repercussions beyond this core area, and potentially well beyond it, for instance reaching out to questions of financial law more generally or even as far as constitutional law (see below section V). Finally, the core findings will be summarised (see below section VI).

II. Survey on Substantive Laws (Rulebook) and Institutions

A. Substantive Laws (Including the Rulebook)

The term 'European Banking Union' refers to the most important reform package in the supervision of credit institutions over the last decades. It became operational only on 4 November 2014, and then still only the first step, the 'Single Supervisory Mechanism' under the lead of the ECB. The second centrepiece, the 'Single Resolution Mechanism' (on resolution of credit institutions) became operational on 1 January 2016, with the deadline for transposition of Banking Resolution and Recovery Directive (BRRD) into national law having passed on 31 December 2014 Only the third centrepiece, a complete Europeanisation/supra-nationalisation of the deposit insurance scheme (intimately linked to recovery and resolution of credit institutions), has not reached so far the point originally envisaged, with the Commission's proposal for European Deposit Insurance Scheme (EDIS) published in November 2015. Finally, the fourth centrepiece, the so-called Single Rulebook, is in a constant process of elaboration.

The importance of this reform becomes still more palpable if one considers that just a few years before, starting with 2010, the whole architecture of European banking supervision had already undergone fundamental reform – on the basis of the very thorough discussion of the high-level de Larosière report (on this reform, which included an institutional overhaul by creation of European System of Financial Supervisors (2010) and new microprudential rules (CRD IV package in June 2013) see section II.B). The legislative measures adopted in October 2013 (and, in the case of the SRM Regulation and BRRD, in 2014) are nothing less than the second large wave of law (after antitrust law) in which *both* a (largely) unitary regulatory regime *and* unitary administration at the EU level have been implemented. As this fact (of transplanting both regulation and administrative implementation to the EU level) has caused antitrust law to serve as one of the main drivers of integration and the subject of many of the leading decisions on EU law in the 1960s and 1970s, it may even be predicted that a similar push in integration could also be triggered by the European Banking Union (see below section V). It may even reach further, affecting all business law more broadly, because it concerns the core factor of capital. This dimension, namely in how far the new regulatory set will indeed trigger a new gigantic push in integration, is the focus of this (series of) chapter(s), in Part 2 of this volume, while the other important aspect will be approached in Part 3, namely whether this development raises fundamental democratic concerns (again). Other more general questions are how deeply the Banking Union affects private and business law. These questions are also briefly touched upon here, but are the focus of a separate inquiry.[8]

In the perception of most beholders, the Banking Union rests on four pillars:[9] the SSM,[10] the SRM,[11] a reshaping of the deposit guarantee scheme,[12] and the Single Rulebook(s) on supervision and recovery/resolution (still under construction). The first three each constitute instruments and pieces of regulation for a sub-area of public intervention: (i) on current supervision (SSM); (ii) on recovery and/or resolution of credit institutions whenever – in a rather exceptional case – such an incisive measure becomes necessary (SSM[13] and SRM); and (iii) (linked to the second) on the question of which deposits remain secured even in such

---

[8] On this question see S Grundmann and J Binder (eds), *The Banking Union Translated into Duties* (2015) Vol 15(3), *European Business Organization Review (EBOR)* which includes S Grundmann, 'The European Banking Union and Private Law'.

[9] In this sense, for instance, the Austrian Parliament summarises the so-called Four Presidents' paper 2012 (EU / ECB / IMF / Eurogroup) with the following structure (http://www.parlament.gv.at/PERK/GL/EU/B.shtml): The European Banking Union encompasses (i) the Single Supervisory Mechanism (SSM), (ii) the Single Resolution Mechanism (SRM), (iii) the harmonised deposit guarantee scheme and (iv) the 'Single Rulebook'.

[10] Council Regulation (EU) No 1024/2013 of 15 October 2013 conferring specific tasks on the European Central Bank concerning policies relating to the prudential supervision of credit institutions, [2013] OJ L 287/63 (based on Art 127(6) TFEU). On the legal basis (in the author's view not really very doubtful), see the very convincing argument by J Ruthig, 'Die EZB in der europäischen Bankenunion' (2014) 178 *Zeitschrift für das gesamte Handelsrecht (ZHR)* 443, esp at 450–60.

[11] Regulation (EU) No 806/2014 of the European Parliament and of the Council of 15 July 2014 establishing uniform rules and a uniform procedure for the resolution of credit institutions and certain investment firms in the framework of a Single Resolution Mechanism and a Single Resolution Fund and amending Regulation (EU) No 1093/2010, [2014] OJ L 225/1 (based on Art 114 TFEU) ('SRM Regulation'). Positive regarding the possibility of creating new regulatory authorities (in the case of the European Banking Union: the Single Resolution Board in Brussels with the Single Resolution Fund) on the basis of the internal market competence (Art 114 TFEU): Case C-270/12 *United Kingdom v European Parliament and Council*, EU:C:2014:18 (on ESMA and its regulatory powers, namely with respect to short-selling). It is with respect to this part of the European Banking Union system in particular that the legal basis is seen sceptically and that an amendment of the treaties is called for, because decisions on resolution of banks are likely to provoke more actual litigation in courts, see, for instance, vice-president of the German Central Bank (*Bundesbank*) Sabine Lautenschläger in *Bundesbank* of 10.02.2014: *Europäische Bankenunion – ein Großprojekt*.

[12] Directive 2014/49/EU of the European Parliament and of the Council of 16 April 2014 on deposit guarantee schemes, [2014] OJ L 173/149.

[13] To the extent that the supervisor is overseeing the recovery procedures and in charge of early intervention.

a situation of resolution (with respect to this third area, however, centralisation of the scheme at the EU-Eurozone level is progressing at a significantly slower pace). On the other hand, (iv) the Single Rulebooks rather constitute a new regulatory technique – cross-cutting all these areas – which, on the basis of the EU regulations and directives, are aimed at achieving a truly uniform supervisory and administrative practice with regard to credit institutions – like a handbook on uniform supervision practice, addressing all practical aspects in great detail. Its relationship to the European Banking Union will be discussed below, but at this point reference has to be made to one crucial point: while the SSM and the SRM (pillars I and II) are restricted to the Eurozone, and pillar III would also have been had centralisation at the EU-Eurozone level been successful, the Rulebooks on banking supervision reach further in their territorial scope of application. They are aimed at rendering more uniform the application of harmonised substantive law, for instance on banking supervision, namely in the CRD IV package or resolution law, ie BRRD. Based on EU-wide measures, they cover the whole of the EU and, in this case, are even based on a set of principles or rules which are applied worldwide in a rather similar way. Indeed, it is not the ECB, but the European Banking Authority (EBA) which is responsible for developing the Rulebooks, for the whole of the EU. In different areas, the Rulebook can adopt rather different forms. What is common to all Rulebooks, however, is the aim of warranting reliable and uniform practical implementation and application of the standards. The criticism made when the SSM was adopted – that this would constitute no more than a first step[14] – has largely been rendered obsolete by the subsequent steps within just one year with the creation of the SRM, and possibility of an ESM backstop for the Single Resolution Fund (SRF).[15] Moreover, the refinement of the Rulebook is an ongoing process.

The first, most general, and probably also most prominent part (or 'pillar'), the SSM adopted and implemented in 2013/14, has two characteristic structural features. First, it applies (only) to a core of the credit industry – those 118 credit institutions in the Eurozone which are 'systemically relevant' – with respect to the current banking supervision which has been entrusted to the ECB, while this institution has only general responsibility of last resort for the proper functioning of the supervisory system at large with respect to the rest of the banking sector. Second, the legal measure adopted has to be seen in a continuity: it is embedded in a regulatory compendium which had already been fundamentally reformed due to the crisis. The SSM Regulation, while establishing a complete system of competences and administrative powers for the ECB, does so on the

---

[14] In this sense namely the president of the German Central Bank (*Bundesbank*) J Weidmann, *Frankfurter Allgemeine Zeitung (FAZ)* of 19.3.2013, that it was meant as a first step only and that the others had to follow soon, was, however, already explicitly mentioned in the 12th recital of the SSM Regulation.
[15] See ESM Guideline on Financial Assistance for the Direct Recapitalisation of Institutions, 8 December 2014 as well as proposals on an ESM backstop to the SRF emerging in 2017.

basis of the reformed substantive law on banking supervision contained in the Capital Requirements Directive IV (CRD IV package[16]) which has fundamentally reformed the requirements on own funds, liquidity and risk diversification with respect to each and every engagement taken by credit institutions, but also reformed or introduced important standards on the internal governance of banks, ie on their organisation (namely general standards for remuneration and for risk management). The SSM Regulation is supplemented by the internal regulations for the ECB as supervisory authority[17] and by the (re-)formulation of the procedural rules on the collaboration with the EBA.[18] Conversely, within the Eurozone, the interplay of supervisory powers and competences in the current supervision exercised by the ECB on the one hand and by the national supervisory authorities on the other is set out in the SSM Regulation itself (on both issues, see below section II.B).

Still more problematic (than the transfer of powers to the ECB for the current supervision) was supra-nationalisation for the second 'pillar'; the creation of a Single Resolution Mechanism for credit institutions. The SRM Regulation,[19] the core measure in this respect, again does not stand alone. Also, this measure, even though it contains much more substantive law (on recovery and resolution) than the SSM Regulation (on current supervision), is based on extensive harmonisation: namely on the BRRD which (only very recently) had harmonised and indeed mostly created from scratch a recovery and resolution regime for credit institutions.[20] Of all harmonisation measures (for the whole of the EU),

---

[16] Directive 2013/36/EU of the European Parliament and of the Council of 26 June 2013 on access to the activity of credit institutions and the prudential supervision of credit institutions and investment firms, amending Directive 2002/87/EC and repealing Directives 2006/48/EC and 2006/49/EC (CRD IV), [2013] OJ L 176/338, and, implementing this directive: Regulation (EU) No 575/2013 of the European Parliament and of the Council of 26 June 2013 on prudential requirements for credit institutions and investment firms and amending Regulation (EU) No 648/2012 (CRR), [2013] OJ L 176/1; transposition, for instance, in Germany via Law Transposing Directive 2013/36/EU, namely Gesetz zur Umsetzung der Richtlinie 2013/36/EU über den Zugang zur Tätigkeit von Kreditinstituten und die Beaufsichtigung von Kreditinstituten und Wertpapierfirmen und zur Anpassung des Aufsichtsrechts an die Verordnung (EU) Nr. 575/2013 über Aufsichtsanforderungen an Kreditinstitute und Wertpapierfirmen [CRD IV-Umsetzungsgesetz]) of 28.8.2013, *BGBl [Official Journal]* 2013 I, p 3395.

[17] Regulation (EU) No 468/2014 of the European Central Bank of 16 April 2014 establishing the framework for cooperation within the Single Supervisory Mechanism between the European Central Bank and national competent authorities and with national designated authorities (SSM Framework Regulation), [2014] OJ L 141/1.

[18] Regulation (EU) No 1022/2013 of the European Parliament and of the Council of 22 October 2013 amending Regulation (EU) No 1093/2010 establishing a European Supervisory Authority (European Banking Authority) as regards the conferral of specific tasks on the European Central Bank pursuant to Council Regulation (EU) No 1024/2013, [2013] OJ L 287/5.

[19] See n 11 above.

[20] Directive 2014/59/EU of the European Parliament and of the Council of 15 May 2014 establishing a framework for the recovery and resolution of credit institutions and investment firms and amending Council Directive 82/891/EEC, and Directives 2001/24/EC, 2002/47/EC, 2004/25/EC, 2005/56/EC, 2007/36/EC, 2011/35/EU, 2012/30/EU and 2013/36/EU, and Regulations (EU) No 1093/2010 and (EU) No 648/2012, of the European Parliament and of the Council, [2014] OJ L 173/190 ('BRRD').

the BRRD/SRM framework is in fact the only one which has been adopted during the second wave of legal measures on the Banking Union, where there was no EU regulatory regime on banks' recovery and resolution before. Here, for the purpose of supra-nationalisation of the administration, a separate EU agency has been created, the SRB in Brussels, which is the owner of the Single Resolution Fund, important for the carrying through of resolution procedures and funded by bank contributions to the amount of €55 billion (see Articles 67–79 of the SRM Regulation and the Intergovernmental Agreement).[21]

The third institutional 'pillar' of a European Banking Union, a truly European Deposit Guarantee scheme, has not, however, been put in place thus far despite the Commission's proposal for the creation of EDIS.[22] Contrary to the initial plans, and because of particularly strong political opposition and disagreement in this respect, no European administrative and joint fund scheme came into being, with the reform so far limited to reform of the already existing harmonisation regime on (national) deposit guarantee schemes (no 'communitisation' of deposit guarantees has taken place as yet, with the EDIS being a reinsurance mechanism at European level rather than a separate new fund at supra-national/ Eurozone level).[23] The core of the (harmonised) regime safeguards certain creditors via (national) deposit guarantee schemes, which within some Member States such as Germany are again split up along the lines of groups of credit institutions, guaranteeing up to €100,000 of deposits in case of insolvencies. This is additionally supplemented by a prioritisation of small and medium-sized enterprises (SMEs) and retail customers as creditors under resolution proceedings within pillar II of the Banking Union – ie SRM.

B. The Institutional Setting: Supervisory Authorities and the ECB

In the following discussion, only the first and second pillar of the supra-nationalisation of banking supervision are considered, as only these, with the

---

[21] Agreement on the transfer and mutualisation of contributions to the Single Resolution Fund, 14 May 2014.

[22] Proposal for a Regulation of the European Parliament and of the Council amending Regulation (EU) 806/2014 in order to establish a European Deposit Insurance Scheme, 24.11.2015, COM(2015) 586 final.

[23] On the dispute regarding whether for a European deposit guarantee scheme a common guarantee fund was needed, see D Gros and D Schoenmaker, 'European Deposit Insurance and Resolution in the Banking Union: European Deposit Insurance and Resolution' (2014) 52 *Journal of Common Market Studies* 529; F Arnaboldi, *Deposit Guarantee Schemes: A European Perspective* (Basingstoke, Palgrave Macmillan, 2014); U Schneider, 'Europäische Bankenunion – ein Etikettenschwindel!' (2012) *EuZW* 721, at 722; and for the concern that a European (!) recovery and resolution scheme would not be operational without a deposit guarantee which therefore, to align effectively, needed to be European as well (just as in the US with the Federal Deposit Insurance Company, FDIC); B Weder di Mauro, 'Zahnlos?' in Friedrich-Ebert-Stiftung (ed), *WiSo-Diskurs: Die Bankenunion – Wer zahlt die Zeche?* (2013) 18, at 19.

full picture of 'Europeanisation' of both the regulatory and the administrative scheme, raise fundamentally new questions. On the other hand, the Rulebook as the fourth element, the uniform 'handbook on practice', also then comes into play.

Three points should be stressed from the outset as they are of more general importance. These are the concerns that the European Banking Union does not reach far enough ('small-scale solution'); that the interplay with other European regulatory agencies is far from being clear ('too complex'); and that the 'independence' of the European supervision, namely of the ECB, may be in conflict with principles of democratic accountability (a concern strongly voiced in Germany in particular).

The concerns that the European Banking Union constitutes only a 'small-scale solution' may initially have been mainly motivated by the fact that then, in 2013, only the SSM had been adopted and had been seen as being 'too little'.[24] This concern has to a considerable extent been taken care of by the adoption, within a year, of the SRM Regulation and also (partially) by the reform of the deposit guarantee scheme (albeit still national with attempts at a European reinsurance mechanism). A concern not met thus far, however, is that the SSM and SRM Regulations introduce a supervision and administrative implementation at the EU level only for a limited amount of credit institutions which are 'systematically relevant', with even this being limited to Eurozone Member States only.[25] The latter may change to some extent due to the fact that non-Eurozone Member States can opt to enter into close cooperation with the SSM.[26] With respect to safeguarding of the Euro stability, there is, however, a significant reason for distinguishing: the Eurozone Member States no longer possess monetary instruments – such as depreciation of their own currency or the steering of the money supply etc – to react to budgetary imbalances, consequently making the isolation of risks stemming from insolvencies of credit institutions a still more urgent concern; conversely,

---

[24] See n 14 above.

[25] Prominent criticism voiced by, for instance: P Legrain, 'Europe's Bogus Banking Union', *Project Syndicate*, 8 April 2014; R Goyal *et al*, *A Banking Union for the Euro Area* (2013) International Monetary Fund Staff Discussion Note 13/01, p 12, available at http://www.imf.org/external/pubs/ft/sdn/2013/sdn1301.pdf; U Schneider and P Mülbert, 'Europäische Bankenunion ohne effektiven Rechtsschutz?', *Börsen-Zeitung* of 5.1.2013. It is true, however, that the restriction of the ECB's direct supervision to those 118 credit institutions constitutes the most incisive modification of what had been the EU Commission's proposal (and Barroso's political announcement of it in September 2012 in his 'State of the Union' speech). Today this restriction is justified by subsidiarity concerns (see recitals 28 and 87 of the SSM Regulation). Under Art 6(4) SSM Regulation, all credit institutions are systematically relevant: (i) whose total value of assets on the balance sheet exceeds € 30 billion or (ii) €5 billion, but also 20 per cent of the GDP of that Eurozone Member State or (iii) any credit institution which is one of the three biggest in that Eurozone Member State or (iv) any credit institution which has requested or received financial assistance directly from the EFSF or the ESM or (v) any other credit institution which the ECB considers to be 'systemically relevant' and therefore subjects to its own supervision. On the list of 123 credit institutions (24 in Germany), see http://www.ecb.europa.eu/pub/pdf/other/ssm-listofsupervisedentities1409en.pdf?59d76de0c5663687f594250ebf228c6b.

[26] UK has been the only country to exclude considering entering into close cooperation with the SSM, even prior to its referendum decision to withdraw from the EU ('Brexit').

budgetary problems of these Member States also influence the stability of the Euro more directly and thereby also the budget and economy of other Eurozone Member States. The other concern is still less 'alarming': while it is true that only 118 credit institutions are under direct supervision of the ECB, they neverthe-less are responsible for the bulk of the banking business in the Eurozone.[27] And while the ECB is directly responsible, with respect to the other 3,000 credit insti-tutions of the Eurozone, only with respect to macroprudential risk supervision (Article 5 SSM Regulation) and not for the classical banking supervision (with power conferred upon the ECB by Article 4 SSM Regulation, and division of tasks within the mechanism outlined in Article 6(5) SSM Regulation), this does not change the situation that the ECB has the ultimate responsibility for the supervi-sory system and is the ultimate 'master' of it in the Eurozone.[28] This is so for three reasons: the ECB – via the national competent authorities – is exclusively compe-tent for issuing the licence to credit institutions and withdrawing it (and also with respect to large block holdings – for the authorisation procedure see Article 14 SSM Regulation), but moreover also can subject any single case and issue under its own supervision if needed (Article 6(5)(b) SSM Regulation); therefore, as per Article 6(1) second phrase of the SSM Regulation, the ECB has the responsibility of last resort for banking supervision in the Eurozone; finally, and more as a ques-tion of factual importance, the practice which the ECB will exercise, and which additionally will have a large impact on the Single Rulebook, is likely also to shape the national practices with regard to less significant institutions within the Bank-ing Union in a similar way as the EU Commission's antitrust practice has done with national antitrust practice. The intimate link between the ECB's supervi-sion and the national authorities' supervision, namely via exhaustive information exchange, is in fact a core characteristic of the (new) concept of integration under-lying the SSM Regulation. Finally, if at all, it is certainly only the ECB's practice (and not that of national supervisors) which can have spill-over into other areas described below in section V.

A second institutional interplay will be important in this respect, now comple-tely at the EU level. Indeed, there are other institutions at the EU level to be considered, most importantly for banking law the EBA, coordinating banking supervision for all EU Member States and also responsible for the drafting of the Single Rulebook(s) in this area, and the European Securities Markets Authority (ESMA). Both were created during the first phase of building the new financial architecture after the financial crisis since 2008 and the Euro crisis since 2010,within the so-called European System of Financial Supervision, ESFS (2010/11), which has been installed on the basis of the high-level de Larosière report. Within the ESFS, supervisory agencies have been created for the three core areas of financial services

---

[27] For figures for this K Lannoo (ed), *ECB Banking Supervision and Beyond*, Report of the CEPS Task Force (Brussels, CEPS, 2014) 27.
[28] Going even further (the 'most powerful EU Institution' altogether): C Schneider, 'Einführung und politische Schlussfolgerungen' in Friedrich-Ebert-Stiftung (above n 23) 4, 5.

and at that time still for *all EU Member States*: for banking supervision (EBA); for securities markets supervision (ESMA); and (not relevant in this context) for insurance supervision (EIOPA).[29] The agencies were only given, however, coordination functions and a core role in the implementing legislation on EU directives, through guidelines and level II technical and implementing regulatory standards (approved by the European Commission). The administrative competence as such still remained with the national agencies. Today, while a representative of the ECB's Supervisory Board is a non-voting member of the Board of Supervisors (Article 40(1)(d) of EBA Regulation, as amended in 2013), it can be assumed that the ECB will exercise a significant coordinatory role with regard to the representatives of the national competent authorities represented in EBA (holding the voting rights). In any case, the role of the ECB as an independent institution installed by the EU Treaties required a readjustment of the inter-institutional equilibrium, namely that it be not subordinated to the agencies (EBA and ESMA) which were created only by secondary law at the EU level, with respect to their coordination powers.[30] With the crisis in Cyprus and in the Spanish Banking sector culminating in 2012 and until early 2013, the balance tipped towards those voices which had asked for more than coordination, and the European Banking Union with the centralisation of administrative implementation constitutes the answer to the concerns formulated, albeit only for the Eurozone. This second phase of a new financial architecture, developed in response to the financial crisis and the Euro crisis encompasses, however, only the Eurozone Member States (and potentially those others entering into 'close cooperation').

This genuinely 'European' banking supervision (in Eurozone-participating Member States) is characterised by 'full independence' (recital 75, Article 19 SSM Regulation). From a German perspective, two points in this arrangement were particularly problematic. First, locating the supervisory function with the ECB,

---

[29] The three authorities of the ESFS are listed in Art 2(2) of Regulation (EU) No 1095/2010 of the European Parliament and of the Council of 24 November 2010 establishing a European Supervisory Authority (European Securities and Markets Authority), amending Decision No 716/2009/EC and repealing Commission Decision 2009/77/EC, [2010] OJ L 331/84: the ESMA (created via Regulation (EU) No 1095/2010 itself, replacing the formerly existing authority for this area, CESR); the EBA (created via Regulation (EU) No 1093/2010 of the European Parliament and of the Council of 24 November 2010 establishing a European Supervisory Authority (European Banking Authority), amending Decision No 716/2009/EC and repealing Commission Decision 2009/78/EC, [2010] OJ L 331/12); and EOPIA, the supervisory authority on insurance undertakings. Moreover, within the ESFS, the authority created, the so-called European Systemic Risk Board (ESRB), was mainly given powers to gather and analyse information, but not classic supervisory powers (see Regulation (EU) No 1092/2010 of the European Parliament and of the Council of 24 November 2010 on European Union macroprudential oversight of the financial system and establishing a European Systemic Risk Board, [2010] OJ L 331/1; already then annexed to the ECB). See, for instance, J Binder, 'Verbesserte Krisenprävention durch paneuropäische Aufsicht? Zur neuen Aufsichtsinfrastruktur auf EU-Ebene', *Zeitschrift für Gemeinschaftsprivatrecht (GPR)* (2011), 34–40; E Ferran and K Alexander, 'Can Soft Law Bodies Be Effective? The Special Case of the European Systemic Risk Board' (2010) 6 *European Law Review* 751.

[30] For how the balancing between EBA and ECB competences and mandates was achieved, see Regulation No 1022/2013 of 22 October 2013 (n 18).

because in the German system and some others (independent) monetary policy is separated from banking supervision (which is under the authority of the minister of finance or independent supervisory authorities). Second, giving 'full independence' to this second function thus vested with the ECB, while in Germany and some other countries the political aspect, namely the democratic accountability, of banking supervision was always stressed and maintained.[31] Independence under Article 19 SSM Regulation has three main aspects, the first two of which are non-renounceable (as they also are from a German perspective). First, within the ECB, monetary policy and price stability function on the one hand (Monetary Union) and the banking supervision function on the other (Banking Union) are segregated, with one 'organ' for banking supervision, the SSB (see Article 25 et seq SSM Regulation), although (imperative under EU primary law) the final decision-taking power had to be with the ECB Governing Board. This brings the EU scheme 'closer' to the German system of institutional segregation where, however, the information flows mean that both functions are closely linked (banking supervision taking place on the basis of Central Bank information). Second, the new European supervision is independent from national supervision (including national ministries – Article 19(1) second phrase of the SSM Regulation). This is already mandated by the principles of supremacy and of general application of Union law. Most disputed was, and still is, the third aspect of independence: the principles of Basel III already ask for 'independence' of banking supervision from influence stemming from political institutions. It had indeed been recognised that the willingness of national supervisory agencies to be 'responsive' to 'political requirements' had at least contributed to the supervisory failure which led up to the financial crisis. The severance of the bond between Member State politics and banking supervision – and thereby also of the chain of contagion in case of financial stress or distress – had been one core aim of the introduction of the European Banking Union (see 6th recital SSM Regulation). Therefore, independence in this third meaning has to be seen as rejecting the notion of political supervision and influence on banking supervision, in favour of a mere accountability to the European Parliament (and the national parliaments) in the form of disclosure and reports, and a reaction by the European Parliament (solely) via nomination to and dismissal from office in the Supervisory Board (see Articles 20 et seq, 26 SSM Regulation). In the core business of supervision, expertise in the supervisory agency should not be watered down by political considerations and order.

---

[31] On both positions – neither one a majority position in Europe – see M Herdegen, 'Europäische Bankenunion: Wege zu einer einheitlichen Bankenaufsicht' (2012) 40 *Zeitschrift für Wirtschafts- und Bankrecht (WM)* 1889; J Ruthig, 'Die EZB in der europäischen Bankenunion' (2014) 178 *Zeitschrift für das gesamte Handelsrecht (ZHR)* 443, esp 466 et seq; L Bini Smaghi, 'Monetary Policy and Supervision: Moral Hazard and Conflicts of Interests?' in E Barucci and M Messori, *Towards the European Banking Union* (Roma, Astrid, 2015) 55; G Hertig, R Lee and J McCahery, 'Empowering the ECB to Supervise Banks: A Choice-Based Approach' (2010) 7(2) *European Company and Financial Law Review* 171, at 175–77.

C. Reaching Beyond SSM, SRM and ESFS: Rulebook and Overall Financial Services Regime

The fourth pillar is different, not referring to a certain area of the law or a particular problem, but rather to the pursuit of uniformity as such: this is the Single Rulebook. It contains the guidelines for the uniform practical application of the CRD IV package. Seen from this perspective, it would seem logical that the EBA is responsible for drafting it.[32] On the other hand, the justification and the need for a Single Rulebook has often been based on the fact that one single institution – and this would be the ECB – cannot act on the basis of diverging practices.[33] This divergence of institutional responsibility and of main thrust may also be the main problem for the drafting of a Single Rulebook in the area of banking supervision. Given the weight of its practice, prestige and high expertise (and its manpower), a strong influence of the ECB on the shaping of the Single Rulebook can be predicted or even already be sensed. On the other hand, it is the idea of a Single Rulebook formulated by the EBA (in close collaboration, of course, with the ECB) which in fact transposes the very idea of the European Banking Union – full uniformity also in the administrative application – to the whole of the Union! This is so because, notwithstanding numerous national discretions possible under the financial regulatory framework, the Rulebook and the guidelines it contains are meant to be so detailed that leeway in interpretation and discretion is eliminated. Even its non-obligatory elements are subject to comply or explain mechanisms. As 'banking supervision practice crystalising in guidelines', the Rulebook in fact extends the idea of administrative uniformity to the whole of Europe. Thus, the real difference between banking supervision inside and outside the Eurozone may not so much be the difference in application of the guidelines contained in a detailed Single Rulebook, but the supervisor itself: in the one case, a supra-national supervisor, in the other (still) a national one.

The other context, reaching beyond the regime of the European Banking Union in the narrow sense is formed by all those areas where an overspill of the regime and the practice of the Banking Union can be forecasted. Among them is private banking law (also in commercial banking, for instance with respect to bank loans or even payment systems) and certainly European capital market law. Therefore, these areas have at least to be taken into account in the context of the present considerations, albeit not thoroughly discussed (see below section V.A).

---

[32] On this competence and on the Rulebook in the area of banking supervision, see namely N Moloney, 'Resetting the Location of Regulatory and Supervisory Control Over EU Financial Markets: Lessons from Five Years On' (2013) 62 *International and Comparative Law Quarterly* 955; U Schneider, 'Inconsistencies and Unsolved Problems in the European Banking Union' (2013) 13 *European Journal of Business Law* 441.

[33] A Lefterov, 'The Single Rulebook: Legal Issues and Relevance in the SSM Context', ECB Legal Working Paper Series, No 15, October 2015. See, however, Art 4(3) SSM, requiring the ECB take into account the domestic transposition of relevant EU directives.

III. Some Theoretical Background on Integration and Regulatory Diversity

This chapter, to a substantial extent, contains more of a positive than of a normative analysis. This is different at least with respect to the question which type of integration dynamism has been triggered *within* the Banking Union framework (see section IV). Therefore, a short summary of the advantages and the disadvantages of regulation at the central, ie the EU level, and of regulation at the decentralised, ie the national level, is needed as background for the assessment of the EU Banking Union which will follow in the next two sections.

As explained, integration and rule-setting at the EU level is understood broadly here: the larger the part of those (components of) decisions which frame the final outcome in the individual case is taken at the EU level, the higher the level of integration. In other words, more uniformity in the guidelines of practical application increases the level of integration, not just the density of rule-setting proper. Given the discretion which supervisory authorities have and given that the discretion now resides primarily with the ECB and no longer with national banking supervisors in many respects, even 'administrative' decisions in the individual cases have their 'regulatory' component and this component is now decided on at the EU level (at least for those 118 banks supervised directly by the ECB, for others potentially via spill-over effects). With the Rulebook, this 'regulatory' or 'rule-setting' side becomes even more evident – and, as explained, the Rulebook shares quite some aspects of the European Banking Union even though it is the EBA which is responsible for its drafting.

When it comes to the advantages and the disadvantages of regulation at the central, ie the EU level, and at the decentralised, ie the national level, the best summaries stem from the literature concerned with regulatory competition (and, as a background for it, also the theory of federalism).[34] Here, the main advantages of rule-setting at the central level – at the EU level, for instance – are summarised as follows:[35] for some areas (such as contract law), the most important

---

[34] See from recent literature: D Cunning and J MacIntosch, (2000) 20 *Int Rev Law & Econ* 141, H Fleischer (2010) 47 *CMLR* 1671, at 1700–03; F Gomez and J Ganuza, 'An Economic Analysis of Harmonization Regimes – Full Harmonization, Minimum Harmonization or Optional Instrument? (2011) 7 ERCL 275; and F Gomez, 'The Harmonization of Contract Law Through European Rules – A Law and Economics Perspective' (2008) 4 *ERCL* 89; S Grundmann and W Kerber, 'European System of Contract Laws – A Map for Combining the Advantages of Centralised and Decentralised Rule-making' in S Grundmann and J Stuyck (eds), *An Academic Greenpaper on European Contract Law* (The Hague/London/New York, Kluwer, 2002) 295–342; W Kerber and S Grundmann, 'An Optional European Contract Law Code – Advantages and Disadvantages' (2005) 21 *European Journal of Law and Economics* 215.

[35] Probably the most systematic account summarising literature (mostly from economics) on the possible advantages and disadvantages can be found in W Kerber, 'European System of Private Laws: an Economic Perspective' in F Cafaggi and H Muir-Watt (eds), *Making European Private Law – Governance Design* (Cheltenham, Edward Elgar, 2008) 65–97 (excellent table summarising the effects at p 76).

advantages of centralisation are those of standardisation, as the ease of transaction is increased. Advantages of standardisation can assume various forms. First, transaction costs for offerors can be reduced when they have the chance to use the same law more frequently or even always – and not divergent laws – namely, if it is easier to have local (cheaper) access to the law used. If this increases the volume of trade of the user, at least of cross-border trade, this leads moreover to economies of scale, where fixed costs can be distributed across a higher number of products, reducing their individual costs. When it comes to a level playing field between the competitors, when the costs of compliance with regulation are substantial (as compared to other costs), standardisation is also needed to allow for a level playing field – without the distortions such costs create. Besides this bundle of advantages of standardisation, there is yet another core advantage, which is that uniform law reduces negative externalities. In other words, it is more likely that interests of all parties affected in the whole territory, for instance the EU (or even beyond), in certain public goods such as financial stability, will be considered. Other important costs avoided by centralisation are seen in potentially reducing clashes and conflicts between different legal orders applied to one phenomenon (homogeneity of the regime applied), fostering easier access to other markets.

On the other hand, the theory of federalism also emphasises the main advantages of decentralised rule-setting, guided by the subsidiarity principle:[36] there is more room for experimentation here, which leads to innovation, which could be a core advantage in dynamically changing times, namely where solutions are untested. In particular this means, that there are, first, more room for offers – in case of decentralised rules-setting they come in a much higher number. There is, second, also more room for errors and therefore also for detecting them and reacting to them – again, a core advantage in a world of high complexity and dynamics (competition as 'a discovery device' – discovery of errors).[37] Closely related to

---

On the following, see, also the accounts in the more general literature on regulatory competition: O Bar-Gill, M. Barzuza and L Bebchuk, 'The Market for Corporate Law' (2006) 162 *Journal of Institutional and Theoretical Economics (JITE)* 134; R Cooter, *The Strategic Constitution* (Princeton, Univ Press, 2000) 130–39; D Esty and D Geradin, 'Regulatory Co-opetition' (2000) *Journal of Economic Law* 235–55, at 240 et seq; K Gatsios and P Holmes, 'Regulatory Competition' in P Newman (ed), *The New Palgrave Dictionary of Economics and the Law*, vol 1, (London, Macmillan, 2002) 271–75, at 273–75; P Gomez (2008) 4 *ERCL* 89–118, at 95–103; K Heine and W Kerber, 'European Corporate Laws, Regulatory Competition and Path Dependence' (2002) 13 *European Journal of Law and Economics* 47; HR Romano, 'Law As a Product – Some Pieces of the Incorporation Puzzle' (1985) 1 *Journal of Law, Economics, and Organization* 225; H Siebert and M Koop, 'Institutional Competition – A Concept for Europe?' (1990) 45 *Aussenwirtschaft* 439; J-M Sun and J Pelkmans, 'Regulatory Competition in the Single Market' (1995) 33 *Journal of Common Market Studies* 67; on innovation and experimentation, see S Cleveland, 'Process Innovation in the Production of Corporate Law' (2008) 41 *UC Davies L Rev* 1829–95, esp at 1868.

[36] See references last note.

[37] See, for instance, F v Hayek, 'Competition as a Discovery Procedure' in *New Studies in Philosophy, Politics, Economics and the History of Ideas* (London, Routledge & Kegan Paul, 1978) 179–90.

this is the advantage that more dispersed and heterogeneous information can be profited from. Yet another advantage of decentralised rule-setting is that it allows for a more varied set of offers, with different regulators being empowered to take into account the local preferences which may be quite heterogeneous in different jurisdictions.

Given the advantages of rule-setting both at the centralised and at the decentralised level – and, simultaneously, also weaknesses at both levels – it was an obvious step to propose – mainly in European literature – a channelling of these advantages and disadvantages by a regulatory order allowing for regulatory competition. In other words: it depends on each type of rule or each segment of regulation whether there are more advantages of centralising decision-making or rule-setting or more advantages of not doing so. Such differentiation should enhance the advantages and reduce the disadvantages of each type of rule-setting as much as possible, and this order would consist mainly of appropriate rules of appropriate level – combining elements of centralisation and of decentralisation.[38] In the following, the above constitutes the basis on which the assessment of single solutions in the regime on the European Banking Union is grounded.

IV. Integration and Remaining Diversity *Within* the European Banking Union

A. A Quick Look Back into History – Differences in Starting Point with Competition Law

Even a short look back into history shows a common thrust between the development (then) in EU antitrust law and (now) in EU banking (supervision) law, but also important differences, mostly of theoretical framing (which then, however, also had substantial practical implications).

On the one hand, it is true that both areas – at a distance of more than half a century – share the main feature: which is that also the bulk of *administrative application* has been shifted to the EU level. Both areas stand out and are indeed unique in this aspect in particular – more so even than with respect to depth of harmonisation and/or unification, ie with respect to the degree of uniformity in *rule-setting*, where already they are also at the upper end of the scale of possibilities

---

[38] See references n 25 above. See in more detail S Grundmann, 'Regulatory Competition in European Company Law – Some Different Genius?' in G Ferrarini, K Hopt and E Wymeersch (eds), *Capital Markets in the Age of the Euro* (The Hague et al, Kluwer Law Int, 2001) 561–95, at 569–76 (principle) and 578 et seqq (different market segments); W Kerber and S Grundmann, 'An Optional European Contract Law Code – Advantages and Disadvantages' (2005) 21 *European Journal of Law and Economics* 215, at 225–27.

which can be found in private and in economic law in the EU. In fact, without EU competition law, the uniform banking law would be difficult to conceive. For the European Banking Union, the problem of combining a certain degree of diversity which still exists in the rules to be applied with a single administrative body being competent, has been taken up and will be discussed in the following section (see section IV.C).

On the other hand, there are also striking differences which influenced the design and the development of the two integration leaps under consideration: in the early times of the European Community, the advantages of diversity and the concept of regulatory competition were not discussed, not sensed, and this theme was not influential. Literature on all these questions and concepts originated in late 1970s onwards and became influential only at the end of the last century (see references in section III). Therefore, if there were limits to the endeavour to shift powers to the EU also at the administrative level, this was due to a lack of political will in the Member States to transfer such powers rather than to an analysis of such advantages and disadvantages. Similarly, the principle of subsidiarity had not yet been enacted. The split of competences in antitrust law was then basically made on the basis of size and of cross-border relevance of the transaction (or merger). A second major conceptual difference would seem to be that, at the time when a uniform antitrust regime was introduced at EU level, the relationship between market regulation and traditional private law (instruments and remedies) was relatively little discussed.[39] Both areas seemed rather far apart (and specialist communities developed accordingly). This was certainly not the case in capital market law when it came into being also in the EU, nor is it today in banking law.

This has substantial repercussions also in the design of regimes and institutions and in the practical application. While for antitrust, uniform law was enacted at least in a core area (as early as in the Treaty of Rome of 1957) and while only one institution at the central level was rendered competent for all the European Community, which later became the European Union, the overall picture is much

---

[39] To some extent, this is astonishing given that one of the founding fathers of European antitrust law, F Böhm, had always stressed the mutual dependence of both orders on each other and even seen the antitrust regime mainly as one helping to maintain meaningful party autonomy for *all* market participants: see F Böhm, 'Privatrechtsgesellschaft und Marktwirtschaft' (1966) 17 *ORDO* 75, at 139 et passim; today this view – market order as facilitating the use of party autonomy rather than limiting it – would seem to have gained ground, certainly in the German theoretical discourse: M Wolf, *Rechtsgeschäftliche Entscheidungsfreiheit und vertraglicher Interessenausgleich* (Tübingen, Mohr, 1970) 8 et seqq, 59 et seqq; C-W Canaris, 'Wandlungen des Schuldvertragsrechts – Tendenzen zu seiner "Materialisierung"' (2000) 200 *Archiv für die civilistische Praxis* 273, at 277 et seq; G Wagner, 'Materialisierung des Schuldrechts unter dem Einfluss von Verfassungsrecht und Europarecht – Was bleibt von der Privatautonomie?' in U Blaurock and G Hager, *Obligationenrecht im 21. Jahrhundert* (Baden-Baden, Nomos, 2010) 24 et seq; particularly for consumer law and self-determination: J Drexl, *Die wirtschaftliche Selbstbestimmung des Verbrauchers* (Tübingen, Mohr, 1998) 282 et seq; similar ideas are expressed in the *capacitas* approach, see the contributions in S Deakin and S Supiot (eds), *Capacitas: Contract Law and the Institutional Preconditions of a Market Economy* (Oxford, Hart, 2009).

more nuanced in the case of the European Banking Union. First, uniform law has still not been achieved, not even in the core part of capital requirements and organisational questions. Single Rulebooks are still to be developed on the basis of legislation enacted at the EU level – ie the CRD IV package (for prudential regulation and supervision) and BRRD (for bank resolution). Moreover, as will be seen, for important areas of (market conduct) supervision, diversity both at the level of rules and of administrative application would still seem to continue to be the core characteristic, namely with respect to consumer protection and codes of conducts imposed on banks. In other words, for certain areas, the advantages of diversity are seen as being high enough to restrict the ECB's regulatory power. Second, while it was always clear that the ECB mandate should be limited to the Eurozone, subsidiarity concerns have explicitly been raised and lead to a still more limited regime where the largest number of banks has been excluded from the supervision by the ECB, even within the Eurozone (see recitals 28 and 87 of the SSM Regulation), and, of course, outside the Eurozone, in the latter case, because the political will was such and because the currencies are still different. Third, even where the ECB decides, there is a significant amount of 'joint decision-making' both at the centralised and at the decentralised levels. All this leads to a picture which is considerably more uniform and 'simple' in the case of antitrust law. And when a lot of the administrative competences were handed back to the Member States in 2013, this was more for practical than for theoretical reasons (work overload) and it was not foreseen that the uniformity in application reached would be challenged swiftly by divergent Member State case law developments.[40]

Similarly, with respect to the interplay of regulation with private law remedies: it is not by chance that a European regime on private law remedies in antitrust law came into being only as late as in 2014.[41] This is totally different in the area of banking law, at least in certain sub-areas, and this makes it much easier to forecast that the Banking Union and the regime established will have significant repercussions in private law rather soon (see below section V.A).

---

[40] See Council Regulation (EC) No 1/2003 of 16 December 2002 on the implementation of the rules on competition laid down in Arts 81 and 82 of the Treaty, [2003] OJ L 1/1; on the astonishment which was caused by highly divergent case law developing then in the Member States, see G. Monti, 'Legislative and Executive Competences in Competition Law' in L Azoulai (ed), *The Question of Competence in the European Union* (Oxford, OUP, 2014) 101, at 107.

[41] Directive 2014/104/EU of the European Parliament and of the Council of 26 November 2014 on certain rules governing actions for damages under national law for infringements of the competition law provisions of the Member States and of the European Union, [2014] OJ L 349/1; on this directive, see on this directive, see S Wisking and K Dientzel, 'European Commission finally publishes measures to facilitate competition law private actions in the European Union' (2014) 35 *European Competition Law Review*, 185; F Haus and M Serafimova, 'Neues Schadensersatzrecht für Kartellverstöße – die EU-Richtlinie über Schadensersatzklagen' (2014) *Betriebsberater (BB)*, 2883–90; substantial discussion before on the Green Paper of 2008, see J Basedow, 'Incentives and Disincentives for the Private Enforcement of EC Competition Law' (2008) *Festschrift for H.-B. Schäfer* 499; G Wagner, 'Should Private Enforcement of Competition Law be Strengthened?' in D Schmittchen,

B. Integration of Administration – Targeted in Application

a. *Key Features Summarised*

In section IV, only the core regulatory part of the European Banking Union is considered, namely the allocation of administrative and regulatory powers within the SSM and the SRM (for repercussions outside this nucleus, see section V). If one wants to summarise the degree of integration, referring mainly to the explanations given above, the following would seem to be the most important features.

There is, first, a restriction in the personal scope of application. Both within the SSM and the SRM, ie within the administrative regime established at the EU level (with the SSB under the ECB and the SRB) and supplanting the regular banking supervision and the recovery (still part of supervision) and resolution decisions at Member State level, the personal scope of application relates only to a limited number of credit institutions. Only 118 banks (or banking groups) from within the Eurozone which are systemically relevant are covered, including, however also branches of banks established outside the Eurozone (Article 4(1)(g) and (i) SSM Regulation) and cross-border groups in the case of SRM (Article 7(2) SRM Regulation). The importance of this restriction can, however, be assessed properly only when the following points are taken into account: the ECB can include any bank if – outside the criteria fixed in the SSM Regulation – it considers them to be systemically relevant (Article 6(4)(5)(b) SSM Regulation; for the SRB see Article 7(2)(a)(ii) SRM Regulation). Moreover, the issuing and the withdrawal of the banking licence and the control of dominant shareholdings are in the hands of the ECB for any (Eurozone) bank (Article 4(1)(a) and (c) in conjunction with Article 6(4) SSM Regulation). Moreover, the ultimate responsibility for the functioning of the banking supervision system – for all banks in the Eurozone – is also allocated to the ECB (Article 2(9) in conjunction with Article 6(1), second phrase SSM Regulation; and, similarly for the SRB, Article 7(1) SRM Regulation). Although the decision-making mechanism is not the same, the most important aspect is common again: the 118 banks or banking groups account for about 80 per cent of the volume of banking activities in the Eurozone.[42]

There is, second, also a restriction of the territorial scope of application, in this case defined by the currency: only banks of participating Member States are subject to the single supervision under the SSM and subject to the single resolution regime under the SRM (see Article 4(1) in conjunction with Article 2(1) SSM Regulation ('credit institutions' of the 'participating Member States') and Article 2(a) in conjunction with Article 4 SRM Regulation). Where a Member State

---

M Albert and S Voigt (eds), *The More Economic Approach to European Competition Law* (Tübingen, Mohr-Siebeck, 2007) 115; V Pinotti and D Stepina, 'Antitrust Class Actions in the European Union: Latest Developments and the Need for a Uniform Regime' (2011) 2 *Journal of European Competition Law & Practice* 24.

[42] Lannoo (n 27) 27.

with a currency other than the euro enters into close cooperation with the SSM, however, it automatically becomes a 'participating Member State' for the purposes of SRM Regulation (Article 6 SSM Regulation and Article 4(1) SRM Regulation). So far no Member State but one (the UK) has excluded making use of this option in the future.[43]

Finally, the material scope of application is restricted, even within areas of supervision (restrictions *rationae materiae*). The core of the ECB's supervision concerns capital requirements of the banks subject to its supervision (namely own funds), their internal organisation (with questions such as remuneration and risk-taking strategies), and 'financial stability' and 'stability of the credit institution(s)' (recitals 6 and 5 and Article 1 first phrase SSM Regulation), but also market integrity ('integrity of the internal market', recitals 10 and 30 Article 1 first phrase SSM Regulation). These reflect the general aims of the Single Supervision Mechanism enshrined in recitals 2–6 of the SSM Regulation (for all three pillars), and also in Article 1 SSM Regulation. On the other hand, concerns about 'consumer protection' are left to the supervision of the national supervisory authorities (recital 28 SSM), and this is understood as also including, for instance, codes of conduct.[44] The typical double function of banking supervision – to be found in many Member States – where both internal capital requirements and organisation *as well as* the relationship to clients are supervised by the same institution, is thus split up between the ECB and national supervisors in the case of systemically relevant banks. A similar division is, however, present within certain Member States – such as the UK – where the conduct and consumer protection supervision is conducted by the Financial Conduct Authority (FCA), with prudential oversight within the remit of Prudential Regulation Authority (PRA). There are two provisos the distinction between consumer protection and market integrity' is not completely clear, and the borderlines may be 'blurred'. Market integrity may also encompass quite a bit of consumer protection.[45] Moreover and related to the first proviso, it would seem as if a consumer protection issue – because of the multitude of parallel cases or because of massive impact on the trust of the public in the financial system or also in particular banks with systemic relevance – could turn into an issue of 'stability'.[46] In this case, the ECB should again be competent as supervisor, as its supervision of 'stability' is meant to be complete, no matter the source of a stability risk. Thus the exception of 'consumer protection', left to national supervisors, can be construed narrowly: it would seem necessarily

---

[43] G Osborne, 'Eurozone approaching moment of truth', *EU Observer*, 15 June 2012.

[44] N Moloney, 'The Investor Model Underlying the EU's Investor Protection Regime: Consumers or Investors?' (2015) 13 *European Business Organization Review* 169.

[45] On this distinction between consumer protection and market integrity, see E Wymeersch, 'The Single Supervisory Mechanism or 'SSM', Part One of the Banking Union' (2014) National Bank of Belgium Working Paper No 255, 14.

[46] See more in detail on this issue S Grundmann, 'The European Banking Union and Private Law' (2015) 16 *European Business Organization Review (EBOR)* 357, at 375.

overridden whenever markets as a whole are affected because mistrust is created ('market integrity'), but also when the volume of the consumer transactions – raising concerns of consumer protection and thus typically also of damages claims or validity concerns – is such that it becomes dangerous for individual systemically relevant institutions or even for the whole of the financial system (as, for instance, in the US subprime loan crisis in 2007/08).

b. Assessment of the Regime

The assessment of the regime focuses on the advantages of centralisation – inserting, however, briefly also the relevant advantages of decentralisation – and this discussion of the advantages of centralisation will be based on three questions: (i) negative externalities on the (common) currency caused by supervisory failure in the banking sector; (ii) negative externalities caused by regulatory arbitrage; and (iii) 'costs' stemming from a non-homogeneous supervision of economic phenomena which form one common unit, which concerns banking groups specifically.

Reducing negative externalities – in areas of third party protection through regulation – and gains from standardisation – for areas where drafting and planning is important, such as contract law – are probably those two gains from centralisation which stand out among those analysed in section III. Therefore, the fact that banking supervision had not been centralised in the European Union until the financial and Euro crisis can probably be explained mainly by the fact that major crises had not occurred previously and that therefore political will (and also questions of path dependency) were stronger than arguments based on cautious analysis of the advantages and disadvantages of centralisation of competences.

i. Negative Externalities on a Common Currency Caused by Supervisory Failure

Indeed, the negative external effects on the (common) currency caused by supervisory failure were so disastrous that, at a certain point, any other solution than centralisation seemed unconceivable: the foremost aim of creating a European Banking Union was to break the link between state budgets (funds) and bank funds (see 6th recital SSM Regulation) which proved to be a vicious spiral in the financial and then the Euro crisis. Both crises have been exacerbated by the mutual dependence between state funds which had to be used for bail-outs of banks and, conversely, of bank funds often invested heavily in state bonds – often mutually speeding up the budgetary problems. In fact, the financial crisis (in addition to its own negative effects) also triggered the Euro crisis, and this development was owed in large part to this link and therefore this link had to be broken (6th recital SSM Regulation). This finding, however, can only justify a change in supervision strategy (setting, for instance, limits to bank investment into state bonds), not yet the passage of competence from the national supervisors to the ECB. This second step is only (strongly) justified – according to the theoretical framework of federalist theory set out above – whenever the negative external effects of a misplaced supervision policy in one country are strongly felt in others. Therefore, within the Eurozone, the passage to a centralised supervision is highly justified, as the enormous repercussions (of suboptimal bank supervision and the ensuing need of bank bail-outs) in other Eurozone countries are so obvious that the countervailing disadvantages of centralisation would seem smaller in any case. There had obviously been gross supervisory failure at the (Eurozone) Member States' level; it is highly plausible that this was in large due to supervisory 'capture', stemming from too close relationships between national politics and national banking systems, which were also responsible for too close a dependence on each other.[47] Breaking also this link of 'intimacy' therefore seems obvious a response. What is probably the main disadvantage of centralisation – reduced knowledge of the local banking business – will be discussed later.

ii. Negative Externalities Caused by Increased Regulatory Arbitrage

This type of negative external effect has, however, to be distinguished from the one stemming from regulatory arbitrage – which can come in addition. Between Member States of different currencies it is only this risk which comes into play and has to be considered. Indeed, from the perspective of negative external effects on (the common) currency, it is not only lack of political will but also a huge difference in the assessment of disadvantages of a decentralised supervision which may be invoked in favour of restricting the (mandatory) competence of the ECB to banks of the same currency (the Eurozone), ie the solution which was found in the scheme enacted. The potential disadvantages of decentralised supervision for Member States or stemming from Member States whose currency is *not* the Euro are completely different from those for Member States or stemming from Member States whose currency is indeed the Euro. Between 'ins' and 'outs' there may be negative external effects from regulatory arbitrage (even though the Single Rule-book is also aimed at minimising this). These effects which are often referred to as 'race to the bottom'. These, however, are of a considerably different weight: while they still may be stronger in a European Union with open borders than globally, they are completely distinct from those on a common currency. Therefore, at least

---

[47] On the concept of 'capture' of public bodies by their constituencies, first discussed for rule-setting rather than administration or adjudication, see ground-breaking G Stigler, 'The Theory of Economic Regulation' (1971) 2 *Bell J Econ Man Sci* 3; and earlier S Huntington, 'The Marasmus of the ICC: The Commission, the Railroads, and the Public Interest' (1952) 614 *Yale Law Journal* 467; and F Böhm, 'Privatrechtsgesellschaft und Marktwirtschaft' (1966) 17 *ORDO* 75–151, at 14 et seqq; further developed by J Laffont and J Tirole, 'The Politics of Government Decision Making. A Theory of Regulatory Capture' (1991) 106 *Quarterly Journal of Economics* 1089; M Levine and J Forrence, 'Regulatory Capture, Public Interest, and the Public Agenda – Toward a Synthesis' (1990) 6 *Journal of Law Economics & Organization* 167; D Sahil, Ch Franz, C Gandrud and M Hallerberg, 'Preventing German Banks Failures: Federalism and Decisions to Save Troubled Banks' (2015) 2 *Politische Vierteljahresschrift*.

from the perspective of the disastrous effects which the named link between state budgets (funds) and bank funds had on the stability of currency, it was indeed *not* mandatory to include in the SSM Member States whose currency was *not* the Euro.

With respect to regulatory arbitrage as the second type of negative external effect, the gains from centralisation are less obvious, for the simple reason that even a single supervisory mechanism for the whole of the European Union would still leave large leeway to regulatory arbitrage on a global level. In this case, it would be regulatory arbitrage in the relationship with non-EU states – as can be seen in the example of the shift of OTC business from New York to London after adoption of the (stricter) Dodd-Frank Act in the US.[48] At least, much more careful analysis would be needed – which is beyond the scope of this chapter. On the other side, the advantage of the ability to experiment in a decentralised supervisory system should not be neglected in an area where innovation and change is as present as in the banking business.

For both relationships and concerns – the non-Eurozone Member State may fear that developments in the Eurozone will heavily affect its own currency or it may fear that regulatory arbitrage may be stronger and more detrimental within a Europe with open borders than globally – it seems indeed appropriate to choose an optional opt-in model.[49] These are concerns to which it is difficult to give a clear answer as with regard to the negative external effects on a common currency area. Diverging assessments – from Member State to Member State – seem plausible.

iii. 'Costs' Stemming From a Non-Homogeneous Supervision of One Common Unit

Much stronger again are the arguments with respect to supervision of banking groups. Within the SSM, banking groups are now supervised by one supervisor, the ECB, not several national supervisors. This also applies with respect to subsidiaries in non-Eurozone Member States (see Articles 4(1)(g) and (i) SSM Regulation). In this respect, the advantages of centralisation would seem to outweigh those of a decentralised solution rather clearly. Economically, banking groups form one coordinated phenomenon while, legally, they consist of separate legal persons. De facto, however, financial distress in parts of the group typically also affects the other parts of the group and in most cases quite heavily – even though the

---

[48] See J Coffee, 'Systemic Risk after Dodd-Frank: Contingent Capital and the Need for Regulatory Strategies beyond Oversight' (2011) 111 *Columbia Law Review* 795; on the regime in the Dodd-Frank Act, see also C Johnson, 'Regulatory Arbitrage, Extraterritorial Jurisdiction, and Dodd-Frank: The Implications of US Global OTC Derivative Regulation' (2014) 2 *Nevada Law Journal* 14, 542.

[49] While this is not an option by market participants (much discussed over the last few years), but an option by Member States, quite a few of the arguments made on the project of an Optional European Sales Law over the last few years, would seem to have some bearing on this question as well. See on this discussion, among others: F Gomez and JJ Ganuza, 'An Economic Analysis of Harmonization Regimes – Full Harmonization, Minimum Harmonization or Optional Instrument?' (2011) 7 *ERCL*

organisation of the group (centralised or decentralised) and measures such as ring-fencing may substantially vary this impact. Certainly, recovery and also resolution plans are impossible without taking into account all parts of the group.[50] In terms of Kerber's systemisation,[51] non-coordinated supervision causes costs of information and of (in)consistency of the legal order applied – which are the two most important cost factors listed there besides those of negative externalities, see above, and trade barriers. The information flow is easier and a uniform decision-making with regard to the whole economic phenomenon ('group') is rendered possible only where they are subject to one and the same supervisory authority. In this respect, it is indeed interesting that Eurozone membership is *not* the decisive factor, but that also non-Eurozone Member States have accepted the SSM to cover (non-Eurozone) subsidiaries of (holding) banks situated in the Eurozone through supervisory colleges.

These features do not exhaust the move towards substantially more integration within the SSM and in the SRM. They are, however, the most significant ones – at least for the current supervision and, partially, recovery planning, albeit not resolution – and certainly very paradigmatic ones. There is, however, not only a move towards substantially more integration. Equally characteristic for a design developed after the turn of the century is a second feature. The regulation is highly nuanced – it is characteristic that the tension between unity *and diversity* is so prominently taken into consideration.

C. Remaining Elements of Diversity *Within* the Banking Union

a. Key Features Summarised

The key factor of diversity would seem to be addressed in Article 4(3) SSM Regulation: wherever national laws may diverge – because transposition of the relevant directive (namely the CRD IV) leaves them discretion or because the Member State used an option right contained in an EU regulation (namely the CRR)[52] – the ECB has to apply the national law of the Member State of the bank at stake, potentially diverging from the one which applies to banks in other Member States. It must, however, be kept in mind that most Member State option rights are limited

---

275, S Grundmann, 'Costs and Benefits of an Optional European Sales Law (CESL)' (2013) 50 *CMLR* 225 [extended version in German in *Archiv für civilistische Praxis* 2012 (212) 502–544].

[50] For these questions, see more in detail R Wiggis, N Tente and A Metrick, 'Cross-Border Resolution - Fortis Group', *Yale Program on Financial Stability*, (2015) Case Study 2014-5C-V1, 12 March 2015, 12, V Babis, 'European Bank Recovery and Resolution Directive: Recovery Proceedings for Cross-Border Banking Groups' (2014) 25(3) *European Business Law Review* 459.

[51] See n 35 above.

[52] See n 16 above.

in time and that discretion left to the Member States in the relevant directive(s) decreases with implementing regulations (for example, the EBA Technical Standards) and even more with a Single Rulebook as it is developed. Therefore, in the long run, a different feature of 'diversity' may even be more relevant for practice.

It is one of the novel features of the SSM that supervisory teams can – or should – be mixed, ie containing employees both of the ECB and of national authorities (when the ECB is competent), but also, albeit only in single cases where the ECB requires this, when a national supervisory authority is competent (see Article 31(1) and Article 7 SSM Framework Regulation). In the first case, typically employees of the Member State of the bank at stake will participate, but only as a minority.[53] The scope of that arrangement is spelt out (at least in part) when the particular importance of conflicts of interests is stressed (see Article 31(3)(4) SSM Regulation), albeit mainly with respect to later employment in the private sector. Having employees of that Member State in the supervisory committee – but only as a minority – reduces the risk of potential regulatory capture being influential in their decision-taking.

A third prominent type of diversity has already been mentioned: (prudential) supervision of aspects of consumer protection and therefore also of compliance with codes of conducts is left to the national authorities. This rule, however, has been interpreted narrowly in this chapter: such questions would then have to nevertheless fall into the competence of the ECB once the 'integrity of the internal market' or the 'stability of credit institutions' or even of the financial system is or are affected.

b. Assessment of the Regime

If the overall scheme is aimed at substantially more uniformity in the core of banking supervision (capital requirements, organisational requirements, uniform application by an independent institution), the remaining diversity of national laws would seem to be of minor importance. The consciously calibrated interplay between (dominant) features of unity and features of diversity may, however, arguably be the one characteristic which most strikingly distinguishes 'full integration' in banking supervision (within the European Banking Union) and 'full integration' in competition law.

The diversity in the composition of supervisory teams, with members coming from the ECB and from the Member State which would otherwise be competent for supervising the bank, is more interesting. It appears to be a novel and promising way of combining advantages of uniformity and of diversity. Diversity in composition – just like diversity in rule-setting (see above section III) – is likely to have the effect that local knowledge can be used more effectively and that therefore

---

[53] For the arrangements envisaged, see more in detail European Central Bank, *Guide to Banking Supervision*, September 2014, pp 14–17.

the knowledge base will be broader.[54] Supervisors from the Member State of the bank at stake are important in this, (often) having better knowledge of the local context, business structure and the particular bank. Participation of such 'local' supervisors potentially may be important for acceptance of policies of the central- ised authority in a given Member State too, for instance in cases such as Greece. On the other hand, mixed composition, namely with the members from that Member State being in a rather small minority, limits the risk that local 'supervi- sory capture' comes in again via the backdoor.

Finally, also the split of competences with respect to areas of supervision (stability and integrity vs consumer protection and codes of conduct) consti- tutes a scheme in which the advantages of unity and diversity may be combined, or where at least the advantages of unity are seen as being strong enough only with respect to the aims of stability and integrity, not with respect to consumer protection. Indeed, consumers typically do not know the law, but at most have a vague feeling that consumer protection may be stronger in one country or the other. Therefore, advantages of uniformity achieved via a centralised super- vision do not seem significant (low economies of scale), one core reason being that for the bank at stake, the supervisor remains the same with respect to all consumer protection concerns even if this is this bank's national supervisor. Conversely, lack of stability of an institution or mistrust in the internal market – in this case that in the Eurozone subjected to supervision – would directly affect other countries as well, as both may have repercussions on that Member State's budget (and hence the stability of the Euro if stabilisation instruments are required) and on the stability of the financial system as a whole. This understanding of where unity is most needed and where it is not so important speaks in favour of the inter- pretation given in cases of overspill: despite recital 28 SSM Regulation, questions of consumer protection or violations of codes of conduct can be taken up by the ECB once the level is reached where the 'integrity of the internal market' or the 'stability of credit institutions' or even of the financial system is or are affected, as outlined above. Thus the division of competences is in reality a functional one, not a strict division by areas of the law.

V. Integration Dynamism Triggered *Beyond* the European Banking Union

The European Banking Union is likely to influence the dynamism of integration beyond its scope proper – which is individual administrative banking supervision

---

[54] This is the basis of the seminal paper by F v Hayek of 1945 on the 'use of knowledge' which, the author's view, is the real starting point of information economics more generally with its find- ing that dispersed knowledge is a superior steering device for economies: see F v Hayek, 'The Use of Knowledge in Society' (1945) 35 *The American Economic Review* 519; see on this paper and the development of information economics: S Grundmann, in S Grundmann, H Micklitz and M Renner, *Privatrechtstheorie* (Tübingen, Mohr-Siebeck, 2015), chapter 12 (and further reference therein).

at microprudential level. This may be so with respect to rule-setting techniques and even with respect to adjudication in courts, probably in most cases in private law matters (see below section V.A). Such influence may, however, potentially also be strong with respect to constitutional principles (see below section V.B). The capital market union might still reinforce these aspects – irrespective of what form it may take (see below section V.C).

A.   Impact on Rule-Setting or Even Adjudication?

a.   Rule-Setting

The first type of impact is related to rule-setting techniques. Here, it may even be argued that this is still a question 'within' the Banking Union, as it is about banking supervision. It does, however, also reach beyond it in at least two respects: The ECB/SRB are not the sole actors in this process and this process is not only about 'administration' (at the centralised level) – as banking supervisor has traditionally been seen – but about the 'administrative' institution as a part of the 'legislative' process as well. Here, the starting point of the considerations in this chapter are the changes introduced with the Lamfalussy architecture of legislation. Already, legal measures (directives or regulations) taken by the European Parliament and the Council were followed by a level II legislation (implementing or delegated), which is much more precise and specifies the details. Administrative agencies such as the ESMA (CESR under the Lamfalussy process prior to 2010 reform) played an important role in this, and the final decision was taken by the European Commission, not by the European Parliament and Council.[55] At level III, ie convergence of regulatory practice, however, there was no competence of an administrative body at the EU level to engage in rule-setting activities in order to eliminate the remaining differences and ensure a completely uniform practice. This, however, is the aim of a Single Rulebook. While the Single Rulebook is to contain guidelines for practice, this blurs the boundaries between administrative acts in single cases and rule-setting.[56] The EBA – which is competent for the elaboration of the Rulebook – thus becomes in part also a 'legislature' (together with the European Commission in adopting the final decisions).

EBA's role is interesting in yet another respect. This agency prepares the Rulebooks for the Eurozone and for the non-Eurozone Member States, from the ECB's perspective: for the 'ins' and for the 'outs'. At the same time, it is always stressed by the insiders of both institutions that this is done in closest collaboration and consultation with the ECB, which is of course is an EU institution as well and directly represented as a supervisor in the EBA. In other words, while the European Commission, as the sole competent body, has created a uniform

---

[55] See references in n 7 above.
[56] See n 5 above.

case practice in competition law, the Rulebook developed by the EBA is likely to be most strongly influenced by ECB's practice (and advice), and will play a similar role in having a uniform case practice guideline in banking supervision matters, but this will be done in a more discursive way – in more of a negotiation process between 'ins' and 'outs'. The main difference will perhaps be that the 'case law practice' will not stand as such, but will be the basis of an ordered guideline for practice. One fact will be of particular importance in this process, which is that the ECB acts in 'full independence' with respect to its banking supervision tasks (recital 75, Article 19 SSM Regulation; as already required by the Basel III principles).[57] In other words, political influence (also by parliaments) on the content of such detailed rules is restricted to mere information (and appointment of members of the SSB). This potential development can perhaps be termed like this: the EBA, with heavy influence from the ECB (acting in 'full independence' from politics), will in reality be the rule-setter with respect to full uniformity in the application of banking supervisory rules, and this will be the case Europe-wide.

In this process, it may even be that similar problems arise as have been the subject of intense discussion in relation to CJEU case law. There, it is hotly debated in how far and under what circumstances the Court may even out systematic inconsistencies in the legal regime, creating a consistent system and shaping the legal regime accordingly (as it has done, for instance, in the case of *Sturgeon*[58]). The main argument for such a role is, of course, that knowledge of the facts may give superior knowledge of inconsistencies in the legal regime.[59] This is an argument which can easily be transposed to the EBA/ECB acting as rule-setters who guarantee the uniform (and consistent) application of banking supervision law in the whole of the Union.

---

[57] On this concept, on the accountability to the European Parliament and national parliaments (and on the dispute whether such 'independence' could be granted), see C Gandrud and M Hallerberg, 'Does Banking Union Worsen the EU's Democratic Deficit? The Need for Greater Supervisory Data Transparency' (2015) 53(4) *Journal of Common Market Studies* 769.

[58] Case C-402/07 and C-432/07 *Sturgeon v Condor Flugdienst GmbH* and *Böck v Air France SA*, EU:C:2009:716. On these issues, see S Grundmann, '"Inter-Instrumental-Interpretation" – Systembildung durch Auslegung im Europäischen Unionsrecht, *RabelsZ* 75 (2011) 882, at 920–23; S Keller, 'Mut zur Lücke – die Fluggastrechte-VO zur Auslegung und Überprüfung vor dem EuGH' *Zeitschrift für Verbraucherrecht (ZVR)* 2011, 228–39.

[59] The strongest roots for such a view of the role of adjudication (bringing in superior knowledge, based on the knowledge of the facts at stake) can probably be found in the theory of hermeneutics. See, path breaking, J Esser, *Vorverständnis und Methodenwahl* (Frankfurt, Athäneum, 1972), esp 7–16 and 116–41; and on this work and the concept: S Grundmann in S Micklitz and M Renner, *Privatrechtstheorie* (Tübingen, Mohr-Siebeck, 2015) ch 1 (and further references therein) (English edition forthcoming 2018); J Köndgen, 'Josef Esser (1910–1999)' in S Grundmann and K Riesenhuber (eds), *Private Law Development in Context: German Private Law and Scholarship in the 20th Century*, (Antwerp/Cambridge/Portland, Intersentia, 2018) 179–203; on hermeneutics more generally: GL Ormiston and AD Schrift (eds), *The Hermeneutic Tradition. From Ast to Ricoeur* (New York, State University of New York Press, 1990); G Bruns, *Hermeneutics. Ancient and Modern* (New Haven, Yale University Press, 1992).

b. Adjudication

Such uniform practice guidelines – in banking supervision – will perhaps not lead to adjudication very often. In case of recovery and resolution proceedings (for the guidance of which the SRB is the prime responsible institution), litigation is already more likely to happen. The greatest influence of the Banking Union developments on adjudication may, however, even reach beyond banking supervision, recovery and resolution proper and be situated in private law. This is not the place to discuss the impact of the Banking Union regulatory compound on private law in some detail.[60] One example may, however, show the dimensions of this: if organisational requirements of banking supervision go so far that the ECB may forbid risky transactions or business strategies even if they would increase shareholder value, the private law equilibrium of a whole area of private law, namely of company law, may be totally changed – with the ensuing need for a detailed readjustment of rules on duties of directors (their ultimate goal no longer being shareholder or also stakeholder welfare).[61] Potentially, this could also affect rules on accounting, rights of shareholders to give instructions, and so on. Moreover, the impact may not be limited to the organisation of banks. Changes in the rules on banking supervision will probably have an impact on their relationship with clients – dictating nullity, if a certain technique is forbidden by the ECB, and potentially deciding on breach of contract or fault (or not) when a certain standard set in the Single Rulebook is not respected. In the present author's view, it will certainly not take 50 years (as in antitrust with the 2014 Directive) until the moment that violation of rules of supervision will lead to nullity claims or claims for damages (and this is to be welcomed). In one area, both regulation and private law are already particularly close to each other: investment services.

The role which the European Banking Union is likely to play in this development is this: a standard established as common European practice is much more likely to influence the courts' interpretation of what is required in legal acts than a national supervisor's practice would be. This is so because the standards in this area are mostly based on EU legal measures, also those standards that can be seen as private law standards. While national courts (who do the bulk of adjudication) traditionally do not feel bound by (national) administrative practice, their attitude is likely to change with respect to the ECB's practice and even more so with respect to a Single Rulebook. This is so for three reasons: national courts will feel more easily bound by such 'standards' set at the EU level with respect to rules

---

[60] See more in detail on this question S Grundmann, 'The European Banking Union and Private Law' (2015) 16 *European Business Organization Review (EBOR)* 357.

[61] J Binder, 'Vorstandshandeln zwischen öffentlichem und Verbandsinteresse – Pflichten- und Kompetenzkollisionen im Spannungsfeld von Bankaufsichts- und Gesellschaftsrecht' *Zeitschrift für das gesamte Gesellschaftsrecht (ZGR)* 2013, 760–801; see also K Langenbucher, 'Finanzinnovationen, Geschäftsleiterhaftung und Corporate Governance in regulierten Branchen' in F Möslein (ed), *Finanzinnovation und Rechtsordnung* (Zurich, Schulthess, 2014) 272–88 and *Zeitschrift für Bankrecht und Bankpraxis (ZBB)* (2013) 16–23.

which themselves are 'European' in origin – or at least they will feel constrained to refer the question to the CJEU if they want to disagree ('the European institutions as prime interpreters of European Law'). They will consider particular expertise in the ECB/EBA as particularly 'persuasive'. And the concept of 'supremacy' of the EU level will be influential even though 'only' an administrative institution acts at the EU level.

B. Impact on 'Constitutional' Questions of Integration?

A short look back in history is helpful also with respect to case law on 'constitutional' questions of integration. Indeed, a considerable part of the CJEU decisions on the 'constitutional' instruments have been decided in the area of competition law: ranging from direct application of EEC/EC/EU Treaty law (primary law)[62] to supremacy of EU law over national law[63] or – more generally – the interaction between national administrations and the EU legal order. Today, this is already part of the *acquis communautaire*, so it cannot be 're-invented' with judgments on the SSM.

Other questions, however, which also are truly constitutional, may be decided for this area in particular and the first cases and disputes already go into this direction: questions of legal basis and subsidiarity will probably be test cases. The Banking Union seems to be the area where such challenges are made more consistently,[64] with statements and challenges made at the level of national constitutional courts, namely the *Bundesverfassungsgericht*, more generally.[65] Banking Union thus may well become the playground for intense judicial assessment of the tension between diversity and unity, and hence also for strongly intensified scholarly debate about these questions – which thus become of prime importance also in practice. Yet another theme is already inherent in the *OMT* case, again one of 'constitutional' dimensions. This is the question of how competences should be arranged in cases where highly specialised and 'superior' knowledge is situated in one body or institution which is democratically less legitimised: whether there are boundaries to the transfer of power; whether such transfer of power, even under the principle of democracy, is possible, or possible in a more extended way if there is democratic accountability (such as constant information provided

---

[62] See case law quoted in Commission Notice on the cooperation between the Commission and the courts of the EU Member States in the application of Arts 81 and 82 EC, OJ 2004 C 101/54, PJ Slot, 'The Past, Present and Future of Competition Law in the European Union', in A Arnull, C Barnard, M Dougan and E Spaventa, *A Constitutional Order of States? Essays in EU Law in Honour of Alan Dashwood* (Oxford, Hart Publishing, 2011).

[63] Case 6/64 *Flaminio Costa v ENEL*, EU:C:1964.66.

[64] Case C-270/12 United Kingdom v European Parliament & Council of the EU, EU:C 2018:18 ['ESMA short-selling case] and Case C-62/14 Peter Gauweiler and Others v Deutscher Bundestag, EU:C:2015:7 [*OMT Programme*], judgment of 16 June 2014.

[65] See *Financial Times*, 'Europe's banking union faces legal challenge in Germany', 27 June 2013.

to European Parliament committees and the power to re-appoint members of the Board); whether the degree of accountability plays a role in this, and what type of accountability – and, most fundamentally: which principle of democracy is enshrined and protected in the European Union?[66]

Finally, the question arises whether the European Union – now mainly through the ECB – will become in yet another area an independent supervisor of EU Member States and national companies, in the same way as the European Commission has become with competition law and state aid law. Indeed, the European Commission was this with respect to antitrust and (to an even greater extent) state aid law. The effects on EU Member State policies of decisions in banking supervision may be similarly strong, in monetary policy, it clearly is (OMT as an example). But has the role perhaps changed: is the EU, contrary to the ordo-liberal model, no longer an independent supervisor, but in part even an actor, namely because the EU – more precisely the ECB as an EU institution – now can invest and decide on a considerable amount of funds?

These questions become all the more important as the breadth of the area is considerable. While it is true that competition law covers all branches and sectors, it nevertheless does so only with respect to restrictions of competition in the large sense. Banking and financial law – namely if the Banking Union is extended to a Capital Market Union – would seem to shape the core factor of finance still more deeply, in a more all-embracing way, even though the area is narrower, covering only finance and not the whole economy.

C. On the Way to a European Capital Market Union?

The features of a European Capital Market Union are still in flux and should therefore be addressed only briefly.[67] The core idea is that dependence on banks and bank loans is too high in the Union – the balance sheet volume being at 250 per cent of EU GDP as opposed to 100 per cent in the US.[68] While, however, fostering finance via capital markets is the ultimate goal, it is not a goal conceived in opposition to bank loans. In other words: capital market finance is to be rendered more attractive, but finance via bank loans is not to be restricted (even though the tightening in the CRD IV has already rendered them more costly, but independent from the project of a Capital Market Union). Therefore, while the project has the potential to modify the model of capitalism in the EU, the ultimate goal is not to do so in opposition to established modes of finance (even though, in practice, this may be the case). There is another main feature which points into the direction that, again, diversity is also an important element of the overall scheme.

---

[66] For first discussions of and answers to these questions, see Gandrud and Hallerberg, n 57.

[67] On the project of a EU Capital Market Union, see more in detail: European Commission, 'Building a Capital Markets Union', Green Paper, 18 February 2015.

[68] *Financial Times*, 'EU banks still pose systemic threat', 21 July 2013.

A prominent concern is to enhance the access of SMEs to (cross-border) capital markets, ie to foster diversity of enterprises.[69]

VI. Conclusions

1. This chapter discusses the question of what role the European Banking Union plays and may play in EU integration dynamics. It discusses this question partly in a positive analysis, in its core – related to the Banking Union itself and its functioning – the question is also assessed in a normative way. The question is discussed on the background of a development which we saw in European Competition Law (antitrust law, merger control and also state aid law), and overall, it forecasts a similar importance for integration dynamism as was experienced much earlier in this other area (potentially as a 'second wave of full integration').

2. The chapter therefore had to relate the concepts of 'Banking Union' and 'integration' to each other and sees both as a continuum of solutions: in the case of the Banking Union, the SSM and SRM form the core – with very far-reaching instruments of uniformity both at the regulatory (rule-setting) level *and* at the administrative level, but only for systemically relevant banks (118) in the Eurozone/participating Member States. In the case of the Banking Union, spill-over effects can, however, be studied both with respect to the non-systemically relevant banks *and* – via the Single Rulebook – also outside the Eurozone, perhaps even beyond banking supervision law itself. Therefore there is the core of the Banking Union to be analysed (sections III and IV), but also the question of spill-over effects (section V, but already to some extent section IV). Integration refers to how much of the final decision (the outcome) is made (or decided on) at the central (ie the EU) level, be it via rule-setting processes or administrative guidelines and practices which become standardised. The big step of the Banking Union is to shift to the central level also administrative implementation – thus striving for much more uniformity in detail than could ever be possible under a judicial system of preliminary reference only, and also than had been possible under the Lamfalussy governance architecture of legislation (which can be seen as a first step in this direction).

3. The survey on the Banking Union is mainly informative. It stresses that the SSM Regulation, rendering the ECB (Frankfurt) competent for ongoing banking supervision, and the SRM Regulation, rendering the SRB (Brussels)

---

[69] N Veron and G Wolff, 'Capital Markets Union: a vision for the long term', Bruegel Policy Contribution 2015/05 (April 2015), see also Report of the Five Presidents, *Completing Europe's EMU*, 22 June 2015.

competent with regard to guidance of recovery and resolution procedures, are grounded in harmonisation of the relevant areas (namely CRD IV and BRRD) which apply to all other banks in the EU, including those not systemically relevant or outside the Eurozone.

4.   The two core interpretative findings in this section on the components of the Banking Union are: (i) even though formally restricted, ECB's practice (and one day perhaps also the SRB practice) – in part via its role in preparation of the Single Rulebook(s) for which EBA is competent, and which cover the whole of the Union – will lead to a uniform and standardised *administrative* practice more generally for all banks in Europe. The weight and the responsibilities of the ECB are such as to warrant this forecast. In one point, however, a huge difference remains between the 'ins' and 'outs': that is, who will be the supervisor to apply such (uniform) guidelines; (ii) it is likely that this will not be restricted to banking supervision proper (including recovery and resolution) even though these are the sole components of the SSM and SRM Regulations (with the Single Rulebooks for each of these segments) which established the Banking Union. This will reach into other areas of banking law and even beyond.

5.   As 'more or less' integration is understood in the sense that this concept describes how much of the final outcome is based on a decision taken at the central level, albeit also in the administrative process, the question of advantages and disadvantages of centralised vs. decentralised decision-making also has to be raised for the Banking Union. The shift of administrative powers to the ECB (from the national supervisors) has to be assessed in this way as well. In the summary of literature on federalism and regulatory competition, mainly economies of scale (for the area of default rules) and the risk of negative external effects (for areas of mandatory regulation), but also the homogeneity of the legal regime are seen as strong arguments for decision-making at the central level, while deeper information and better experimentation would speak for decentralisation. Even more important than analysing these advantages and disadvantages separately is combining them in an intelligent competition order for regulatory competition. Whether the Banking Union can be seen as such is the core question of the section for the remainder of the discussion.

6.   Banking Union is the second large area after competition law in which also administration (not only rule-setting) was shifted to the central (EU) level and therefore is good to compare. Contrary to the latter, however, it came into being when regulatory competition, the balancing of unity and diversity, and the link between regulation and private law tools were part of the policy and scholarly discourse. Therefore, the Banking Union is much more consciously about instruments combining unification and differentiation. Diversity at least in parts (such as for the supervision on codes of conduct), with respect to countries covered and in institutions, is combined with unity in a nuanced way.

7.   When it comes to elements of unification, it might appear that the (uniform) supervision by the ECB covers *only 118* systemically relevant banks and *only in the Eurozone*. This impression is, however, misleading. Rather, the ECB has the overall responsibility for all banks of the Eurozone and instruments to exercise it, and for non-Eurozone banks, it is likely that the Single Rulebook – issued by the EBA, but heavily influenced by the ECB and also its extended practice – will result in uniformity in practice as well. The main difference remaining is that the national supervisor may remain as the supervisor outside the Eurozone.

8.   From the perspective of advantages and centralisation, the stronger the case for centralisation, the stronger the negative external effects are. Here the disastrous links between bank funds and state funds (budgets) come into play: the former investing into bonds of the latter, the latter bailing out the former. The negative effects are, however, much stronger inside the common currency than outside because inside, budgetary deficits caused by bail-outs affect the stability of the currency of others as well. These links led to the situation where the financial crisis did not remain only a financial crisis, but moreover turned into a Euro crisis. Hence the Eurozone had to be included into a centralised regime (more likely to break the detrimental link described). For the non-Eurozone, this is less clear, as the external effects are much minor, and an optional model (as adopted) may even be preferable. Negative external effects stemming from regulatory arbitrage are less of an argument for unification, as this arbitrage would take place anyhow (globally). There is, however, a strong argument for consistency and better information flow for supervising groups of banks in a uniform way and by one deciding body. Therefore, the inclusion even of non-Eurozone subsidiaries into the SSM is laudable (exception from the principle that the non-Eurozone is left 'outside').

9.   In practice, the most important elements of diversity (*within* the Banking Union) may be the following two. Consumer protection in the banking business (and the supervision on codes of conducts) is left to the national supervisory authorities while the ECB is responsible for the 'stability' of individual (systemically relevant) institutions and of the overall financial system plus 'market integrity'. Thus, only those elements which carry a high risk of cross-border contagion and negative externalities are subject to centralised supervision, but it is important to note that massive violation of consumer rules may result in stability problems (with a shift of competence to the ECB). Similarly, the mixed supervisory teams can be explained as a conscious mix of diversity (fostering close knowledge) and unity (combating 'capture'). The consciously calibrated interplay between the (dominant) features of unity and the features of diversity constitute probably the one characteristic which most clearly distinguishes 'full integration' in banking supervision (within the European Banking Union) and 'full integration' in competition law.

10. With respect to rule-setting, it would seem as if administrative bodies become highly prolific and important regulators in detail, moreover, the interplay

between the EBA and the ECB may be such that, while the EBA is competent to draft the Rulebook, with final approval of the European Commission, the content may well be influenced mostly by the ECB. Thus, the Rulebook is in to a large extent one pillar of the full integration project of the European Banking Union. For several reasons (such as the concept of supremacy, high, specialised expertise and natural 'competence' for EU law matters), the ECB's practice and the Rulebook are likely to have an intense impact also on adjudication (by national courts). This may even increasingly be the case in private law matters – and perhaps these may even become the most important area in this respect.

11. The Banking Union is likely to have an effect on 'constitutional' issues and the case law referring to them. Just as competition law was influential with respect to direct application and supremacy of EU law (among many others), the Banking Union may be influential with respect to unity and diversity (with questions of legal basis) and with respect to the definition of what the EU model of democracy requires. In some aspects, the Banking Union might even be pushing the constitutional transformation further, where its composite parts (such as the SRB), are themselves, and independently of the national, decentralised level, subject to provisions of EU law (in this case EU state aid law).[70]

12. The EU Capital Market Union would be about enhancing access to capital markets in the EU – partly because bank finance is seen as being too prominent. Enhancing the former has, however, not been combined purposefully with restricting the latter. Moreover, the fostering mainly of SMEs is designed rather to increase diversity than to reduce it, despite the fact that the overall thrust is, of course, towards more unity in capital market law.

---

[70] See Art 18 SRM Regulation.

5

Banking Union and the European Economic Constitution

A Brief Comparison of Regulatory Styles in Banking Regulation and Competition Law

HEIKE SCHWEITZER

I. Introduction

The (unfinished) Banking Union sets out the cornerstones for European banking regulation. Drawing consequences from the financial crisis of 2008, it strives to codify, for the field of banking, a set of fundamental principles of any private market activity: the concurrency between risk-taking and liability, a well-organised market exit in case of insolvency and the separation between private banking and the state. The harmonisation of the regulatory structure for banking and the centralisation of supervision at the European level shall ensure a level playing field between banks. The European Commission is striving to establish a European Deposit Guarantee Scheme as another pillar of banking regulation to prevent bank runs.[1] This framework shall lay the basis for workable competition in banking markets while responding to the specificities of banking. Whereas some have identified an inherent conflict between competition and financial stability in banking markets, the Banking Union, together with the 'Single Rulebook', is meant to ensure their compatibility. Certainly, the legal acts that, together, constitute the Banking Union are acts of secondary European Union (EU) law. Yet they directly relate to the goals of the EU as set out in Article 3(3) of the Treaty on European Union (TEU) and Protocol 27,[2] that is, to establish an internal market with a system of undistorted competition, based on balanced economic growth and price stability. The fundamental principles underlying the Banking Union may thereby

---

[1] See European Commission, Proposal for a Regulation amending Regulation (EU) 806/2014 in order to establish a European Deposit Insurance Scheme, COM(2015)586 fin, 24.11.2015.
[2] Protocol No 27 on the internal market and competition, [2008] OJ C 115/309.

be said to share in the 'constitutional' status of Article 3(3) TEU. The principles of individual liability and market exit in case of failure are essential for any market economy.

The 'social market economy' that the TEU subscribes to is an economic order based on individual economic freedoms and decentralised coordination. Article 16 of the Charter of Fundamental Rights[3] protects the 'freedom to conduct a business in accordance with Community law and national laws'. The reliance on, and protection of, individual economic rights is characteristic for the Union's legal order. In a supranational regime with comparatively weak democratic legitimacy, the protection of individual economic rights is a separate source of legitimacy.[4] The EU has been most successful where it has been able to set rules that allow for the decentralised coordination between economic actors in the exercise of their individual economic choices under the rule of law. Competition rules are paradigmatic. In the EU, they are combined with a particular enforcement style. The EU Commission and the national competition authorities (NCAs) enjoy strong enforcement powers,[5] but they typically intervene *ex post*,[6] within the framework of an essentially non-discretionary, rule-based regime, and will not intervene into economic planning, which remains the task of each economic actor alone.

EU banking regulation, on the other hand, has come to cultivate a very different regulatory style. While it is meant to give force to fundamental legal and economic principles, it currently does so by way of a much more managerial, regulatory regime, characterised by tight supervision and a broad empowerment to intervene into the economic decision-making by individual banks *ex ante* based on a discretionary assessment of risks.

This chapter will claim that there is a tension between the 'constitutional' anchorage of the Banking Union in Article 3(3) TEU with Protocol 27 and the regulatory style described above. There is no doubt that in any economic order, financial stability is a fundamental goal that allows for far-reaching interventions into individual autonomy.[7] But in order to remain in line with the goal of a competitive order grounded in individual economic rights, in particular decentralised decision-making, it would be more appropriate to shift to a different regime forcefully advocated by Martin Hellwig[8] and others:[9] high capital

---

[3] Charter of Fundamental Rights of the European Union, [2012] OJ C 326/391.

[4] See E-J Mestmäcker, 'On the Legitimacy of European Law' in E-J Mestmäcker, *Wirtschaft und Verfassung in der Europäischen Union* (Baden-Baden, Nomos, 2006) 133, in particular 147 et seq.

[5] As set out in Council Regulation (EC) No 1/2003 of 16 December 2002 on the implementation of the rules on competition laid down in Articles 81 and 82 of the Treaty, [2003] OJ L 1/1.

[6] With the exception of merger control and the law of state aid.

[7] For a critical view of the absence of an explicit financial stability mandate of the ECB in the European Treaties see M Hellwig, *Financial Stability, Monetary Policy, Banking Supervision, and Central Banking*, Preprints of the Max Planck Institute for Research on Collective Goods 2014/9, at 18–19.

[8] A Admati and M Hellwig, *The Bankers' New Clothes* (Princeton, Princeton University Press, 2013), in particular p 79.

[9] A Admati, P DeMarzo, M Hellwig and P Pfleiderer, *Fallacies, Irrelevant Facts, and Myths in the Discussion of Capital Regulation: Why Bank Equity is Not Expensive*, Stanford University Working Paper Series 2011.

requirements for all banks, combined with a more hands-off regulatory approach with regard to entrepreneurial decisions. The argument is not that the existing regulatory framework would contravene EU law. But the argument will be made that the alternative regulatory style would be a significantly better fit with the constitutional structure of the EU.

The introduction has to end with a caveat: in contrast to most other contributions to this volume, this chapter is not written by an expert in the field of banking or financial market regulation, but from the perspective of a competition lawyer.

II. The Economic Constitution of the European Union

The European Treaties have established 'a new legal order for the benefit of which the States have limited their sovereign rights, in ever wider fields'. Contrary to traditional international law, the subjects of this legal order 'comprise not only Member States but also their nationals'.[10] In its Opinion 1/91 of 14 December 1991, the Court of Justice of the European Union (ECJ) has called the Community Treaties a 'constitutional charter'.[11] As set out in Article 2 TEU, the Union is founded on the shared values of respect for human dignity, freedom, democracy, equality, the rule of law and respect for human rights. Despite the expansion of EU law in ever more policy fields, its hard substantive core is the internal market (Article 3(3) TEU), based on the fundamental economic freedoms as set out in the Treaty on the Functioning of the European Union (TFEU), and comprising a system of undistorted competition (Protocol 27). These rules have direct effect in the national legal orders and enjoy primacy over the law of the Member States.

The rights-based model of the creation of a common market has been the basis of an intense cross-border interaction between firms and individuals and of the evolution of what may be called a European 'private law society'.[12] At the same time it has been criticised as a driver of a 'neoliberal' model of negative integration.[13] In this perspective, economic liberties are 'normatively reduced' liberties.[14] According to the critics, Europe is in need of a greater exercise of political autonomy – or of 'positive integration' – namely of a political model of integration, going hand in hand with more political constraints imposed on markets. The financial crisis has been regarded as proof of the failure of 'neoliberalism', a concept typically left undefined.

---

[10] Case C-26/62 *Van Gend en Loos*, EU:C:1963:1.

[11] CJEU, Opinion 1/91 of 14 December 1991, para 21.

[12] For the concept of a 'private law society' see F Böhm, 'Privatrechtsgesellschaft und Marktwirtschaft' (1966) 17 *ORDO Bd* 75.

[13] See, eg, F Scharpf, *Regieren in Europa* (Nordenstadt, GRIN, 1999) 47 et seq.

[14] J Habermas, *Die postnationale Konstellation* (Frankfurt am Main, Suhrkamp, 2005) 142.

A long time ago, Benjamin Constant contrasted the balance between political liberty and individual independence in ancient and in modern times.[15] According to Constant, the social basis of the emphasis on political liberty in ancient times was a constant active participation of the people in the exercise of collective power – in the making of the laws and in the day-to-day monitoring of their implementation, ie a very concrete share and a real influence in the exercise of sovereignty. In modern times, on the other hand, the individual can no longer see the influence s/he exerts. Given this new reality, modern liberty, to an important part, 'consist[s] of the peaceful enjoyment of private independence':

> The true modern liberty is individual liberty. Political liberty is its guarantee, which is why we must have political liberty, too. But to ask today's people to sacrifice their entire individual liberty to political liberty … is the surest means of detaching them from the latter, after which it won't take long to rob them of the former.

Considering the amount of legislation passed at the European level, creating a stark contradiction between positive and negative integration is unpersuasive. Markets are social institutions in need of rules. In particular financial markets and banking – which are fundamental but complex infrastructures of a market economy – 'laissez faire' is not an option. Their systemic relevance requires a sound legal structure to contain risk. While distinguishing between negative and positive integration in the banking sector is nonsensical, a distinction can be made between different types of regulatory structures. Within the EU, harmonisation based on Article 114 TFEU must – in principle[16] – be based on the goal to promote a smooth cross-border exercise of individual rights. This argues for a legislative, rule-based and essentially non-discretionary model of regulation.

A rule-based model of regulation can be contrasted with a more managerial, executive mode, which is characterised by more ad hoc discretionary interventions based on risk assessments case-by-case. In his book 'Le bon gouvernement', Pierre Rosanvallon has analysed the shift from the legislative to the executive branch in European democracies.[17] It is a shift which intervenes more intensively into individual economic rights, because it does not provide a sound basis for individual planning. Furthermore, it is a mode of governance in need of greater public control. The EU economic constitution is built on the strength and legitimacy of the rule of law, as prominently highlighted in the ECJ's Opinion 1/91.[18] It is less fit to accommodate a managerial mode of governance.

---

[15] B Constant, *The Liberty of the Ancients Compared with that of the Moderns* (1819), available at http://oll.libertyfund.org/titles/constant-the-liberty-of-ancients-compared-with-that-of-moderns-1819.

[16] For a critique of the evolution of the more recent ECJ's jurisprudence in this regard see M Nettesheim, 'Die Tabak-Urteile des EuGH: Lifestyle-Regulierung im Binnenmarkt' 2016 *EuZW* 15, 578.

[17] See P Rosanvallon, *Le bon gouvernement* (Paris, Le Seuil, 2015).

[18] CJEU, Opinion 1/91 of 14 December 1991, para 21. See also C Joerges, 'Integration Through Law and the Crisis of Law in Europe's Emergency' in D Chalmers, M Jachtenfuchs and C Joerges (eds), *The End of the Eurocrats' Dream: Adjusting to European Diversity* (Cambridge, CUP, 2016) 299, at 301.

III. The Constitutional Relevance of the Banking Union

From the signing of the Treaties of Rome in 1957 onwards, the fundamental economic freedoms and competition rules have constituted the core of the European economic constitution. Yet, the concept has expanded over time. With the setting up of the Monetary Union and the introduction of the Euro as its currency in 2002, the Monetary Union has become part of the economic constitution. This is reflected in the Union Treaties in Article 3(4) TEU and Article 119 et seq TFEU. According to Article 119(1) TFEU:

> ... the activities of the Member States and the Union shall include ... the adoption of an economic policy which is based on the close coordination of Member States' economic policies, on the internal market and on the definition of common objectives, and conducted in accordance with the principle of an open market economy with free competition.

According to Article 120 TFEU:

> Member States shall conduct their economic policy with a view to contributing to the achievement of the objectives of the Union, as defined in Art. 3 TFEU ... The Member States and the Union shall act in accordance with the principle of an open market economy with free competition, favouring an efficient allocation of resources ...

Article 3(3) TEU contains an important commitment to price stability, which the European Central Bank (ECB) is entrusted to maintain (Article 127 TFEU).

Member States must avoid excessive government deficits (Article 126(1) TFEU). The EU will not be liable for or assume the commitments of Member States (Article 125(1) TFEU). Rather, the Member States, in taking on public debt, shall be subject to market discipline.

The financial crisis of 2008 has tested the limits of this legal regime, as Member States had to step in to save national banks at the brink of insolvency.[19] A number of important lessons were drawn from this critical experience.

First, while banking regulation and financial market regulation is not itself part of the formal constitution of the EU, it is so closely interconnected with the monetary system that a banking crisis can easily challenge the legal principles on which the monetary system is based. In substantive terms, the financial system and the banking system is part of the fundamental constitutional structure on which market economies and civil societies are built. As Lenin observed, if you want to destroy civil society, you must devastate its monetary and financial system.

---

[19] For a good account of the financial crisis of 2008 see eg M Hellwig, *System Risk in the Financial Sector: An Analysis of the Subprime-Mortgage Financial Crisis*, De Economist 157/2 (2009) 129; H-W Sinn, *Kasino Kapitalismus* (Berlin, Econ, 2010); J Goddard, P Molyneux and J Wilson, 'The Financial Crisis in Europe: Evolution, Policy Responses and Lessons for the Future' (2009) 17(4) *Journal of Financial Regulation and Compliance* 362. From a US perspective: Financial Crisis Inquiry Commission, *Final Report of the National Commission on the Causes of the Financial and Economic Crisis in the United States*, January 2011, available at www.gpo.gov/fdsys/pkg/GPO-FCIC/pdf/GPO-FCIC.pdf.

Second, if the economic and monetary system is so intricately interconnected with the financial and the banking system, it is essential to bring the regulatory structure of the latter into conformity with the first. This is what the Banking Union sets out to do.

IV. The Structure of the Banking Union

The Banking Union may be regarded as an attempt to create a legal framework for the European banking system that ensures its conformity with the basic principles of the European economic constitution: it shall establish an internal market for banking services with undistorted competition; it shall ensure that the banking sector functions in conformity with fundamental principle of the concurrency of risk-taking and liability; and it shall make market exit in case of failure viable. In implementing these principles, it must take account of the specialty of the financial and the banking system: its nature as an infrastructure for the whole of economic activity, and its interwovenness with the well-functioning of the monetary system.

The Banking Union strives to translate these principles into concrete rules, namely prudential rules to be applied to banks, a regime of banking supervision, and a regime for market exit.

A. Harmonisation of Substantive Rules – Single Rulebook

The so-called 'Single Rulebook' is not formally a part of the Banking Union; yet, it may be considered to be its substantive foundation. The term 'Single Rule-book' refers to the common prudential rules that all banking institutions in all (currently) 28 Member States have to respect. The rules are meant to promote the financial stability of banks, and thereby the stability of the banking system, while at the same time ensuring a level playing field for banking competition. Fully harmonised rules increase the transparency of regulation and the efficiency of the internal market for banking. Also, regulatory competition in financial market regulation would likely lead to a race to the bottom,[20] while the additional risks for financial stability created by the exploitation of regulatory loopholes in a divergent regulatory landscape could hardly be contained within national boundaries but would quickly spread across the EU.[21]

---

[20] A Pacces and D Heremans, 'Regulation of Banking and Financial Markets' in A Pacces and RJ Van den Bergh (eds), *Encyclopedia of Law and Economics: Regulation and Economics*, 2nd edn (Cheltenham, Elgar, 2012) 35.
[21] ibid, 35.

The core of the relevant prudential rules is contained in the so-called 'CRD IV-package', namely the Capital Requirements Directive IV (CRD IV)[22] concerning access to the activity of credit institutions and investment firms, as well as rules for prudential supervision; and Regulation 575/2013 on prudential requirements for credit institutions and investment firms (CRR),[23] setting out, *inter alia*, own funds requirements, requirements limiting large exposures, liquidity requirements and reporting requirements. Importantly, the 'CRD IV-package' is meant to implement the Basel III capital requirements. It is supplemented by a broad set of Regulatory Technical Standards drafted by EBA/ESMA.

B. Centralisation of Supervision and Partially Direct Enforcement of Rules

One of the two main pillars of the Banking Union is the Single Supervisory Mechanism (SSM) as contained in:

- Council Regulation (EU) No 1024/2013 conferring specific tasks on the ECB concerning policies relating to the prudential supervision of credit institutions (Article 127(6) TFEU).[24]
- Regulation (EU) No 1022/2013 amending Regulation No 1093/2010 establishing a European Supervisory Authority (EBA) as regards conferral of specific tasks on the ECB.[25]
- Regulation (EU) No 468/2014 of 16 April 2014 establishing the framework for cooperation within the SSM between the ECB and national competent authorities.[26]

The SSM sets up a harmonised and partially centralised supervisory structure for the banking sector in order to ensure a uniform interpretation and application of the prudential rules to banks so as to avoid regulatory arbitrage based on regulatory practice, and in order to weaken the link between state and 'national' banks and the concomitant national bias in financial supervision.[27]

More specifically, the SSM subjects so-called 'significant credit institutions' established within the Eurozone States – currently around 120 groups of

---

[22] Directive 2013/36/EU of 26 June 2013 on access to the activity of credit institutions and the prudential supervision of credit institutions and investment firms ..., [2013] OJ L 176/338.

[23] Regulation (EU) No 575/2013 of 26 June 2013 on prudential requirements for credit institutions and investment firms ..., [2013] OJ L 176/1.

[24] [2013] OJ L 287/63.

[25] [2013] OJ L 287/56.

[26] ECB/2014/17, [2014] OJ L 141/1.

[27] For a careful discussion see T Tröger, 'The Single Supervisory Mechanism – Panacea or Quack Banking Regulation?' (2014) 15 *EBOR* 449.

credit institutions, and approximately 1,200 entities – to the direct supervision of ECB. Non-Eurozone States can participate in the centralised supervision regime on a voluntary basis (Article 7 Regulation 1024/2013). For the non-participating Member States, a Memorandum of Understanding between the ECB and the competent authorities regulates a mode of cooperation – in particular a regular mode of consultation and a mode of cooperation in emergency situations – with regard to the performance of supervisory tasks (Article 3(6) Regulation 1024/2013).

The concept of 'significant credit institutions' is defined in Article 6(4) Regulation 1024/2013. According to this provision, banks with a total value of assets exceeding €30 billion, or with a ratio of total assets over the GDP of the relevant Member State in excess of 20 per cent, with a total value of assets above €5 billion, or any bank that receives direct assistance from the European Stability Mechanism (ESM) will qualify as 'significant institutions'. In addition, institutions with subsidiaries in more than one Member State and where the cross-border assets/liabilities represent significant part of total assets/liabilities will be subjected to the ECB's control.

Vis-à-vis these credit institutions, the ECB possesses comprehensive supervisory competences (Article 4 Regulation 1024/13). The ECB has to authorise the relevant institutions; assess acquisition or disposal of qualifying holdings; and ensure compliance with the whole set of prudential requirements (own funds, securitisation, large exposure limits, liquidity, leverage; supervision of governance arrangements and risk management; stress tests; supervision of credit institutions on consolidated basis; application of higher requirements for capital buffers if necessary, etc).

C. Single Resolution Mechanism

The second core pillar of the Banking Union is the Single Resolution Mechanism (SRM), namely a harmonised regime for market exit for banks. For all EU Member States, the Bank Recovery and Resolution Directive 2014/59/EU[28] (BRRD) sets out a single rulebook for the resolution of banks and large investment firms, some common resolution tools and resolution powers for the relevant national resolution authorities and a framework for cooperation among them when dealing with a failure of cross-border banks. The Directive follows the principle of minimum harmonsisation.

For the Eurozone Member States, Regulation (EU) No 806/2014[29] ('SRM Regulation') establishes, in addition, a Single Resolution Board with centralised

---

[28] [2014] OJ L 173/190.
[29] Regulation (EU) No 806/2014 of 15 July 2014 establishing uniform rules and uniform procedure for the resolution of credit institutions and certain investment firms in the framework of a Single Resolution Mechanism and Single Resolution Fund, [2014] OJ L 225/1.

resolution powers, as well as a Single Resolution Fund. The Council Implementing Regulation (EU) 2015/81[30] specifies uniform conditions of application of Regulation No 806/2014, and, in particular, the *ex ante* contributions to the Single Resolution Fund.

D. European Deposit Guarantee Scheme

The European Commission has envisioned a European Deposit Guarantee Scheme, which would become an important third pillar of the Banking Union. However – partly due to opposition from Germany – this scheme is not yet in place. Instead, the Deposit Guarantee Scheme Directive 2014/49/EU (DGSG)[31] sets out a common minimum standard for national deposit guarantee schemes.[32]

V. Banking Union – Constitutional Principles and Regulatory Styles

In its attempt to implement fundamental principles of a market economy in the field of banking regulation, the Banking Union has opted for a strongly managerial and discretionary style. It is a style that fits well with a regime with a strong executive branch, but within the EU, the executive branch possesses comparatively weak legitimacy.

A. Constitutional Principles Underlying the Banking Union

As a system of decentralised coordination, any market relies on a well-functioning regime of incentives. Among them is the principle of liability for losses, as a counterpart to the appropriation of profit.[33] Also, undistorted competition requires that firms that fail in a competitive environment have to exit the market.

Yet, the banking sector is special. The provision of credit to the industry and to consumers has an infrastructural quality. As the last financial crisis has impressively confirmed, financial stability is an indispensable institutional basis for the whole of the economy.

[30] Council Implementing Regulation (EU) 2015/81 of 19 December 2014 specifying uniform conditions of application of Regulation (EU) No. 806/2014 …, [2015] OJ L 15/1.
[31] [2014] OJ L 173/149.
[32] For a discussion see B Clarke, 'Deposit Guarantee Schemes' in M Haentjens and B Wessels (eds), *Research Handbook on Crisis Management in the Banking Sector* (Cheltenham, Elgar, 2015) 345.
[33] W Eucken, *Grundsätze der Wirtschaftspolitik*, 7 edn (Berlin, Mohr Siebeck, 2004) 279. See also R Posner, *Antitrust Law* (Chicago, Chicago University Press, 2001) 27–28.

There has been some debate about the compatibility of competition in the banking sector with financial stability. In the 1930s, Frank Knight observed that competition between banks for the expansion of credit will lead to excessive leverage, and is hence at odds with financial stability and must be regulatorily contained.[34] Minimum capital requirement are an important limit to such competition. According to the Chicago School of the 1930s, capital requirements were to be high. Fiat money creation was to be left to monetary policy – contained by well-defined rules.[35]

Empirical evidence on the link between the degree of competition in banking and financial stability is mixed.[36] The EU banking sector is not exempted from the application of competition rules. A strong regulatory framework for competition in banking is all the more important; a framework, namely, that impedes excessive leverage in the granting of credit and that ensures a level playing field, with no possibilities for regulatory arbitrage with regard to the essential safeguards for financial stability. The stricter, and fully harmonised prudential regulation of the 'Single Rulebook' and the centralised supervision and enforcement regime within the SSM are meant to ensure just that.

An essential part of the competitive process is the possibility of market exit in case of failure. Where failing firms are systematically bailed out by the state, moral hazard problems are bound to arise. The incentives of firms will be skewed towards risk-taking:[37] while the relevant firms can pocket the gains, they will not have to pay the (full) price in case of failure. In the banking sector, however, the market exit of one credit institution can lead to contagion and put the stability of the whole system at risk. Banks may turn out to be 'too big to fail',[38] 'too interconnected to fail'[39] or 'too many to fail'.[40] The exit of one market player can trigger a more generalised loss of confidence in other market actors and lead to a domino

---

[34] For an abbreviated version of his concerns see F Knight, 'The Ethics of Competition' in F Knight, *The Ethics of Competition* (London, Routledge, 1997) 45. See also A Turner, *Between Debt and the Devil* (Princeton, Princeton University Press, 2016) 57.

[35] See J Benes and M Kumhof, *The Chicago Plan Revisited*, IMF Working Paper 12/202, August 2012, available at www.imf.org/external/pubs/ft/wp/2012/wp12202.pdf.

[36] See eg J Boyd and G De Nicolo, 'The Theory of Bank Risk Taking and Competition Revisited' (2005) 60 *Journal of Finance* 1329; K Schaeck and M Cihak, 'Banking Competition and Capital Ratios' (2012) 18 *European Financial Management* 836; K Schaeck and M Cihak, 'Competition, Efficiency, and Stability in Banking' (2013) 43(1) *Financial Management* 215.

[37] D Zimmer and L Rengier, 'Enflechtung, Fusionskontrolle oder Sonderregelung für systemrelevante Banken? Ansätze zur Lösung des "Too-big-to-fail"-Problems' (2010) *ZWeR* 105, at 109.

[38] W Silber, *When Washington Shut Down Wall Street. The Great Financial Crisis and the Origins of America's Monetary Supremacy* (Princeton, Princeton University Press, 2008), A Sorkin, *Too Big To Fail: Inside the Battle to Save Wall Street* (London, Penguin, 2010), B McLean and J Nocera, *All the Devils are Here. The Hidden History of Financial Crises* (London, Penguin, 2010).

[39] D Zimmer, 'Finanzmarktregulierung – Welche Regelungen empfehlen sich für den deutschen und europäischen Finanzsektor?' (2010) 3 *NJW-Beilage* 101.

[40] E Liikanen et al, *High-Level Expert Group on reforming the structure of the EU banking sector*, October 2011, p 12.

effect. During the financial crisis of 2008, the Member States have therefore stepped in to save financial institutions on a broad scale. The principles of liability and market exit in case of failure were thereby severely compromised – despite the European Commission's effort to uphold some important limits in saving banks, namely within the framework of state aid control.[41] Severe distortions of competition are one of the lasting legacies. The necessary process of market consolidation has not taken place.[42] Instead, the EU, and in particular the European Monetary Union, continues to struggle with the negative feedback loop between the failure of banks and the (near) failure of sovereigns.[43]

The SRM is designed to break up this negative feedback loop and to reconcile the competitive logic with financial stability by establishing a special framework for the market exit of banks. The Single Resolution Fund will step in if there is a bank insolvency. National governments shall no longer be responsible for a possible bail-out. Access to the fund depends on a prior 'bail-in' of equity holders and creditors of a failing bank with 8 per cent of total assets of the institution. In substance, the 'bail-in' re-establishes the link between risk-taking and liability, and attenuates the concomitant moral hazard. The distortions of competition that the concept of 'systemic relevance' of banks has caused in the past will thereby be significantly diminished.

The attempt to re-establish an adequate exit and incentive regime while taking account of the specificities of banking have been broadly appreciated. The Banking Union has started to establish an institutional architecture at EU level that is, in principle, committed to overcoming regulatory arbitrage, the co-dependence of national states and bank and political capture of banking supervision.

---

[41] See European Commission, 'The recapitalisation of financial institutions in the current financial crisis', [2009] OJ C 10/2; European Commission, 'Communication on the treatment of impaired assets in the Community banking sector', [2009] OJ C 72/1; European Commission, 'Communication on the return to viability and the assessment of restructuring measures in the financial sector in the current crisis under the State aid rules', [2009] OJ C 195/9; European Commission, 'Communication on the application, from 1 January 2011, of State aid rules to support measures in favour of banks in the context of the financial crisis', [2010] OJ C 329/7; European Commission, 'Communication on the application, from 1 January 2012, of State aid rules to support measures in favour of banks in the context of the financial crisis', [2011] OJ C 356/7; European Commission, 'Communication on the application, from 1 January 2013, of State aid rules to support measures in favour of banks in the context of the financial crisis', [2013] OJ C 216/1. See also A Sutton et al, *Bank State Aid in the Financial Crisis: Fragmentation or Level Playing Field?*, CEPS Task Force Report, October 2010; D Gerard, 'Managing the Financial Crisis in Europe: The Role of EU State Aid Law Enforcement' in M Merola, J Derenne and J Rivas (eds), *Competition Law at Times of Economic Crisis – In Need for Adjustment?* (Bruylant, Brussels, 2013) 231 et seq.

[42] M Hellwig, *Yes Virginia, There is a European Banking Union! But It May Not Make Your Wishes Come True*, Preprints of the Max Planck Institute for Research on Collective goods 2014/12 (2014), at p 8: '... the post-Lehman policy of bailing out most banks has prevented the adjustment of market structure that is necessary if the intensity of competition is to be reduced to a level where banks do not have to take unconscionable risks in order to survive because there is too much capacity in the market'.

[43] See Liikanen, *High-Level Expert Group* (n 40) 4 et seq.

B. The Banking Union's Regulatory Style – Constitutional Caveats

Nonetheless, it is not evident whether the regime set out by the Banking Union will really re-establish well-functioning decentralised coordination and workable competition in the banking sector – in other words: a well-functioning market regime.

The resilience of the market exit regime as set up by the SRM has been questioned by many.[44] It remains potentially underfinanced, in particular with regard to immediate liquidity needs of large institutions.[45] The handling of cross-border insolvencies affecting both EU and non-EU States remains an open flank, in particular when different resolution regimes apply to legally independent subsidiaries in different countries.[46] Also, the SRM sets up a highly regulatory regime – the differentiated treatment of creditors in the 'bail-in' procedure is an example in point.[47]

A first recent test case – the de facto bail-out of Monte dei Paschi di Siena, an Italian Bank, by way of a capital injection by the Italian State[48] – has corroborated the doubts. Apparently, the link between banks and the state that the SRM meant to sever is still alive.

The persistent privileges for government bonds, which banking regulation continues to treat as safe assets, ensure the continuity of the link between states and banks.[49]

What is more, the regulatory style for which the EU has opted with the Banking Union – and in the field of financial regulation more broadly – is a novel one at the European level: a style far removed from the rule-based approach that guides the EU in the field of competition law, ie the other prominent field where the EU possesses direct enforcement powers. In interpreting Article 101 and Article 102

---

[44] Hellwig, *Yes Virginia* (n 42); Hellwig, *Financial Stability* (n 7); J Gordon and J-W Ringe, 'Bank Resolution in the European Banking Union: A Transatlantic Perspective on What It Would Take' (2015) 5 *Columbia Law Review* 1297, at 1347 et seq; G Zavvos and S Kaltsouni, 'The Single Resolution Mechanism in the European Banking Union: Legal Foundation, Governance Structure and Financing' in M Haentjens and B Wessels (eds), *Research Handbook on Crisis Management in the Banking Sector* (Cheltenham, Elgar, 2015) 117.

[45] Highlighted by Hellwig, *Yes Virginia* (n 42) 19 et seq.

[46] Hellwig, *Financial Stability* (n 7) 32. See also Gordon and Ringe, 'Bank Resolution' (n 44) 1364 et seq, arguing for a 'single-point-of-entry' system similar to the regime used in the US.

[47] See in more detail: C Hadjiemmanuil, 'Special Resolution Regimes for Banking Institutions – Objectives and Limitations' in W-G Ringe and PM Huber, *Legal Challenges in the Global Financial Crisis: Bail-Outs, the Euro and Regulation* (Oxford, Hart Publishing, 2014) 209, S Grundmann, 'Bankenunion und Privatrecht' (2015) 179(5) *ZHR* 563, at 586 et seq.

[48] See *Financial Times*, 'Italy's cabinet approves Monte dei Paschi bailout', 23 December 2016.

[49] For a proposal to remove the privileges see J Andritzky, N Gadatsch, T Körner, A Schäfer and I Schnabel, 'Removing Privileges for Banks' Sovereign Exposures – A Proposal' (2016) 1 *European Economy* 139 et seq. See also A van Riet, *Government Funding Privileges in European Financial Law: Making Public Debt Everybody's Favourite* (2016) Tilburg CentER Discussion Paper. For the persisting political character of banks see also Hellwig, *Yes Virginia* (n 42) 9.

TFEU, the European Commission is bound by the case law of the Union courts. It does not possess discretion in the interpretation of the law.[50] It is, in other words, the TFEU that governs – the task of the executive is to enforce the law. The regulatory style of EU banking regulation as it is currently designed is, however, a different one. As the EU regime of banking regime shies away from imposing high capital requirements, it has to engage in a close monitoring of possible risks. But sources of risk are diverse, and the conditions of their realisation are difficult to foresee. By necessity, a regulatory model built on risk monitoring will therefore be a highly discretionary regime. Power shifts from the legislator to the executive.

The discretion in the identification of relevant risks must be accompanied by strong, discretionary enforcement powers. Given the EU's experience in EU competition law enforcement, it does not come as a surprise that the ECB's enforcement powers as foreseen in the SSM follow, in important respects, the model of Regulation 1/2003 on the implementation of Articles 101 and 102 TFEU.[51] But the legitimacy requirements for strong enforcement powers within a strongly managerial model differ from the legitimacy requirements of enforcement powers in a rule-based model. An executive that acts highly discretionarily would seem to need a higher degree of democratic legitimacy. The ECB does not possess such legitimacy. It is deliberately conceived of as an independent agency (Article 19 Regulation 1024/2013) – and is potentially affected by conflicts of interest when engaging in both monetary policy and banking regulation.

C. Enforcement Powers in the SSM – Inspirations from Competition Law

In the EU, decentralised law enforcement by national courts and agencies is the rule. With regard to banking regulation, the SSM has set up a supervisory and enforcement structure with centralised powers of the ECB for 'significant credit institutions' in the Eurozone States, and with a strong position of the ECB in the network of national authorities. In doing so, it has clearly taken inspiration from EU competition law, where the Commission was endowed with centralised enforcement powers in 1963.[52] Regulation 1/2003, which has replaced Regulation 17/62 from May 2004 onwards, has been said to decentralise EU competition law enforcement; indeed, Regulation 1/2003 requires NCAs and national courts to apply EU competition rules alongside national rules (Article 3

---

[50] For a detailed analysis see H Schweitzer, 'Judicial Review in EU Competition Law' in I Lianos and D Geradin (eds), *Research Handbook on EU Antitrust Law* (Cheltenham, Elgar, 2013) 491.

[51] Council Regulation (EC) No 1/2003 of 16 December 2002 on the implementation of the rules on competition laid down in Articles 81 and 82 of the Treaty, [2003] OJ L 1/1.

[52] Regulation 17/62 implementing Articles 85 and 86 of the Treaty, [1963] OJ 13/204.

Regulation 1/2003). But at the same time, it has reinforced, rather than weakened, the position of the Commission within the European network of competition authorities (Article 11(6) Regulation 1/2003 and Article 16 Regulation 1/2003).

While EU competition law and banking regulation differ in many respects, there is a similar interest in a uniform interpretation of the relevant rules that impedes regulatory arbitrage and gives weight to the public European regulatory purpose, and in a speedy and effective enforcement. A centrepiece of the supervisory and enforcement regime in banking therefore is the establishment of the ECB as an independent agency with centralised, direct supervisory and enforcement powers for significant credit institutions in the Eurozone states whose activities will likely have cross-border effects (Article 9 with Articles 4 and 5 Regulation 1024/2013), and with important powers within the network of national competent agencies (NCAs) as established by Article 6 Regulation 1024/2013.

The ECB's powers with regard to significant credit institutions in the Euro States resemble the Commission's enforcement powers in the field of competition law in many respects: The ECB may request information from Eurozone credit institutions, from financial holding companies and persons belonging to those entities as well as from third parties to whom the entities have outsourced functions (Article 10 Regulation 1024/2013; see Article 18 Regulation 1/03). The ECB may require the submission of documents, examine books and records and obtain written or oral explanations (Article 11 Regulation 1024/2013; see Article 19 and Article 20 Regulation 1/03). The ECB has a right to conduct on-site inspections on business premises of the legal persons referred to in Article 10 (Article 12 Regulation 1024/2013; see Article 20 Regulation 1/2003). And the ECB possesses remedial powers vis-à-vis credit institutions which are modelled on the Commission's remedial powers in the field of competition law (Article 16 Regulation 1024/2013; compare to Articles 7–10 Regulation 1/2003). The ECB's powers even reach beyond the EU Commission's power in competition law, in that they encompass the power to enforce national law.[53]

Regulation 1024/2013 provides a framework for the close cooperation of the ECB with both the national competent authorities participating in the Eurozone (Article 6 Regulation 1024/2013) and with the competent authorities of non-participating Member States (Articles 3(6) and 7 Regulation 1024/2013). The national competent authorities participating in the Eurozone are bound by a duty to cooperate in good faith, and by an obligation to exchange information (Article 6(2) Regulation 1024/2013). The centralisation of powers within the SSM clearly exceeds the centralisation of powers under Regulation 1/2003. The ECB shall thereby be enabled to implement European policies quickly across all participating Member States. To a significant extent, the national competent authorities are turned into subordinated European agencies.

---

[53] Which raises the question whether the ECJ will also be competent for the judicial review of decisions taken by the ECB under national law.

VI. Managerial Regulation vs Rule-based Approach

Where, in competition law, the strong enforcement powers of the European Commission relate to the enforcement of non-discretionary rules, such that the preconditions for intervention are specified in the competition rules as interpreted by the European courts, EU banking regulation combines a regime of strong, centralised enforcement powers with a discretionary regime of *ex ante* risk regulation. As the risk scenarios are highly variable, and as the probability of the realisation of relevant risks is difficult to predict, the ECB enjoys broad discretion as regards the preconditions for intervention. More particularly, the ECB is entitled to impose 'all necessary measures' on credit institutions when the credit institutions do not meet the prudential requirements; or when the ECB has evidence that they will likely breach the requirements; or when the arrangements, strategies, processes and mechanisms implemented by the credit institution, or the own funds and liquidity held by it do not ensure a sound management and coverage of risk (Article 16(1) Regulation 1024/2013). Where one of these preconditions is met, possible remedial actions include, *inter alia*: obliging the institutions to hold own funds in excess of prescribed capital requirements; requiring the reinforcement of relevant processes or strategies; obliging credit institutions to restrict or limit the business, operations or network of institutions or the divestment of activities that pose excessive risks, or requiring a risk reduction; imposing limitations upon variable remuneration; requiring institution to use net profits to strengthen own funds; restricting or prohibiting a distribution to shareholders; imposing liquidity requirements (Article 16(2) Regulation 1024/2013).

Remedial discretion is thereby broad – but it is broad in competition law, too. What distinguishes EU banking regulation from EU competition law is both the breadth of the empowerment to intervene and the power to intervene also into corporate governance structures and business strategies.[54] Which evidence will make it likely that credit institutions will breach prudential requirements? Under which preconditions are doubts regarding the sound management and coverage of risks justified? Contrary to EU competition law, EU banking regulation does not only rely heavily on a regime of 'preventive' regulation (as does competition law and state aid law), but leaves open the type of risk and the threshold of probability of risk realisation that may justify intervention. The obvious justification for this broad regulatory discretion is the great variety of possible risks to financial stability and the absence of reliable knowledge of causalities, hence the great and inevitable uncertainty in the prediction of harm, combined with a need to intervene early in order to prevent immense harm to the economy.

---

[54] See Grundmann, 'Bankenunion und Privatrecht' (n 47), at 581.

In such a situation, we are left with a choice between two different regulatory styles:

- A managerial hands-on regulatory regime of the type provided for in Regulation 1024/2013; a regime within which the regulatory authority will need to try to track markets and banking behaviour closely, based on as much information as possible, a close interaction with the supervisees and extensive efforts to predict market developments and outcomes, and combined with a broad discretion to intervene whenever sufficiently severe concerns arise.

- A regulatory regime which provides for strong safeguards against any form of unforeseen risks – safeguards which significantly moderate incentives to put the viability of a credit institution at risk, protect against contagion and reduce the cost of crisis for the economy.[55] In banking, high capital requirements for credit institutions have been said to fulfil this function. Prominently, Admati and Hellwig have called for a substantial raising of the capital requirements for banks.[56] Capital requirements can be specified in clear-cut rules. Day-to-day supervision and regulation could then take a more 'arm's length' style. Some monitoring of market developments and risk scenarios would still be necessary, but the need for (additional) behavioural regulation and intervention would be significantly reduced.

Different regulatory styles have different advantages and disadvantages. A broad and evolving literature has tried to categorise and compare them.[57] In the aftermath of the financial crisis of 2008, the pendulum has swung away from a trend towards a more horizontal and cooperative style of regulation, involving self-regulation, co-regulation and voluntary compliance, back towards a more vertical approach, relying on stringent hierarchical oversight and strong powers to intervene.

Even if a vertical style of regulation is indeed called for in banking supervision, the current combination of an hierarchical style with broad discretion in rule-setting and a subsequent flood of detailed, specific rules, combined with a

---

[55] See O Jorda, B Richter, M Schularick and A Taylor, *Bank Capital Redux: Solvency, Liquidity, and Crisis* (2017) NBER Working Paper No 23287. The authors argue that particularly low capital requirements are not a good indicator of an upcoming crisis. This does not imply that very high capital requirements can be safeguard against crisis.

[56] Admati and Hellwig, *The Bankers' New Clothes* (n 8), at 79.

[57] See generally J Black, *Rules and Regulators* (Oxford, Clarendon Press, 1997); J Black, 'Paradoxes and Failures: "New Governance" Techniques and the Financial Crisis' (2012) 75(6) *The Modern Law Rev* 1037; OECD, *Best Practice Principles for Regulatory Policy: Regulatory Enforcement and Inspection* (2014); O Lobel, 'New Governance as Regulatory Governance' in D Levi-Four (ed), *The Oxford Handbook of Governance* (Oxford, OUP, 2012); D Awrey, 'Regulating Financial Innovation: A More Principles-Based Alternative?' (2011) 5(2) *Brooklyn Journal of Corporate, Financial and Commercial Law* 273; RF Weber, 'New Governance, Financial Regulation, and Challenges to Legitimacy: The Example of the Internal Models Approach to Capital Adequacy Regulation' (2010) 62(3) *Administrative Law Review* 783, J Dalhuisen, 'The Management of Systemic Risk from a Legal Perspective' in M Andenas and G Deipenbrock (ed), *Regulating and Supervising European Financial Markets* (New York, Springer, 2016).

broad discretion in decision-making and in remedial powers, comes at a high cost, namely a loss of transparency, and a constriction of competitive leeway, combined with a possible race to creatively circumvent the more specific rules, or, to the extent that the rules are kept relatively open and flexible, loss of predictability of interventions for the regulated institutions. Simultaneously, a tight hierarchical model of regulation based on detailed rules and case-by-case powers to intervene relies on the ability of a regulatory agency to identify and address relevant risks in a timely fashion. In the past, financial regulation has failed to create trust in this ability.

A regulatory model based on high capital requirements would involve regulatory costs of its own. While still staying with the vertical mode of regulation, it would, however, diminish many of the risks described above.

Lawyers are not well placed to compare economic costs and benefits. Yet, beyond a pure cost-benefit analysis, the strongly managerial style of the Banking Union raises legal concerns, too.

The concern that the delegation of broad discretionary powers upon a European agency raises issues of legitimacy within the European legal framework can no longer be considered dispositive after the ECJ's judgment in the *ESMA* case:[58] The UK had claimed, *inter alia*, that a delegation of highly discretionary powers to the ESMA – a European agency – was in conflict with the ECJ's *Meroni* judgment of 1958. According to *Meroni*, the institutional structure set up by EU primary law implies a specific balance of powers that must not be altered by a delegation of discretionary powers to bodies other than those established by the European Treaties. In particular, a delegation of discretionary powers, which may 'according to the use which is made of it, make possible the execution of actual economic policy', may 'bring about an actual transfer of responsibility' for which there is no basis in primary law.[59] In its *ESMA* decision, the ECJ found that the delegation of powers of intervention into financial market transactions granted to the ESMA by Article 28 of Regulation No 236/2012 – *inter alia* the power to prohibit, or impose conditions on, the entry by natural or legal persons into a short sale or a transaction which creates, or relates to, a financial instrument in cases of a threat to the orderly functioning and integrity of financial markets or to the stability of the financial system – was no breach of general principles of EU law. According to the ECJ, the exercise of those powers was sufficiently circumscribed by various conditions and criteria limiting the ESMA's discretion, and it did not confer any autonomous power on the ESMA that went beyond the bounds of the regulatory framework established by the ESMA Regulation.[60]

---

[58] Case C-270/12 *UK and Northern Ireland v European Parliament and Council of the EU*, EU:C:2014:18 ('*ESMA*').

[59] Case 9/56 *Meroni v High Authority*, EU:C:1958:7.

[60] C-270/12 *ESMA*, at paras 43 et seq. See, in particular, paras. 53–54: '... the powers available to ESMA under Article 28 of Regulation No 236/2012 are precisely delineated and amenable to judicial review in the light of the objectives established by the delegating authority. ... Contrary to the

The reasoning of the *ESMA* judgment has been questioned.[61] Yet, as regards the case of the exercise of discretionary regulatory powers by the ECB with a view to banking supervision, the concerns regarding the legal basis for a delegation of powers to an independent agency seem to be less pronounced at first sight, as the ECB's mandate is firmly anchored in EU primary law and encompasses an involvement in the prudential supervision of credit institutions. According to Article 127(5) TFEU, the 'ESCB shall contribute to the smooth conduct of policies pursued by the competent authorities relating to the prudential supervision of credit institutions and the stability of the financial systems'. According to Article 127(6) TFEU, the Council 'may unanimously … confer specific tasks upon the European Central Bank concerning policies relating to the prudential supervision of credit institutions …'.

Nonetheless, substantial concerns relate to the potential conflicts of interest between prudential supervision of credit institutions and monetary policy, and the negative effects that the combination of an intermingling of both competencies may have on the responsible exercise of either task.[62] Monetary policy can negatively affect the financial stability of banks. Despite efforts to clearly separate the exercise of monetary policy from the ECB's banking regulation activities,[63] the ECB can – and arguably has – taken these effects into account in relevant decisions on monetary policy. The same is true when the ECB is acting as a lender of last resort and has to decide on the financial viability of the institutions to which it grants credit. Vice versa, the ECB may take its monetary policy decisions into account when exercising its banking regulation mandate. Yet, as an institution endowed with strong institutional independence, the ECB lacks the legitimacy to balance the different goals of price stability – the ECB's primary goal – against the goal of safeguarding the financial stability of credit institutions.[64] A more rule-based, non-discretionary model, namely a shift to a comparatively simple, high capital requirements, would alleviate the conflict of interest; that can otherwise only be solved by way of a currently unattainable modification of the TFEU.

---

applicant's claim, those powers do not, therefore, imply that ESMA is vested with a "very large measure of discretion" that is incompatible with the FEU Treaty …'.

[61] See, eg, D Ritleng, 'Does the European Court of Justice Take Democracy Seriously?' (2016) 53(1) *Common Market Law Review* 32, interpreting the ESMA judgment as one out of a series of judgments that stand for a concept of output legitimacy, instead of input legitimacy, and thereby 'does not fit well with the traditional understanding of representative democracy'. See also R Priebe, 'Agenturen der Europäischen Union – Europäische Verwaltung durch eigenständige Behörden' (2015) 7 *EuZW* 268.

[62] For such concerns see, *inter alia*, Hellwig, *Financial Stability* (n 7), at 26. Article 127(6) TFEU is a weak legal basis for the ECB's supervisory powers. For a summary of the relevant concerns: M Lehmann, 'Die Ausgestaltung grenzüberschreitender Bankenaufsicht als ordnungspolitisches Problem' (2013) 64(1) *ORDO* 327, at 342, with further references.

[63] See on this: Grundmann, 'Bankenunion und Privatrecht' (n 47), at 574–75.

[64] Lehmann, 'Die Ausgestaltung' (n 62), at 342. For a critical analysis see also GT Kuile, L Wissink and W Bovenschen, 'Tailor-made Accountability Within the Single Supervisory Mechanism' (2015) 52(1) *Common Market Law Review* 155.

Beyond the issue of the legitimacy of executive discretion and conflicts of interest – and possibly most fundamentally – the breadth of the regulator's authorisation to preventively intervene and to impose behavioural obligations strongly compromises credit institutions' right and ability to compete. Decentralised decision-making (and risk-taking) on the basis of private law is replaced by regulation. Such regulation may lead to the imposition of some sorts of coordinated behaviour, enforce collusive market outcomes and significantly constrain the ability to compete.

If, by contrast, competition on credit and risk expansion with low safeguards were outlawed by way of high capital requirements, credit institutions would regain entrepreneurial discretion to compete on a broad variety of other parameters. A simple rule-based regime of high capital requirements would seem to be a better fit with the constitutional value of competition than a complex, discretionary managerial regime.

6

Technocratic and Centralised Decision-making in the Banking Union's Single Supervisory Mechanism

Can Single Market and Banking Union Governance Effectively Co-exist in a Post-Brexit World?

NIAMH MOLONEY

I. EU Financial Governance in Steady State?

This chapter is concerned with the centralisation of supervisory and regulatory decision-making relating to banks and banking governance through the Banking Union's Single Supervisory Mechanism (SSM) and with the functional and institutional implications.[1] The chapter also addresses the interaction between the euro-area SSM and the single banking market's major institutional actor, the European Banking Authority (EBA). These two institutions sit within and are shaped by the wider system of EU financial governance, which has been undergoing major reforms.

The contours of EU financial system governance have undergone an epochal re-shaping over the last eight years. This re-shaping began in autumn 2008 and did not begin to slow down until approximately mid-2014.[2] It is now axiomatic that regulation, supervision, supporting institutional structures, and the very purpose of the financial system and of financial intermediation – and of the benefits of an integrated financial system – have, over the crisis-era, all experienced intense reconsideration in the EU.[3] Something of a sea-change in the pace of reform and reconsideration is now identifiable, however.

[1] This analysis is dated as at August 2016 and reflects the materials available at that time.

[2] On 15 April 2014 the European Parliament adopted a final series of crisis-era reforms in its last plenary session before the 2009–2014 parliamentary term closed. For an assessment see N Moloney, *EU Securities and Financial Markets Regulation* (Oxford, Oxford University Press, 2014).

[3] From the extensive literature see, eg, Moloney, *EU Securities* (n 2); D Mügge, *Europe and the Governance of Global Finance* (Cambridge, Cambridge University Press, 2014); T Porter (ed),

From a market perspective, the stability of the EU financial system is, albeit slowly, being secured. The most recent annual surveys (April 2016) from the European Central Bank (ECB) and the European Commission on financial integration and financial stability are cautiously optimistic on financial system conditions.[4] They report on a financial system which is now more resilient, albeit still prone to short-term volatility shocks and vulnerable to risks related to the current low-yield environment. They also report on improving, if still fragile, levels of financial integration. Capital ratios in EU banks, to take one indicator of progress, have significantly strengthened. The July 2016 stress test of a sample of 51 banks (39 within the Banking Union/SSM zone) showed that Common Equity Tier 1 capital ratios had strengthened to 13.2 per cent on average across the sample as at December 2015 (an increase of some €180 billion on 2013), and that in stressed adverse conditions this would fall to 9.4 per cent by 2018. The EBA interpreted this result as showing 'resilience in the EU banking system as a whole'.[5] Particular difficulties remain, notably with respect to the persistence of non-performing loans across the EU banking sector and with the Italian banks in particular,[6] but progress is being reported.[7]

With respect to regulatory governance, with the Capital Markets Union agenda, launched in autumn 2015, EU policy priorities are shifting away from the previously overwhelming pre-occupation with financial stability to concern for the productive capacity of the EU financial system. The EU financial system is being characterised more in terms of its funding function and less in terms of its capacity to generate stability risks. An ambitious set of reforms which are designed to strengthen funding markets are underway.[8] Attention is also turning to review and calibration of the crisis-era reforms and to assessing their impact on growth and funding.[9]

With respect to the institutional underpinnings of EU financial governance, the concern of this chapter, a degree of stability has also been achieved. Like the

---

Transnational Financial Regulation after the Crisis (London, Routledge, 2014); and E Ferran, 'Crisis-driven Regulatory Reform: Where in the World is the EU Going?' in E Ferran, N Moloney, J Hill and JC Coffee, *The Regulatory Aftermath of the Global Financial Crisis* (Cambridge, CUP, 2012) 1.

[4] Commission, 'European Financial Stability and Integration Review' (2016) ((SWD) 2016 146) and ECB, 'Financial Integration in Europe' (2016) ('2016 Financial Integration Report').

[5] EBA, '2016 EU-Wide Stress Test', 29 July 2016.

[6] As has been widely reported: eg, R Sanderson and C Jones, 'Essential Repairs', *Financial Times*, 11 July 2016, 11.

[7] SSM Chair Nouy noted in the March 2016 ECB report on banking supervision that the European banking sector 'is much better prepared to cope with unexpected headwinds than just a few years ago' (ECB Banking Supervision, 'ECB Annual Report on Supervisory Activities 2016' (2016) ('2016 SSM Annual Report') 7).

[8] Originally announced in summer 2014 by European Commission President Juncker ('A New Start for Europe: My Agenda for Jobs, Growth, Fairness and Democratic Change', speech to European Parliament, Strasbourg, 15 July 2014) and since then the subject of a major Commission reform agenda: Commission, 'Green Paper on Building a Capital Markets Union' (COM (2015) 63) and Commission, 'Action Plan on Building a Capital Markets Union' (COM (2015) 468). See further N Moloney, 'Capital Markets Union: "Ever Closer Union" for the EU Financial System' (2016) 41 *European Law Review* 307.

[9] See, eg, Commission, 'Call for Evidence. EU Regulatory for Financial Services', September 2016.

major global economies which grappled with securing the optimal regulatory response to the financial crisis and with implementing the G20 reform agenda, the EU adopted a swathe of regulatory governance reforms (the 'Single Rulebook'). But it also sought, on a scale not replicated in any major global economy, to rebuild its institutional governance structure for the EU financial system. In phase one, the European System of Financial Supervision (ESFS) and its constituent European Supervisory Authorities (ESAs) was established (2011) to support the optimal supervision and regulation of the single financial market. In phase two, the EU established the major Banking Union institutions: the SSM and the Single Resolution Mechanism (SRM) (2014–2015). The Banking Union reforms were designed to stabilise the euro area – which came under existential threat as the financial crisis turned into a sovereign debt and euro-area crisis over 2010–2012 – by means of institutional reforms directed to the management of the mutualisation of the fiscal risks arising from bank failure and the related supervisory risks and costs.[10]

The first review of the ESFS and the ESAs, up and running since 2011, has been positive and the related institutional and constitutional technology deployed appears to be relatively robust.[11] Banking Union, a later development, has moved from abstraction, to political commitment, to design, and, finally, to operation. The SSM took over supervision of SSM-zone credit institutions on 4 November 2014, while the SRM commenced operations in March 2015 when the Single Resolution Board first undertook its activities.[12] Proposals have recently been made for the third institutional leg of Banking Union: the European Deposit Insurance Scheme (EDIS).[13] Initial stakeholder indications as regards Banking Union augur well. The establishment of the SSM was assessed by the European Parliament in March 2016 as successful, both operationally and with respect to supervisory quality.[14]

---

[10] For reviews of the reform process see, eg, D Ioannou, B Leblond and A Niemann, 'European Integration and the Crisis: Practice and Theory' (2015) 22 *Journal of European Public Policy* 155; D Howarth and L Quaglia, 'Banking Union as Holy Grail: Rebuilding the Single Market in Financial Services, Stabilizing Europe's Banks, and 'Completing' Economic and Monetary Union' (2013) 51 *Journal of Common Market Studies* 103; and N Moloney, 'Resetting the Location of Regulatory and Supervisory Control over EU Financial Markets: Lessons from Five Years On' (2013) 62 *International and Comparative Law Quarterly* 955.

[11] Commission, 'Report on the Operation of the European Supervisory Authorities and the European System of Financial Supervision' (2014) (COM (2014) 509).

[12] For discussions of the SSM and SRM see, eg, J-H Binder and C Gortsos, *The European Banking Union* (Baden-Baden, Beck/Hart/Nomos, 2016); K Alexander, 'A Legal and Institutional Analysis of the Single Supervisory Mechanism and the Single Resolution Mechanism' (2015) 40 *European Law Review* 154; D Busch and G Ferrarini, *European Banking Union* (Oxford, Oxford University Press, 2015); N Moloney, 'European Banking Union: Assessing its Risks and Resilience' (2014) 51 *Common Market Law Review*; B Wolfers and T Vorland, 'Level the Playing Field: The New Supervision of Credit Institutions by the European Central Bank' (2014) 51 *Common Market Law Review* 1463; the discussions in the *European Journal of Banking Law* (1)(2014), edited by P Mülbert and U Schneider; and E Ferran and V Babis, 'The European Single Supervisory Mechanism' (2013) 13 *Journal of Corporate Law Studies* 255.

[13] European Commission, 'Proposal for a European Deposit Insurance Scheme (EDIS)', COM (2015) 586.

[14] European Parliament, *Resolution on Banking Union – Annual Report* (2015) (P8_TA-PROV (2016)0093), 10 March 2016.

Major claims are already being made for the nascent Banking Union, including that its construction can be credited with the recent improvement in levels of financial integration.[15] Much remains uncertain, however, including the nature of the 'fiscal backstop' required to provide 'last resort' support to banks in Banking Union and the related role of the European Stability Mechanism.[16] In addition, it is not clear if powerful centripetal forces will be unleashed by the euro-area Banking Union on single market banking governance.[17] To this cocktail of uncertainty can be added the risks and challenges posed by the UK's decision to withdraw from the EU following the referendum held on 23 June 2016 ('Brexit'). While the UK was not a participant in the SSM, its withdrawal from the EU banking system and from the structures which support the single market, notably the EBA, is likely to have far-reaching effects.

But even allowing for this fragility and dynamism a staging post of sorts has been reached as regards Banking Union. The SSM, the major concern of this chapter, has passed its first serious political and operational test, in the form of the 2013–2014 Comprehensive Assessment by the ECB of the banks directly supervised by it within the SSM, and is now adopting a business as usual posture. In particular, it is gaining experience with the operationally critical Supervisory Review and Evaluation Process (SREP) which all supervisors of EU banks must undertake annually under the major EU banking measure – the Capital Requirements Directive IV/Regulation 2013 (CRD IV/CRR).[18] The ECB heralded 2015 as an important year in which 'European banking supervision took a great step towards harmonised and unbiased supervision' as the SSM undertook a harmonised SREP assessment of the banks within the ECB's direct supervision.[19] In addition, evidence is emerging on the nature of the relationship between the SSM and the EBA. More generally, transparency on SSM operations is increasing with a raft of speeches, answers to European Parliament questions, market-oriented communications on the SREP, letters to bank management, and other communications, including extensive annual reports, all shedding some light on SSM operations.

Analysis of the SSM has an inevitably speculative hue at present given its still nascent character, uncertainty relating to the impact of Brexit on current institutional arrangements and institutional preferences and incentives, and

---

[15] The ECB has linked the establishment of Banking Union to the ongoing improvement in levels of financial integration: 2016 Financial Integration Report (n 4) 53.

[16] Euro area Member States have agreed to provide national credit lines to the Single Resolution Fund and have committed to start work on a common backstop in September 2016 ('Council Conclusions on a Roadmap to Complete Banking Union', 17 June 2016 (Press Release 353/16)).

[17] On the EBA/ECB relationship see E Ferran, 'European Banking Union and the EU Single Financial Market: More Differentiated Integration or Disintegration' in B de Witte and E Vos (eds), *In Between Flexibility and Disintegration in the State of EU Law Today* (Chelthenham, Elgar, 2014).

[18] Directive 2013/36/EU [2013] OJ L176/338 and Regulation EU No 575/2013 [2013] OJ L 176/1.

[19] 2016 SSM Annual Report (n 7) 4.

functional uncertainty as to the outcome of the SSM's approach to bank super-vision. Nonetheless, as noted above, the wider governance environment within which the SSM operates is now relatively stable as is the EU financial system, while empirical observation of the SSM can now be engaged in more easily. Analysis of the institutional and functional implications of the SSM can there-fore be undertaken with at least some degree of certainty. Accordingly, section II considers SSM decision-making. It sets out the major institutional features of centralised decision-making within the SSM and considers the institutional and functional implications. Section III moves beyond the SSM to consider the inter-action between the SSM and the single banking market, and speculates as to the impact of Brexit on the fragile institutional ecosystem which supports the SSM and the EBA and the implications of this. Section IV concludes.

II. Centralised Decision-making and the SSM: Internal Effects

A. SSM Governance

Banking Union's SSM applies to euro-area Member States on a mandatory basis and to other Member States which choose to join the SSM on a volun-tary basis (together, 'participating Member States') and to their deposit-taking institutions only.[20]

The SSM within Banking Union is of a very different character to the EBA within the single market. The 2011 ESA reform was evolutionary, rather than revolutionary, reflecting its three main influences. First, the pre-existing secto-ral, soft-law-based 'Lamfalussy committees' of national supervisors (for banking markets (CEBS), insurance markets (CEIOPS), and securities markets (CESR)) provided a politically, functionally and constitutionally expedient organisational template for the ESAs. But their availability allowed the Member States to side-step more ambitious institutional designs, including, for example, a 'twin peaks' model based on conduct and prudential financial governance rather than on sectoral governance, which might have been more efficient. Second, the institu-tional design of the ESAs, and the strong soft law quality of their functionality (outlined in section III), was shaped by the crystallisation over the financial crisis

---

[20] Two legislative instruments support the SSM: Council Regulation (EU) No 1024/2013 [2013] OJ L 287/63, conferring specific tasks on the European Central Bank (2013 ECB/SSM Regulation); and Regulation (EU) No 1022/2013 [2013] OJ L 287/5, revising the governance and powers of the European Banking Authority to reflect the ECB/SSM (2013 EBA Regulation, revising the 2010 EBA Regulation (EU) No 1093/2010 [2010] OJ L 331/12 – references to the EBA Regulation are to the 2010 Regulation as revised). Articles 1, 2, and 6 of the 2013 ECB/SSM Regulation set out the scope of the SSM and limit it to the deposit-taking institutions of participating Member States, with some limited exceptions relating to holding company structures.

of the fiscal costs of supervisory failure and of supervisory decisions. This hardened Member State resistance in some quarters to the mutualisation of risk and to related EU-level supervisory decision-making. Third, the EU Treaties limited the extent to which radical institutional designs could be entertained. The EU Treaties, and particularly the single market competence (Article 114 of the Treaty on the Functioning of the European Union (TFEU), which provided the legal basis for the ESAs although it is primarily concerned with rule harmonisation), were placed under some strain by the establishment of the ESAs. But the prevailing market, political, and institutional conditions were such that there was limited appetite for more imaginative institutional re-designs which would have required Treaty change.

The Banking Union/SSM reforms are significantly more ambitious and novel. The ESAs are charged with quasi-rule-making and with the support of supervisory coordination, as outlined in section III. By contrast, the SSM is executive in nature. It operates under the EU's harmonised banking rulebook (primarily the behemoth CRD IV/CRR regime) and brings the supervision of the euro area's some 6,000 banks (non-euro-area Member States may join the SSM on a voluntary basis, but have yet to do so), directly and indirectly, under the supervisory oversight of the ECB. As at August 2016, the ECB is directly responsible for the supervision of 129 'significant' euro-area banking groups (by size of bank assets, systemic importance, and relevance to the national economy in question), representing 82 per cent of banking assets within the euro area, and has related rule-making, supervision, and enforcement powers. In practice, ECB direct supervision is managed through 'Joint Supervisory Teams' (JSTs) headed by ECB supervisors but including supervisors from the relevant national competent authority (NCA).[21] These JSTs follow the SSM's SREP methodology for bank supervision.[22] Where a bank which the ECB directly supervises has cross-border operations outside the euro area and across the EU, the ECB sits in the relevant college of supervisors and is subject to coordination by EBA in this regard. The ECB also oversees the supervision of the other 'less significant' (some 3,100) euro-area banks by their NCAs within the SSM,[23] including by means of ECB rules, soft law, and supervisory guidance.[24] These different coordinating measures include a common methodology (the Risk Assessment System (RAS) model) for the national risk assessment systems which are deployed in the national SREPs undertaken by SSM NCAs of their 'less significant' banks.[25] The ECB is empowered to take supervision away from these SSM NCAs of

---

[21] For a recent description of how the JSTs operate see 2016 SSM Annual Report (n 7) 30–36.
[22] ibid.
[23] Some 3,100 banks had been identified as 'less significant' by the ECB at end December 2015 and as outside direct ECB supervision (ibid, 43).
[24] On the mechanism-based nature of the SSM and the allocation of supervisory competence within the SSM see E Ferran, 'European Banking Union: Imperfect But it Can Work' in Ferrarini and Busch, *European Banking Union* (Oxford, Oxford University Press, 2015) 56 and Moloney, 'European Banking Union' (n 12).
[25] 2016 SSM Annual Report (n 7) 43–44.

'less significant banks' and is responsible for the authorisation of all banks, of whatever size, within the Banking Union/SSM zone. The SSM is accordingly a network-based mechanism. At the core of the mechanism sits the ECB, which at the time of writing directly supervises 129 banking groups and which retains overall oversight of all other banks. Outside the ECB, a network of NCAs within the SSM either supports the ECB within ECB JSTs on the supervision of their 'significant' banks; or directly carries out the supervision of their 'less significant' banks, subject to ECB oversight and supervisory templates and protocols.

Despite its novel conferral of direct supervisory and related enforcement powers on a central EU authority, and although it was forged in unique conditions as the euro area came under existential threat, the SSM and its decision-making structures reflect two long-standing features of EU financial system governance. First, the SSM is based on a re- or up-cycling of an existing institutional template (in this case, the ECB[26]).[27] SSM decision-making governance has been shaped by this institutional re-cycling. Second, decision-making governance has been shaped by the many political and constitutional compromises which are typically a feature of institutional design for EU financial governance. The design constraints which SSM design faced – political, institutional, and constitutional – were very considerable.[28] It remains to be seen whether the many and often ingenious governance compromises and constitutional sleights of hand which have followed, and which are designed to work around the many constraints, will allow the ECB to operate effectively. A representative sample of the related decision-making challenges follows.

First, reflecting the ECB's origins as a monetary authority, the organisational governance of the ECB with respect to its SSM decision-making functions is in part designed to address the conflict of interest risks attendant on the ECB (or any bank supervisor) combining monetary and supervisory functions. Article 25 of the 2013 ECB/SSM Regulation establishes the principle that monetary policy and supervisory functions must be separated.[29] This principle is supported by the location of de facto decision-making power on SSM matters within the new ECB Supervisory Board (2013 ECB/SSM Regulation, Article 26).[30] The Supervisory

---

[26] SSM Chair Nouy suggested that the ECB was 'the perfect and natural home for meeting the SSM challenge' and that 'for a new European supervisory authority starting its work, the ECB's long-established services and its credibility as an institution are tremendous assets': 'ECB Banking Supervision, Annual Report on Supervisory Activities' (2015) ('2015 SSM Annual Report') 4.

[27] On the political, functional, and legal logic of the ECB choice see Moloney, 'European Banking Union' (n 12) and Ferran, 'European Banking Union' (n 24).

[28] On the origins of the SSM reforms see the references above at n 12.

[29] The ECB must carry out its supervisory tasks without prejudice to and separately from its tasks relating to monetary policy and other tasks, and these supervisory tasks must neither interfere with nor be determined by its tasks relating to monetary policy: 2013 ECB/SSM Regulation, Art 25(2).

[30] Internal procedures, including organisational separation of staff, apply in support: ECB, SSM Report. *Progress in the Operational Implementation of the Single Supervisory Mechanism Regulation*, 2014/2, 9–10. These procedures are governed by ECB Decision 2014/39 on the implementation of separation between the monetary policy and supervisory functions of the ECB. In practice, these procedures usually apply in relation to information exchange: 2016 SSM Annual Report (n 7) 18.

Board is responsible for the ECB's supervisory functions and is composed of a Chair (currently Danièle Nouy) – proposed by the ECB,[31] approved by the Parliament, and appointed by the Council, excluding non-participating Member States;[32] Vice Chair (currently Sabine Lautenschlager) – proposed by the ECB from the ECB Executive Board, approved by the Parliament, and appointed by the Council;[33] four ECB representatives – appointed by the ECB Governing Council;[34] and one representative of the relevant banking NCA in each SSM-participating Member State.[35] The four ECB representatives must not perform functions directly related to the monetary functions of the ECB.[36] The governance barrier which the Supervisory Board provides is malleable,[37] however, in that, reflecting Treaty constraints (noted below) the Supervisory Board may not adopt supervisory decisions. These must be formally adopted by the ECB Governing Council which is dominated by euro-area central bank governors. A 'silent assent' procedure applies under which a Supervisory Board decision is 'deemed adopted', unless the Governing Council objects within a specified period (ECB/SSM Regulation, Article 26(8)). The governance barrier is also buttressed by a Mediation Panel which provides a mechanism for the resolution of differences by participating NCAs which arise following an objection by the Governing Council to a Supervisory Board draft decision (ECM/SSM Regulation, Article 25(5)). Whether or not this arrangement is sufficiently robust so as to ensure appropriate segregation of supervisory and monetary decisions, and to at the same time support functional effectiveness in decision-making, remains to be seen, although initial indications augur well, as noted below.

Second, the ECB's decision-making governance on SSM matters has been shaped by the interplay between the ECB's Treaty-based independence guarantee (Articles 130 and 282(3) TFEU), which can be regarded as applying to its new supervisory functions,[38] and the SSM-specific independence requirement (ECB/SSM Regulation 2013, Article 19),[39] on the one hand; and, on the other, the potentially conflicting need for accountability controls which reflect the ECB's new

---

[31] On the basis of an open competition.

[32] Art 26(1) and (3). The Chair may be removed, on specified conditions, by the Council, on a proposal by the ECB and approval by the Parliament. The Council and Parliament may inform the ECB that they consider the conditions for removal of the Chair to be fulfilled and the ECB must respond (Art 26(4)).

[33] Art 26(1) and (3).

[34] Art 26(1) and (5).

[35] Art 26(1).

[36] Art 26(5).

[37] On the difficulties of separating both functions see, eg, J Carmassi, C di Noia and S Micossi, 'Banking Union: A Federal Model for the European Union with Prompt Corrective Action', *CEPS Policy Brief* No 282, September 2012.

[38] The Treaty independence guarantee applies to the exercise of ECB 'powers' generally (Art 282(3) TFEU), although Art 130 TFEU applies the guarantee to ECB powers and tasks and duties conferred by the Treaty and the Statute of the European System of Central Banks and of the ECB. See further Wolfers and Voland, 'Level the Playing Field' (n 12) 1487–88.

[39] Under Art 19, when carrying out tasks conferred by the 2013 ECB/SSM Regulation, the ECB and NCAs within the SSM must act independently (as must Supervisory Board members).

supervisory functions. The business of supervision is operational and granular and shapes institutions' balance sheets, business models, and strategies. Accordingly, while operational independence is essential for effective supervision it must be tempered by accountability controls. The ECB's SSM-specific accountability regime is similar to the wider (Treaty-based) ECB accountability regime, being broadly based on institutional reporting devices. But it is more intrusive, reflecting the more acute need for accountability in the operational supervision context.[40] The ECB is declared to be accountable to the European Parliament and Council with respect to the implementation of the 2013 ECB/SSM Regulation (2013 ECB/SSM Regulation, Article 20(1)). Related regular reporting and review requirements apply and extend beyond the Parliament and Council to the euro group and Commission,[41] while the European Court of Auditors is empowered to examine the ECB's exercise of its supervisory functions when examining the operational efficiency of the ECB (2013 ECM/SSM Regulation, Article 20). Particular obligations apply as regards the European Parliament,[42] including with respect to the appointment and removal of Supervisory Board members, as noted above. Reporting obligations are also imposed with respect to reporting to national Parliaments of participating Member States (2013 ECB/SSM Regulation, Article 21). The ECB is, in addition, subject to a range of due process requirements, including the establishment of an Administrative Board of Review empowered to review ECB decisions addressed to natural or legal persons (2013 ECB/SSM Regulation, Article 24), while ECB acts can be reviewed by the Court of Justice of the EU (Articles 263–266 TFEU). It remains to be seen whether this degree of accountability threatens the ECB Treaty independence guarantee, or, conversely, whether it is sufficient, given the implications of supervisory decision-making and the potential for third-party effects.

Third, contortions in decision-making governance have followed from the Treaty requirement that ultimate decision-making control within the ECB must be located within the ECB Governing Council (Article 129 TFEU). The related implied exclusion of any non-euro-area Member State which chooses to join the Banking Union and the SSM from the ECB's supreme decision-making body (which body must hold a veto over ECB Supervisory Board decision-making)

---

[40] Ferran and Babis, 'The European Single Supervisory Mechanism' (n 12) 270–73.

[41] The ECB must, eg, submit an annual report to the European Parliament, Council, Commission and euro group; this report must be presented by the ECB Supervisory Board Chair to the Parliament and the euro group; the Chair of the ECB Supervisory Board may, at the request of the euro group, be heard on ECB supervisory tasks; and the ECB must reply to questions put to it by the Parliament or euro group (Art 20(2)–(5)).

[42] The Chair of the ECB Supervisory Board must participate in hearings where requested by the European Parliament and hold confidential discussions with the Chair and Vice Chairs of the competent committee of the Parliament where such discussions are required for the exercise of the Parliament's Treaty powers, and the ECB must cooperate sincerely with any investigations by the Parliament, subject to the TFEU (Art 20(5), (8) and (9)). In practice, ECB and European Parliament relations are governed by the Interinstitutional Agreement between the European Parliament and ECB on Co-operation on Procedures Relating to the SSM, 12 October 2013.

seriously disrupted the SSM negotiations.[43] The compromise solution includes a complex procedure under which non-euro-area NCAs can raise specific concerns as to a Governing Council decision (2013 ECB/SSM Regulation, Article 7). The resilience of this arrangement if non-euro-area Member States join the SSM in any numbers, is doubtful. And given that the success of the SSM depends, to some extent at least, on 'early adoption' by the euro 'pre-ins',[44] this decision-making model, which presupposes a significant loss of autonomy by the pre-ins over ECB decision-making, is inherently unstable.

B. SSM Decision-making: Early Lessons

While the SSM decision-making process is complex, initial indications augur well for the SSM's ability to take decisions.

From a regulatory perspective, the major procedural rules critical for managing relations between the ECB and NCAs within the SSM have been adopted through the ECB's 2014 SSM Framework Regulation.[45] Further, Rules of Procedure governing the Supervisory Board, the legal framework for the SSM Administrative Board of Review and Mediation Panel, and legal arrangements governing the separation of monetary and supervisory functions within the ECB were all adopted over 2014[46] and an ECB regulation on bank reporting of supervisory financial information followed in 2015.[47] The ECB has also adopted an important regulation which governs how it will exercise the different national options and discretions which are conferred by EU law on SSM NCAs[48] and issued a related Guide.[49]

From a supervisory perspective, the initial allocation of significant banks to ECB direct supervision has been concluded and subsequent refinements have been made.[50] The important 2013–2014 Comprehensive Assessment of the 130 largest banks in the euro area, required before the ECB took over direct bank supervision,[51] was broadly successful (section III). The detailed, granular, and

---

[43] Sweden threatened to veto the discussions and to require a Treaty amendment to revise ECB governance requirements in order to reflect the importance of the non-euro-area to the future development of Banking Union.

[44] See Ferran, 'European Banking Union' (n 24).

[45] Regulation (EU) No 468/2014, [2014] OJ L 141/1 (ECB/2014/17).

[46] Collated in ECB Banking Supervision, 'Legal Framework for Banking Supervision', Volume II, July 2015.

[47] ECB Regulation, ECB/2015/13.

[48] The ECB is empowered to exercise such discretions in relation to the banks it supervises directly: 2013 ECB/SSM Regulation, Art 4(3).

[49] Regulation (EU) 2016/445 of the ECB [2016] OJ L 78/60 and ECB Banking Supervision, *ECB Guide on Options and Discretions Available in Union Law* (2016).

[50] The 2016 SSM Annual Report noted that nine other institutions have been classified as significant since the initial 2013–2014 Comprehensive Assessment: (n 7) 29.

[51] The Assessment's scope was wider than the 123 banking groups which ultimately came within ECB direct supervision in November 2014.

operationally critical SSM SREP procedural manual, which governs the supervision of the significant banks directly supervised by the ECB, has been constructed and a related approach to supervision adopted (based on 'constrained expert judgment'); the SSM SREP has also been subject to continual review.[52] The Joint Supervisory Teams, composed of ECB and NCA members and which supervise the 129 banking groups currently under direct ECB supervision, have been set up and are carrying out SREP supervisory reviews. Related remedial measures have been required of directly supervised banks. Thematic supervisory reviews of particular areas (including risk governance) have also taken place.[53] A major review of the internal risk models which significant banks use to assess their capital requirements has been launched.[54] Directions have been given to the management of banks directly supervised by the ECB as to SSM supervisory priorities, including through CEO letters[55] and general SSM supervisory statements.[56] The ECB is also refining its supervisory approach. In response to the results of the July 2016 stress tests, for example, it is to deploy the 'capital guidance' technique in its 2016 SSM SREP assessments of significant banks. Under this new approach, which is designed to take into account the impact of stress tests and to support forward and adverse scenario planning by banks, the ECB will provide forward guidance to banks on their desired capital levels which will be above the required level of binding capital, but which will not be legally binding, and non-compliance with which will not lead to specific remediation measures, although failure to meet the guidance will lead to intensified supervision.[57] The ECB has also adopted processes governing how the ECB oversees the supervision by NCAs of their 'less significant' banks, including joint supervisory standards and a common methodology for the RAS of these banks.[58]

The ECB's first March 2015 annual report on the operation of the SSM did not underplay the scale of the initial effort. As summarised by Chair Nouy, 'It required harmonised, comprehensive and clearly defined supervisory standards and processes; practical infrastructures such as functional and tested IT systems; and appropriate governance structures for swift and effective decision-making' and included the requirement to undertake the Comprehensive Assessment – 'an

---

[52] ECB Banking Supervision, 'SSM SREP Methodology Booklet' – 2015 edition (2016); and 2016 SSM Annual Report (n 7) 30–36.

[53] 2016 SSM Annual Report (n 7) 37–40.

[54] ibid., 6.

[55] eg, in January 2016 Chair Nouy wrote to the management of significant banks on the ECB's supervisory expectations regarding their internal capital and liquidity review systems (the ICAAP and ILAAP).

[56] ECB Banking Supervision, 'SSM Supervisory Statement on Governance and Risk Appetite' (2016).

[57] Letter from Chair Nouy to MEP Giegold, 11 July 2016. The capital guidance approach follows the recommendation by EBA that if NCAs were concerned as to any capital shortfalls revealed by the 2016 stress test they could use capital guidance to address concerns relating to banks' ability to meet their capital requirements in stressed conditions: EBA, EBA Clarifies the use of 2016 EU-wide Stress Tests Results in the SREP Process, 1 July 2016.

[58] 2016 SSM Annual Report (n 7) 41–45.

exercise of unprecedented magnitude'.[59] On a purely executive basis the challenge was immense. But, and at the risk of reductionism, it has been met insofar as the SSM is operational and the first cycle of SREPs of directly supervised banks has completed. In March 2016 the ECB could report that some 1,500 supervisory decisions had been made, including 213 SREP decisions and 921 authorisation procedures.[60] It also reported on the workings of the monetary/supervision separation principle, which seems to be working effectively with most instances where the relevant procedures were required relating to information exchange, although not in relation to individual banks.[61]

It is not yet possible to assess whether good outcomes will follow and, in particular, whether the ECB will meet its mandate to 'contrib[ute] to the safety and soundness of credit institutions and the stability of the financial system within the Union and each Member State' (2013 ECB/SSM Regulation, Article 1). But at the very least a degree of decision-making effectiveness and a significant capacity to take complex decisions at the Supervisory Board level can be assumed. This is all the more the case as the ECB has signalled that it is to streamline its supervisory decision-making procedures, including through delegation mechanisms – which suggests a degree of institutional effectiveness and confidence in decision-making.[62] The inevitably large size of the ECB Supervisory Board, composed currently of 19 euro-area NCAs and six others (the Chair, Vice Chair, and four ECB representatives) does not, therefore, seem to be generating inefficiencies. Similarly, the need for the Governing Council to follow the 'negative assent' procedure does not seem to be obstructing the ability of the ECB Supervisory Board to notionally take decisions.

More generally, there are indications that the complex decision-making procedures are not leading to destructive tensions between the ECB and NCAs, at least in this start-up phase. In addition to the raft of supervisory decisions which have been adopted, the ECB has adopted a regulation and guide which set out how it will exercise the different national options and discretions (ONDs) available to NCAs of significant banks directly supervised by the ECB.[63] This action is designed to remove the risk that ONDs (of which there are some 150 across CRD IV/CRR), where not appropriately justified, might have a material effect on the overall level of prudence in the bank capital framework, obstruct market and public comparison and review of capital ratios, lead to regulatory arbitrage, and obstruct the ECB in supervising banks effectively.[64] But their removal also

---

[59] ibid, 4.

[60] ibid, 12.

[61] ibid, 18.

[62] ibid, 12.

[63] cf above (n 49). The regulation addresses horizontal ONDs which apply to all banks and the Guide addresses those ONDs which apply on a bank-by-bank basis (there are some 122 in all).

[64] ECB Banking Supervision, 'Public Consultation on a draft Regulation and Guide of the ECB on the exercise of options and discretions available in Union law. Explanatory Memorandum' (2015) 2–3.

removes a significant channel for NCA supervisory discretion and for the imposition of national preferences.[65] ONDs have, however, been of concern to the ECB since the establishment of the SSM, as well as to the Commission, Parliament, and Council,[66] given their distorting effects. The discretion which ONDs give to Member States and NCAs in relation to the components of capital, for example, has been associated with a distortion in the capital levels of euro-area banks recorded by the Comprehensive Assessment of some €126.2 billion.[67] Particular difficulties have arisen in relation to different national approaches to Deferred Tax Assets and whether these assets can be counted as capital – the Basel III Agreement requires that their treatment as capital be phased out within five years at the end of which they must be deducted from capital, but CRD IV/CRR provides for a 10 year phase-out. The ECB Supervisory Board was, however, able to reach agreement on reducing the transition period to six years.[68] Overall, the adoption of the regulation and guide suggests a productive relationship between the ECB and NCAs, for the moment at least,[69] and that the Supervisory Board is able to manage national preferences and interests.

There are, however, significant challenges ahead. Pressure may be placed on the pivotal ECB/NCA relationship and political tensions may emerge as the ECB moves into a 'business as usual' posture. There were few incentives for NCAs or the Member States to disrupt the build-up phase of the SSM or the initial Comprehensive Assessment given the acute sensitivity of the EU financial system, and euro-area sovereign debt markets in particular, to signals as to the effectiveness of Banking Union. But national preferences may become more pressing as the SSM beds in and as its consequences for local significant banks become clearer. The ECB has, for example, been uncompromising with respect to the challenging low-interest-rate environment banks are operating in and called for banks to rethink their business models.[70] In addition, its forward supervisory agenda is ambitious. Its 2016 agenda, for example, includes potentially sensitive priorities with respect to business models and profitability drivers; credit risk, non-performing loans, and the quality of banks' internal assessment models; risk governance and data quality; and liquidity.[71] Particular tensions may emerge if a perception develops

[65] Chair Nouy has trenchantly suggested that many of the ONDs 'are the mere reflection of unquestioned traditions, pure national interest and regulatory capture': 2016 SSM Annual Report, above (n 7) 4–5.

[66] The removal or reduction of ONDs has been called for in, eg, Commission, 'Towards the Completion of the Banking Union' (2015) (COM (2015) 584); European Parliament, Resolution of 10 March 2016 on the Banking Union – Annual Report 2015 (O8_TA-PROV(2016)0093); and Council Conclusions on a Roadmap to Complete Banking Union, 17 June 2016 (Press Release 353/16).

[67] 2015 Explanatory Memorandum (n 64) 5.

[68] ibid, 8.

[69] The OND initiative was led by a High Level Group on which the ECB and NCAs were represented (ibid, 6).

[70] As reported in C Jones, 'ECB Supervisor Rejects Banks' Complaints', *Financial Times*, 24 March 2016, 8.

[71] 2016 SSM Annual Report (n 7) 7–9.

that the ECB is adopting a 'one size fits all' model or deploying supervisory benchmarks in a manner which is seen as insufficiently discriminating. In particular, the obligation on the ECB to have full regard to the diversity of credit institutions, their size and business models' (2013 ECB/SSM Regulation, Article 1) may, as supervisory decisions shape bank profitability, become a source of pressure and a potential focus point for national interests. The European Parliament, which has emerged as having some appetite for holding the ECB to account, has recently focused on the proportionality of ECB action and its approach to the SREP, and has queried how the ECB relies on supervisory benchmarks and peer group analyses in developing supervisory approaches.[72] Over 2016, the ECB was careful to highlight its proportionate approach to supervision and to underline the concessions which are made to smaller banks, including with respect to supervisory reporting.[73] While it has been robust with respect to the need for a harmonised supervisory approach, it has acknowledged the importance of the proportionality principle.[74] Operationally, the SSM SREP Methodology is based on a common methodology (based on an assessment of business models; governance and risk management; capital; and liquidity and funding) and a decision-making process which allows for peer comparisons.[75] But the Methodology also underlines the importance of proportionality and flexibility. The intensity of supervisory engagement is based on a bank's risk profile and size, and decisions on the outcome of an SREP are built on three elements: data-gathering from the bank (phase 1); an automated scoring process (phase 2); and a supervisory judgment (phase 3).[76] This approach is designed to ensure the 'right balance' between a common approach which ensures consistency across SSM banks and the necessary supervisory judgment which takes into account the specificities and complexity of an institution.[77] But pressure for greater differentiation in the ECB's supervisory approach, and for the diversity of euro-area banks to be reflected to a greater extent in its supervisory approach, may become significant, particularly if the operating environment for banks continues to be challenging. All this will test whether ECB decision-making within the SSM can withstand pressure from national preferences while taking into account appropriately justified national interests and concerns.

---

[72] See the 2016 European Parliament Resolution (n 14) para 36 and the Letter from Chair Nouy to MEP Giegold on the proportionality of accounting requirements, the review of less significant banks, and the SREP and related supervisory benchmarking and peer group analyses, 20 November 2015.

[73] eg, Speech by Vice Chair Lautenschläger, 'European Banking Supervision – Much Achieved, but Still Much to Do', Frankfurt, 1 June 2016.

[74] Statement on the Principle of Proportionality: applicability in the Single Supervisory Mechanism, Letter to MEP Giegold, 2 October 2015.

[75] SSM SREP Booklet (n 52).

[76] The automated score which emerges in phase 2 can be improved by one notch and worsened by two notches by the exercise of supervisory judgment.

[77] SSM SREP Booklet (n 52) 9.

Whether or not the current accountability regime is effective in holding the ECB to account is also likely to be tested.[78] The effectiveness of the ECB's wider accountability regime, particularly with respect to its monetary functions, has long been contested.[79] With respect to SSM-specific accountability, the notion of 'output legitimacy', which relates the accountability and wider legitimacy of the ECB to the achievement of its objectives,[80] may suggest there are grounds for optimism. The objectives imposed on the ECB in its SSM capacity are not as finely grained as the objectives which are imposed on the EBA (reflecting the EBA's status as an agency),[81] or those which typically define national supervisory action.[82] These objectives include that the ECB contribute to the safety and soundness of credit institutions and the stability of the financial system within the EU and each Member State (2013 ECB/SSM Regulation, Article 1). But they provide at least something of a benchmark against which the ECB can be held accountable. In addition, the range of institutional reporting obligations to which the ECB is subject provides channels through which its effectiveness in meeting its objectives can be challenged and made transparent. As noted above, the European Parliament is proving to have an appetite for holding the ECB to account. Searching questions have been posed to the ECB by MEPs[83] and the 2016 European Parliament resolution on the ECB's activities over 2015 saw the Parliament challenge the ECB on, for example, the need for improvements in involving NCAs more effectively in JSTs; the need to take account of any unintended consequences of supervisory action; the need to avoid double reporting obligations; the costs of high capital requirement; greater transparency, including on the SREP; and cooperation with other EU actors, including the EBA.[84]

What then might be suggested from the early evidence as to the centralisation of banking governance decision-making within the SSM? It is too early to assess the functional effectiveness of SSM decision-making with respect to the achievement of optimal outcomes for the euro-area banking zone, whether in terms of, for example, financial stability or the transmission of credit to the real economy.

---

[78] For a sceptical view on the robustness of the new accountability regime see Wolfers and Voland, 'Level the Playing Field' (2014) (n 12) 1481–82, suggesting that national accountability frameworks for domestic supervisors are stronger.

[79] See, eg, W Buiter, 'Alice in Euroland' (1999) 37 *Journal of Common Market Studies* 181 and F Amtenbrink and K van Duin, 'The European Parliament before the European Parliament: Theory and Practice After Ten Years of Monetary Dialogue' (2009) *European Law Review* 561.

[80] eg E Jones, 'Output Legitimacy and the Global Financial Crisis: Perceptions Matter' (2009) 47 *Journal of Common Market Studies* 1085.

[81] 2010 EBA Regulation, Art 8.

[82] Detailed strategic and operational objectives apply to the UK Financial Conduct Authority and Prudential Regulation Authority, eg, under the Financial Services and Markets Act 2000, Articles 1B–1E and 2C–2B.

[83] MEP Giegold eg, has queried the proportionality of the SREP process and how the ECB ensures that supervisory discretion is not abused: Letter from Chair Nouy to MEP Giegold, 20 November 2015.

[84] 2016 European Parliament Resolution (n 14) paras 6–8, 21, 37, and 41.

But it can be suggested that the SSM has shown procedural effectiveness, particularly in adopting an operating framework which includes the SSM SREP and by successfully having adopted a related series of supervisory decisions. It can also be suggested that there are some indications that the ECB is aware of the need to show discrimination and proportionality in how it deploys the SSM SREP in relation to significant banks. Initial indications also suggest sensitivity to its accountability obligations and a willingness to engage with the European Parliament. A fairly positive score card can therefore be suggested, with the major caveat that the implications of SSM supervisory decisions are not yet clear.

III. SSM Decision-making, the EBA and Brexit: ESFS Effects

A. The EBA and Banking Governance

The centralisation of decision-making in relation to banking governance by the SSM is likely to have effects beyond the Banking Union zone and to have an impact on single market banking governance.

The institutional governance of the single market in financial services is managed through the ESFS which is composed of: the NCAs which provide the foundations of the system; the three sectoral ESAs which are charged with a range of quasi-regulatory and supervisory/supervisory coordination functions – the European Securities and Markets Authority (ESMA), the EBA, and the European Insurance and Occupational Pensions Authority (EIOPA), and their coordinating Joint Committee; and the European Systemic Risk Board (ESRB), which monitors the EU financial system for system-wide risks. The SSM structures sit somewhat awkwardly within the ESFS, with the ECB taking on certain of the functions of NCAs in relating to banking supervision within the SSM zone.

The ESFS has quasi-rule-making and supervisory functions over the single market as a whole. Financial rule-making at the legislative, 'level 1' level, is the prerogative of the European Parliament and the Council of the EU. Delegated, administrative 'level 2' rule-making is the prerogative of the European Commission.[85] The ESAs, however, can be mandated by level 1 measures to propose a particular form of administrative rule to be adopted/endorsed by the Commission: the 'Binding Technical Standard' which can take the form of a 'Regulatory Technical Standard' (under Article 290 TFEU) or an 'Implementing

---

[85] The Lamfalussy framework which governs the organisation of regulatory governance in the EU financial system is composed of level 1 legislation, adopted by the co-legislators; level 2 administrative rules, adopted by the Commission and advised/supported by the ESAs to different extents; level 3 soft supervisory coordination/convergence measures adopted by the ESAs; and level 4 enforcement of Member States breaches by the Commission.

Technical Standard' (Article 291 TFEU). The complex procedural arrangements which apply under the founding ESA Regulations to the proposal by an ESA and the adoption by the Commission of a Binding Technical Standard are designed to protect the position of the ESAs as the location of technical expertise in EU financial governance. These procedures are also designed to preserve the constitutional pre-eminence of the Commission as the location of administrative rule-making power. The ESAs can in addition adopt different forms of soft law, primarily Guidelines in relation to which NCAs must 'comply or explain'.

Supervisory decision-making remains for the most part at Member State level with the NCAs (although with the ECB with respect to significant banks), according to the allocation-of-competence rules contained in EU financial law. Cross-border activity in the single financial market is legally anchored to, and supervised by, the 'home' State of a market participant (typically its State of registration/incorporation). Only a limited and enumerated range of supervisory functions are reserved to the host State. Coordination between multiple 'home' supervisors (which is required for group structures composed of subsidiaries registered in different Member States) is typically carried out through colleges of supervisors. The ESAs have a primarily coordinating role in relation to supervision and have been conferred with: a range of soft coordination and convergence powers, including oversight functions in relation to colleges of supervisors; a limited range of binding powers to direct NCAs in specified circumstances (breach of EU law, emergency conditions, and in binding mediation situations); and, in the case of ESMA, direct powers of supervision in relation to a discrete group of actors and activities, including credit rating agencies, trade repositories, commodity positions, short selling, and the sale of products (in relation to the latter, the EBA also has direct supervisory powers).

Decision-making in relation to these competences is the prerogative of the ESAs' Boards of Supervisors. The Boards are quasi-inter-governmental in nature, being primarily composed of the relevant NCAs – only NCAs can vote. They also display a supranational quality, however, as, for the most part, they operate on the basis of a 'qualified majority vote' under which one or more dissenting NCAs may be subject to a binding decision taken by coalitions of NCAs on the Board. Experience since 2011 suggests that consensus is the more typical Board decision-making model, reflecting the still youthful nature of the ESAs, their incentives to establish their credibility and capacity, and the sensitivity of the pivotal ESA/NCA relationship. Board minutes do, however, increasingly note the taking of decisions by a majority.[86] In addition, the influence of the European Commission, a non-voting observer on ESA Boards, on ESA decision-making cannot be entirely discounted,

---

[86] The EBA Board minutes note, eg, the majority position in favour of disagreeing with a Commission revision to a draft Technical Standard proposed by EBA: EBA Board of Supervisor Minutes, 8 September 2015 (EBA BS 2015 332 rev1).

not least given its role, noted below, in 'endorsing' certain forms of ESA action. It can be regarded at times as having a potentially chilling effect.[87]

Accordingly, in the single EU banking market EBA operates as a quasi-rule-maker and carries out a series of supervisory coordination and convergence functions, including in relation to bank colleges of supervisors. By contrast, the ECB is an operational supervisor and is subject to the EU banking rulebook, which is shaped by the EBA, as well as to the EBA's supervisory convergence and other measures (2013 ECB/SSM Regulation, Article 4). In principle, the EBA and ECB spheres of competence are distinct. But the potential for destructive tension and confusion, and for related prejudice to the single market, is not insignificant.

With respect to EBA's quasi-rule-making powers, caucusing by a coalition of SSM NCAs on its Board of Supervisors (the ECB is a non-voting member of the Board (2010 EBA Regulation, Article 40(1)(d)) could, in theory, limit the EBA's effectiveness with respect to single market regulatory governance. In addition, the threat arises of the ECB operating as a competing standard-setter to the EBA. The ECB is empowered to adopt rules relating to the SSM, as well as 'instructions' and 'guidelines' (2013 ECB/SSM Regulation, Article 4(3) and 6) which are very likely to acquire a quasi-regulatory quality. The ECB is charged with following EBA soft law under Article 4 of the 2013 ECB/SSM Regulation[88] and can only adopt rules with respect to the organisational and operational modalities of banking supervision within the SSM (such as the 2015 ECB regulation governing the exercise of ONDs within the SSM). But the potential for conflict is there, at least until the institutional landscape settles. The possibilities for tension are all the greater as EBA/ECB communication channels are not as strong as they might be. The ECB is a permanent non-voting member of the EBA Board of Supervisors but the EBA is not a permanent non-voting observer on the ECB Supervisory Board. By contrast, a European Commission representative may participate as a non-voting observer on the ECB Supervisory Board (2013 ECB/SSM Regulation, Article 26(11)). The SSM rules of procedures allow the EBA to be invited, but this invitation is a function of ECB secondary law. The ECB's first annual report on supervision noted that EBA had been invited to Supervisory Board meetings, but only on an ad hoc basis and where single market interests so required.[89] A 'double-lock' voting device has, however, been used to support EBA and the wider single market against SSM/ECB-led caucusing on the EBA Board of Supervisors. Separate simple majorities within the participating and non-participating blocs are required for the purposes of reaching the qualified majority required for the Board of Supervisors' quasi-rule-making activities.[90]

---

[87] Particularly, eg, with respect to ESA soft law activity, including the adoption of Guidelines, and where the boundaries of ESA action may be unclear. See further Moloney (n 2) chapter X.

[88] As it acknowledged in its ECB Banking Supervision, Guide to Supervision, September 2014, 3.

[89] 2015 SSM Annual Report (n 26) 17.

[90] 2010 EBA Regulation, Art 44(1). The double-lock arrangement also applies to the Board panels which are constituted to take decisions in relation to a breach of EU law by an NCA or in relation to the imposition of a binding mediation decision on an NCA.

Potential difficulties also arise with respect to supervisory decision-making. Supervision is the core function of the SSM. But ECB/SSM supervision poses potential complications for EBA across two dimensions in particular: the borderline between rules and supervisory practices/decisions can be a thin one in the banking sphere; and EBA has a distinct supervisory mandate which includes promotion of SREP convergence, the adoption of guidelines on supervisory practices, stress-testing, and participation in the colleges of supervisors in which the ECB, as a direct supervisor, participates.[91] As a result, the potential for EBA/SSM tensions and overlaps is not insignificant.

B. Early Lessons

Initial evidence at the time of writing suggests that EBA and the ECB are learning to play a complex governance game to some effect and that the destabilising centripetal effects which the SSM may generate for single market banking governance may be weaker than first predicted.

With respect to quasi-rule-making governance, there is little evidence of Banking Union/SSM caucusing thus far.[92] In addition, EBA appears to have strengthened its credibility as a quasi-rule-maker, limiting the risks to its position. EBA is considered to have safely navigated a complex range of issues with respect to the development of 'level 2' rules under CRD IV/CRR.[93] It has also adopted a vast array of related soft Guidelines and similar measures. The outcome is an interactive CRD IV/CRR rulebook of immense scale and depth.[94] EBA has also engaged in an array of activities which underline its centrality to the development of the CRD IV/CRR regime. To take only a handful of examples, it acts as custodian for the massive supervisory disclosures ('COREP' and 'FINREP') now made under CRD IV/CRR by EU banks; produces regular reports on risks and vulnerabilities in the EU banking sector;[95] monitors the impact of the new banking rulebook;[96] and advises the Commission on the impact of proposed rules.[97] Sitting at the centre of this dense data network affords the EBA the potential to increase its

---

[91] 2010 EBA Regulation, Arts 20a, 29, 22, and 21.

[92] As was repeatedly noted by witnesses to the 2014–2015 Inquiry by the UK House of Lords European Union Select Committee: House of Lords, European Union Committee, 'Fifth Report of Session 2014–2015, The Post-Crisis EU Regulatory Framework: Do the Pieces Fit?' (2015).

[93] eg, Mazars, 'Review of the New European System of Financial Supervision. Part 1: The Work of the European Supervisory Agencies'. Study for the ECON Committee (2013) (IP/A/ECON/ST/2012-23).

[94] An interactive single rulebook which embeds relevant administrative rules, BTSs, and EBA soft law within the CRD IV/CRR is hosted by EBA: available at www.eba.europa.eu/regulation-and-policy/single-rulebook/interactive-single-rulebook.

[95] For an example see EBA, 'Risk Assessment of the European Banking System', December 2015.

[96] eg EBA, 'Overview of the Potential Implications of Regulatory Rules for Banks' Business Models' (2015) and EBA, 'CRD IV-CRR Monitoring Exercise', March 2016.

[97] eg, EBA, 'Report on the Leverage Ratio Requirements under Article 511 of the CRR' (EBA-Op-2016-13) (2016).

credibility as a quasi-regulator. To similar effect, the EBA also monitors potential divergences in the application of CRD IV/CRR,[98] including with respect to the quality of own funds (capital) and the degree of convergence taking place.[99] There are likely to be limited incentives accordingly for the ECB to displace the EBA as the seat of technical expertise on the development of EU banking regulation.

Certainly, the public record shows some degree of unanimity between the EBA and the ECB on rule-making matters. The ECB has acknowledged the 'main task' of the EBA as developing the banking rulebook and has reported on its participation in a number of EBA working groups in this regard.[100] In reaching a position on its approach to the exercise of ONDs, to take another example, the ECB drew on EBA standards and noted that certain of its policy stances could not be finalised until certain EBA initiatives were complete.[101] The ECB and EBA have also found common ground internationally. In December 2014, the EU was found to be 'materially non-compliant' in applying the Basel III regime (through CRD IV/ CRR) under the Basel III Regulatory Consistency Assessment Programme (RCAP) assessment of compliance.[102] Among the difficulties was the EU's failure to define 'capital' with sufficient clarity and in line with the Basel III regime. EBA and the ECB were vocal in reinforcing the Basel Committee's RCAP concerns and in calling for greater consistency in the banking rulebook, particularly with respect to the definition of capital.[103] Accordingly, there are some indications of a potential EBA/ECB axis of technocracy emerging. The European Commission has also emerged, not unexpectedly given the threat that the ECB poses to its rule-making prerogatives, as a champion of the EBA's single market role and has emphasised the EBA's quasi-rule-making functions, contrasting them with the predominantly supervisory role of the ECB within the SSM.[104]

A similarly optimistic assessment of initial EBA/ECB relations can be suggested with respect to supervisory governance. The ECB's first Comprehensive Assessment (2013–2014) and the EBA's related 2014 pan-EU stress test provided an early test case for EBA/ECB relations, but seems to have been a relatively smooth process with regard to institutional coordination. Under the 2013 ECB/SSM Regulation the ECB is required to carry out a Comprehensive Assessment of significant banks before it takes over their supervision (Article 33(4)). The ECB is also empowered to conduct stress tests, albeit in cooperation with EBA (2013 ECB/SSM

---

[98] See, eg, EBA, 'Reply to Commission's Request for an Overview of Possible Errors and Inconsistencies in CRD IV/CRR Observed via the Single Rulebook Tool' (EBA/2016/D840) (2016).

[99] eg, EBA, 'Report on the Monitoring of Additional Tier 1 (AT1) Instruments of EU Institutions' – Second Update – Draft (2016),

[100] 2016 SSM Annual Report (n 7) 61.

[101] ibid, 65 (although the ECB allowed for some divergence to support the transition to new rules) and 2015 Explanatory Memorandum (n 64) 6.

[102] Basel Committee, Regulatory Consistency Assessment Programme (RCAP), Assessment of Basel III Regulation – European Union, December 2014, 4.

[103] See, eg, 2015 SSM Annual Report (n 26) 51.

[104] Commission, 'Staff Working Document, Report on the Operation of the ESA and ESFS' (SWD (2014) 261) (2014) 23–24.

Regulation, Article 4(1)(f)). The first ECB Comprehensive Assessment was based on two exercises: an asset-quality review (or an assessment of the quality of loan assets on banks' balance sheets and the extent to which they were impaired); and the stress-testing of the capital held against the reviewed balance sheet under 'base-line case' and 'stressed' scenarios. EBA however, is charged with considering, at least annually, whether it is appropriate to carry out EU-wide stress tests and with disclosing the results (2010 EBA Regulation, Article 22). EBA is also, for the purposes of running stress tests, empowered to request related information directly from financial institutions and to request NCAs to conduct specific reviews and onsite inspections (Article 32(3a)). The Comprehensive Assessment accordingly saw the powers of the ECB and EBA intersecting with potentially troublesome effects. EBA had strong incentives to exert control over the 2014 pan-EU stress tests, which were folded into the ECB's Comprehensive Assessment, in order to protect its institutional position, particularly as its member NCAs were reported to have softened the impact of the earlier 2011 EBA stress test.[105] The ECB had similarly strong incentives, however, to establish its executive capacity and to ensure that the Comprehensive Assessment would allow it to commence supervision in a strong position. The allocation of stress-testing functions appears, however, to have been relatively efficient. EBA set the common methodology and scenarios for the 2014 pan-EU stress test;[106] these applied to the stress-testing of non-euro-area banks by their relevant NCAs[107] as well to the stress-testing of euro-area banks which was overseen by the ECB as part of its wider Comprehensive Assessment. In addition, the ECB's related asset-quality review was based on an EBA Recommendation.[108] Executive and quasi-rule-making functions were accordingly allocated between the ECB and the EBA.

Since then, institutional coordination appears to be reasonably effective. In 2015 the ECB undertook a small Comprehensive Assessment of an additional nine banks.[109] The Assessment did not include an EBA stress-test element given the smaller scale of the exercise. EBA did not carry out a pan-EU stress test in 2015 but instead published the results of a pan-EU 'transparency exercise' which was

---

[105] EBA was reportedly prevented by its NCAs from exposing the true scale of losses at major EU banks, leading Chancellor Merkel to charge NCAs with acting from 'misguided national pride': S Fleming and A Barker, 'Credibility Test', *Financial Times*, 12 December 2013, 10.

[106] EBA produced the stress test 'common methodology' to be applied by all EU banks and the macro-economic scenarios for the stress test: EBA, 'EBA Publishes Common Methodology and Scenario for the 2014 EU Banks Stress Tests', Press Release 29 April 2014. An 'adverse scenario' used in the stress test was developed by the European Systemic Risk Board.

[107] EBA's concern to highlight the pan-EU nature of the stress test was clear from the outset. Its FAQ on the stress test described it as providing a 'common foundation on which national authorities can base their supervisory assessment of banks' resilience' and as being initiated and coordinated by EBA: EBA, '2014 EU-Wide Stress Test: Frequently Asked Questions', 29 April 2014.

[108] EBA, 'Recommendations on the Asset Quality Review' (EBA/RC/2014/04).

[109] ECB Banking Supervision, 'Note on the 2015 Comprehensive Assessment' (2015). The Assessment applied to a group of banks which either would become significant in 2016 or became significant in 2014 and had not been included in the original Assessment.

based on supervisory reporting data and which provided detailed bank-by-bank data.[110] A subsequent large-scale stress test, coordinated by EBA and in which the ECB was closely involved, took place in 2016, however, and further illustrates the nature of ECB/EBA coordination. Given the scale of the earlier 2014 EBA exercise, the 2016 EBA stress test was based on a smaller sample of banks, but the filter for the sample reflected the ECB's supervisory jurisdiction as it was based in part on the test for 'significance' for the purposes of direct ECB supervision (the 51 banking groups tested included 39 banking groups supervised by the ECB). EBA developed the methodology for the 2016 stress test and acted as a data hub, publishing the results of the test, while the ECB was responsible for ensuring that the banks it supervised applied the methodology correctly and for testing the reliability of banks' assumptions, data, estimates, and results through quality assurance procedures.[111] A coordinated EBA/ECB position on how to use the 2016 stress test for the purposes of supervision also emerged, with the ECB adopting a new approach to 'capital guidance', following EBA's direction in this regard.[112] The ECB in addition undertook a parallel stress test, based on EBA's methodology, for the remaining significant banks outside the EBA 2016 stress test group.[113]

Other signs also augur well. A particular stress point for ECB/EBA relations as regards supervisory governance concerns the SREP, which requires supervisors to review, *inter alia*, the resilience of bank capital and risk management and which also governs how supervisors can/should apply additional capital requirements and other supervisory tools. As required under Article 107 of CRD IV, EBA has produced extensive Guidelines on how the SREP should be undertaken,[114] reflecting the risks to the single market, including with respect to supervisory consistency, arbitrage risks, and transaction costs, which could arise were divergences in the SREP process to emerge. These Guidelines form part of the EBA's 'Single Supervisory Handbook' which 'sets out supervisory best practices for methodologies and processes' for the EU as a whole (as required under 2010 EBA Regulation, Articles 8 and 29(2)). EBA is also charged with promoting the convergence of SREP practices (EBA Regulation, Article 20a). In addition, Article 107 CRD IV requires the EBA to assess the reports which NCAs must make to it regarding

[110] EBA, 'Report – 2015 EU-wide Transparency Exercise' (2015).

[111] EBA, '2016 EU-wide Stress Test: Frequently Asked Questions', 29 July 2016. EBA summarised the allocation of competence as follows: 'The EU-wide stress test is initiated and coordinated by the EBA and undertaken in cooperation with the Competent Authorities (the ECB-Banking Supervision for the euro area banks), the European Systemic Risk Board ... and the European Commission.' The Commission provided the baseline scenario for the test and the ESRB provided the adverse scenario.

[112] See Nouy Letter (n 57).

[113] ECB Banking Supervision, 'ECB to stress test 39 euro area banks as part of the 2016 EU-wide stress test', Press Release, 5 November 2015.

[114] EBA, Guidelines on Common Procedures and Methodologies for the Supervisory Review and Evaluation Process' (EBA/GL/2014/13) (EBA SREP Guidelines). The Guidelines did not come into force until 2016.

their SREPs for the purposes of developing SREP consistency, and the EBA to report annually to the European Parliament and Council on the degree of convergence being achieved.[115] The EBA therefore has a critical role to play in promoting single-market-wide convergence between ECB/SSM SREP practices and those of NCAs which do not participate in Banking Union.

The ECB, as a supervisor of significant banks, is subject to the CRD IV/CRR SREP requirement. It is also responsible for ensuring consistent SREP practices across the SSM generally with respect to the SREPs carried out by NCAs of less significant banks. In this regard, it is required to follow the EBA's SREP Guidelines (2013 ECB/SSM Regulation, Article 4). But supervision is a granular operational activity and divergences may arise in how the ECB delivers supervision within the SSM through the SREP process and the EBA's Guidelines and other measures in this area.

Thus far, however, the distinct roles of the EBA and the ECB appear to be synchronised. The ECB has highlighted that its supervisory procedures are designed to follow and be complementary to the EBA Single Supervisory Handbook/SREP Guidelines,[116] and its SSM SREP Methodology Booklet for significant banks contains multiple references to EBA's SREP Guidelines.[117] EBA, for its part, appears to have the appetite to review the SSM's application of its SREP Guidelines. In its 2015 Report on supervisory practices, which pre-dated the ECB's undertaking of SREP activities as well as the coming into force of EBA's SREP Guidelines in 2016, EBA noted that the ECB's SREP activities will 'ensure more unified supervisory practices in SSM Member States' but it warned that 'EBA's role is particularly important in ensuring that relevant standards and guidelines are consistently implemented across the Single Market'.[118] In its 2016 Report, which included review of the first set of SREPs carried out by the ECB, EBA noted that the SSM was having a significant impact on supervisory convergence within the SSM zone, driven by a consistent SSM process for significant banks and by joint supervisory activities, and reported on visits to SSM NCAs designed to gain insights into their SREP practices.[119] It also noted that the consistency of the SREP for significant banks supervised by the ECB was checked through extensive peer comparisons and horizontal analyses and that the SSM had continued to complete and refine its methodology.[120] Initial indications therefore seem to augur well for an appropriate differentiation of tasks between EBA and the SSM in relation to

---

[115] eg, EBA, 'Report on the Convergence of Supervisory Practices' (EBA-Op-2016-11) (2016).
[116] 2015 SSM Annual Report (n 26) 52–53. The 2016 Annual Report (n 7) 31 similarly notes that its SREP methodology is in line with the EBA SREP Guidelines.
[117] In the Booklet the ECB notes that it follows the EBA SREP Guidelines and that its Methodology implements the Guidelines: (n 52) 2 and 4; eg, the building block approach on which the SSM SREP is based (business model analysis; governance and risk management; risks to capital; and risks to liquidity) follows the EBA Guidelines.
[118] EBA, 'Report on Convergence of Supervisory Practices' (n 115) 4.
[119] ibid, 4 and 12.
[120] ibid, 13.

the SREP, but it is as yet too early to predict whether euro-area/SSM preferences may come to shape the SSM SREP to the detriment of single market banking governance. It can, however, be predicted, based on the tone and content of its 2016 Annual Report on Supervisory Convergence, that EBA will be vigilant in monitoring divergences and in ma king them transparent.

A similar conclusion might be drawn from EBA's prioritisation of its work in relation to colleges of supervisors for cross-border banks in which the ECB sits where a college covers SSM and non-SSM banks. Under the 2010 EBA Regulation, Article 10 and under CRD IV/CRR, EBA is conferred with a range of coordinating and monitoring powers in relation to bank colleges of supervisors. Immediately prior to the ECB taking on its SSM supervisory powers, EBA's extensive review of colleges in 2014 and its plans for 2015 suggested a strong interest in establishing ownership with respect to the oversight of colleges.[121] Notably, the 2015 review noted the 'important changes' to the institutional setting of euro-area banks with ECB SSM supervision and EBA's commitment to continuing its role in colleges 'to strengthen the co-operation between SSM, non-SSM and third country supervisory authorities'.[122] The EBA's 2016 report was similarly alert to the EBA's role in protecting the single market interest, noting the 'unquestionable need for authorities to reassess their roles and competences under the new institutional setting, and to review colleges' settings and functioning'.[123]

Something of a delicate institutional minuet is therefore well underway as both the ECB and the EBA learn to navigate a fragile institutional environment in which their respective incentives are distinct and powerful. But initial signs augur well as to the productive nature of the learning process and as to the ability of the EBA and the SSM to co-exist.

C. EBA, Brexit, and the SSM: Is there a Role for the EBA in EU Banking Governance Post Brexit?

On Brexit the single market will lose a strong advocate for the need to protect single market governance from euro-area interests and euro-area caucusing. As is clear from the now over-taken February 2016 New Settlement,[124] the UK was in the vanguard of efforts to ensure single market governance was not dominated by euro-area interests and that further institutional centralisation was resisted.

---

[121] EBA, 'Establishment of the EBA Colleges Action Plan for 2014 and Establishment of the EBA Colleges Plan for 2015' (2015).
[122] EBA, 'Report on Convergence of Supervisory Practices' (n 115) 7.
[123] EBA, 'Report on the Functioning of Supervisory Colleges in 2015 and 2016 EBA Colleges Action' (2016).
[124] Decision of the Heads of State or Government Meeting Within the European Council, Concerning a New Settlement for the United Kingdom with the European Union, European Council Meeting, 18 and 19 February 2016 EUCO 1/16 (Annex 1).

Earlier, the UK was the driving force behind the 'double-lock' which applies to EBA Board of Supervisors decision-making and which is designed to prevent euro-area caucusing. The implications of the UK's withdrawal are as yet unclear, but some tentative predictions can be offered as to the nature of the SSM/EBA relationship post Brexit.

The withdrawal of the UK from the EU will remove one of the major frictions preventing the further integration of institutional governance within the euro area. 'SSM-like' structures with centralised decision-making might accordingly develop for the euro-area insurance and capital markets.[125] But it is not clear that EBA's role will significantly change, at least in the medium term. There are at present nine EBA members who are not members of the euro area or participants in the SSM; this will be reduced to eight with the exit of the UK. Whether or not the single market interest which EBA is charged with supporting will become subsumed within the SSM interest, and thereby lead to related calls for a change to EBA's role, will depend on whether or not those eight members become members of the SSM. While there are incentives for the 'pre-in' euro-area Member States to join the SSM ahead of time, there are also considerable counter-incentives.[126] At present, only Denmark has made a clear statement of support for joining the Banking Union,[127] although other non-euro-area Member States are supportive.[128]

There is, of course, a temporal inevitability here. If only one or two more Member States either join the euro or choose to participate in the SSM, network effects are likely to develop which make the case for SSM participation compelling, particularly if the reputation of the ECB is not, in the meantime, damaged. In addition, the double-lock which protects non-SSM Member States is to be reviewed when the number of non-participating Member States reaches four (2010 EBA Regulation, Article 81a).[129] But it does not necessarily follow that the ECB within the SSM will take over the EBA's functions even if there is greater alignment between single market and SSM NCAs.

---

[125] See further N Moloney, 'International Financial Governance, the EU, and Brexit: the 'Agencification' of EU Financial Governance and the Implications' (2016) 17 *European Business Organization Law* 451.

[126] See further Moloney, 'European Banking Union' (n 12) and Ferran, 'European Banking Union' (n 24).

[127] The Danish central bank called for Denmark to join the Banking Union in 2014: Danish Nationalbank, 'Danish Participation in the Banking Union' (2014) 4th Quarter *Danmark's Nationalbank Monetary Review*, 41. This was followed by a positive report from the Ministry of Business and Growth in May 2015 and a related supportive statement from two government ministers: Press Release, Ministry of Business and Growth, 11 May 2015.

[128] Bulgaria and Romania have indicated their support while the Czech Republic, Hungary, and Poland are adopting more of a sceptical or 'wait and see' approach: P Hüttl and D Schoenmaker, 'Should the "outs" join the European Banking Union?' *Policy Contribution*, Issue 2016/3, February 2016.

[129] In addition, in relation to Board decisions regarding enforcement action against a fellow NCA or in relation to binding mediation, the required panel decision, previously subject to a form of double-lock procedure, is to be taken by a simple majority which includes one non-SSM NCA: 2010 EBA Regulation, Art 44(1).

If the SSM zone and the single banking market were to become aligned in terms of membership the need for the supervisory coordination which EBA currently provides would be reduced, but it would not be removed entirely. The EBA's supervisory remit is wider than that of the ECB/SSM. The ECB/SSM currently deals only with prudential matters relating to credit institutions (2013 ECB/SSM Regulation, Article 1). The EBA's mandate, however, includes consumer protection,[130] in relation to which its activities are increasing, and it extends beyond deposit-taking institutions.[131] It also includes financial crime, with the EBA conferred with a number of roles in relation to the EU's anti-money laundering regime, for example. It is not, of course, impossible that the ECB's competences are extended in the future to match those of EBA. The more likely outcome, however, is that the risks of creating a vastly powerful institution are likely to minimise political, institutional, and market support for such a change. While the EBA's role may therefore change somewhat, and might become more focused on conduct governance and consumer protection, it is unlikely to be subsumed within the ECB.

The EBA similarly has a wider regulatory remit than the ECB has.[132] It has also developed a strong and tested technical capacity, which underscores the risks and uncertainties of transferring its regulatory powers to the ECB – particularly as the ECB will be preoccupied with bedding in its supervisory functions for some time. The EBA has in addition developed productive relationships with the European Parliament, Council, and Commission in relation to administrative level 2 rule-making. It is not at all clear that these institutions would substitute the EBA, which, as an agency, has a constrained operating environment which limits its competences as a rule-maker, and over which the institutions can exert significant oversight powers, for a mighty ECB. The constitutional conundrums which any such transfer would pose would also be significant. Assuming that the ECB were to be conferred with the EBA's advisory and BTS proposal functions in relation to administrative rules, it is not clear how, for example, the ECB's independence requirement could be met in a situation where the ECB, as a quasi-regulator, was subject to endorsement by the Commission and oversight by the European Parliament and Council. And any conferral of direct administrative rule-making powers on the ECB would require a major overhaul of the Treaty rules governing administrative rule-making which the institutions are unlikely to have the appetite for, particularly given the severe difficulties which the most recent Lisbon Treaty reforms generated.

---

[130] 2010 EBA Regulation, Art 10. See, eg, EBA, 'Guidelines on Product Oversight and Governance' (EBA/GL/2015/18) (2015) and its regular monitoring of consumer market risks (EBA, 'Consumer Trends Report' (2016)).

[131] It has recently been charged with advising the Commission in relation to prudential requirements for investment firms: EBA, 'Report on Investment Firms' (EBA/Op/2015/20) (2015).

[132] It coordinated with ESMA and EIOPA, eg, on the development of the administrative rules for the consumer-focused Packaged Retail and Insurance-based Investment Products (PRIIPs) regime: ESMA, EBA, EIOPA, Final Draft RTSs (JC 2016 21) (2016).

It may also follow that the EBA will be strengthened by the withdrawal of the UK. The UK voice on the EBA appears to have been strong and distinctive, reflecting the particular features of the UK banking market as well as the UK concern to ensure that the EBA operated within the constraints that apply to EU agencies. This was apparent recently, for example, over discussions on the EBA Guidelines on the CRD IV/CRR remuneration regime,[133] in relation to which the UK took a different position to the majority EBA position as regards the proportionate application of certain of the Guidelines.[134] In the absence of the UK it may be that the EBA Board of Supervisors will come to collective positions more easily and will be more willing to take action which strengthens EBA's position but which pushes at the boundaries of the powers of EU agencies.

Predictions as to the impact of Brexit are fraught with risk. But it is not unreasonable to suggest that the EBA and the ECB/SSM are likely to continue to co-exist, in some form, for the medium term at least.

IV. Conclusion

This chapter has considered the evidence which has recently emerged from the SSM in relation to its centralisation of decision-making over regulatory and supervisory banking governance in the Banking Union zone. Its conclusions are modest but relatively optimistic.

Internally, the SSM seems to have established a functional and productive decision-making capacity, although the nature of the outcomes for the EU financial system of its supervisory decisions remains to be seen. Externally within the wider ESFS, while the risks of destructive tension between the EBA and the ECB were considerable, as were the risks of the EBA's effectiveness being prejudiced by SSM caucusing, initial indications appear positive. The EBA and the ECB appear to be carving out their respective spheres of competence and there is a welcome robust quality to the EBA's engagement with the ECB.

These conclusions are necessarily provisional. National preferences may come to exert pressure on the SSM. The impact of Brexit on EBA/ECB relations remains to be seen, as does the extent to which NCA membership of the SSM and of the single market in banking becomes aligned, with implications for the current institutional arrangement. At present, a continuation for the medium-term of the current arrangement, albeit with some adjustments, can be predicted reasonably safely. But the likelihood of a more long-term configuration of EU banking governance, and the nature of any consequences for the centralisation of decision-making, must remain in the realms of speculation at present.

---

[133] EBA, 'Guidelines on Sound Remuneration Policies' (EBA/GL/2015/22) (2015).

[134] PRA and FCA Statement on Compliance with the EBA Guidelines on Sound Remuneration Policies, 29 February 2016.

7

Single Resolution Board

Lost and Found in the Thicket of EU Bank Regulation

AGNIESZKA SMOLEŃSKA*

I. Explaining the Complex Regulatory Architecture of EU Bank Oversight

The complex and multi-peak institutional regulatory architecture[1] put in place for European Union financial sector oversight in the aftermath of the crisis seems to support the argument that democratic values are at odds with modern finance.[2] This is because the highly technical and voluminous banking regulation, coupled with the imperative of swift action (and therefore executive discretion) in the face of a crisis, make the 'lure of technocracy' all the stronger,[3] impairing channels of democratic control. European Union (EU) reforms since 2008 reflect this technocratic push in terms of granularity of the new rules and by putting in place an array of new financial regulators.[4]

---

* The author gratefully acknowledges comments from participants of the Multidisciplinary Research Workshop 'Political Economy of Regulation' organised by Max Weber Program in May 2016, in particular Masha Hedberg and Anna Chadwick, where an earlier version of this chapter was presented. The chapter benefited greatly from further discussions and comments from Adrienne Heriter, Delvinder Singh and Mattia Guidi. Errors remain my own.
[1] Regulatory architecture is understood here in terms of public governance arrangements in the financial sector, that is how power and competences are allocated between various agencies and institutions, see 'Regulatory Architecture: What Matters?', chapter 27 in J Armour, D Awrey, PL Davies, L Enriques, JN Gordon, CP Mayer and J Payne, *Principles of Financial Regulation* (Oxford, Oxford University Press, 2016).
[2] D Rodrik, *The Globalization Paradox: Democracy and the Future of the World Economy* (New York, Norton, 2011).
[3] J Habermas, *The Lure of Technocracy* (Cambridge, Polity, 2015).
[4] Literature on bank regulation traditionally distinguishes between supervision and regulation, that is between those authorities which apply and enforce the rules and those which make them, essentially following the traditional separation of powers doctrines. Given the significance of administrative rule-making in financial regulation context, term 'regulators' is used here in a broader sense to denote all those public authorities responsible for regulating particular aspect of bank behaviour or enforcing particular rules.

The Banking Union[5] – with its two institutional pillars of Single Supervisory and Resolution Mechanisms – is but a fraction of the overall regime, which also includes the rule-makers (the European Supervisory Agencies, such as the European Banking Authority (EBA) and the European Commission),[6] supervisors of financial institutions other than banks,[7] systemic supervisors,[8] competition authorities[9] and consumer protection agencies[10] – in addition to central banks, acting in their capacity as monetary policy authorities, and national (and perhaps eventually also EU) treasuries. The EU financial oversight architecture thus includes authorities pursuing distinct objectives, but also operating within different jurisdictional spaces: EU, Eurozone and national. Even by the notorious EU standards of arcane institutional arrangements, this Byzantine architecture stands out. The question which inevitably arises – and is the theme of this book – is whether given the implications of this complex technocratic design, the death of democracy in the EU is a foregone conclusion. This chapter does not seek to answer such a fundamental quandary – addressed in this book by Professor Möllers (Chapter 8). Rather, it adopts a reconstructive approach in building on alternative legitimating theories,[11] to explain – by reference to the principles of the EU legal order – the importance of deliberation in-built in the regulatory processes occurring within the overall architecture.

Complexity of institutional design raises questions of democratic legitimacy where it obscures ultimate responsibility and accountability for decisions made externally,[12] thereby exasperating public choice problems in an area which, due to knowledge-intensity is prone to capture by insiders and forbearance by supervisors, both of which are held to have contributed to the crisis. Arcane architecture can

---

[5] For an overview of the Banking Union see D Busch and G Ferrarini (eds), *European Banking Union* (Oxford, Oxford University Press, 2015), JH Binder and C Gortsos, *The European Banking Union: A Compendium* (Munich, CH Beck, 2016); specifically on the Bank Recovery and Resolution Directive (BRRD) see JH Binder and D Singh (eds), *Bank Resolution: The European Regime* (Oxford, Oxford University Press, 2016).

[6] N Moloney, 'Technocratic and Centralized Decision-making in Banking Union's Single Supervisory Mechanism: Can Single Market and Banking Union Governance Effectively Co-exist in a Post Brexit World?', Chapter 6 in this volume.

[7] For example insurance and money market supervisors.

[8] On the macroprudential role of the European Systemic Risk Board (ESRB) see E Ferran and A Kern, 'Can Soft Law Bodies Be Effective? Soft Systemic Risk Oversight Bodies and the Special Case of the European Systemic Risk Board' (2011) *Cambridge Law Legal Studies Research Paper Series*.

[9] On cooperation between financial regulators and competition authorities, see E Carletti and A Smoleńska, *Co-operation Between Competition Agencies and Regulators in the Financial Sector: 10 Years on from the Financial Crisis*, OECD Background note.

[10] On the rationale behind the creation of Consumer Financial Protection Bureau in the US see E Warren, 'Unsafe at Any Rate' (2007) 5 *Democracy*.

[11] Where legitimacy is an essential feature of any regulatory system, see E Pan, 'Organizing Regional Systems: The US Example' in N Moloney, E Ferran and J Payne (eds), *The Oxford Handbook of Financial Regulation* (Oxford, Oxford University Press, 2015) 109.

[12] V Schneider, 'Governance and Complexity' in D Levi-Faur (ed), *The Oxford Handbook of Governance* (Oxford, OUP, 2012) 134.

thus propagate socially suboptimal outcomes,[13] though it is not necessarily their direct cause. Rather when understood in structural terms, as a characteristic of a system comprising multiple institutional actors locked in joint decision-making processes, complex regulatory architectures allow for externalisation of conflict between different regulatory objectives, which in the alternative remains hidden from the public eye.[14] This allows a diversity of experimental approaches, as well as uncertainty as to the optimal policy implementation and solutions, to come to the fore, thereby setting conditions which encourage expert deliberation and inter-institutional accountability.[15] The approach adopted here therefore argues that characteristics of the overall institutional design ('fragmentation'), and of individual procedures which join heterogeneous actors in common deliberation ('joints') are a source of legitimacy for the overall architecture, in particular where they allow for diversity and expert deliberation. Such an approach to regulatory architectures in the EU builds on the multi-level EU governance literature,[16] where it explores coordination of decision-making and policy implementation in cases where multiple authorities pursue divergent intermediate goals within formally and informally structured exchanges of information and cooperation mechanisms. It is further in the context of such complex, multi-level governance arrangements, that political science literature has explored the questions of throughput and process-oriented legitimacy: an approach which informs the perspective of regulatory processes adopted here.[17] Two characteristics of EU regulatory architecture for banking add additional layers to these frameworks, however: the temporal differentiation (ie different authorities are in the lead at different periods and act with different time horizons) and the micro/macro distinction (where within the framework individual banks are subject to the regulatory architecture in a two-fold manner, ie both in their own capacity and as part of the banking system). While these dimensions are only partially explored

---

[13] On regulatory failure literature see JJ Laffont and J Tirole, 'The Politics of Government Decision Making: A Theory of Regulatory Capture' (1991) 106 *Quarterly Journal of Economics* 1089; DC Hardy, *Regulatory Capture in Banking* (2006) International Monetary Fund Working Paper WP/06/34. For crisis-specific considerations see E Monnet, S Pagliari and S Vallee, 'Europe Between Financial Repression and Regulatory Capture' (2014) *Bruegel Working Paper* 08/14. In the alternative the argument can be made that accountability undermines the independence of technocratic institutions, whose *raison d'etre* is the their insulation from direct political process. See eg M Guidi 'Accountability Mechanisms: The Case of the European Banking Union' (Working Paper on file with author).

[14] See for this argument D Masciandaro and M Quintyn, 'The Governance of Financial Supervision: Recent Developments' (1991) 5 *Journal of Economic Surveys* 30.

[15] See eg I Chiu, 'Power and Accountability in the EU Financial Regulatory Architecture: Examining Inter-Agency Relations, Agency Independence and Accountability' in M Andenas and G Deipenbrock, *Regulating and Supervising European Financial Markets: More Risks than Achievements* (New York, Springer Berlin Heidelberg, 2016).

[16] See for authoritative approach L Hooghe and G Marks, *Multi-Level Governance and European Integration* (Lanham, Rowman & Littlefield, 2001).

[17] V Schmidt, 'Democracy and Legitimacy in the European Union Revisited: Input, Output and "Throughput"' (2013) 61 *Political Studies* 1.

here, the legislative choice to introduce them into the overall framework (leading to fragmentation) reflects the multi-dimensional, dynamic and time-variant nature of public intervention in the financial sector in temporal and aggregation terms, which necessarily increases the importance of joint procedures to ensure coherence.

The specific mandates of actors within multi-peak regulatory architecture allow for additional insights to be drawn from an EU law perspective. First, such fragmentation puts in place a system of checks and balances ('institutional balance'), in compliance with general EU rule of law principles. Second, it is through and within the interaction between actors within the overall architecture that the abstract EU Treaty objectives become articulated. This is because implementation of distinct financial regulation policies should be consistent in the pursuit of general public good-type objectives such as economic growth or integration, as provided for in the Treaties, which are the basis on which power and tasks are conferred to distinct EU authorities.

To explore the viability of an approach which looks to the procedural 'joints' within the EU regulatory architecture as sources of its legitimacy, the design of the Single Resolution Mechanism (SRM)[18] is explored in this chapter. The choice of the SRM is motivated by its relatively recent vintage (no specific resolution authorities existed prior to the financial crisis) and the perceived constrained role of the Single Resolution Board (SRB) as an agency under the EU legal order in particular.[19] The specificity of the SRM is further explored in section III, which explores the SRB as a new agency created by the SRM Regulation. The detailed procedural interaction between the SRB and other authorities is analysed in the context of resolution planning in section IV. Section V draws a number of tentative conclusions with regard to the characteristics of the resolution-planning processes in the context of the overall design of EU financial regulation architecture, where EU law simultaneously requires deliberation and cooperation, and assumes conflict of interest and/or mandates between distinct institutions. First, however, some words of explanation are required as to why an inter-institutional and process-oriented approach is particularly explanatory in the context of complex regulatory architectures such as that put in place for the oversight of EU's financial sector.

---

[18] Regulation (EU) No 806/2014 of the European Parliament and of the Council of 15 July 2014 establishing uniform rules and a uniform procedure for the resolution of credit institutions and certain investment firms in the framework of a Single Resolution Mechanism and a Single Resolution Fund and amending Regulation (EU) No 1093/2010, OJ 2014 L 225/1 ('SRM Regulation').

[19] Following BRRD, crisis management measures are the implementation of resolution schemes in cases of banks failing, see Art 2(1)(102) of Directive 2014/59/EU of the European Parliament and of the Council of 15 May 2014 establishing a framework for the recovery and resolution of credit institutions and investment firms and amending Council Directive 82/891/EEC, and Directives 2001/24/EC, 2002/47/EC, 2004/25/EC, 2005/56/EC, 2007/36/EC, 2011/35/EU, 2012/30/EU and 2013/36/EU, and Regulations (EU) No 1093/2010 and (EU) No 648/2012, of the European Parliament and of the Council, OJ 2014 L 173/190 ('Bank Recovery and Resolution Directive' – BRRD).

II. Legitimacy and Accountability

EU's Banking Union, and financial regulatory architecture more broadly, are typically considered by reference to individual regulatory objectives and institutions rather than as a whole. As has been suggested above, however, it could argued that it is the terms of inter-institutional engagement which – by holding the 'EU house for finance' together – are a source of legitimacy of the overall institutional design, as it is only through the interaction between distinct policies and actors that EU Treaty objectives can be articulated. In addition, traditional methods for assessing legitimacy (such as input and output),[20] are hardly applicable in the context of complex regulatory architectures.

Specifically, given the fragmentation of policy objectives, the application of traditional input-oriented approaches to expert delegation is limited. In other words, though technical and expert knowledge has been held to be sufficient to lend authority to new independent regulatory institutions,[21] such an approach does not explain technocratic delegation within complex regulatory architectures, where fragmentation of oversight provides evidence of heterogeneity of knowledge and expertise as well as the variety of interests pursued within the framework. Similarly, output legitimacy orientation seems unhelpful, given the generic nature of objectives such as 'financial stability' (even when framed in technical terms), as well as lack of clarity with regard to hierarchy between different objectives.[22] Furthermore, in the case of the concrete resolution-planning exercises discussed below, the success of preventive measures in building up endogenous institutional and sectoral resilience has the unfortunate feature of being unobservable outside of crisis. It is puzzling, therefore, that evaluations of the SRM have been predominantly output-oriented: can the system be considered 'credible', 'can it work' when a bank goes bust?[23] Where bank crisis management has been associated with significant costs imposed on the taxpayer, the question of sufficiency of the Single Resolution Fund (SRF)[24] to fend off the need for public assistance is considered to be the primary benchmark for evaluation.[25] While first resolution cases of Banco

[20] G Monti, 'Independence, Interdependence, and Legitimacy' in D Ritleng (ed), *Independence and Legitimacy in the Institutional System of the European Union* 1st edn (Oxford, Oxford University Press, 2016); Schmidt (n 17).

[21] C Zilioli, 'Accountability and Independence: Irreconcilable Values or Complementary Instruments for Democracy? The Specific Case of the European Central Bank' in *Mélanges En Hommage à Jean-Victor Louis. Vol 2* (Bruxelles, Éditions de l'Universite de Bruxelles, 2003).

[22] See section III.B for consideration of conflicts of interest which may occur between different authorities.

[23] MF Hellwig, 'Yes Virginia, There Is a European Banking Union! But It May Not Make Your Wishes Come True' (2014) MPI Collective Goods Preprint; E Ferran, 'European Banking Union, Imperfect, But It Can Work' in Busch and Ferrarini (n 5).

[24] On the evolution of approaches to Banking Union and SRF backstop see in particular, European Commission, *Further Steps Towards Completing Europe's Economic and Monetary Union: A Roadmap*, (2017) Brussels, COM(2017) 821.

[25] Here conflicting assessments have been made. C Hadjimmanuil argues the size of the backstop will be insufficient, see: C Hadjiemmanuil, 'Bank Resolution Financing in the Banking Union' (2015)

174   *Agnieszka Smoleńska*

Popular in 2017 provide some empirical evidence for such assessments, the truly innovative aspect of crisis-prevention and resolution-planning roles, which are the focus of this chapter,[26] escape output-oriented frameworks.

By contrast, in the highly technical areas such as those overseen by the financial regulators, an inter-institutional and procedure-oriented approach can prove more helpful.[27] Even where elaborate institutional architectures can be expected to breed inter-institutional tensions,[28] and power struggles,[29] the deliberative supranationalism of Joerges and Neyer sees particular value emerge from such legally required expert exchanges, where these are constrained by a problem-solving orientation and a clear mandate with weak formal voting procedures, allowing for deliberative and bargaining interaction.[30] Deliberative approaches are thus particularly explanatory in the context of procedures such as those within the remit of the SRB outside of crisis management proper, that is resolution planning, as will be explored in Section IV.[31] This is because a deliberative framework relies on the various understandings public actors bring to the table, with common procedures, including consultation and exchanges of information, creating 'arenas of justification' and exploring differences in current understanding of 'public interest'.[32] A number of characteristics of the EU regime – such attempts to break through siloed regulatory approaches by introducing requirements of exchange and structured consultations – reinforce similarities with deliberative supranationalism models. Assessing the overall regulatory architecture, and the resolution-planning procedures in particular, from the perspective of inter-institutional relations, sees the value of (public) expert deliberative processes which re-politicise insulated and technical policy choices within a complex architecture, overcoming the typical criticism of SRM design being a 'hybrid monster'.

LSE Law, Society and Economy Working Paper Series, 6/2015. W De Groen and D Gros meanwhile estimate the SRF to be sufficient in all but extreme circumstances, see WP De Groen and D Gros, *Estimating the Bridge Financing Needs of the Single Resolution Fund: How Expensive Is It to Resolve a Bank?* (Brussels, CEPS, 2015).

[26] Following BRRD, crisis-management measures are the implementation of resolution schemes in cases of banks failing, see Art 2(1)(102) of Directive 2014/59/EU of the European Parliament and of the Council of 15 May 2014 establishing a framework for the recovery and resolution of credit institutions and investment firms and amending Council Directive 82/891/EEC, and Directives 2001/24/EC, 2002/47/EC, 2004/25/EC, 2005/56/EC, 2007/36/EC, 2011/35/EU, 2012/30/EU and 2013/36/EU, and Regulations (EU) No 1093/2010 and (EU) No 648/2012, of the European Parliament and of the Council, OJ EU 2014 L 173/190 (BRRD).

[27] See in particular Schmidt (n 17) on the concept of 'throughput' legitimacy.

[28] See Moloney (n 6).

[29] M Busuoic, 'Friend of Foe? Inter-agency Co-operation, Organizational Reputation, and Turf' (2016) 94 *Public Administration* 40.

[30] See J Falke, 'Comitology After Lisbon: What is Left of Comitology as We Have Praised It?' in C Joerges and C Glinski (eds), *The European Crisis and the Transformation of Transnational Governance: Authoritarian Managerialism versus Democratic Governance* (Oxford, Hart Publishing, 2014).

[31] See Title II BRRD, 'Preparation', which covers tasks of resolution authorities such as resolution and recovery planning.

[32] O Gerstendberg and C Sabel, 'Directly-Deliberative Polyarchy: An Institutional Ideal for Europe?' in C Joerges and R Dehousse (eds), *Good Governance in Europe's Integrated Market* (Oxford, Oxford University Press, 2002).

Quite the opposite – some procedures within the architecture can be conceived in terms of inter-institutional accountability,[33] especially where traditional control and dismissal accountability models are less readily available in regimes which rely heavily on the concept of independence of technocratic authorities.[34] Political science frameworks which focus on inter-institutional relations, however, rely on the 'distinctiveness' of individual actors, that is, characteristics which clearly distinguish one authority from others in the eyes of their peers and supervised entities.[35] Before considering resolution-planning procedures specifically and the extent to which deliberative models are applicable to these, the next section will look in detail at how the SRB is to be distinguished from other financial regulators.

III. What is 'Specific' about the Single Resolution Board?

The Banking Union, as it has been implemented in the EU, and well described in this book, rests on two institutional pillars relating to supervision and resolution: the Single Supervisory Mechanism (SSM) and the Single Resolution Mechanism (SRM), underpinned by substantive regulations (the Single Rulebooks) outlined in the Capital Requirements Directive (CRD) IV package and the Bank Recovery and Resolution Directive (BRRD) for the two pillars respectively.[36] While it cannot be excluded that the complexity of Banking Union's architecture is the inevitable result of constitutional constraints as well as political economy explanations relating to the reluctance of certain Member States to centralise powers with the European Central Bank (ECB) or at the EU level, to make sense of the consequent architecture, a crucial step is understanding precisely the distinctiveness of the SRB's mandate. Such an approach is also suggested by recent political science research emphasising reputational distinctiveness as a key factor in ensuring successful cooperation between agencies.[37] Of course, there are rather obvious features which distinguish resolution authorities from other regulators: their very creation reflects the idea that specific technical expertise (such as with regard to

---

[33] M Everson and E Vos, 'Unfinished Constitutionalization: The Politicised Agency Administration and Its Consequences', (2016), Paper presented at TARN Conference, 'Constitutionality, powers and legitimacy of EU agencies or agency-like bodies' 10–11 November 2016, EUI, Florence.

[34] On notions of inter-institutional accountability within regulatory networks see Monti (n 20), on politicisation of administration and inter-institutional accountability see M Everson and E Vos (n 33).

[35] On role of reputational distinctiveness and intra-agency accountability, see Busuioc (n 29).

[36] For BRRD, see n 19 above, Directive 2013/36/EU of the European Parliament and of the Council of 26 June 2013 on access to the activity of credit institutions and the prudential supervision of credit institutions and investment firms, amending Directive 2002/87/EC and repealing Directives 2006/48/EC and 2006/49/EC (CRD IV). See S Madaus, 'Bank Failure and Pre-emptive planning' in M Haentjens and B Wessels (eds), *Bank Recovery and Resolution: A Conference Book* (The Hague, Eleven International Publishing, 2014) 50.

[37] See n 29 above.

the banking sector's structure) is required to achieve the stated goals of resolution, that is developing a capacity to identify interdependencies between actors and the banking system's critical functions.[38] The rationale behind ringfencing of resolution from other modes of intervention further stems from possible conflicts of interest between orderly management of failing or likely to fail banks and competition or other ongoing supervision type concerns.[39] At the same time to say that resolution authorities' *raison d'etre* is the complexity of the matter within their mandates is not to say very much.[40] A deeper exploration of the SRM finds its distinctiveness rests on two pillars: (a) the institutional set-up, and specifically the ways in which it differs from the SSM; and (b) the uniqueness of the SRB's mandate which focuses on 'critical functions' provided by the financial sector and 'public interest in financial stability' as unique concepts in EU law.

A. Institutional 'Specificity'

The SRM is a dynamic regulatory mechanism with a structure corresponding to its tasks;[41] it is composed of the 'core' SRB and national resolution authorities (NRAs) in participating Member States, with the SRB exercising overall responsibility for the functioning of the SRM.[42] The SRB – following the wording of the SRM Regulation – is a 'specific' Union agency.

Where the SRM is one of the pillars of the Banking Union, analysis of the mechanism has typically drawn on comparison with the SSM. Such a juxtaposition is flawed, however, for a number of reasons. First, while the SSM's legal basis can be found in a pre-existing competence to confer specific tasks with regard to prudential supervision of credit institutions on the ECB under Article 127(6) TFEU, the SRM was created with reference to the non-specific Article 114 TFEU, as an EU agency with the *Meroni* doctrine limitations this entails as per Court of Justice of the European Union jurisprudence.[43] Resolution law competences were therefore not conferred on an existing institution in line with a preconceived possibility under the Treaty, as was the case with the Single Supervisory Board (SSB), but a new EU body was created with specific tasks and objectives, which

---

[38] See V de Seriere, 'Recovery and Resolution Plans of Banks in the Context of the BRRD and the SRM: Some Fundamental Issues' in Busch and Ferrarini (n 5). Still, the EU state aid regime, prior to the enactment of the BRRD regime has been held to have served as a *de facto* resolution regime, see speech of Commissioner Joaquín Almunia, *Banks in distress and Europe's competition regime: On the road to the Banking Union*, 25 September 2013.

[39] Art 3(3) BRRD, recital 24 SRM Regulation.

[40] On in-depth analysis of BRRD implications also for daily operations of the supervised banks see T Huertas, *Safe to Fail – How Resolution Will Revolutionise Banking* (Basingstoke, Palgrave Macmillan, 2015).

[41] Art 43 SRM Regulation.

[42] Art 7 SRM Regulation.

[43] S Weatherill, 'Limits of Legislative Harmonization Ten Years After Tobacco Advertising: How the Court's Case Law Has Become a Drafting Guide' (2011) 12 *German Law Journal* 827.

must be interpreted functionally in the context of internal market.[44] The existence of EU competence for resolution, allowing for the creation of a new agency in particular, was considered necessary to ensure the functioning of the internal market given cross-border externalities of insufficient supervisory coordination in rescuing failing large financial institutions and distortions of the internal market generated by bank bailouts.[45] This rationale is reflected also in the differences in the scope of application of the two pillars. Credit institutions within the SRB's remit automatically include 'significant' banks as in the case of the SSB under the SSM Regulation,[46] with national authorities competent for the remaining banks.[47] The SRB's mandate however extends specifically also to 30 additional cross-border groups.[48] The SRM's 'significance test' design in this sense is more sensitive to cross-border and internal market bank activities than the SSM.[49]

Furthermore, while both the SRM and the SSM employ 'similar legal technology'[50] to repartition responsibilities between the 'core' (SRB) and the national authorities (NRAs), EU's resolution mechanism does so in a more dynamic and variable manner. In particular, the full composition of the supranational 'core' changes in the case of SRB. The agency's Executive Board, tasked with taking decisions with regard to resolution plans,[51] is composed of five full-time members (including the Chair),[52] in its executive formation; however, compulsory participation is required by those NRAs in which the bank under consideration is established, or has subsidiaries or branches. The five permanent members of the Executive Board are responsible for ensuring that executive decisions are 'coherent, appropriate and proportionate' despite the variable composition of

---

[44] See to this end, para 45 of Case C-217/04 *UK v European Parliament and Council*, EU:C:2006:279.

[45] On specific problems related to coordination of cross-border bank groups: PH Thomas, *Dexia: Vie et Mort D'un Monstre Bancaire* (Paris, Les Petits matins, 2012); RZ Wiggins, N Tente and A Metrick, 'European Banking Union C: Cross-Border Resolution – Fortis Group' (2015) Yale Program on Financial Stability Case Study 2014-5C-V1; on the costs of bank bailouts see H Hakenes and I Schnabel, 'Bank Bonuses and Bailouts' (2014) 46 *Journal of Money, Credit and Banking* 259; on 'financial trilemma' proclaiming in interconnected financial markets it is impossible to simultaneously enjoy free movement of capital, financial stability and independent monetary policy see D Schoenmaker, *Governance of International Banking: The Financial Trilemma* (Oxford, Oxford University Press, 2013). See also Legal Service of the Council of the European Union, Opinion on the Proposal for a Regulation of the European Parliament and of the Council establishing uniform rules and a uniform procedure for the resolution of credit institutions and certain investment firms in the framework of a Single Resolution Mechanism and a Single Bank Resolution Fund and amending Regulation (EU) No 1093/2010 of the European Parliament and of the Council, Interinstitutional File 2013/0253.

[46] This echoes the scope of Single Supervisory Board, as per Art 6(4) SSM Regulation.

[47] On division of tasks within SRM see Art 7 SRM Regulation.

[48] See Art 7(2)(b) SRM Regulation.

[49] For the list of cross-border groups see https://srb.europa.eu/sites/srbsite/files/5_for_publication_srb_website_list_of_other_cross_border_groups_1februar.pdf.

[50] N Moloney, 'European Banking Union: Assessing Its Risks and Resilience' (2014) 51 *Common Market Law Review* 1609.

[51] See Art 50(1) SRM Regulation.

[52] See Art 53(1) SRM Regulation.

the Board.[53] Furthermore, while being an institutionally distinct body, the SRB is embedded in a broader network of financial services' oversight as its executive sessions are attended not only by the European Commission (formally the agency's principal under EU delegation doctrine), but also the ECB[54] as permanent observers with a right of voice and access to *all* documents.[55] On an *ad hoc* basis the EBA may be invited to the meetings of the Executive Board, while resolution authorities of non-participating Member States shall be present when agenda items include deliberation on a banking group that has subsidiaries or significant branches in those non-participating Member States.[56] Further, the SRM Regulation envisages inviting representatives of the European Stability Mechanism to meetings of the Board.[57]

Implementation and enforcement of the decisions of the SRB rely on the national authorities: for example the determination of the minimum requirement for 'bail-in'-able funds (MREL) as discussed below in section IV.B, is to be addressed to NRAs, which are subsequently in charge of the implementation of this decision in respect of individual banks.[58] Decentralised implementation of the SRB's decisions in this case can be explained by fiscal implications of bank failure and resistance of Member States to give up their competences in this area,[59] though once the legislative choice was made to create a new agency, the EU constitutional doctrine of delegation stepped in, setting down a number of constraints with significant implications, well explored in literature.[60] These constraints on discretionary powers of agencies mean that the dynamics between the 'core' of the Mechanism and the national authorities as well as other institutional actors (European Commission, Council), are very different than in the case of the SSM.[61] Horizontally, or rather transversally with regard to other EU bodies, the EU delegation doctrine requires that at all stages of resolution planning the Commission is competent to set the boundaries of the SRB's discretion[62] and enjoys broad access

---

[53] Art 53(5) SRM Regulation, on decision-making procedures in the executive session for individual entities and cross-border groups see Art 55 SRM Regulation.

[54] The Article does not specify, however, if this concerns the monetary or prudential supervision arm of the ECB.

[55] Art 43(3) SRM Regulation.

[56] Art 53 SRM Regulation.

[57] See recital 35 and Art 30(6) SRM Regulation requiring that 'The Board shall endeavour to cooperate closely with any public financial assistance facility including the European Financial Stability Facility (EFSF) and the European Stability Mechanism (ESM), in particular in the extraordinary circumstances referred to in Art 27(9) and where such a facility has granted, or is likely to grant, direct or indirect financial assistance to entities established in a participating Member State'.

[58] See Arts 12(1), (13) and (14) SRM Regulation on the decision-making mechanism for significant banks, and Art 29 on implementation of decisions under the SRM Regulation.

[59] For an analysis of the legislative process and the drivers of the final SRM design see S Fabbrini and M Guidi, 'The European Banking Union: A Case of Tempered Supranationalism?', Chapter 9 in this volume.

[60] N Moloney (n 50) 1660; P Van Cleynenbreugel, '"Meroni" Circumvented?: Article 114 TFEU and EU Regulatory Agencies' (2014) 21 *Maastricht Journal of European and Comparative Law* 64.

[61] See S Grundmann, 'The European Banking Union and Integration', Chapter 4 in this volume.

[62] Recital 24 SRM Regulation.

to information, in particular the Board shall inform the Commission of 'any action it takes in order to prepare for resolution'.[63] In relation to the SRB's interaction with the ECB under resolution and pre-resolution procedures, the SRB must also transmit information from the Frankfurt supervisor back to its Brussels principal.[64] Vertically, within the Mechanism itself, the limits of the SRB's autonomy translate into limits on the type of decisions it can take with respect to market actors, hence the competences of NRAs are broader than those of national competent authorities under the SSM, also with regard to 'significant' institutions falling directly within the scope of the Board's purview. The SRB can take limited operational action, depending entirely on the NRA,[65] and there are limits to the direction that the SRB can make vide national authorities,[66] though the post-*ESMA* reading of delegation powers seems to allow the Board to override NRAs in certain cases.[67]

The degree of centralisation within the SRB is dynamic, where the fullest degree of delegation to the core[68] happens where the Board takes the decision on the resolution scheme adoption, with the potential use of the SRF.[69] The everyday SRM governance technology is more polyarchical than within the SSM, given the operational reliance on NRAs, cross-membership on its Board of various institutions,[70] and also – as will be shown below – through reliance on external input in the preparatory stages of resolution planning, involving broad consultations and exchanges of information. The SRM is therefore more akin to other types of networked, agency-led EU governance arrangements, and these should form the basis for any comparison and assessment, rather than the legally and conceptually very different SSM. At the same time, the SRB is indeed a 'specific', new type of an EU agency – the SRM Regulation affirms the independence of the Board, including that it shall not take nor seek instructions from other Union institutions

---

[63] Art 30(1) SRM Regulation, see also recital (26) which states that '... as an observer to the meetings of the Board, the Commission should, on an ongoing basis, check that the resolution scheme adopted by the Board complies fully with this Regulation, balances appropriately the different objectives and interests at stake, respects the public interest and that the integrity of the internal market is preserved ...'.

[64] Art 13(2) SRM Regulation thus requires the SRB to act as an intermediary between the supervisor/ECB and the European Commission.

[65] See Moloney (n 50) 1649.

[66] D Adamski, 'The ESMA Doctrine: A Constitutional Revolution and the Economics of Delegation' (2014) 39 *European Law Review* 812, at 822.

[67] Moloney (n 50) 1658.

[68] Albeit in a constrained way, where the decision-making procedure involves cumbersome cooperation between the Commission and the Council, and where the NRAs are charged with the final implementation of the resolution scheme.

[69] Art 18 SRM Regulation. Though the decision-making procedure for adoption of resolution scheme includes the Council as well as the European Commission in assessing the discretionary aspects of the scheme and state aid rules under Art 19 SRM Regulation. See I Angeloni and N Lenihan, 'Competition and State Aid Rules in the Time of Banking Union' in E Faia et al (eds), *Financial Regulation: A Transatlantic Perspective* (Cambridge, Cambridge University Press, 2015).

[70] Which naturally is asymmetrical, though the Memorandum of Understanding (MoU) between the SRB and the ECB sets down provisions for the SRB's participation in meetings of the SSB when relevant; such participation remains however at the discretion of the ECB, see para 5 of MoU.

or bodies, from any government of a Member State, or from any other public or private body.[71] The supranational character is further confirmed by qualified majority decision-making both in plenary and executive sessions[72] as well as the Board being the owner of the SRF.[73]

B. Distinctiveness of Resolution Policy Aims

The distinctiveness of the SRB is also evident in its mandate and objectives. Resolution policy aims to prevent, and in any case limit, the consequences of bank failure, given their disruptive effect on the broader economy and to minimise or in fact prevent the costs of any collapse from being imposed on the taxpayers.[74] Through clarifying *ex ante* processes and distribution of losses (eg through bail-in of the bank's creditors), the regime seeks to reduce moral hazard and remove perverse incentives associated with implicit bank subsidies, while bringing certainty for banks, their shareholders and creditors.[75] In this sense, the objective of resolution is making the system resilient *ex ante*[76] and banks safe to fail[77] by policy implementation being done in a forward-looking manner.[78] The SRM Regulation, following the wording of the BRRD, thus includes among the objectives of resolution: ensuring the continuity of critical functions; curtailing negative effects of bank failure on financial stability by preventing contagion and maintaining market discipline; and protecting public funds, depositors and creditors.[79] These objectives should nevertheless be read in the context of 'public interest in financial stability',[80] where EU resolution regime aims also at curtailing financial dominance.[81]

---

[71] Art 47 SRM Regulation, consider also recital (89) BRRD which recalls the need for a large margin of discretion in crisis management by resolution authorities.

[72] Art 52(1) SRM Regulation.

[73] Art 67 SRM Regulation. The modalities for the calculation of contributions of SRF are, however, set down in the Intergovernmental Agreement, see F Fabbrini, 'On Banks, Courts and International Law: The Intergovernmental Agreement on the Single Resolution Fund in Context' (2014) 21 *Maastricht Journal of European and Comparative Law* 444.

[74] European Council, *Conclusions of the European Council of 28/29 June 2012*.

[75] On argument that resolution law can be used by regulators to create 'constructive certainty' see Huertas (n 40).

[76] R Baldwin, M Cave and M Lodge, 'Regulation: The Field and the Developing Agenda' in R Baldwin, M Cave and M Lodge (eds), *The Oxford Handbook of Regulation* (Oxford, Oxford University Press, 2012) 10.

[77] See D Singh, 'Recovery and Resolution Planning: Reconfiguring Financial Regulation and Supervision' in Binder and Singh (n 5) 51; Huertas (n 40).

[78] CW Calomiris and S H Haber, *Fragile by Design: The Political Origins of Banking Crises and Scarce Credit* (Princeton, Princeton University Press, 2015).

[79] See Art 31(2) BRRD, Art 14(2) SRM Regulation.

[80] See S Cappiello, 'The Impact of the New Resolution Regime on "Banking as Usual"' in European Central Bank, *From Monetary Union to Banking Union, on the Way to Capital Markets Union New Opportunities for European Integration* (ECB Legal Conference, 2015) 191.

[81] MF Hellwig, 'Financial Stability and Monetary Policy' (2015) Preprints of the Max Planck Institute for Research on Collective Goods 2015/5.

Particularly noteworthy here is the focus on 'public interest in financial stability'[82] and 'protecting critical functions' – two areas protected specifically by the resolution authorities within the overall regulatory architecture.[83] Over the course of the crisis, 'financial stability' in various guises (such as 'financial stability of the euro area' or 'stability of the financial system'), has emerged as a new guiding objective in the EU constitutional landscape.[84] In the context of resolution law, it has been understood as a procedural step to determine whether the law applicable to a case of bank failing or likely to fail should be the EU resolution law or national insolvency law.[85] Potential interference with Article 16 of the EU Charter of Fundamental Rights,[86] also in the context of crisis jurisprudence of the European Court of Human Rights,[87] makes clear the significance of emphasis on public interest, as a necessary consideration where rights to conduct business, but also property, are interfered with. The focus of this test is, however, inward looking: that is, its crux is the interconnectedness of one bank with the system as a whole. 'Critical functions', meanwhile, are a relatively novel concept – seeking to distinguish and protect those functions of banking which serve the real economy, such as deposit-taking and lending to small and medium-sized entities (SMEs). Where these tests are conditions for the implementation of a resolution scheme,[88] the SRB is tasked with determining *ex ante* what they might be, also outside of the design and implementation of a resolution scheme. The responsibilities of the SRB in this regard must be read in the context of the general principles of the SRM outlined in the Regulation,[89] that is, through the lens of impact and inter-linkages of the banking sector with the broader economy or society as a whole,[90] thereby exceeding in terms of scope concerns of endogenous systemic stability only, which informed the pre-crisis regulatory design.[91] To that end, considerations of proximity to failure do not play the same role in banks' assessment under early intervention by the supervisor[92] as under resolution planning, that is, low

---

[82] See recital 46 SRM Regulation.

[83] On protecting public interest in financial stability see M Haentjens and B Wessels, 'Conclusions' in M Haentjens and B Wessels, *Research Handbook on Crisis Management in the Banking Sector* (Cheltenham, Edward Elgar Publishing, 2015). On critical functions see E Hupkes 'The Last Frontier: Protecting Critical Functions Across Borders' in E Wymeersch, K Hopt and G Ferrarini, *Financial Regulation and Supervision: A Post-Crisis Analysis* (Oxford, Oxford University Press, 2012).

[84] K Tuori, *European Constitutionalism* (Cambridge, Cambridge University Press, 2015).

[85] See Art 18 SRM Regulation, for detailed outline of resolution and recovery planning procedures see D Singh, 'Recovery and Resolution Planning' in Binder and Singh (n 5).

[86] Numerous references to the EU Charter, and in particular potential interference with the right to property and right to protect business, are made in BRRD and SRM. See eg recital 46 SRM Regulation.

[87] *Grainger v United Kingdom*, App No 34940/10, ECtHR (2012).

[88] Binder and Singh (n 5).

[89] Under Art 5 SRM Regulation these include integrity and unity of the internal market as well as 'financial stability, fiscal resources, the economy, the financing arrangements, the deposit guarantee scheme or the investor compensation scheme' of any Member State.

[90] See recital 49 SRM Regulation.

[91] E Davis, 'Towards a Typology for Systemic Financial Instability', http://bura.brunel.ac.uk/handle/2438/916.

[92] Art 27 BRRD, not reproduced in the SRM Regulation.

probability of default does not exclude intervention by resolution authorities.[93] EU resolution law thus is not just a pre-insolvency regime[94] or a crisis-containment mechanism,[95] its preventive focus on 'public' functions of private banks being one of the novelties of the post-crisis architecture.[96] Emphasis on protection of depositors in resolution further helps clarify those critical functions and the relevant public interest test with regard to proportionality analysis of any infringements of the right to property (eg in the case of bail-in) or freedom to conduct business (where authorities intervene in ownership and management structures).

The SRM further seeks to tackle a number of specific failures which occurred under the pre-crisis regulatory architecture: in particular time inconsistency of supervisory action. EU resolution law addresses this not only by creating an independent agency at the EU level (thereby addressing also national capture concerns), but specifically by having a countercyclical orientation, much like macroprudential policy of leaning against the wind, where the trade-offs and externalities are to be assessed through the lens of long-term rather than short-term impact of intervention in the financial sector. Differences in the assessment from (micro-prudential) supervisory and resolution perspectives can arise, for example where the time factor leads to divergent assessment of the desirable size of the entities from a static (risk diversification of large institutions) or more dynamic (consequences of them failing) view.[97] Resolution planning further seeks to escape the legal technology constraints which arise at proximity to failure such as exasperation of information asymmetries[98] or lack of tools to deal with systemic effects of failure of complex banks.[99] Resolution allows, much like reflexive legal strategies,[100] for the dynamic effect of resolution plans to kick in, with theoretical exercise in 'planning for failure' in the future translating into aligning banks' structures and activities in the present. It is the long-term, forward-planning orientation as well as consideration of effects of financial instability which extend beyond the financial system itself (ie connecting it to the real economy), which distinguish resolution from other modes of public intervention in the financial

---

[93] See Cappiello (n 80).

[94] On differences between bank insolvency and resolution see S Schelo, *Bank Resolution and Recovery Directive* (Alphen aan den Rijn, Kluwer Law International, 2015). For an in-depth juxtaposition between bank resolution and insolvency see G Moss, B Wessels and M Haentjens (eds), *EU Banking and Insurance Insolvency* 2nd edn (Oxford, Oxford University Press, 2017) and A Dombret, 'Solving the Too-Big-To-Fail-Problem for Financial Institutions' in AR Dombret and PS Kenadjian (eds), *The Bank Recovery and Resolution Directive: Europe's Solution for 'Too Big to Fail'?* (Berlin, De Gruyter, 2013).

[95] P Honohan and L Laeven (eds), *Systemic Financial Crises: Containment and Resolution* (Cambridge, Cambridge University Press, 2005).

[96] See Haentjens and Wessels (n 83) 567.

[97] See Cappiello (n 80).

[98] Consider that information asymmetries play a key role in underlying instability of bank intermediation, as shown in the traditional bank run model, D Diamond and PH Dybvig, 'Bank Runs, Deposit Insurance, and Liquidity' (1983) 91(3) *Journal of Political Economy* 401.

[99] R DeYoung, M Kowalik and J Reidhill, 'A Theory of Failed Bank Resolution: Technological Change and Political Economics' (2013) 9 *Journal of Financial Stability* 612.

[100] J Black, 'Proceduralizing Regulation: Part I' (2000) 20 *Oxford Journal of Legal Studies* 597.

sector. The dynamic nature of resolution objectives, as well as the time-variant nature of the tools at the disposal of resolution authorities, implies that the post-crisis regulatory architecture is mobile, thereby making the 'joint' mechanisms all the more important and – in line with basic tenants of any architectural design – their proper functioning a precondition of the edifice's overall resilience.

The SRB is thus a 'specific' agency in EU constitutional terms, but also one with a very distinct mandate among other financial regulators. Where the function of resolution powers is to pursue specific notions of financial stability and protection of critical banking functions, with an explicitly 'public' and long-term angle, EU law doctrine on delegating powers to agencies requires additional factors be taken into account. First, given the constitutional constraints of delegation to agencies under Article 114 TFEU outlined above, and in particular the *ENISA* and *ESMA* judgments, the relevant public interest in financial stability and critical functions need to be construed in the context of functioning of EU internal market as a whole. While a duty of care for the internal market underpins the SSM,[101] arguably there the principle is much more of a general nature, not guiding the interpretation of the tasks conferred on the SRB within the regulatory architecture. Considerations of integrity of the internal market are a necessary condition for legality of the decisions taken by the SRB, with the non-discrimination principle forcefully reaffirmed under the SRM Regulation.[102] The SRB's legal basis – even as its scope is limited to banks in participating Member States – means the public interest in financial stability relates to the EU as a whole, a point of particular relevance, for example, in the context of cross-border groups operating both within the Banking Union and in non-participating Member States.

IV. Resolution Planning and 'Going Concern' Cooperation Between Financial Regulators

The SRB's uniqueness, as outlined in the previous section, is helpful in understanding its role and tasks in procedures outside of resolution, that is, in crisis prevention and resolution planning.[103] As far as crisis management is concerned,[104] when an individual bank is deemed failing or likely to fail, the SRB is charged with preparation and implementation of resolution schemes, which outline the use

---

[101] See Art 1 SSM Regulation and parallel phrasing in Art 6 SRM Regulation.

[102] Art 6 SRM Regulation, see also E Ferran, 'European Banking Union and the EU Single Financial Market: More Differentiated Integration, or Disintegration?' in A Ott, E Vos and B De Witte (eds), *Between Flexibility and Disintegration: The Trajectory of Differentiation in EU Law* (Cheltenham, Edward Elgar Publishing, 2017).

[103] On distinctions between crisis management, containment and resolution preceding the 2007–08 financial crisis see Honohan and Laeven (n 95).

[104] See Art 2(1)(102) BRRD for the definition of 'crisis management measures' as a resolution action or appointment of a special manager.

of resolution tools (sale, bridge bank, bail-in, asset separation) to achieve resolution objectives.[105] Beyond crisis management proper, however, the SRB's tasks are manifold also in stable states when banks are going concerns, and include crisis prevention measures,[106] preparation of resolution plans, and assessment of recovery plans.[107] In the context of resolution planning, the SRB assesses banks' 'resolvability',[108] identifies their 'critical functions', and determines the minimum eligible own funds and liabilities requirement (MREL).[109] Resolution planning thus combines measures with direct impact upon going concern operation of financial institutions with a partly theoretical exercise of preparation for failure.

As has already been suggested above, resolution planning procedures foresee ample coordination between the various institutions of the EU's regulatory architecture. This coordination can be explained in two ways. First, in exercising these tasks the SRB interferes with day-to-day micro-prudential supervision exercised by the SSM – without coordination there is a risk of conflicting commands being issued by different regulators. Second, exchange and coordination allows for pooling of information and deliberation on policy implementation. Coordination between authorities is procedurally organised at the level of individual procedures under the relevant provisions of the Single Rulebook as well as in the SRM Regulation which sets down general principles for cooperation[110] and requires a specific Memorandum of Understanding to be concluded between the ECB and the SRB.[111] The Memorandum covers a broad range of arrangements for cooperation and exchange of information, emphasising that supervision and regulation are mutually dependent, and that mutual trust is necessary with regard to treatment of information. Various modes of information provision, consultation and cooperation are distinguished depending on the phase of resolution action: planning, early intervention and resolution. Specific areas of cooperation include on-side inspections, drafting of the annual SRB work programme and determining order of priority of claims in resolution.[112] Provisions for settlement of any disputes related to information exchange are made under the MoU, though these are limited to bilateral settlement of disputes, in the last instance at the level of senior management and Board Members of the SRB and Executive Board of the ECB.[113]

---

[105] See Art 18 SRM Regulation outlines the resolution procedure, including its interaction with state aid rules.

[106] See Art 2(1)(103) BRRD.

[107] Arts 8 and 10(2) SRM Regulation.

[108] Art 10 SRM Regulation.

[109] Art 12 SRM Regulation.

[110] Arts 30–32 SRM Regulation set down an obligation to cooperate with ECB/SSM, Council, Commission ESFS/ESM, modalities of information exchange between the Board and NRAs as well as cooperation with authorities in non-participating Member States.

[111] See recital 4 and para 12 of Memorandum of Understanding on cooperation and information exchange concluded between the Single Resolution Board and the European Central Bank on 22 December 2015 ('ECB/SRB MoU').

[112] These additional areas of cooperation (not outlined in BRRD or SRM Regulation) seem to impose requirements solely on the SRM.

[113] See Art 30(7) SRM Regulation and para 15 ECB/SRB MoU.

MoUs are nonetheless soft-law instruments, and in terms of cross-border super-visory cooperation have been notoriously weak over the course of the crisis.[114] Further, information asymmetries with regard to information obtained from supervised entities will be present, in particular given the ECB's double role as a monetary and supervisory authority, notwithstanding provisions made for Chinese walls between the two sets of tasks.[115] Where powers of investigation directly by the SRM are already limited, any asymmetry is reinforced further by one-sided insti-tutional cross-membership, where the ECB has a permanent observer on the SRB Board, while the same privilege is not extended to the Banking Union's resolution authority.[116] The comparative advantage of the supervisory mechanism over that of resolution in these terms is strong, even if the legislative framework attempts to alleviate any asymmetries through proceduralisation of cooperation procedures, specifically in the context of resolution planning.[117] However, as has already been suggested, the distinctiveness of the SRB relies also in its nature as a regulator one-step-removed from ongoing direct supervision, exercising a mandate embedded in forward-looking public interest and internal market considerations, meaning such asymmetries might not necessarily impede on its ability to perform its tasks: different objectives require different tools.

Where resolution plans are 'an essential component of effective resolution',[118] EU resolution law distinguishes between recovery (prepared by the bank under the guidance of the supervisor) and resolution plans (drawn up by the resolu-tion authority).[119] Resolution plans outline actions to be taken under a number of instability scenarios, under the assumption that control over the troubled bank has been transferred to the public authorities.[120] The plans are the basis of, but not necessarily the same as, resolution schemes, adopted in relation to a concrete bank failure,[121] although any deviation should be duly justified by effectiveness concerns.[122] Resolution plans are to include: a demonstration of how critical functions[123] and core business lines could be legally and economically separated from other functions so as to ensure their continuity ('continuity of critical

---

[114] E Hupkes, '"Living Wills" – An International Perspective' in AR Dombret and PS Kenadjian (eds), *The Bank Recovery and Resolution Directive: Europe's Solution for 'Too Big to Fail'?* (Berlin, De Gruyter, 2013) 72.

[115] The MoU between ECB and the SRB is cosigned, on the SSB side by representatives of both the monetary and the supervisory arm of the ECB.

[116] The MoU makes provisions for 'institutional representation' of the Chair of the SRB at Supervisory Board meetings for items relating to the tasks and responsibilities of the SRB, para 5.1.

[117] E Wymeersch, 'The Single Supervisory Mechanism or "SSM", Part One of the Banking Union' (2015) *National Bank of Belgium Working Paper*.

[118] See recital 25 BRRD.

[119] R Hockett, 'Macroprudential Turn: From Institutional Safety and Soundness to Systematic Financial Stability in Financial Supervision' (2014) 9 *Virginia Law & Business Review* 201.

[120] See Art 6(2) SRM Regulation. In a sense, instability scenarios mirror the stress testing approach of supervisors.

[121] Art 18(1) and (6) SRM Regulation.

[122] See recital 67 and Art 23 SRM Regulation.

[123] For definitions see Art 2(1)(35) BRRD.

functions'); provisions for the financing of resolution without public support (including Emergency Liquidity Assistance (ELA) facilities provided by central banks); a description of critical interdependencies of the bank; and a communication plan.[124]

The SRB's Executive Board draws up the resolution plans for banks within its remit,[125] thereby determining also the potential impact of a given credit institution on the system as a whole: with regard to institutions which are not systemic, this requirement can be lifted or relaxed via simplified resolution-planning obligations.[126] In preparation of the resolution plans, the SRB relies on information provided by the NRAs, which must duly share any relevant information, notwithstanding the investigatory powers which the SRB enjoys itself.[127] The SRB/ESM MoU further provides – to avoid duplication of information requirements on banks – that where any information to be requested from the bank by the SRB is already in the possession of the ECB, the latter will provide it to the former, in line with the procedures for information exchange outlined above.[128] In preparing the plans, broad inter-institutional consultation is required: in particular the SRB must consult the ECB, national supervisory authorities and NRAs, including the resolution authorities of non-participating Member States where a significant branch is located.[129] The SRB further takes part in multi-jurisdictional EU group resolution-planning exercises for entities active in non-participating Member States.[130] The *ex ante* consultation requirement is coupled with an *ex post* information requirement. In particular, the SRB must transmit the resolution plans to the ECB, even where representatives of both the Commission and the ECB are present in executive sessions of the Board.[131] In contrast to the US, resolution plans are not made public,[132] and in fact are made under very restrictive confidentiality requirements.

---

[124] BRRD Annex furthermore outlines specifically the list of relevant considerations, and in particular the areas which the SRB should take into account when making the decision. The comprehensiveness of that list at the same time reinforced the proceduralisation of the assessment (with impact on review).

[125] Art 7 and Art 54(2)(a) SRM Regulation.

[126] Art 11 SRM Regulation; this is not the case though with regard to institutions which are under direct supervision of the SSB as per Art 6(4) SSM Regulation.

[127] Art 8(4) SRM Regulation.

[128] See para 1.3 ECB/SRB MoU.

[129] No representation is provided for authorities from branches of non-EU Member States.

[130] Recital 91 SRM Resolution recalls that SRB replaces national authorities in the context of resolution colleges, as provided for in the BRRD. Article 32 SRM Regulation further provides for the framework of cooperation between SRB and resolution authorities of non-participating Member States, including where 'the Board, the ECB and the resolution authorities and competent authorities of the non-participating Member States shall conclude memoranda of understanding describing in general terms how they will cooperate with one another in the performance of their tasks under Directive 2014/59/EU. … the Board shall conclude a memorandum of understanding with the resolution authority of each non-participating Member State that is home to at least one global systemically important institution'. Note though that Article 31(2) SRM Regulation disapplies BRRD provisions concerning resolution collages among the NRAs of participating Member States. Furthermore, disagreement in these collegiate bodies is mediated by the EBA.

[131] Arts 13 and 43(3) SRM Regulation.

[132] For the rationale underpinning secrecy surrounding resolution plans, including commercial interests, see recitals 36 and 86 BRRD.

They are to be updated at least annually, though any revision can be prompted by the ECB/national competent authorities (NCAs)[133] or banks themselves, making the procedure an interactive one rather than purely top-down. Finally, in addition to substantive information necessary for resolution planning, the SRB relies on other EU bodies for detailed rules on the drafting process: that is, the technical regulatory standards prepared by EBA and approved by the European Commission on the basis of BRRD.[134]

Where the resolution-planning procedure sets the general terms of cooperation with other EU institutions, such as consultation and exchange of information, as well as the role of other rule-making bodies (in particular the EBA), two concrete assessments embedded in the resolution-planning process provide further insight into the logic of inter-institutional cooperation embedded within EU's regulatory architecture: that is, the assessment of the bank's resolvability and the determination of MREL. In particular, in the context of these two exercises, the level of proceduralisation of inter-institutional cooperation and consultation becomes even more granular.

A. Resolvability Assessment

Elimination of reliance on public support in cases of bank failure is central to the paradigm shift marked by the new EU resolution law, and the assessment of resolvability conducted by the Board to this end is meant as a credible commitment. Put bluntly, 'if [authorities] cannot figure out how to do the job in theory, then hope for anything other than bail-out in practice must be slim'.[135] Resolvability assessment is to be conducted both in the context of resolution plans prepared by the SRB and recovery plans prepared by banks under the supervision of competent authority (ie the supervisor). In the case of the latter, the SRB shall make recommendations to the supervisors on any actions proposed by the entity as part of the recovery plan, which could adversely impact the use of resolution tools.[136] Resolvability means that the institution can be wound-down without '(a) extraordinary public financial support beside the use of the Fund ...; (b) any central

---

[133] Article 8(12) SRM Regulation.

[134] Commission Delegated Regulation (EU) 2016/1075 of 23 March 2016 supplementing Directive 2014/59/EU of the European Parliament and of the Council with regard to regulatory technical standards specifying the content of recovery plans, resolution plans and group resolution plans, the minimum criteria that the competent authority is to assess as regards recovery plans and group recovery plans, the conditions for group financial support, the requirements for independent valuers, the contractual recognition of write-down and conversion powers, the procedures and contents of notification requirements and of notice of suspension and the operational functioning of the resolution colleges, C/2016/1691.

[135] JE Castañeda, DG Mayes and G Wood (eds), *European Banking Union: Prospects and Challenges* (Routledge, Taylor & Francis Group, 2016) 46.

[136] Art 10(2) SRM Regulation, for BRRD parallel see Art 17. For comment see Cappiello (n 80).

bank emergency liquidity assistance; or (c) any central bank liquidity assistance provided under non-standard collateralisation, tenor and interest rate terms.[137] It further excludes reliance on ELA,[138] the Eurozone incarnation of the conventional function of central banking – the lender of last resort, which does not necessarily imply that a bank is failing or likely to fail, but rather that it operates in a liquidity-constrained environment. Exclusion of ELA from resolvability scenarios could be held to interfere with the performance of functions within the remit of ECB (naturally the monetary rather than supervisory arm).[139] On the other hand, however, given the somewhat dubious use of ELA during the financial crisis,[140] this provision highlights that the objective of decoupling the loop between states and their banks extends to the dependencies between central banks and credit institutions in the context of smooth transmission of monetary policy, thus raising the threshold for endogenous resilience of the supervised banks – the building up of which lies precisely within the mandate of the SRB (section III).

Beyond aiming at reducing the dependence on public support, the assessment of resolvability includes wider considerations, reflecting the broad notion of public interest in financial stability discussed above. A credit institution is to be deemed resolvable if its winding-up through normal insolvency proceedings or through resolution is possible without 'adverse consequences for financial systems ... and with view to ensuring the continuity of critical functions'.[141] The assessment of resolvability thus raises the central question of which banking operations are critical or socially useful, in the sense of being critical to the functioning of economies of Member States and of the EU as a whole.[142] The assessment is to be carried out after consulting the competent authorities, including the ECB.[143] Incorporating the broader macroprudential and cross-border perspective, the ESRB is also to be consulted inasmuch as it issues relevant warnings and recommendations[144] and EBA insofar as it develops the relevant criteria in considering the identification and measurement of systemic risk. While the SRM Regulation does not make clear what are the modalities under which the SRB is to take the outcome of these consultations into account, given the (annually) repeated game-type arrangement of resolution planning, and resulting institutional incentives for cooperation, broad formally mandated consultation implies a role for the SRB in reconciling

---

[137] Art 10 SRM Regulation.

[138] Within the EU framework ELA provided by the national central banks within the European System of Central Banks (ESCB) see M O'Connell, 'The Legal Framework for the Provision of Emergency Liquidity Assistance within the ESCB' (2013) 3 *Zeitschrift für Europarechtliche Studien* 261.

[139] For this argument see I Angeloni and N Lenihan in Faia et al (n 69).

[140] G Psaroudakis, 'State Aids, Central Banks and the Financial Crisis' (2012) 9 *European Company and Financial Law Review* 194.

[141] Art 10(4) BRRD.

[142] On the question of 'what is banking?' see eg G Gorton, *Slapped by the Invisible Hand: The Panic of 2007* (Oxford, Oxford University Press, 2010) arguing the post-crisis context blurs the lines between various forms of financial activity, not all of which can be defined as banking proper.

[143] Art 10(1) SRM Regulation.

[144] Art 10(5) SRM Regulation.

the micro- and macro perspectives in drawing up of resolution plans, in particular where it relies on other authorities – including the NRAs and the supervisor – for the enforcement of any measures related to removing impediments to resolvability once these are identified.[145] After all, even where resolvability assessment plays a central role in limiting negative externalities of failure, and in many ways is *the* policy to counter the 'too-big-to-fail' problem,[146] the powers which the SRB enjoys to remove structural, operational impediments to resolvability within the supervised banks are limited. Where in its assessment of recovery plans or preparation of resolution plans, the Board identifies obstacles to a controlled resolution process, it prepares a report addressed to the bank (in cooperation with supervisors), analysing the substantive impediments to effective implementation of resolution tools, including suggestions of any legal and structural measures to ensure resolvability, bearing in mind – given the right to freedom of business – the bank's business model.[147]

The bank concerned has up to four months to propose measures to tackle the identified shortcomings. The Board is required to forward this information to competent authorities (supervisors), the EBA and the resolution authorities of non-participating Member States where significant branches of the entity are located. Where the measures proposed by the bank are not deemed to be enough, the Board will take a decision (after consulting the supervisor and the designated macroprudential authority), instructing the NRA to require the bank to take a particular set of measures, such as revising intra-group financial arrangements, limiting exposures, divesting specific assets, refraining from entering new business lines or issuing new MREL instruments. It is useful to recall here that the Single Supervisor has at its disposal similarly incisive powers of direction as part of the Supervisory Review and Evaluation Process.[148] Where in the case of SRM these powers are more precisely formulated (eg requiring restriction of existing business lines; operational and legal changes to the entity's structure or issuance of liabilities), the SRM Regulation emphasises the principle of proportionality, where the requirement imposed is proportionate when it takes into account 'the effect of the measures on the business of the institution, its stability and its ability to contribute to the economy, on the internal market for financial services and on the financial stability in other Member States and the Union as a whole'.[149] Further instructions

---

[145] Though Art 17 of ESRB Regulation sets the framework outlining the follow-up to recommendations of the ESRB.

[146] eg Dombret (n 94).

[147] Art 10(7) SRM Regulation; JH Binder, 'Resolution Planning and Structural Bank Reform within the Banking Union' in J Castañeda, DG Mayes and G Wood (eds), *European Banking Union: Prospects and Challenges* (Abingdon, Routledge, Taylor & Francis Group, 2016).

[148] See Art 4(1)(i) and 16(2) SSM Regulation and Art 104 CRD IV. See section IV.C for further discussion on duplicated procedures between supervisors and resolution authorities.

[149] Art 10(10) SRM Regulation stipulates in particular that 'the Board shall take into account the threat to financial stability of those impediments to resolvability and the effect of the measures on the business of the institution, its stability and its ability to contribute to the economy, on the internal market for financial services and on the financial stability in other Member States and the Union as a

on the application of measures to reduce or remove impediments to resolvability are covered by the EBA Guidelines.[150]

Three elements are key here. First, the assessment of the resolvability of the Banking Union's banks is to be done in the context of a broader macroprudential framework (under the remit of ESRB) as well as the EU-wide framework for legal harmonisation ('Single Rulebook') and supervisory convergence ('Single Handbook for Supervision') developed by EBA. Despite being an element of a resolution plan for a single institution, the assessment of resolvability is to include considerations from a broad range of vantage points, including micro- and macroprudential aspects. The SRB plays a central coordinating role between stances of distinct authorities (including NRAs) in addition to its own, inviting deliberation on a number of under-defined, yet central concepts, such as 'critical functions'. Proceduralisation of consultation here creates a space for inter-institutional deliberation, through exchange of information, and operational reliance on other authorities for implementation.

Second, the power of direction of the Board is significantly limited with regard to resolution planning, with the intermediating role of the NRAs in directing the credit institutions to remove impediments to resolvability. Reliance on other actors for enforcement underpins the deliberative nature of the resolution-planning process: a form of consensus around the resolution plans can be assumed to be necessary. At the same time, notwithstanding convergence of practice which might occur in the networked SRM, the dynamics of these processes are likely to differ across participating Member States, depending on the national supervisory architecture, culture and tradition. Further with resolution law being a new area of law in the EU, it is likely to be shaped through the interaction with other, not yet harmonised, areas of law, such as national insolvency law. These factors lend an experimentalist aura to the process, even if within the dynamic SRM centralisation, the overall SRB oversight addresses public capture and related forbearance concerns at the national level, at least through increased (intrainstitutional) transparency and accountability.[151]

Third, resolvability assessment connects recovery and resolution-planning tasks, where a similar assessment is carried out by the resolution authority with regard to a plan it draws up itself, and with regard to a plan drawn up by the bank. In the case of the former SRM authorities (SRB via the NRAs) can direct the institution to remove impediments to resolvability. In the context of recovery

---

whole. The Board shall also take into account the need to avoid any impact on the institution or the group concerned which would go beyond what is necessary to remove the impediment to resolvability or would be disproportionate.'

[150] European Banking Authority, 'Guidelines on the specification of measures to reduce or remove impediments to resolvability and the circumstances in which each measure may be applied under Directive 2014/59/EU', 19 December 2014.

[151] See CJ Lindgren, 'Pitfalls in Managing Closures of Financial Institutions' in Honohan and Laeven (n 95) 76.

plans, developed in a somewhat more intensive supervisory relationship, the SRB's powers are limited to the general power to make recommendations to the supervisor.[152] Nevertheless, the broad definition of financial stability provided for in the SRM Regulation, implies that any proportionality tests applicable in the case of any requirements imposed by the SRB in the context of resolvability assessment must be different than when similar powers are exercised by the supervisor. This introduces important caveats distinguishing the two procedures, which can be conceived also as duplicating each other as a form of checks and balances and a mechanism of expert inter-institutional accountability.[153]

B. MREL Amount Calibration[154]

As part of resolution planning, the resolution authorities are to set the minimum requirement for own funds and eligible liabilities (ie the loss absorption and recapitalisation amounts, known as MREL) – a key post-crisis innovation oriented at ensuring resolution tools and bail-in in particular, can be made operational in crisis, but also that the costs of failure are distributed between the shareholders and the banks' creditors. The SRB sets this ratio for each institution under its direct responsibility, though a minimum of 8 per cent is set for access to the SRF or other extraordinary public support.[155] The MREL requirement indicates the level of own funds and liabilities, which can be made subject to write down and conversion powers both under resolution and in the context of early intervention measures. Its objective is to ensure that the institution's CET1 ratio, necessary to meet the requirement for continuing authorisation under the CRD IV requirements, can be met under stressed and crisis scenarios. As far as it is to include 'bail-in'-able debt, MREL further creates a specific, new type of a stakeholder, a creditor liable to absorb losses outside of insolvency procedures – the holder of 'bail-in'-able bonds. The SRB is not only competent for setting this amount, but also has the power to exclude certain types of liabilities from bail-in.[156] The setting of MREL in a bank group context implies making a choice between single-point-of-entry and multiple-point-of-entry strategies in relation to cross-border banks, that is, deciding on whether resolution in a cross-border context will be coordinated or fragmented along border lines.[157] The import of setting the amount

---

[152] In the case of recovery planning, the resolvability assessment focuses on the impact of the actions proposed by the entity itself, on provisions related to cooperation between supervisor and the resolution authority see para 7 ECB/SRB MoU and Art 10(2) SRM Regulation.

[153] See further section IV.C on the implementation of the early intervention measures.

[154] Although as of December 2017 the MREL requirement is undergoing significant changes, the general principles of are likely to remain the same.

[155] Art 27(7)(a) SRM Regulation.

[156] See Art 44(3) BBRD.

[157] See recital (80) BRRD.

for daily business conduct of banks and the market is self-evident, inasmuch as MREL alters the relationships between actors of bank governance in particular.[158]

In setting the MREL requirement, the SRB consults with the supervisor,[159] and specifically – as outlined in the MREL Implementing Technical Standards (ITS)[160] – it relies on and requests any specific information from the SSM.[161] The SRB exercises discretion with regard to the amount of MREL, though whenever it deviates from the level calculated automatically pursuant to the ITS, it must provide the supervisor with a reasoned explanation of its decision in a form of inter-institutional accountability.[162] At the same time, in terms of organising between different types of authorities, the SRB coordinates group entity supervision and with authorities responsible for subsidiaries both in non-participating Member States and third countries.[163] This is of particular importance as the so-called 'living wills' were seen in the early phases of the crisis as a means to overcome cross-border coordination problems where intra-group financing and support was found lacking over the course of the crisis.[164] Under original BRRD design, the SRB sets the MREL amount on an individual basis for each of bank's subsidiaries.[165] The requirement decision[166] will be addressed to the NRAs, which have the power to implement the instruction of the Board with respect to banks. Similarly, the verification and enforcement of MREL is to be conducted through NRAs.[167]

---

[158] For a commentary on bank corporate governance implications see S Grundmann, C Petit and A Smoleńska, 'Banking Governance: The EU Regime' in F Barrière (ed), *Le traitement des difficultés des établissements bancaires et institutions financières: Approche croisee* (Paris, LexisNexis, 2017).

[159] Art 12(1) SRM Regulation and Art 45(6) BRRD.

[160] Where SRM continues to apply in tandem and in parallel with the BRRD, the position of the Board and its competences vide the determination of MREL are further affected by the European Commission's legislative competences under Art 45(18) BRRD and Art 12(18) SRM Regulation. In the process of adoption of MREL Delegated Regulation (see n 161 below), EBA expressed dissent over amendments proposed by the European Commission to its draft standards which in its view would undermine their effectiveness. Such rare open disagreement further brings attention to the role of the Commission as the overarching institution for the post-crisis EU framework, bringing the various modes of intervention – supervision and resolution, but also legislative/convergence measures – under a common umbrella, raising the question of the extent to which it is well placed to reconcile tensions which exists between them. See EBA, 'EBA expresses dissent', Press release, 9 February 2016.

[161] See Art 1(2) Commission Delegated Regulation (EU) 2015/1450 of 25 May 2016 supplementing Directive 2014/59/EU of the European Parliament and of the Council with regard to regulatory technical standards specifying the criteria relating to the methodology for setting the minimum requirement for own funds and eligible liabilities, OJ 2016 L 237/1 ('MREL Delegated Regulation').

[162] Art 1(6) MREL Delegated Regulation.

[163] Art 45 BRRD and MREL Delegated Regulation.

[164] E Avgouleas, C Goodhart and D Schoenmaker, 'Living Wills as a Catalyst for Action' (2010) 4 DSF Policy Paper.

[165] Art 12(9) SRM Regulation, see also Art 45(9) BRRD which provides for the procedure for coordination between group level authority and other resolution authorities, including a mediating role for the EBA where no decision can be reached. In any case, decision of the group-level resolution authority is binding on Member States concerned.

[166] Art 12(13) SRM Regulation.

[167] See Art 12(14) SRM Regulation, especially: 'Board shall address its determination to the national resolution authorities. The national resolution authorities shall implement the instructions of the Board in accordance with Art 29. The Board shall require that the national resolution authorities verify

While MREL might be the cornerstone of the new regulatory paradigm, centralisation under the SRB is limited to the determination of the amount required, with the resolution authority reliant on other authorities for information input, as well as implementation and enforcement.

C. Early Intervention and Recovery Plans as Alternatives to Resolution

Where the SRB coordinates the process of resolution planning by drawing also on the expertise of other EU bodies and national authorities, the grey area between crisis prevention through resolution-planning and crisis-management measures in the Banking Union is the dominion of the SSB, under whose authority recovery plans are to be implemented as early intervention measures under BRRD/SSM Regulation framework.[168] Bank resolution is the last resort scenario, which is why the responsibility for recovery – public intervention in the daily management of the bank under the spectre of resolution, which still does not entail complete takeover by public authorities – is held by the supervisor. The rationale for distinguishing between responsibilities for recovery and resolution plans is not clear, with international experts of the International Monetary Fund (IMF) recommending both competences to be granted to the resolution authority.[169] Given the choice of the EU legislator, Section 2 of the BRRD concerning recovery planning is not replicated in the SRM Regulation, but nevertheless its provisions apply with respect to the SRB inasmuch as it is the competent resolution authority for significant banks within the Banking Union.[170] The 'specific' agency thus plays a role in recovery and early intervention procedures led by the supervisor, in particular with regard to: (a) assessment of resolvability aspects of the recovery plan as discussed above;[171] and (b) monitoring the implementation of early intervention procedures (which entails preparation of resolution schemes).

Early intervention measures[172] include the implementation of actions outlined in the bank's recovery plan, and can include change of senior management and management body of the bank in question, at the request of supervisor or when

---

and ensure that institutions and parent undertakings maintain the minimum requirement for own funds and eligible liabilities.'

[168] Note that way BRRD covers both recovery and resolution, provisions related to the former are only included in the SSM Regulation, not the SRM Regulation. Specifically on the SREP processes, which are the pre-recovery phase, and competences of the supervisor in this regard see also Art 4 SSM Regulation and Art 104 CRD IV Directive.

[169] See T Tressel, 'Single Resolution Mechanism' in C Enoch and IMF (eds), *From Fragmentation to Financial Integration in Europe* (Washington, IMF, 2014) 247.

[170] See Art 5 SRM outlining the relationship between SRM and BRRD.

[171] Under Art 6(4) BRRD the supervisor shall transmit the recovery plan to the resolution authority, which in turn can make recommendations for action to be taken by the bank, in particular with regard to resolvability.

[172] Art 27 BRRD.

particular indicators are triggered.[173] The supervisor shall inform the SRB of any measures it intends to take under the procedure. At the same time, ECB and NCAs are required to transmit without delay any information necessary for the finalisation of a resolution scheme at this stage to the SRB, including specific information necessary for valuation of assets and liabilities.[174] In one of the rare examples of the Board's direct powers with respect to credit institutions, it has the power to require the institution to contact potential purchasers in preparation for resolution.[175] A requirement of consistency is further in place between early intervention measures adopted by the supervisor and the process of preparation of a resolution scheme by the SRB.[176] Proportionality of actions taken by the authorities could be proposed as one possible benchmark for consistency in this context, especially given the emphasis on proportionality under the SRM Regulation. There are clear limits, however, to how incisive supervisory action can be in this regard without triggering fears of the institution actually failing or being likely to fail.[177] The parallelism which exists between the role of the supervisor and resolution authorities in early intervention measures and resolution raises numerous questions, including the role which such a grey area plays in transition to the new resolution regime, which only came into force fully in 2016. For the purposes of the present inquiry, however, what is key is duplication itself, where the role of supervisors under the early warning mechanism mirrors that of the resolution authorities under resolution planning – creating a system of checks and balances under the overall regulatory architecture, and thus contributing to inter-institutional accountability. The proceduralisation of cooperation under these procedures meanwhile, creates yet another deliberative space between the authorities involved, for example with regard to particular tools used, and their market impact.

V. Resolution-Planning 'Joints' of the Banking Union Regulatory Architecture

Even as the complexity and multi-stage procedures installed at the heart of EU financial regulatory architecture can be seen to impede not only the effectiveness of the Banking Union, but also prevent democratic control over the technocratic decision-making procedures, the above considerations have sought to explore the position of the SRB from a somewhat different angle. The future-oriented and

---

[173] Art 28 BRRD.

[174] Art 13(2) SRM; RZ Wiggins, M Wedow and A Metrick, 'The European Banking Union B: The Single Resolution Mechanism' (2015) *Yale Program on Financial Stability Case Study* 2014-5B-v1.

[175] ie potential implementation sale of business tool, Art 39 BRRD see L Enriques and G Hertig, 'Shadow Resolutions as a no-no in a Sound Banking Union' in Faia et al (n 69) 160.

[176] Art 13(5) SRM Regulation.

[177] This determination can be made both by the supervisor and the resolution authority (SRB) under Art 18(1) SRM Regulation.

contingency-planning nature of the resolution-planning procedures, despite the scope for direct regulatory remedies, such as removal of impediments to resolvability, and imposition of new regulatory requirements, such as the imposition of MREL, mean that the exercise is one step removed from the immediacy of day-to-day supervision. Within such space, the consultative nature of the process, with the SRB collecting inputs from and sharing information with multiple authorities, creates space for much needed expert and informed deliberation, in particular with regard to the aspects central to the SRB's mandate, that is, the public interest in financial stability or critical bank functions. Deliberation being understood here – building on the models discussed in section II – as creating 'arenas for justification' where distinct actors are engaged in common and cyclical procedures substantiating the aims of the overall bank regulatory architecture, understood as ensuring the soundness and safety of the banking sector which nonetheless underpins the EU's real economy and contributes to the attainment of overall EU Treaty objectives. Such deliberation relies on the interactions between the authorities, but also – in the specific case of the SRM – internal organisation aspects.

The SRM is not a 'top-down cooperative mechanism'[178] to the extent that the SSM is – the centralisation drive under the resolution pillar of the Banking Union is much more nuanced and variable. As was shown in the preceding sections, the role of the SRB, also outside of crisis management proper, is less prominent and centralised, but nonetheless significant, in particular in the context of preparatory resolution procedures where it plays the role of the coordinator of inputs various other modes and levels of public intervention in the banking sector in the EU, and Banking Union specifically. These procedures however take place under constitutional constraints on the SRB resulting from EU law, requiring that the role of other institutions at EU and national level within the agency's internal bodies is substantial and the implementation of the SRB's decisions reliant on the NRAs. At the same time, even with the limitations on the position of the SRB, the agency operates under a strong mandate of public interest in financial stability, which is highly sensitive to cross-border effects within the internal market. Given the reliance of the system on consultations and exchanges of information, as well as the decentralised nature of implementation, the system is reminiscent of the experimentalist-type modes of governance emerging in highly technical, expertise-heavy fields of EU policy-making as they only partially centralise rule enforcement.[179] The EU has a long tradition of relying on soft methods of governance, especially in contentious fields, where deliberation and process-orientation at EU level has particular value given the diversity of national legal and financial

---

[178] G Lo Schiavo, 'The Single Supervisory Mechanism: The New Top-Down Cooperative Supervisory Governance' in F Fabbrini, EMH Ballin and H Somsen (eds), *What Form of Government for the European Union and the Eurozone?* (Oxford, Hart Publishing, 2015).

[179] See CF Sabel and J Zeitlin, 'Learning from Difference: The New Architecture of Experimentalist Governance in the EU' in CF Sabel and J Zeitlin (eds), *Experimentalist Governance in the European Union: Towards a New Architecture* (Oxford, Oxford, University Press, 2010).

systems, and especially where uncertainty as to the optimal final arrangement prevails.[180] The formal resolution-planning procedures,[181] which rely extensively on exchange, consultation and cross-representation of bodies within the overall regulatory architecture bear the characteristics of deliberative supranationalism models, but with two crucial caveats.

First, where the formal inter-institutional consultations under the SRM have been meticulously outlined by the legislator, they invite not only deliberation through consultation and common fora, but assume heterogeneity of viewpoints on matters where actors involved are likely to have diverging interpretations or time-scales of considerations. An assumption of conflict between the functions and mandates of different authorities in fact underpins the fragmentation of modes of intervention in the banking sector.[182] While the tension between ECB's role as the supervisor and a monetary policy authority is already well discussed,[183] this tension is further problematised under the resolution-planning framework with regard to ECB's role as the lender of last resort,[184] including in the context of contested application of state aid and resolution law on ELA to liquidity-constrained institutions.[185] Further scope for inter-institutional disagreement centres around the perceived trade-off between probability of bank failure and *ex ante* policies oriented at lowering costs of failure. A notable example in this regard is the initial opposition of the ECB to the burden-sharing requirements of the European Commission in 2013 under state aid rules.[186] A further trade-off concerns the enforcement of competition rules in the sector and maintaining safety and soundness of individual banks.[187] Externalisation of these conflicts, ie the fact that 'arenas of justification' can take place not only within the formalised procedures, but also in public, invite inter-institutional accountability in terms of a heavier burden of proof and reasoning requirements, but potentially also external accountability of the regulatory architecture as a whole – paving the way for throughput legitimacy as defined by Vivien Schmidt.[188]

In this context, a key difference between actors concerns also their relationship vis-à-vis the supervised banks, and the differentiated scope for forbearance these entail. The intensive day-to-day supervisory relationship creates a symbiotic relationship between the banks and the supervisor – a relationship which is much

---

[180] F Knight, *Risk, Uncertainty and Profit* (Chicago, University of Chicago Press, 1971).

[181] This is in addition to the informal contacts and exchanges of knowledge, see eg provisions for these under MoU between the SRB and the ECB.

[182] For an overview of various interests in resolution see C Gandrud and M Hallerberg, 'Who Decides? Resolving Failed Banks in a European Framework' (2013) *Bruegel Policy Contribution*.

[183] C Goodhart and D Schoenmaker, 'Should the Functions of Monetary Policy and Banking Be Separated?' (1995) 40 *Oxford Economic Papers* 539.

[184] O'Connell (n 138).

[185] See I Angeloni and N Lenihan in Faia et al (n 69).

[186] On letter sent by M Draghi to the European Commission see Reuters, *Draghi asked EU to keep state aid rules for banks flexible*, 18 October 2013.

[187] See Carletti and A Smoleńska (n 9).

[188] Schmidt (n 17).

less intense in the case of resolution authorities, also where in many cases they do not rely directly on information provided by the banks. This point is key when one considers forbearance as one of the factors increasing implicit subsidies in the sector, associated with excessive risk-taking and moral hazard.[189] Such considerations reveal also the tension between the practical orientation of the ECB (with regard to resolvability assessment for example), where supervision is an ongoing exercise, and resolution planning, which remains a forward-looking (planning for failure) and a partially theoretical exercise, thus constituting a feat of imagination and contingency planning. The SRB is therefore less constrained by the immediacy of action, and as such can adopt a longer-term, dynamic perspective.

Given the distinctiveness of actors involved, the tensions which can emerge between actors are not necessarily an unfortunate resultant of constitutional constraints. Indeed Moloney criticises the tension which can emerge 'between the SRB, as the independent, expert competent agency, and the Commission, as the constitutional location of executive decision-making power but also of potentially conflicting functions (including with respect to the approval of any State aid to be provided to an institution in resolution), [signalling] a degree of instability at the heart of the SRM'.[190] Such instability, however, allows for bargaining and deliberation over policies and ideas, especially where the divergent mandates of institutions are considered and further brought into the picture. Supervision by the SSM focuses on soundness and safeness; macroprudential policy of ESRB on broader systemic risks; the EBA on fostering convergence across the internal market and supervisory practices; the European Commission – also though its state aid practice – on competition in the internal market. The mandate of resolution authorities meanwhile, beyond reducing *ex ante* the cost of bank failure, encompasses protection of clients and depositors, avoiding adverse effect on financial stability of failure and ensuring the continuity of critical functions (already a broad definition, reaching into the social context of banking).[191] Such diversity of intermediate objectives is required by deliberative models, allowing also for inter-institutional accountability. The balancing between these divergent objectives meanwhile occurs through enmeshed procedures – such as those of resolution planning – through the course of abstract and under-defined objectives of the regulatory architecture as a whole gain substance.

Second, the exchange within the institutional architecture takes place in a multi-level and transversal manner – no longer do we function in the dichotomy national–supranational in the context of governance of EU banking markets. Rather, the institutional design incorporates the geographical scope dimension

---

[189] K Tuori, 'From Expert to Politician and Stakeholder? Constitutional Drift in the Role of the ECB' in E Fossum and A Menendez, *The European Union in crises or the European Union as crises?* (Oslo, Arena Reports, 2014), Goodhart and Schoenmaker (n 183).

[190] Moloney (n 50) 1661.

[191] See Art 14(2) SRM Regulation.

in a much more nuanced way, with diverging and overlapping scopes, requiring consultation and exchange between authorities at EU level (Commission, ESRB, EBA), Eurozone level (SRB, SSM, ECB), the level of other Member States (non-participating NRAs), and national levels (NRAs and NCAs). Where the political economy analysis of crisis reforms has focused on the divisions between Member States as creditors and borrowers, the SRM resolution-planning procedures superimpose another layer of potential conflict between different financial national ecosystems and introduce yet another purely Eurozone scope.[192] Further, where complexity of resolution procedures has been criticised for 'not cleanly [allocating] power across supranational and intergovernmental interests [resulting in] some risk of it being obstructed by national interests', arguably resolution planning will have to play a significant role in reconciling differences between different traditions of relationships between public authorities and their banks, precisely through the deliberation procedures outlined above.[193] The 'one-step-removed' institutional framework might facilitate overcoming coordination problems notorious in the case of cross-border groups, where theoretical nature of resolution planning could facilitate good will cooperation and trust between national authorities of the SRM, under the ultimate spectre of binding centralisation in crisis management, that is resolution.[194]

Notwithstanding these distinct characteristics of the resolution-planning procedures, a number of key features of deliberative supranationalism are nonetheless evident when the interaction of the SRB with other actors within the overall regulatory architecture is considered. *Ex ante* resolution planning under EU resolution law provides a space for a very specific type of expert deliberation between authorities, with broad consultation – as outlined above – required by the legislator both at horizontal (or rather transversal given the SRB's 'agency' nature with respect to other EU institutions) or vertical (NRAs) levels, coupled with exchanges of information and joint, enmeshed procedures, where the SRB relies on implementation of its policies on other authorities. Further, a number of specific 'arenas for justification' exist under resolution law, in particular where there is apparent duplication (or parallelism)[195] of tasks and roles: this is the case with regard to two types of 'living wills': the recovery and resolution plans. Such duplication, together with a strong principle of separation between authorities and entrenched notions of independence, acts as a system of checks and balances

[192] See GR Underhill, 'The Political Economy of (Eventual) Banking Union' in T Beck (ed), *Banking Union for Europe – Risks and Challenges* (London, CEPR, 2009).
[193] E Monnet, S Pagliari and S Vallee, 'Europe Between Financial Repression and Regulatory Capture' (2014) Bruegel Working Paper 08/14; on varieties of capitalism arguments with regard to EU financial sector see L Quaglia, 'The Politics of Financial Services Regulation and Supervision Reform in the European Union' (2007) 46(2) *European Journal of Political Research* 269.
[194] F Lupo-Pasini and RP Buckley, 'International Coordination in Cross-Border Bank Bail-Ins: Problems and Prospects' (2015) 16 *European Business Organization Law Review* 203, 216.
[195] Recital 4 of SRB/ECB MoU.

and inter-institutional accountability,[196] though only to a certain extent given the differences in mandates of the supervisor and the resolution authority.[197] In particular, symmetry is required for such a 'checks and balances' system to work. Where causes of the last financial crisis are attributed to deficiencies in public reasoning, with oversimplified indicators and private reasoning substituting public reasoning and deliberation, non-inclusive decision-making and fragmented regulation and supervision encouraging regulatory arbitrage as contributing factors,[198] formally structured deliberation between public authorities around key under-defined concepts, such as the notion of financial activities 'critical' to the real economy, can improve expert policy-making in highly technical areas, also by showcasing externally the heterogeneity and range of regulatory perspectives and objectives to the broader public.

Deliberation in resolution planning – a competence of the SRB under a broad mandate of public interest in financial stability and protection of bank critical functions – further facilitates realising interdependencies between systems across various levels (notably not only national–supranational, but also Eurozone–EU scopes) and reconciling the fragmented (multi-peak) nature of post-crisis regulation in the financial sector. A space for competences and mandates to overlap and interact though (formally) structured exchanges allows for cross-filtration of perspectives and ideas is in this sense created under the SRM. The weak and decentralised nature of implementation and enforcement of resolution plan elements *ex ante* – that is, MREL and requirements to remove impediments to resolvability – reinforces the importance of the deliberative element at the decision-making stage.

VI. The SRB in the Thicket of EU Bank Regulation and the Value of 'Constraints'

The SSM seeks to *ex ante* build up resilience in the banking sector in a forward-looking manner as means to prevent bank crises.[199] Further, the SRB, as an EU agency, is the institutional response to particular problems of coordination related to financial integration in the EU.[200] In many ways, this being the result of the

---

[196] Tressel (n 169) 184.

[197] See Tucker on the notion of 'activity structure of a financial system resilience regime', P Tucker, 'The Design and Governance of Financial Stability Regimes: A Common-Resource Problem That Challenges Technical Know-How, Democratic Accountability and International Coordination' (2016) *CIGI Essays in International Finance* 3.

[198] M Goldmann *The Financial Crisis as a Crisis of Democracy: Towards Prudential Regulation through Public Reasoning*, Society of International Economic Law (SIEL), 3rd Biennial Global Conference, July 12–14, 2012, Working Paper No 2012/05.

[199] See Financial Stability Board, 'Key Attributes of Effective Resolution Regimes for Financial Institutions' (2011).

[200] See B Haar, 'Organizing Regional Systems: The EU Example' in Moloney, Ferran and Payne (n 11).

specific constitutional context within which the SRM was created – that is, the internal market and constraints on delegation of powers to agencies – the second pillar of EU's Banking Union is more composite than the pillar of the SSM. Not only is the degree of centralisation more variable than in the case of the SSM, being a function of time, state of the supervised bank and the sector as a whole, but on the less-centralised side of the spectrum – where the SRB engages in crisis prevention, planning tasks – the mechanism is heavily reliant on broad consultations and exchanges of information within a complex institutional architecture of financial regulators. Such complexity in regulation has hardly been praised,[201] though some have already argued for the benefits in terms of inter-institutional accountability that it can foster.[202] The approach outlined above takes this argument further by showing how given the distinct institutional set-up and mandate of the SRB, the agency plays a particular role in enabling exchange and deliberation with various national, Eurozone and EU authorities, setting up a system of inter-institutional deliberation and accountability under normal times procedures such as resolution planning, given also the cross-membership of those other authorities within the SRB's internal structures. This creates space for example for the elaboration of public interest in financial stability – one overarching telos of financial regulation – through interaction between various distinct authorities within the architecture.[203] Such a space seems warranted in particular where resolution in concerned with the highly contentious redistribution of losses caused by bank failure, but also more broadly given the role which banks play for the economy as a whole and where technicality of the subject matter is seen to impede traditional forms of democratic control.

By acknowledging the complexity of the regulated subject matter and heterogeneity of possible regulatory approaches the legitimacy of EU's overall regulatory architecture is revealed, where the polyarchical design of resolution-planning procedures coupled with extensive formal consultation procedures creates a space for deliberation and diversity.[204] To this end, the design of the EU resolution law overcomes temporal distinctions (crisis/containment/normal times)[205] and objectives (financial stability, breaking state-bank nexus, broader considerations of real economy impact of bank failure and therefore socially valuable

---

[201] AG Haldane, 'The Dog and the Frisbee', Speech delivered on 31 August 2012.

[202] See I Chiu, 'Power and Accountability in the EU Financial Regulatory Architecture: Examining Inter-Agency Relations, Agency Independence and Accountability' in M Andenas and G Deipenbrock, *Regulating and Supervising European Financial Markets: More Risks than Achievements* (New York, Springer Berlin Heidelberg, 2016) and P Iglesias-Rodríguez, *Building Responsive and Responsible Financial Regulators in the Aftermath of the Global Financial Crisis* (Cambridge, Intersentia, 2015).

[203] HP Minsky, *Stabilizing an Unstable Economy* (New York, McGraw-Hill, 2008); MA King, *The End of Alchemy: Money, Banking and the Future of the Global Economy* (New York, Norton & Company, 2016).

[204] On procedural legitimacy in agency studies see M de Bellis, 'Procedural Rule-Making of European Supervisory Agencies (ESAs): An Effective Tool for Legitimacy?' *TARN Working Paper Series* 12/2017.

[205] A Gelpern, 'Financial Crisis Containment' (2009) 41(4) *Connecticut Law Review* 493.

aspects of banking). Rather than setting the regulators up for 'a permissive consensus'[206] between technocrats, the SRM in the planning stage requires various – potentially conflicting – vantage points of other authorities within the regulatory architecture, to be brought into view through the procedure creating 'arenas of justification'. Where this is partially a result of EU's constitutional constraints on delegation, the inter-institutional consequence is the establishment of channels for coordination and cooperation as procedural requirements on the SRB's decision-making via EU law. While not experimentalist strictly, as defined by Sabel and Zeitlin, the combination of centralised and decentralised decision-making within the SRM adds a further layer of variability within the system, combining horizontal and transversal deliberation processes (through consultation, cross-membership on 'single' Boards and exchanges of information) with possibilities for vertical experimentation between national and centralised ('single') authorities in implementation and rule enforcement. It is the design of the 'joints' of the regulatory architecture – which bring together the distinct financial regulators, such as in the case of resolution planning, which allow for a source of legitimacy of the regulatory architecture as a whole to emerge: it is only *through* those inter-institutional connections that the overall aims of EU regulatory framework become articulated.

---

[206] See PL Lindseth, 'Power and Legitimacy in the Eurozone: Can Integration and Democracy Be Reconciled?' in M Adams et al (eds), *The Constitutionalization of European Budgetary Constraints* (Oxford, Hart Publishing, 2014).

PART III

European Banking Union, Democracy and Technocracy

8

Some Reflections on the State of European Democracy with Regard to the Banking Union and the ECB

CHRISTOPH MÖLLERS

I. Introduction

In democratic theory we wonder how to define democracy, either as a form of rational deliberation[1] or as a space of contestation between ideologies or preferences.[2] But if we accept for a moment that both elements may be needed in practice, despite their incommensurability in theory, we have to look at both in order to ask some relevant questions: (1) Where are the dividing lines of political contestation in the European Union (EU)? (2) What do they mean for the European Central Bank (ECB) and the complex reform that is labelled the 'Banking Union'? (3) Does it generally help to look for compensatory mechanisms under the heading of 'accountability', and (4) what are its implications for the evaluation of the ECB?

A few words concerning the approach taken here: as you can see from its first two sentences, this chapter is relatively agnostic with regard to the question of the 'right' democratic theory. Instead of applying some particular model of democracy to the structure of the EU, it will try to pin down some contradictions in the self-understanding of the actors with regard to their own legitimacy and the legitimacy of the entities they created. A methodological buzz-word for this approach could be 'rational reconstruction', but not only do the results rather seem to lead to an irrational reconstruction, the claim of this chapter is also much more modest. It will try to shed some light on the difficult knot of legitimacy narratives that appear in this context.

---

[1] The main sources of this idea are the rational republicanism of Kant and Rousseau and the pragmatism of Dewey's theory of democracy.

[2] One hesitates to attribute this idea to Schmitt's concept of the Political, it seems to be better enshrined in the practice of parliamentary opposition (which is excluded by Schmitt).

II. Overlapping Lines of Political Contestation in the EU

Democracy in the EU takes place along lines of contestation that are overlapping and blurred. At least three of them can be identified. First, the debate on austerity and budgetary restraint illustrates that there still is a meaningful distinction between the political right and left on the European level. There are other debates confirming this point.[3] But with regard to the Euro-crisis this line, second, overlaps with the differing interests of givers and takers within and outside the Eurozone. Even countries that do not fully endorse austerity may have an interest in controlling other countries that received guarantees (Italy). Even countries that received guarantees themselves may have an interest in seeing a formally equal treatment of other receiver countries (Ireland/Portugal versus Greece). Even countries that did not receive support may not play along the same political lines, independent from their governments' political ideology (France, Italy versus Germany).[4] Moreover, all of these differing views may be legitimate from a domestic democratic point of view. Let us take the German case. Its stance on austerity may be politically, morally and economically flawed; a short-sighted and selfish plea for the kind of 'ordo-liberalism' nobody else believes in.[5] But it is surely representative of the views of a majority of voters whose taxes are in question. The fact that the democratically legitimate decision may be the wrong decision is a neglected truism in democratic theory.

Third, there is the political process as we see it playing out within the European Parliament (EP). For the EP, the right/left divide is less important than the distinction between the grand coalition of Europeanists and the opposition of Eurosceptics from the right and the left.[6] This constellation is not necessarily undemocratic. A role model for this could be the Swiss system, in which the government was backed by an all-party coalition for decades. But this kind of political conflict needs compensatory mechanisms such as a robust federalism and a lively system of direct democracy. For the EU, the all-party centrism raises the question as to where the much-debated 'politicisation' of the European Commission may lead. At the moment, regarding the EURO-complex, politicisation of the Commission would mean it would have to take sides in conflicts between Member States, something the Commission seems to carefully avoid.

It is not entirely clear how meaningful democratic contestation along these overlapping and blurred lines can be possible. Though this is nothing entirely new for the student of federal polities, the example of the United States shows

---

[3] Migration and social policy would be other examples.

[4] For the debate between France and Germany about the Banking Union: D Howarth and L Quaglia, 'Die Bankenunion als Krönung der Wirtschafts- und Währungsunion?' (2015) 38 *Integration* 44, 50–51.

[5] 'Of Rules and Order', *The Economist*, 9 May 2015.

[6] Euro-scepticism is better represented in the EP than in the average national parliament: P Manow and H Döring, 'Electoral and mechanical causes of divided government in the European Union' (2008) 41 *Comparative Political Studies* 1349.

that things could be easier. Since the early American Republic, the emerging two-party system showed an amazing ability to integrate questions of economic policy, foreign politics and the politics of federalism into a coherent dualism of two parties:[7] and the Federal Bank was one of the most important objects of its contestation.[8]

This indeterminacy of political camps corresponds to the ambiguous definition of the project that requires democratic justification. The Europeanisation of the banking supervision is a consequence of the Euro-crisis and this makes it a politically deeply ambivalent project. On the one hand, banking supervision could be seen as a leftist project, an attempt to tame capitalism's most dubious players; on the other hand, the ECB has acquired a problematic reputation during the crisis as a defender of the system and a promoter of austerity. On the one hand, the Banking Union is a milestone in deepening European integration; on the other hand, it is not only contributing to further fragmentation between the States of the Eurozone and the other Member States, its actual genesis and the diversity of its legal fundaments also express a considerable lack of trust in the legitimacy and viability of European solutions while pursuing them. On the one hand, there are many angles from which the legitimacy of the ECB–Banking Union combination seems dubious; on the other hand, it is also unclear which solution could be accepted as enjoying a satisfying degree of democratic legitimacy under the given circumstances. Today, endorsing one model of democracy for the European institutions means endorsing a contested political program, not a settled constitutional principle.

In any case, recourse to democratic legitimacy introduces a new normative layer beyond the actual political norm-making processes. But this does not mean that it can ignore what is going on in a given polity. It has to reconstruct the constitutional framework in a critical fashion.[9] But the way in which the Banking Union came into being makes this especially difficult, because its rationales as well as its legal fundaments are so contradictory and range from an allegedly normal common market legislation to intergovernmental agreements outside the formal EU framework.

III. A View on the ECB

A. Framework Expertise: The ECB as an Institution

In no democracy do all institutions enjoy the same level of democratic legitimacy. We would hesitate to endorse a system in which this standard was achieved; it

---

[7] So coherent that the parties could switch sides in the Federal conflict.

[8] For the early republic: S Elkins and E McKittrick, *The Age of Federalism* (New York, Oxford University Press, 1994); CR Henning and M Kessler, 'Fiscal Federalism: US History for Architects of Europe's Fiscal Union' (2012) *Bruegel Essay and Lecture Series*.

[9] C Möllers, *The Three Branches: A Comparative Model of Separation of Powers* (Oxford, Oxford University Press, 2013) 51–109.

would be a polity without a judicial branch that deserves that name. Put simply, in a democracy all institutions must have a democratic pedigree, but not all institutions must be democratic. We can attribute a first-order democratic legitimacy to an institution that is democratically responsible according to the standards of its own order, and a second-order democratic legitimacy if the institution is institutionalised through a democratic decision, though it is not in the same way democratically responsible.

From a legal point of view, the ECB can claim a maximum amount of institutional legitimacy within the European legal order. It enjoys an explicit constitutional status,[10] though it is not as completely insulated from external control as it has claimed to be.[11] One might even argue that its constitutional status as an independent organ has deeper roots than the rule of Article 130 of the Treaty on the Functioning of the European Union (TFEU). Pierre Rosanvallon has argued for the German Bundesbank that its independence had a constitutive mandate stemming from the German experience with inflation in the early 1920s.[12] This argument seems to still be valid from the viewpoint of the German public, but it is also somewhat ironic given the fact that an expertocratic institution is built on a narrative that is at least factually contestable. While the Weimar Republic was successful in dealing with inflation by democratic and politically responsible means (!), it finally collapsed under the consequences of deflationary politics.

But from a democratic perspective, the constitutional status of the ECB is a vice rather than a virtue, and one might wonder if even second-order legitimacy can be attributed to it. While the independent US Federal Reserve is a creature of Congress, of an egalitarian and reversible political process, the ECB is basically set in institutional stone. Even if there were a political process on the European level, this process would not be able to amend its fundamental structure.[13] But democratic legitimacy is created by the ability to change. Put differently: political constitutionalism is built on the fundamental trust of all members of a community that majoritarian decisions will be acceptable for all possible minorities, ie for everybody. This trust does not exist between the Member States that created the ECB. Especially, it does not exist between France and Germany.[14] Moreover, the constitutional status of the ECB is part of an institutional environment in which the meaning of the highest political offices is unclear and contested. The role of an EU head of government is opaquely distributed between the Presidents of Council, the Commission and the heads of important Member State governments. Consequently, the President of the ECB assumes a role and authority that

---

[10] Art 13 TEU, Art 282 TFEU.

[11] Case C-11/00 *Commission v ECB*, EU:C:2003:395; Case T-496/11 *UK v ECB*, EU:T:2015:133.

[12] P Rosanvallon, *Democratic Legitimacy: Impartiality, Reflexivity, Proximity* (Princeton, Princeton University Press, 2011) 115–19.

[13] AS Binder, *The Quiet Revolution: Central Banking Goes Modern* (New Haven, Yale University Press, 2004) 8–9.

[14] But for a much more fine-grained account: H James, *Making the European Monetary Union* (Cambridge MA, Harvard University Press, 2012) ch 8.

is remarkably weightier than that of any other head of a central bank. Would it be possible to imagine an American Republic in which the office of the Chairman of the Federal Reserve is older, more deeply constitutionally entrenched and less contested than the office of the President of the United States? Functionalism has created an institutional monstrosity.[15]

In a traditional transmission-belt model of democratic administration, the lack of political legitimacy is compensated by a clear statutory mandate. This was the German argument for a normative focus on price stability for the ECB, in contrast to the Federal Reserve which is also obliged to take employment into consideration. Despite many challenges from governance theory there is still a good case to be made for well-defined mandates, but the definition of a mandate only functions in specific contexts. Even if one accepted the restrictive economic approach of the ECB mandate as a matter of policy, it could be wondered whether it makes sense as an institutional solution, given the factual dependence between monetary and economic policies. Can this mandate really prevent the ECB from becoming a democratically illegitimate economic government? Or does it rather work like the mandate of a hypothetical environmental agency that must put all its resources in the protection of clean water while ignoring air pollution? As a matter of fact, there is a political process going on within the ECB concerning its own mandate, and this process is less of an indicator of usurpation of competences[16] than of an ill-designed legal framework. Setting up a Central Bank as the guardian of a currency without other political actors in the field of economic policy at hand implies that this institution does not only apply rules, but also sees itself responsible for the survival of the currency. This kind of protection will always work beyond a given mandate.

Within the existing political framework, the ECB is more problematic for left-wing politics than for conservatives, and more problematic for sovereigntists than for Europeanists. The combination of liberal monetary politics as executed in the Outright Monetary Transactions (OMT) and quantitative easing (QE) programmes on the one hand and its tough stance towards the Greek government on the other has allowed the ECB to escape a definition in clear political terms. But this achievement can also be seen as a problem. Maybe the ECB did not feel at liberty to be more flexible towards the Greek government because it had already used up its political credit with regard to other Member States. This is mere speculation, but it illustrates that the independence of the ECB, contrary to what is often assumed, may not be increased through the European construction: as the argument goes, the ECB is an institution without a clear political counter-process. Hence, its independence may be even bigger and more problematic than

---

[15] 'Monstro simile' – Pufendorf's comment on the Holy German Empire was meant as description rather than as an evaluation.
[16] This is, of course, the view of the German Federal Constitutional Court's preliminary ruling: Judgment of 14 January 2014, 2 BvR 2728/13.

in the case of national central banks.[17] But the fragmentation of European politics could make the Bank even more dependent. It might be much more difficult for an independent agency to please fighting factions than to cope with a political process from which it is supposed to deviate occasionally. The bad news is that this kind of dependence does not produce any convincing form of legitimacy because it is hidden within a structure that claims expertise and independence from politics. The specific problem of the ECB may be not too much independence, but a complex mix of informal dependence.

This problem becomes more dramatic because this political conflict is not only part of the environment of the ECB, but of its internal discourse. The federal structure of the Governing Council led to an internalisation of the conflict between the Member States, albeit with different decision-making rules. One does not have to take sides in this conflict to see that this threatens the core of the ECB's claim to legitimacy. If decisions are taken according to political criteria in the first place, then this should be done in the open and left to elected officials.

A final problem for the ECB lies in the dramatic loss of credibility with regard to expertocratic arguments in the field of economic politics. The decline of expertise on the European level began perhaps with the now infamous paper of the European Commission for Economic and Monetary Union (EMU),[18] and it went on with the policy recommendations of the International Monetary Fund (IMF), especially for Greece, that were endorsed and executed by the 'institutions'. To be sure, there is no governing without expertise, and no expertise without flaws. But the misrepresentations of these institutions were not simple mistakes – they were not accidental. They were the result of an institutional political agenda that was clothed in the language of the economically factual. Neither independent expertise nor democratic politics explains these errors, but, rather, the agenda of institutions that pursue their self-preservation.

B. Federalism and a Weaker Case for Independence: The SSM

The political context that finally led to the Single Supervisory Mechanism (SSM) was defined by the fear of supranational centralism. Politically, it was a debate between sovereigntism and regulatory efficiency. In a typical move, it was an attempt to square the circle by connecting national agencies. The long expert discussion around the establishment of the European System of Financial Supervision (ESFS) with the European Securities and Markets Authority (ESMA), the

---

[17] G Majone, 'Rethinking European Integration after the Debt Crisis' (2012) *UCL Working Paper* 3.
[18] European Commission, Directorate-General for Economic and Financial Affairs, 'One money, one market: an evaluation of the potential benefits and costs of forming an economic and monetary union' (Brussels, 1990).

European Insurance and Occupational Pensions Authority (EIOPA) and the European Banking Authority (EBA) while the crisis was already under way seemed to assume that the political (democratic?) costs of centralised banking supervision would be higher than its economic gains. Banking supervision seemed to be too big to be placed under just another specialised agency. It seemed also to be too heavy for the European Commission.

It is, therefore, not an accident that the agency that was finally entrusted with the task of banking supervision was not a newly created entity, but the ECB itself. While this choice may have practical and legal advantages, especially the somewhat stretched competence of Article 127(6),[19] and while it allows the new structure, at least partly, to participate in the organisation and the legal dignity of a treaty organ, it seems otherwise not self-evident. The rationale for independence that has become widely successful for central banks does not apply to banking supervision authorities. In some countries banking supervision is part of the duties of the central bank, in many others this is not the case and in some, this part of their duties is not shielded through independence. The supervision of banks is a typical regulatory task that is different from monetary politics. To give this kind of task to a central bank may be an indicator of a problem – be it on the side of the banking system (too big), be it on the side of the institutions (not legitimate enough), or be it on both sides. The quest for a legitimate exception from the normal case of democratic administration is more difficult to meet. And the chosen solution was not the result of a comparative analysis of the right distribution of regulatory tasks; rather, it followed from a situation in which there was no political will to more regulatory integration, but the general crisis-driven impression that it was necessary to do it anyhow.

But, again, what would have been the normal case of democratic administration in the EU? Without picking up on the eternal debate on European democracy it is fair to say that neither the European Commission nor the Council nor any other specialised agency seem to be natural candidates of a democratically responsible administrative structure. A weak inter-administrative solution failed with the ESFS. The Commission cannot claim the democratic mandate for the EU that a national government can claim for its State. In other words: the distinction between independent and democratically responsible government does not work. But the fact that the task was given to the ECB expresses considerable doubts concerning the legitimacy of the other institutions. The Banking Union delivers a heavy load of administrative responsibility, but without the right political structure to carry it.

---

[19] Reading the affirmative debate in the literature, the author feels like a German formalist in conceding that the words 'concerning policies relating to' sound as being designed to *exclude* the kind of supervision powers the ECB received through Council Regulation 1024/2013. The point is not that the words allow for that meaning – they clearly do not – but rather that the unanimous procedure allows the words to be ignored.

C. A Framework for Legitimate Capital Distribution: SRM

If the Single Resolution Mechanism (SRM) is any different from the SSM in terms of its legitimacy, it is because of the distribution of capital involved. Beyond the important technical problems of coping with defunct banks, the special regime that was needed to set up the SSM has similarities to the European Stability Mechanism (ESM) structure. Member States like Germany were not ready to agree to the distribution of considerable amounts of capital into a supranational structure. Therefore, an Intergovernmental Agreement had to be signed that allowed national parliaments to be included in the procedure.[20] From the perspective of German constitutional law this is probably a valid legal point, not just the argument of a government that hides behind its constitution in order to avoid an unwanted outcome.[21] For the EP, its exclusion from what it regarded to be an important element of a normal legislative procedure was the most problematic element of the whole Banking Union structure. Is there any criterion from democratic theory which may resolve this clash of democratic representations?

As long as the capital that is flowing into the mutual resolution fund is raised by a national system of taxation, the argument for national participation has its merits. To be sure, the unity between raising and spending money from a single constituency is not self-evident in a federal polity, and it is explicitly not so in the German system in which federal and state tax and spending powers are intertwined in an almost incomprehensible manner. But for a polity like the EU, which has not even started to seriously raise taxes from its citizens, it would seem odd to claim spending powers of such a degree. Any plan to tax the Europeans through the EU would challenge the legitimacy of the EU even more. A visionary European political process would yearn for a tax power that could make the EP a more relevant actor. No representation without taxation. But as long as this is lacking, the normative nationalism keeps a strong point.

The choice of Article 114 TFEU as the legal basis for the SRM/SRM remains odd, though it may be justified as matter of doctrine by the recent jurisprudence of the Court of Justice.[22] This is illustrated by its institutional outcome: a decision-making structure that includes basically all the national, supranational and intergovernmental bodies that have stakes.[23] As a matter of coherence, it is irritating when the normal legislative procedure leads to an organisational structure that deviates so far from the normal institutional balance. The legal constitution and the political constitution of the EU do not converge in their evaluation of the SRM and Single Resolution Board (SRB). The cluelessness in the legislative process

---

[20] Howarth and Quaglia, 'Die Bankenunion' (n 4) 56.

[21] M Ruffert, 'The European Debt Crisis and European Union Law' (2011) 48 *Common Market Law Review* 1777, 1789–90.

[22] Case C-270/12 *UK v EP & Council* EU:C:2014:18.

[23] N Moloney, 'European Banking Union: Assessing its Risks and Resilience' (2014) 51 *Common Market Law Review* 1609, 1638–42.

for the SRB, in which the ECB, the Commission and the European Council were presented as candidates,[24] is a disturbing sign of the fundamental disorientation of the European political process regarding where decision-making powers that are considered to be highly relevant ought to be allocated.

IV. Democracy, Accountability and Independence

The legal debate on the legitimacy of the original ECB and the Banking Union has mostly been centred on issues other than those discussed here so far, above all on the notion of 'accountability' and its compatibility with independence. Some conceptual clarifications are necessary.

First, accountability has become a central category in European and international institutional law, obviously because it is generally understood as a compensatory mechanism. Where public authorities cannot claim a convincing degree of democratic legitimacy they must, at least, be held accountable. While the meaning of accountability is far from settled, one basic definition may be stipulated. In order to be considered accountable, a public authority must document its own actions. This documentation may concern what it is actually doing and the reasons why it is doing so. A satisfying form of accountability will give the audience to whom one is accountable some say in defining under which conditions the requirements of accountability are satisfied. This means that accountability entails not only a general duty to report but also a duty to answer concrete questions. A second, yet practically immensely important, question is whether accountability will be connected to any sanctions. If it is not, accountability will remain necessary but also weak in adding any legitimate value to the action of a public authority. The strongest accountability mechanism is judicial review. It receives its strengths from the independence of the reviewer, from the legitimacy of the reviewed standard, and from the power to strike down the reviewed act. An executive act receives democratic legitimacy when it is plausibly connected to a democratically created rule. But the judicial review of this act does not produce, as such, greater *democratic* legitimacy.

Put so simply, it becomes clear that accountability cannot compensate for democratic legitimacy because it is a condition of democratic legitimacy. No egalitarian political procedure, an election, a plebiscite, would make any sense if it were not based on a record of what has been done or will be done as a consequence of a democratic decision. In practice, such requirements are far from fulfilled, as the eternal fight for governmental information in all democracies shows. But analytically, there is no democratic legitimacy without accountability, but only accountability without democratic legitimacy. Accountability cannot compensate for any lack of democratic legitimacy. This take on the relation between

---

[24] Howarth and Quaglia, 'Die Bankenunion' (n 4) 53–55.

accountability and democracy is not belied by the theory of deliberative democracy. The idea that democracy is legitimate because it enables an exchange of justificatory reasons is not meant to substitute egalitarian procedures through rational deliberation, though it is sometimes interpreted this way, especially by lawyers and technocrats.[25] One interesting twist of the use of deliberation and accountability lies in the avoidance of facts by giving 'reasons': the ECB prefers to give its own rationale for a decision instead of providing raw data.[26] This expresses the idea that the democratic discourse is an exchange of arguments that can be substituted through an intra-institutional debate between economic philosopher-kings.

But the model of deliberative democracy assumes that egalitarian procedures should be designed in a way that allows public deliberation.[27]

Second, the debate about the compatibility of accountability and independence of the ECB often relies on a lack of conceptual clarity with regard to the meaning of independence.[28] There are no particular forms of accountability that protect independence while others do not. As long as accountability concerns only the record of the action of a public authority, independence cannot be endangered by it. Can the fact that the public knows what a public authority is really doing have repercussions on its course of action? Obviously, it can. But these repercussions do not concern its independence, because this refers only to a normative concept of independence regarding elements like re-appointment, hierarchy, budget – all of them depending on a legal structure. Independence is a legal form that restricts the normative attribution of an action to a designated actor, though her actions are, unavoidably, dependent on others. There is no such thing as factual independence, but only different ways of dependence. The German debate on the ECB shows how misleading the conflation of normative and factual independence can be. One common political argument against the OMT programme was that it would undermine the independence of the ECB by connecting national economic politics with the functioning of the Bank. Maybe, this is not altogether wrong as a matter of fact. But the obvious irony remains that national politicians try to influence ECB policy by reminding it of its independence.

This does not mean that there might not be a functional case for the secrecy of some administrative agendas and, therefore, for some limits to accountability. But the reasons for secrecy apply equally to independent and politically responsible

---

[25] A powerful example is AM Slaughter, *A New World Order* (Princeton, Princeton University Press, 2004) 213–16.

[26] D Curtin, '"Accountable Independence" of the European Central Bank: Seeing the Logics of Transparency' (2017) 23(1–2) *European Law Journal* 28.

[27] C Lafont, 'Is the Ideal of a Deliberative Democracy Coherent?' in S Besson and JL Marti, *Deliberative Democracy and Its Discontents* (Aldershot, Ashgate, 2006) 3.

[28] The whole debate on 'accountable independence' seems to conflate the categories in question: P Magnette, 'Towards "Accountable Independence"? Parliamentary Controls of the European Central Bank and the Rise of a New Democratic Model' (2000) 6 *European Law Journal* 326; eg C Zilioli and M Selmayr, 'The Constitutional Status of the European Central Bank' (2007) 44 *Common Market Law Review* 355, 364.

authorities, to Central Banks and Foreign Ministries. Again, there is no special relation between independence and accountability.

V. Accountability of the ECB

A. Transparency and Internal Deliberations

All in all, the ECB seems to show a relatively weak record with regard to transparency.[29] Much debated are the minutes of the meetings of the Governing Council and the decision of the ECB to have them published, albeit in an anonymised manner.[30] At first glance, it is not entirely clear in which cases the preparation of decisions of a public authority should come under public scrutiny. There is at least a weak argument for spaces of reflection and debate within any public administration. But in the case of the Governing Council, it is the federal structure of the body and of the entire Euro-system that makes this argument dubious. What is the character of this body and its deliberations? Is it a debate among experts that may improve the quality of decision-making and prevent the body from capture through idiosyncratic economic models?[31] Or is it a federal organ in which a political process is constituted? The twist of this question lies in the fact that the first alternative makes it less necessary but politically easier to publish the minutes, while the second one makes it both more necessary and more difficult to do it. The federal political process within the bank[32] cannot create the kind of legitimacy that the ECB claims to have. And, again, if there is a struggle between German and Italian central bankers then it becomes unclear why we should insulate the Bank from, let us say the Council, in which the same struggle could take place.

The main reason to withhold information such as uncensored minutes seems to be that a complete disclosure could create pressure on members of the Governing Council within their national public spheres.[33] This presumes that there is no

---

[29] Curtin, '"Accountable Independence" of the European Central Bank' (n 26). For a quantitative model, giving the ECB middle grades: SCW Eijffinger and PM Geraats, 'How Transparent Are Central Banks?' (1006) 22 *European Journal of Political Economy* 1.

[30] ECB, ECB to adjust schedule of meetings and to publish regular accounts of monetary policy discussions in 2015, Press Release, 3 July 2014, available at https://www.ecb.europa.eu/press/pr/date/2014/html/pr140703_1.en.html; C Jones, 'Publication of ECB minutes will end a decade of silence', *Financial Times*, 20 July 2014.

[31] This is the general argument for collegiality in Central Banks governing bodies: Binder, *Quiet Revolution* (n 13) ch 2.

[32] The oral argument in the German FCC case between the member of the Executive Council, Asmussen, and the President of the Bundesbank seemed at some moments like a debate between policy makers.

[33] Curtin, '"Accountable Independence" of the European Central Bank' (n 26). C Jones, 'European Central Bank to publish account of meetings', *Financial Times*, 18 December 2014.

serious political process at the European level. But this presumption is based on a categorical mistake similar to the conflation of formal and factual independence: it is the duty of the members of the Governing Board to resist political pressure. But this duty would be useless, if there is no possibility of public pressure. The same argument could be used to introduce unsigned judgments of criminal cases in a country with an aggressive 'yellow press'. The ECB cannot escape the political environment that has already taken hold of its internal debate by keeping these debates a secret.

B. The ECB and the Parliaments

Parliamentary accountability is a fuzzy concept.[34] It has already been seen that mere duties to report that are not connected to any kind of sanctions cannot add much to the legitimacy of the reviewed act. The accountability mechanism has to have some meaningful connection to the powers of parliament, be they legislative or appointment powers, as well as to its procedures. Not every public act becomes more legitimate through contact with parliamentarians. The most plausible function of parliamentary accountability is to inform future legislation. But as far as the ECB claims to be on equal footing with the whole EU and basically not be bound by secondary legislation[35] this rationale of accountability becomes futile. Another function could lie in supporting the control functions of the EP with regard to the Commission. But if the ECB informs the EP without any of these relationships, it becomes hard to see where the use of this kind of accountability structure lies. This is all the more true because the systematic difference between information for a parliament and information for the general public remains unclear. The fact that the ECB has been in a constant 'monetary dialogue' with the EP should, therefore, not be over-estimated, because one may doubt if this dialogue allows the EP to seriously review the ECB.[36] In addition to that, such a review would be a dead end, because in most cases it could not lead to any legislative action – legislative action that cannot be considered to be an interference with the independence of the ECB.

When the Interinstitutional Agreement between the ECB and the EP gives the latter the right to secret meetings between members, the Chair of the SSM Supervisory Board and the Chairmen of the ECON committee,[37] the legitimating value

---

[34] Möllers, *Three Branches* (n 9) 118–21.

[35] For this maximalist position: C Zilioli and M Selmayr, 'The Constitutional Status' (n 28) eg. 378–79. It reminds of pre-modern models of church and state.

[36] For a moderate assessment after 10 years: F Amtenbrink and K van Duin, 'The European Central Bank Before the European Parliament: Theory and Practice After Ten Years of Monetary Dialogue' (2009) 34 *European Law Review* 561.

[37] Art I 2, para 10, Interinstitutional Agreement between the European Parliament and the ECB on the practical modalities of the exercise of democratic accountability and oversight over the exercise of the tasks conferred on the ECB within the framework of the Single Supervisory Mechanism, [2013] OJ L 320/2.

of such a procedure can be easily and precisely assessed: it is zero. The informed MEPs cannot talk about their knowledge, so that there is not even the trace of a relevant political process this kind of 'accountability' could lead to. Strictly speaking, single members of a representative body do not have any legitimacy of their own, they can only claim it as part of the necessary division of labour every legislative process needs to have. And even if they could make this claim, it would be far from clear what a secret parliamentary process should look like. If there are no justifications, there are at least explanations for such institutional arrangements. One is that they serve to forge legitimacy. Another is that they satisfy the participating institutions.[38]

Structures as different as the SRB and the relations between the ECB and EP seem to be justified by the same underlying assumption: the assumption that the connection of different institutions that claim diverse types of legitimacy creates a legitimate whole. This assumption is obviously wrong. To the contrary, legitimate institutions need a certain homogeneity and autonomy for their own procedures and they need to be distinguished from other institutions. Legitimacy cannot be created by simply involving 'all actors – perhaps in different ways …'.[39]

The most relevant accountability structure for the members of the Executive Board is therefore the consultation of the EP, under Article 283(2) TFEU. Here lies at least a form of *ex ante* participation in which the Parliament could mediate the process to the public. The failure of some candidates for the office of European Commissioner in their hearings before the EP was a major step for the creation of a democratically responsible Commission.

VI. Conclusion

The complex matrix of political contestations within the EU makes it nearly impossible to construct a democratic ideal against which to measure the development of the Banking Union. Instead, it can be seen that the participants of the process are deeply disoriented about where to allocate legitimate executive power within the EU. The rise of the ECB as an administrative entity beyond its classical central banking functions is not only due to its expertise and experience in banking supervision,[40] but also to an institutional void in which no other candidate was as trustworthy and as constitutionally entrenched. Regarding the state of the law, the ECB seems like a rather over-justified institution.

---

[38] The whole complicated system of inter institutional agreements seems to rely on the odd assumption that the legitimate relation between public powers can be stipulated by them. Legitimacy becomes a self-referential game of affected institutions.

[39] eg GT Kuile, L Wissink and W Bovenschen, 'Tailor-Made Accountability within the Single Supervisory Mechanism' (2005) 52 *Common Market Law Review* 155, 164.

[40] National banking supervisors do not hesitate to argue that the ECB is lacking both.

The classical EU solution for such a lack of legitimacy is to create institutional ties between all the actors in a voluntary manner through agreements, hoping that this will create legitimacy. But there is no systematic reason to believe that it will: organs cannot control their own legitimacy, nor do asymmetric 'dialogues' convey any form of political legitimacy. To put it extremely simply: talking to a parliamentarian does not make me democratic. Talking to a parliamentarian in secret is not different from not talking to her. Therefore, accountability mechanisms are not able to compensate for this problem. They are not bad as such, and they may help to inform the public about what is going on, but this kind of information remains a necessary, not a sufficient, condition for democratic legitimacy. They may become problematic when they create the illusion that progress regarding the question of legitimacy is made.

'Now that it is independent, and since the European Parliament rejects the idea of applying the classic model of parliamentary control to the ECB, new models of democratic legitimation must be invented.'[41] Well, if it were possible to invent new forms of democracy for every institutional arrangement, it would be better to forget about democracy as a matter of theory in the first place. The most dangerous temptation for any legitimacy discourse lies in the need to find solutions for everything, instead of developing critical arguments.

---

[41] Magnette, 'Towards "Accountable Independence"?' (n 28) 338.

9

The European Banking Union: A Case of Tempered Supranationalism?

SERGIO FABBRINI AND MATTIA GUIDI

I. Introduction

The Banking Union (BU) can be considered the most important integrative project of the Economic and Monetary Union (EMU) after the single currency.[1] It is part of the complex set of measures approved by EMU and European Union (EU) authorities for dealing with the Euro crisis, which have 'had a profound impact on the constitutional order of the EU and its Member States'.[2] It is constituted by the Single Supervisory Mechanism (SSM), entered into force in November 2014, the Single Resolution Mechanism (SRM), become operative in January 2016, and a European Deposit Insurance Scheme (EDIS), which is still in the book because of the opposition coming from Northern European Member States (Germany in particular).[3] The project of a BU has been in the EU pipeline for a long time. However, with the Four Presidents' Report of June 2012, the BU has become a formal project of the EU political authorities, further celebrated by the Five Presidents' Report of June 2015. The aim of the project has been to break the vicious nexus between banking and sovereign debt crises, eradicating national supervisory forbearance and reducing banks' moral hazard. The BU has thus been seen as an indispensable institutional regime for preserving the integrity of the EMU through the reduction of fragmentation of the financial markets.[4]

The first two pillars have been introduced through a complex set of legal measures. The SSM was introduced through Regulation 1024/2013 ('SSM Regulation' henceforth), based on Article 127(6) of the Treaty on the Functioning of the European Union (TFEU), which aimed at creating a system of centralised

---

[1] N Véron, 'Europe's Radical Banking Union' (2015) *Bruegel Essay and Lecture Series*.

[2] A Hinarejos, *The Euro Area Crisis in Constitutional Perspective* (Oxford, Oxford University Press, 2015) 1.

[3] A Posen and N Véron, 'Europe's Half a Banking Union', *Europe's World*, 15 June 2014.

[4] E Barucci and M. Messori (eds), *Towards the European Banking Union: Achievements and Open problems* (Rome, Astrid, 2014).

banking supervision under the authority of the European Central Bank (ECB). The SRM was introduced through Regulation 806/2014 ('SRM Regulation'), Directive 59/2014 ('Bank Recovery and Resolution Directive' – BRRD) and the 'Agreement on the transfer and mutualisation of contributions to the Single Resolution Fund' of 14 May 2014 ('Intergovernmental agreement' – IGA), and it was designed to deal with banks that are 'failing or … likely to fail' (Article 18.1, SRM Regulation). The SSM consists of a centralised supervisory system, based on a single legal framework and a supervisory authority constituted by both the ECB and national authorities – which form a network that resembles the architecture of EU competition policy. The ECB is the body responsible for its functioning, although the European Banking Authority (EBA) sets the supervisory rules and practices in order to preserve the interest of the Member States not participating in the SSM. The SRM consists instead of a much less centralised system than the SSM. In particular, the role of the ECB is limited at the advantage of an *ad hoc* body, the Single Resolution Board (SRB), and national resolution authorities.

The aim of this chapter is to understand the institutional nature of the BU, and notably whether it epitomises the logic of supranationalism or intergovernmentalism. It will be organised as follows: first, it will reconstruct the basic process of negotiation that led to the institutional features of the first two pillars of the BU; second, it will discuss the institutional structure of those two pillars in order to detect their institutional logic; third, it will derive from the BU's experience some considerations on the inter-institutional relations between supranational and intergovernmental actors in the EMU decision-making process. These inter-institutional relations are structurally conflicting. This is why this chapter identifies the BU as a case of a supranational project yet constrained by intergovernmental interests and considerations – according to the definition here, an example of tempered supranationalism.

II. The Making of the BU

Although the idea of creating a BU had been put forward by the European Parliament (EP) as early as 2000,[5] it was only with the emergence of the 2008 financial crisis that the possibility of uploading banking supervision and resolution mechanisms to the EU level became more realistic.[6] Both mechanisms have received

---

[5] See European Parliament resolution on the Commission communication on implementing the framework for financial markets: Action Plan (COM(1999) 232 – C5-0114/1999 – 1999/2117(COS)), available at: www.europarl.europa.eu/sides/getDoc.do?pubRef=-//EP//TEXT+TA+P5-TA-2000-0180+0+DOC+XML+V0//EN.

[6] See European Parliament resolution of 7 July 2010 with recommendations to the Commission on Cross-Border Crisis Management in the Banking Sector (2010/2006(INI)), available at: www.europarl.europa.eu/sides/getDoc.do?type=TA&language=EN&reference=P7-TA-2010-0276#def_1_1.

decisive input from the European Council's President report of 26 June 2012.[7] The report, entitled 'Towards a genuine Economic and Monetary Union', was prepared in collaboration with the presidents of the Commission, of the Eurogroup and of the ECB, and proposed – among other reforms – an 'integrated financial framework [which] elevates responsibility for supervision to the European level, and provides for common mechanisms to resolve banks ...'.[8] This document was followed by a formal European Commission proposal that was then approved by the EU legislators: 'A Roadmap towards a Banking Union'[9] and a subsequent document 'A blueprint for a deep and genuine economic and monetary union: Launching a European Debate',[10] of November 2012, which defined the strategy to pursue. In this phase, the stress was on supervision and resolution.

It is, however, worth noting that the two pillars of SSM and SRM followed different procedures. The SSM was approved by the Council under unanimity rule, following Article 127(6) TFEU, which calls for such a procedure where the members of the Eurozone want to 'confer specific tasks upon the European Central Bank concerning policies relating to the prudential supervision of credit institutions'. For the SRM, instead, the adoption has been carried out through the ordinary legislative procedure (using Article 114 TFEU as a legal basis). It must be stressed that the debate and the negotiation on both institutions proceeded, in part, together, as they were obviously intertwined. However, given the different content, timing and decision-making procedures, it is better to analyse the development of each one separately.

A. The Single Supervisory Mechanism

A draft proposal for a Council Regulation creating a SSM was elaborated by the European Commission on 12 September 2012.[11] The most relevant difference between the Commission's proposal and the text finally approved by the Council on October 2013 concerned the scope of the ECB's powers vis-à-vis those of national supervisory authorities. The initial proposal of the Commission envisaged a fully hierarchical institutional structure, similar to the one in place for monetary policy, in which the ECB would have been exclusively competent for banking supervision in all the Eurozone countries and for all Member State banks. Obviously, given

---

[7] See H Van Rompuy, 'Towards a Genuine Economic and Monetary Union' (26 June 2012) EUCO 120/12, available at www.consilium.europa.eu/uedocs/cms_data/docs/pressdata/en/ec/131201.pdf.

[8] ibid, 3.

[9] European Commission, *A Roadmap Towards a Banking Union*, Communication of 12 September 2012, COM/2012/510)

[10] European Commission, 'A blueprint for a deep and genuine economic and monetary union: Launching a European Debate', Communication of 28 November 2012, COM/2012/777.

[11] Proposal for Proposal for a Council Regulation conferring specific tasks on the European Central Bank concerning policies relating to the prudential supervision of credit institutions, COM/2012/0511 final – 2012/0242 (CNS).

that the ECB could not possibly supervise more than 6,000 banks, the national authorities would have carried out most supervisory activities, though under the ECB's control.

It soon became evident that this proposal was not enjoying the necessary (unanimous) support by the Member States' governments. In particular, German savings banks (*Sparkassen*) started to voice their concerns about the proposed plan. The main issue they pointed to was the high administrative costs that an ECB-led supervision would have imposed on them. German savings banks claimed that they posed no systemic threat to the stability of the Eurozone financial system, and that the national regulator was in a better position to assess their situation. On the other hand, supporters of the Commission's proposal argued that the strong reciprocal links between German *Sparkassen*, their relationship, through ownership stakes and mutual guarantees, with larger banks, and the overall huge size of their combined assets justified their full inclusion in the proposed SSM.[12] ECB President Mario Draghi, on the other hand, explicitly endorsed the draft proposal.[13]

The negotiations on the SSM proceeded quite quickly in the first months of 2013, with a general informal agreement reached in March. A cornerstone of this agreement was, indeed, a separation between significant banks, whose supervision had to be delegated to the ECB, and all the others, which had to remain under the authority of national supervisors.[14] Another point of bargaining regarded the need to separate the ECB monetary policy activities from the banking supervision ones.[15] The solution finally reached by the Council was a compromise: although the national supervisory authorities remain formally competent for small banks, the framework for cooperation between ECB and national authorities (Regulation 468/2014 of the ECB) substantially reduced the latter's leeway. However, it must be noted that, given the unanimous decision-making procedure, Germany was able to veto the approval of a SSM which would have given the ECB direct supervisory powers on its savings banks.

B. The Single Resolution Mechanism

The negotiation process leading to the adoption of the SRM was longer and more complex, for three main reasons. First, the procedure required the involvement of the EP, which means (i) more readings before the adoption and (ii) more players with a potential veto taking part in the decision-making process. Second, the

---

[12] See for instance 'Germany's small banks fight union plans', *Financial Times*, 2 December 2012.

[13] See 'One regulator for all banks, says Draghi', *Financial Times*, 6 December 2012.

[14] See 'EU agrees on ECB bank regulatory role', *Financial Times*, 19 March 2013.

[15] See 'EU set to clash on bank deal as Germany sees treaty limit', *Bloomberg Business*, 14 April 2013, available at www.bloomberg.com/news/articles/2013-04-13/eu-set-to-clash-on-bank-deal-as-germany-sees-treaty-limit.

resulting policy was achieved through a combination of three different acts: the SRM Regulation, the BRRD and the IGA. Third, the policy choice regarded, among other things, the transfer of national funds to the EU level, in a fund managed by an institution insulated from the direct control of Member States.

The Commission put forward its draft proposal in July 2013, after the European Council reiterated (see the European Council conclusions of the December 2012[16] and June 2013[17] meetings) its request to the EU legislators to complete the remaining steps of the BU, and after an informal agreement on the SSM had already been reached. The main stages in the decision-making processes leading to the adoption of the SRM were the following:

(1) The Commission proposal of 10 July 2013.[18]
(2) The Council agreement of 18 December 2013, proposing a (large) number of amendments to the Commission proposal.[19]
(3) The negotiation between EP and Council, consisting of several trilogue meetings in February and March 2013,[20] leading to the adoption of the SRM Regulation in the first reading on 14 July 2013.

All in all, if it is considered how complex and ambitious the SRM is, the process was relatively short, lasting only one year in total. Despite different views regarding the legal instruments to be used, with regard to the composition of the Single Resolution Board (SRB) and the nature of the Single Resolution Fund (SRF), the EP and the Council were able to strike a deal. Although the bargaining concerned a large number of provisions in the SRM Regulation, it is worth stressing that the changes proposed in each stage of the negotiation process concerned three relevant issues: (i) the composition of the SRB, (ii) the resolution procedure, and (iii) the legal instrument used to transfer funds to the SRF and the managing of the transitional period.

---

[16] European Council, 'Conclusions' (14 December 2012) EUCO 205/12, available at www.consilium. europa.eu/uedocs/cms_data/docs/pressdata/en/ec/134353.pdf.

[17] European Council, 'Conclusions' (28 June 2013) EUCO 104/2/13, available at www.consilium. europa.eu/uedocs/cms_data/docs/pressdata/en/ec/137634.pdf.

[18] 'Proposal for a regulation of the European Parliament and of the Council establishing uniform rules and a uniform procedure for the resolution of credit institutions and certain investment firms in the framework of a Single Resolution Mechanism and a Single Bank Resolution Fund and amending Regulation (EU) No 1093/2010 of the European Parliament and of the Council' (2013) COM/2013/0520, available at eur-lex.europa.eu/legal-content/EN/TXT/HTML/?uri=CELEX:52013PC0520&from=EN.

[19] Council of the European Union, 'Proposal for a regulation of the European Parliament and of the Council establishing uniform rules and a uniform procedure for the resolution of credit institutions and certain investment firms in the framework of a Single Resolution Mechanism and a Single Bank Resolution Fund and amending Regulation (EU) No 1093/2010 of the European Parliament and of the Council' (19 December 2013) 18070/13, available at data.consilium.europa.eu/doc/document/ST-18070-2013-INIT/en/pdf. A document with the modifications proposed by the Council is available at: data.consilium.europa.eu/doc/document/ST-17742-2013-INIT/en/pdf.

[20] See Council of the European Union, 'Single Resolution Mechanism' (7 February 2014) 6187/14, available at data.consilium.europa.eu/doc/document/ST-6187-2014-INIT/en/pdf; Council of the European Union, 'Single Resolution Mechanism' (3 March 2014) 6956/14, available at data.consilium. europa.eu/doc/document/ST-6956-2014-INIT/en/pdf.

C. The Composition of the SRB

As shown in Table 9.1, in its initial draft regulation, the Commission proposed a SRB whose members of the executive session would be four, only two of whom would have been appointed by the Commission and the Council together, while the EP was only meant to be heard before the final appointment decision was made. One of the two other members was to be appointed by the Commission and the other by the ECB. With this proposal, the power of the two supranational institutions was asserted vis-à-vis the interests of the intergovernmental institutions: the Commission reserved for itself the right to appoint one member of the SRB, and the ECB, although excluded from the management of the SRF, would have had a chance to influence the composition of the Board, given its strong involvement in the banking supervision activity. On the other hand, the Council had the power to co-decide (with the Commission) on the appointment of the Executive Director and Deputy Executive Director, the two most important members – because, in case of a tie in the executive session, the head would have had a casting vote. At the same time the EP got only a consultative role. However, the supranational logic of the proposal was significantly watered down in the final text.

Table 9.1 Changes that occurred in the various stages of the negotiation on the SRM Regulation regarding the appointment of the members of the SRB in its executive session

	Commission Proposal (July 2013)	**Council Agreement (December 2013)**	**Final Text (July 2014)**
Commission	Appoints two of four members with the Council, one out of four autonomously	Appoints all five members together with the Council ($\downarrow$)	Appoints all six members together with the EP and the Council ($\downarrow$)
Council	Appoints two out of four members with the Commission	Appoints all five members together with the Commission ($\uparrow$)	Appoints all six members together with the EP and the Commission ($\downarrow$)
European Parliament	Only consulted	Only consulted (=)	Appoints all six members together with the Commission and the Council ($\uparrow$)
SRB	Not involved	Not involved (=)	Consulted ($\uparrow$)
ECB	Appoints one member out of four autonomously	Not involved ($\downarrow$)	Not involved (=)

Note: The symbols indicate whether the institution gained or lost power in that stage of the negotiations.

In the Council agreement of December 2013, the ministers of the Member States changed the initial text considerably, by assigning more powers to themselves while at the same time reducing the power of the other bodies. They increased by one the number of members of the SRB in its executive session, and proposed to appoint all of them, together with the Commission – in this way, they ensured that they would have a veto power (as an institution) on the composition of the Board. None of the supranational institutions was to gain power from the set-up proposed by the Council: the EP remained confined in its consultative role, while both the Commission and the ECB lost the power to appoint autonomously one of the members of the Board.

As one could expect, this arrangement was not well received by the supra-national institutions, and by the EP in particular, whose approval was needed for the Regulation to pass. In the negotiations following the Council agree-ment, therefore, the EP managed to get an active role in the appointment of the now six executive members of the SRB. The procedure that was finally agreed prescribes, regardless of the technical legal wording, a role for the EP that is equivalent to that of the Commission and the Council. In this way, it can be argued that the Commission has seen its power in this procedure further reduced, because it now has to reach an agreement not only with the Member States' ministers, but also with the members of the EP. The same can be argued regard-ing the Council, which had to accept the EP's involvement in the appointment procedure. Moreover, the Commission is now asked to consult the SRB before appointing the new members. Although the effect of this provision should not be overestimated, it certainly signals an interest in preserving the independence of the institution.

D. The Resolution Procedure

The procedure for resolving a failing bank, which entails the use of money from the SRF, was also the object of a contrasted negotiation. In contrast to the two other aspects analysed in this section, however, the round of negotiations between the Commission, Council and EP, carried out in the first months of 2014, did not substantially change the compromise reached by the finance ministers in December 2013. The evolution of the SRM Regulation in this regard is shown in Table 9.2. As can be seen, in the first proposal, the Commission had granted itself a decisive role. According to that text, the Commission was the only body respon-sible for initiating a resolution procedure. The SRB could issue a recommendation to the Commission, suggesting that a procedure should be initiated, and it was responsible for drafting the resolution scheme, but it had no autonomous power. It was to have acted as an agent of the Commission.

Table 9.2 Changes that occurred in the various stages of the negotiation on the SRM Regulation regarding the adoption of a resolution procedure

	Commission Proposal (July 2013)	Council Agreement (December 2013)	Final Text (July 2014)
Commission	With our without recommendation from the SRB, it can initiate a resolution procedure	Together with the Council, it can block or amend a resolution scheme ($\downarrow$)	Together with the Council, it can block or amend a resolution scheme (=)
Council	Not involved	Together with the Commission, it can block or amend a resolution scheme ($\uparrow$)	Together with the Commission, it can block or amend a resolution scheme (=)
European Parliament	Not involved	Not involved (=)	Not involved (=)
SRB	Can recommend initiation of a resolution procedure to the Commission	Can initiate a resolution procedure ($\uparrow$)	Can initiate a resolution procedure (=)

Note: The symbols indicate whether the institution gained or lost power in that stage of the negotiations.

The Council completely reversed this logic in its revised draft. It gave to the SRB alone the power to initiate a resolution, thus making it independent from the Commission. On the other hand, to compensate for this relevant power, it envisaged the possibility for the Council (within 24 hours) to propose amendments or even block the scheme prepared by the Board. In order to avoid politicising this decision, however, it proposed that this power of the Council could be exercised only after a proposal of the Commission. What this meant, in practice, is that both institutions had to agree on the amendments or on the veto for these to be effective. The text agreed upon by Council and EP made some stylistic modifications but, regarding the substance, only changed the timing for the Commission and Council's intervention, making it shorter. In the Council's formulation, the Board could object to the amendments proposed by Commission and Council, and in that case 24 more hours were given to consider the SRB's notice. This made it possible for this *navette* to last up to 48 hours. The final text has instead set a maximum of 24 hours for the whole procedure. It could be argued that shortening the time for amending the resolution scheme makes it less likely for the Commission and the Council to exercise their power – thus strengthening the position of the Board in this delicate decision.

E. The Legal Instrument Used to Transfer Funds to the SRF and the Managing of the 'Transitional Period'

The rationale of the SRM is that the fund(s) used to ensure the continuity of a bank's essential functions should come from fees levied on the banks themselves, and not from the national or EU budget. Although the principle was clear and shared by all the actors from the beginning, the way in which it should be applied was less so. The following three questions in particular were highly controversial (see Table 9.3): (1) what should the legal basis be for setting up this system? (2) How quickly should the Fund be constituted? (3) How long should it take before the SRF is fully mutualised? The choice regarding the first question has important consequences for the competence of the Court of Justice of the European Union (ECJ) and for the ability to modify those rules in the future. While a regulation is approved by the EP and by the Council voting under qualified majority rule, an intergovernmental agreement is instead adopted only by the States under unanimity rule, and can be changed only with the approval of all the contracting parties. Similarly, the application of an intergovernmental agreement is not subject to the ECJ competence. The Member States' governments are the only enforcers of those rules and, at the same time, their behaviour has to be supervised only by their national constitutional courts.[21] The second question concerns the length of the period in which the Fund will not be fully operational. Banking crises occurring in this period run the risk of being dealt with in the same way as the crises which originated the European sovereign debts crisis, ie by national governments with public budgets. The third issue regards the position of financially weaker States: the mutualisation of the funds implies, for instance, that a Greek bank could be resolved with funds coming (in part) from other countries as well, if the contributions raised in Greece were not sufficient. This will not happen (or will happen only partially) until the end of the transitional period.

Table 9.3 Changes that occurred in the various stages of the negotiation on the SRM Regulation regarding the legal instrument used to transfer funds to the SRF and the managing of the 'transitional period'

	Commission Proposal (July 2013)	**Council Agreement (December 2013)**	**Final Text (July 2014)**
Legal Instrument	The Fund was established and the funds mutualised only on the basis of the Regulation	The system for transferring national funds to the SRF is laid down in an IGA (↓)	The system for transferring national funds to the SRF is laid down in an IGA (=)
Length of the Transitional Period	Transitional period of 10 years before the Fund reaches its full target level	Transitional period of 10 years before the Fund reaches its full target level (=)	Transitional period of 8 years before the Fund reaches its full target level (↑)
National Compartments	No national compartments	National compartments gradually merged during the transition period (↓)	National compartments gradually merged during the transition period (=)

Note: The symbols indicate whether the EU institutions lost or gained power vis-à-vis the Member States.

---

[21] F Fabbrini, 'On Banks, Courts and International Law: The Intergovernmental Agreement on the Single Resolution Fund in Context' (2014) 21 *Maastricht Journal of European Law* 444.

In the first proposal of the Commission, the mutualisation was covered by the SRM Regulation, relying on a disposition of the BRRD. The length of the transitional period was set to 10 years, and there was no mention of national compartments, meaning that each country was supposed to contribute to the Fund in proportion to its banking sector's size, but in the case of a crisis the money from the Fund would have been used regardless of where it came from. This approach, 'supra-national' from the beginning, was radically challenged by the Council, especially under German influence.[22] In particular, Germany's finance minister Schaeuble wanted the Fund to be composed of 'a network of national funds',[23] with no full mutualisation.

Not surprisingly, the compromise reached in the Council agreement of December 2013 marked a clear step back in terms of supranationalisation compared to the original Commission proposal. On the one hand, the transfer of funds from national resolution authorities to the SRF was now expected to be dealt with through an Intergovernmental Agreement (IGA) concluded by all members of the Eurozone. On the other, until the end of the transitional period, the contributions transferred from national authorities were set to remain formally separated in the SRF so that, in case of a resolution procedure involving one country's bank, the funds disbursed by that country's banks should be used entirely before funds from other countries were used. The IGA was unnecessary for setting up a resolution fund. However, through the IGA, the national governments of the Eurozone have created a financial regime separated from the EU legal order. In the final stage of negotiations with the EP, although the EP argued strongly for not unpacking the SRM in a Regulation and an IGA, the only change that it was able to persuade the Council to accept was the shortening of the transitional period from 10 to 8 years.

The Council position was that the legal basis for the Regulation, Article 114 TFEU (concerning approximation of law for the strengthening of the internal market), did not allow the EU legislators to impose a taxation on banks operating in Member States.[24] Therefore, the IGA was necessary in order to avoid the uncertainty related to possible appeals to the ECJ in such a sensitive policy area. However, a particular provision included in the IGA shows that the Member States also used it to protect themselves from future unwanted evolutions of the SRM. Article 9 of the IGA, indeed, states that if the SRM Regulation is changed against the will of a Member State with regard to the resolution procedure, the SRB's decision-making rules or other salient provisions, that Member State might invoke a 'fundamental change of circumstances' clause to block a particular measure, asking the ECJ to verify if such change has occurred. The 'fundamental change of circumstances' clause is a general rule regulating international treaties, codified

---

[22] See 'Berlin rejects Brussels' attempt at grabbing power to shut banks', *Financial Times*, 10 July 2013.
[23] 'Germany's SPD hints at greater solidarity with troubled EU states', *Financial Times*, 12 December 2013.
[24] Hinarejos, *The Euro Area Crisis* (n 2) 46.

by the Vienna Convention of 1969. The fact that it could be invoked for blocking the application of an action resulting from a change in a EU Regulation is equivalent, in practice, to recognising that each contracting party of the IGA has a veto power over modifications of the SRM Regulation: the uncertainty derived from the possibility that one State could in future block a resolution invoking this clause will prevent any change that would not be agreed by all the Eurozone Member States. The use of the IGA as a legal instrument, and the provision set out in Article 9 in particular, had the effect of weakening the supranational character of the SRM.

F. The Stalemate on EDIS

The constant inter-institutional tension between supranational actors and national governments has finally stalled the negotiation regarding the third pillar of the BU, the EDIS. The Five Presidents' Report of June 2015[25] made it clear that it was necessary to accelerate the process for setting up the latter. The Report states that:

> the current set-up with national deposit guarantee schemes remains vulnerable to large local shocks (in particular when the sovereign and the national banking sector are perceived to be in a fragile situation), common deposit insurance would increase the resilience against future crises. A common scheme is also more likely to be fiscally neutral over time than national deposit guarantee schemes because risks are spread more widely and because private contributions are raised over a much larger pool of financial institutions. Setting up a fully-fledged EDIS will take time, but taking concrete steps in that direction should be a priority already ... using the possibilities under the current legal framework.[26]

The Report also offers some suggestion on how to devise the common deposit guarantee scheme. For instance, it might 'be privately funded through *ex ante* risk-based fees paid by all the participating banks in the member states and devised in a way that would prevent moral hazard. Its scope should coincide with that of the Single Supervisory Mechanism'.[27] The Commission thus submitted a draft proposal for a 'Regulation of the European Parliament and of the Council, amending Regulation (EU) 806/2014 to establish a European Deposit Insurance Scheme'[28] on November 2015, but also this proposal has not met friendly ears in the European Council and in the ECOFIN. In particular, the German government has publicly

---

[25] JC Juncker, D Tusk, J Dijsselbloem, M Draghi and M Schulz, 'Completing Europe's Economic and Monetary Union' (22 June 2015) The Five Presidents' Report, available at https://ec.europa.eu/priorities/publications/five-presidents-report-completing-europes-economic-and-monetary-union_en.

[26] ibid, 11.

[27] ibid.

[28] See 'Proposal for a regulation of the European Parliament and of the Council amending Regulation (EU) 806/2014 in order to establish a European Deposit Insurance Scheme' (2015) COM (2015) 586, available at http://eur-lex.europa.eu/procedure/EN/2015_270.

opposed the proposal, fearing that it would create the institutional condition for a mutualisation of debts. Indeed, the third pillar of the BU is far away from entering into the pipeline of the negotiations.

III. The Institutional Outcome: The SSM

Because of the stalled negotiation with regard to the third pillar, the analysis in this chapter of the institutional structure of the BU will concern the only two pillars that have been set up: the SSM and the SRM. Although the activities carried out in implementing both mechanisms are strictly related to each other, the institutional structure of the two is significantly different. This section will analyse the specific features of both pillars with regard to three aspects: (a) the tasks conferred to existing and newly created institutions in the framework of the SSM and SRM (ie which policies are established); (b) the procedure for appointing the members of these institutions (ie who chooses those who decide); and (c) the decision-making process for, respectively, supervision and resolution activities (ie how decisions are made).

A. SSM: Policies

The SSM assigns to the ECB (in cooperation with national supervisory authorities) the prudential supervision of the most 'significant' banks of the Eurozone – although the mechanism can be extended to other countries that may request so. All banks in the participating Member States that either:

(1) have assets of more than €30 billion,
(2) have assets which constitute at least 20 per cent of their home country's GDP,
(3) have requested or received assistance from the European Financial Stability Facility (EFSF) or the European Stability Mechanism (ESM), or
(4) are among the three most significant ones in the country,

are directly supervised by the ECB. The ECB, following a notification of a national authority or acting on its own initiative, can also decide to consider a financial institution significant if its cross-border activities represent a relevant part of its total assets and liabilities (Article 6(4), SSM Regulation). The prudential supervision on all the other banks is still carried out by national supervisory authorities, but in a much more centralised framework than before, in which the national supervisory procedures are adopted by the ECB, and all national supervisory activities must be notified to the ECB (Article 6(7), SSM Regulation).

The prudential supervision on the most significant banks consists of a wide range of supervisory and investigatory powers. In particular, the ECB has been delegated, among others, the power to request information (Article 10), conduct investigations (Article 11), conduct on-site inspections (Article 12), grant authorisations to operate in a participating Member State (Article 14), assess the acquisition of qualifying holdings in banks (Article 15). The ECB and the national authorities, in the framework of the SSM, must act independently from EU and national political authorities. At the same time, the ECB must also interact with the EP and the Council: it must submit to them an annual report and it can be heard by parliamentary committees or by the Eurogroup. However, this relation cannot be configured as a form of accountability of the ECB towards EU institutions.[29]

B. SSM: Appointment Procedures

The tasks conferred on the ECB in the SSM are carried out by a Supervisory Board (SB), that is, 'an internal body' (Article 26(1), SSM Regulation) of the ECB. The SB is composed by a Chair, a Vice-Chair who is also a member of the Executive Board of the ECB, four other members appointed by the Governing Council of the ECB, and one representative of the national competent authority per participating Member State. Unlike the other members of the SB, the Chair and Vice-Chair are appointed through a process that involves not only the ECB and the national authorities, but also the EP and the Council (acting under qualified majority voting). All in all, the SB is a body clearly dominated by the ECB, which controls the appointment of all the members except the Chair. The Chair, which is the member of the SB enjoying the highest independence from the ECB, has some autonomous powers and functions: she or he presides a Steering Committee which sets the agenda of the SB meetings, has a casting vote in case of a tie, and deals with representatives of the EP and Eurogroup. However, the Chair's ability to steer the activities of the SB is constrained by the other SB members. The term of office of the Chair is five years, and it is not renewable.

C. SSM: Decision-making Process

The independence of the SB from Commission, Council and EP is reinforced by the decision-making procedures. The SB, indeed, is the only decision-making body, and it decides by simple majority – in case of a draw, the Chair has a casting vote. The only exception is when the SB adopts regulations 'necessary to organise or specify the arrangements for the carrying out of the tasks' of banking supervision (Article 4(3), SSM Regulation); in this case it must do so using the qualified majority voting system used in the Council – this means that the authorities of

---

[29] For an overview of accountability mechanisms, see M Guidi, *Competition Policy Enforcement in EU Member States*, pp. 53–58 (Basingstoke, Palgrave Macmillan, 2016).

the biggest countries have a decisive weight in shaping the rules of the game. That said, neither the Commission, nor the EP or the Council are involved in the SSM decisions. A representative of the Commission can participate in the meetings of the SB as an observer, but the representative has no access to confidential information. So, the SSM Regulation is very strict and explicit in insulating the SSM not only from the influence of the EP and the Council, but also from that of the Commission.

D. SSM: Overall Institutional Logic

It is plausible to argue that the SSM functions according to a supranational logic, although supranationalism has an evident technocratic character. The ECB was the most effective entrepreneur for the launch, design and implementation of the SSM[30] and the main beneficiary of the project. The ECB is responsible for its functioning. To this end, it can issue guidelines and instructions to national authorities, it may decide to exercise a direct supervisory powers on national institutions, it sets the supervisory standards to be met in the BU. It is the ECB that grants and withdraws banking licences or assesses acquisitions and disposals of specific holdings in credit institutions. It is the ECB that has to verify the compliance of supervised banks with prudential requirements and has to verify the respect, by the supervised banks, of appropriate governance arrangements (like the competence of the management, their remuneration practices, their capacity to prevent and manage financial risks). It is the ECB that has the power to check whether recovery plans are effectively pursued by credit institutions under supervision. The ECB has also the authority of early intervention in those credit institutions in breach of prudential requirements. It is plausible to argue, as Henning[31] does, that the ECB behaved as a strategic actor in a politically fragmented monetary union.

Of course, the SB is distinct from the ECB, although it is located within the ECB building. The ECB is in charge of monetary policy, where the SB is in charge of banking supervision. Indeed, a mediation panel has been set up in order to solve disagreements between the ECB Governing Council and the SB (Regulation 673/2014 of the ECB). In order to stress the independence of the SB, it has been avoided to redouble its governance structure in an executive and plenary session (as in the SRB see below), with the latter constituted by national authorities. The SB directs the supervision of the 128 major banking groups, representing 85 per cent of bank total assets, that have already been subject to comprehensive assessment of risks and asset quality (Asset Quality Review – AQR), followed by

---

[30] S De Rynck, 'Banking on a Union: The Politics of Changing Eurozone Banking Supervision' (2016) 23 *Journal of European Public Policy* 119.

[31] R Henning, 'The ECB as a Strategic Actor: Central Banking in a Politically Fragmented Monetary Union' in J Caporaso and M Rhodes (eds), *Political and Economic Dynamics of the Eurozone Crisis* (Oxford, Oxford University Press, 2016).

a stress test. The SSM thus strengthens the role of the ECB and at the same time it benefits from the latter's independence from national authorities. Through the SSM an important step towards a financial union has been made. However, the role assigned to the supranational ECB has ironically deepened the democratic deficit of the SSM, because the ECB itself does not meet the basic criteria of transparency.[32] However, it is probably implausible to expect technocracy to be democratised.[33]

IV. The Institutional Outcome: The SRM

The decision to establish a SRM derived from the shared recognition, by EU and national authorities, that domestic insolvency procedures were insufficient for dealing with national banks' crisis, nor they were institutionally justifiable. In fact, the burden of bank crises has been traditionally offloaded onto the shoulders of national taxpayers, thus further aggravating national public debt. The Regulation and the Directive promoting the SRM have reversed this approach. It is up to shareholders to bear the first losses of the bank's failure, thus followed by unsecured creditors. Only after the private sector has absorbed a quota of bank losses are national governments allowed to intervene with public resources, as a last resort's institutions. Through the institutionalisation of the bail-in principle, the SRM has introduced a radical change of the paradigm organising the relation between a bank and the holders of bank accounts.[34]

The rationale for the establishment of the SRM has been twofold: on the one hand, by creating a stable system for dealing with bank failures, it aims at reducing the risk of national and European financial crises; on the other, by establishing the principle that the banks themselves contribute to resolution funds, and that shareholders and creditors must be the first to bear the costs (through the so-called bail-in tool), it aims at preventing taxpayers from paying for bank failures through public budgets.[35] One of the main reasons for creating the SRM was to avoid the vicious circle that transformed a financial crisis in a large scale sovereign debt crisis. This happened because some governments increased their deficits to repay the losses that private banks had incurred. By doing so, however, they paved the way for speculation on their sovereign bonds and on the whole EMU.

---

[32] C Gandrud and M Hallerberg, 'Does Banking Union Worsen the EU's Democratic Deficit? The Need for Greater Supervisory Data Transparency' (2015) 53 *Journal of Common Market Studies* 769.

[33] M Everson, 'Banking on Union: EU Governance Between Risk and Uncertainty' in M Dawson, H Enderlein and C Joerges (eds), *Beyond the Crisis: The Governance of Europe's Economic, Political and Legal Transformation* (Oxford, Oxford University Press, 2015).

[34] S Micossi, G Bruzzone and J Carmassi, 'The New European Framework for Managing Bank Crises (November 2013) *CEPS Policy Brief* No. 304.

[35] The involvement of shareholders and creditors, through the so-called 'bail-in tool', in the resolution of banks is also meant to avoid moral hazard. The expectation of having to pay the price of bank mis-management should reduce moral hazard and act as an incentive to actively monitor the management's activities.

A. SRM: Policies

The SRM has been established to manage failures of credit institutions of all the Member States participating in the SSM. The term resolution indicates 'the restructuring of an institution in order to ensure the continuity of its essential functions'.[36] As in the case of the SSM, there is a division of labour between EU and national authorities. The resolution of the banks supervised by national supervisory authorities is carried out by the national resolution authorities, while the resolution of significant banks supervised by the ECB is managed by the SRB at EU level. However, while the SB is located in Frankfurt, the SRB has been located in Brussels in order to make clear, even symbolically, its distance from the ECB and its independence. The practical management of bank failures in the SRM takes the form of resolution schemes adopted by EU or national authorities, which include a variety of operations aimed at preserving market stability.[37] For the resolution scheme, as we have seen, the SRM Regulation allows EU authorities to use money from an SRF, established through an intergovernmental agreement that merges together contributions raised at the national level.

B. SRM: Appointment Procedures

The outcome of the negotiation between the Council and the EP has been a SRB completely and symbolically separated from the ECB – therefore very different from the SB, which is an internal body of the ECB. This choice is clearly reflected in the appointment procedures. In contrast with the SSM, the ECB is completely excluded from the process. The members of the SRB are of two types: six members take part in the executive sessions, in which all the most relevant decisions (included the adoption of resolution schemes) are taken; representatives of the national resolution authorities participate, together with the six other members, in the plenary sessions.

The six members that participate in executive sessions are appointed, for five years without possibility of renewal, through a complex procedure (Article 43, SRM Regulation) involving all of the three EU decision-makers: a list of candidates for the six posts is proposed by the Commission, and must be approved by the EP; after the EP's approval, the Council, acting by qualified majority voting, implements the appointments. In simpler terms, all of the three institutions have a veto

---

[36] See European Commission, 'A single rulebook for the resolution of failing banks will apply in the EU as of 1 January 2015' (31 December 2014) IP/14/2862, available at: europa.eu/rapid/press-release_IP-14-2862_en.htm?locale=en.

[37] See SRM Regulation, recital 59: '… The relevant resolution tools should include the sale of the business or shares of the institution under resolution, the setting up of a bridge entity, the separation of the performing assets from the impaired or under-performing assets of the failing entity, and the bail-in of the shareholders and creditors of the failing entity'.

power over the choice of the six main members of the SRB. Yet the last decision pertains to the national governments in the Council.

C. SRM: Decision-making Process

With regard to the decision-making process, the SRB has less autonomy than the SB in banking supervision. The process for passing resolution schemes (Article 18, SRM Regulation, see Figure 9.1) is initiated by the SRB, and then transmitted to the Commission, which, within 24 hours, can endorse or object to it. If the Commission does not endorse the scheme, it can (within 12 hours) propose the Council (i) to object to it (if it deems that the resolution is not in the public interest), or (ii) to propose that the amount of the fund provided for should be modified (in this case, the SRB can, within eight hours, draft another scheme in accordance with the request of Commission and Council). It is important to note that the Council, in approving or rejecting the Commission's proposal, decides by simple majority.

Figure 9.1 The resolution procedure (Article 18, SRM Regulation)

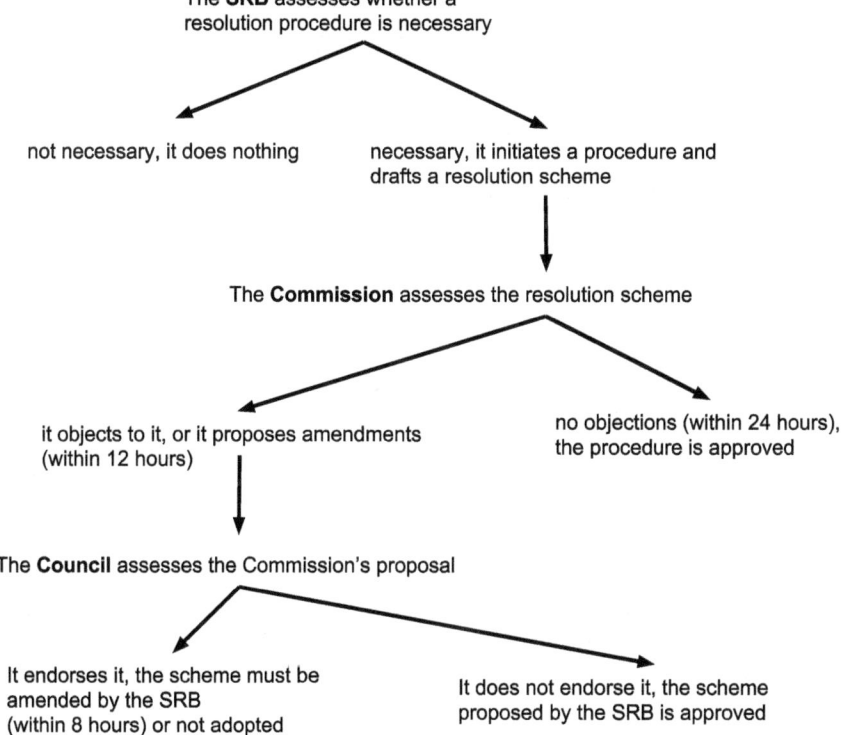

The **SRB** assesses whether a resolution procedure is necessary

not necessary, it does nothing

necessary, it initiates a procedure and drafts a resolution scheme

The **Commission** assesses the resolution scheme

it objects to it, or it proposes amendments (within 12 hours)

no objections (within 24 hours), the procedure is approved

The **Council** assesses the Commission's proposal

It endorses it, the scheme must be amended by the SRB (within 8 hours) or not adopted

It does not endorse it, the scheme proposed by the SRB is approved

Certainly, the Commission has another means to intervene in this process, that is by assessing that the use of the SRF is incompatible with EU competition policy regarding state aid (Article 19, SRM Regulation). If the Commission detects such incompatibility, it may ask the SRB either to revise the draft resolution scheme or to block its adoption. In the latter case, however, the Council can overrule the Commission's opinion by deciding, unanimously, that the use of the Fund is compatible with the internal market rules. In this procedure there is a tension between the technical role of the Commission as a EU competition enforcer and the political role of the Council that takes over if the need to avoid a financial crisis must prevail.

More generally, the SRB emerges as a chiefly technical institution (similar to the ECB), whose power is influenced by the Commission but constrained by the Council. The rationale for the Commission intervention is different in the two cases analysed above. In the standard procedure, the Commission is supposed to evaluate whether the resolution proposed by the SRB is 'necessary in the public interest' (Article 18(1), SRM Regulation): this is a political assessment, for which the Commission is involved because of its executive role. In the second case, the Commission is, instead, involved as an independent enforcer of EU competition policy. As regards the Council, the majority required for its interventions is related to the nature of its mandate and makes a decision more, or less, likely. In the standard procedure, when deciding by simple majority, the Council acts as a legislative chamber of the bicameral EU legislature. When the Council is called to overrule the Commission's assessment on state aid, it acts as a purely intergovernmental body subject to the unanimity requirement. In both cases, it is the Council that has the last word on the Commission's objections, although the latter are more difficult to be refuted as the Council has to vote unanimously against them.

D. SRM: Overall Institutional Logic

Because bank resolution has inevitable financial implications, the national governments have control over the last decision of the resolution process. The Commission may object or ask for amendments to the SRB assessments, but then the Council has the power not to endorse the Commission's proposal, letting the original scheme of the SRB be approved. In this process, the influence of the ECB is also limited. The ECB may communicate to the SRB and the Commission that a bank is failing or likely to fail for several reasons (breach of regulatory requirements, assets lower than liabilities, losses eroding a significant share of capital, inability to repay a debt), but the SRB can then repeat the assessment conducted by the ECB in order to verify the critical conditions of the bank. If the ECB alarm is confirmed, the SRB will adopt a resolution scheme detailing the use of resolution tools within the framework of the SRF. The resolution scheme enters into force after 24 hours, unless the Commission objects to it. If that happens, it is up to the Council to make the final decision. If the scheme implies the mobilisation of public funds, then the Commission has to ensure that the use of public funds does not contravene the prohibition of state aid, as required by the EU antitrust legislation. The process is extremely complex, involving a panoply of political actors and implicating an inevitable politicisation of the decision finally taken.[38] Moreover, the SRB governance, with its redoubling of an executive and plenary sessions, increases the influence of national resolution authorities to the detriment of supranational ones. Indeed, the plenary sessions (constituted by representatives of the resolution authorities of all the participating Member States) have the power to decide (through a majority of 2/3 representing 50 per cent of the paid contributions) the use of liquidity support of significant size (more than 20 per cent of the capital paid into the fund or when the total disbursement exceed €5 billion). After all, the SRF has been set up through an IGA external to EU law. The IGA has decided the transfer of national contributions to national compartments of the Fund outside of any EP control. This is why the SRM is highly influenced by intergovernmental interests: it is structured around institutions whose functioning is largely controlled by national governments.

V. Conclusions

The BU is the most important project pursued by the EMU after the adoption of the single currency. This chapter has shown that its negotiation process and institutional outcomes have been largely constrained by the contradictory forces that constitute the EMU. The EMU, since its inception in the Maastricht Treaty, was based on the combination of a supranational institution (the ECB) exclusively in charge of monetary policy and intergovernmental institutions (the ECOFIN and the then informal European Council become a formal institution of the EU with the 2009 Lisbon Treaty) coordinating nationally decentralised economic policies. At the same time, the policies of the common and then single market continued to be managed through the supranational framework (inclusive of both supranational institutions such as the Commission and the EP). This was the structure of the Maastricht compromise, then confirmed by the Lisbon Treaty – a compromise that has created a dual constitution, one intergovernmental and the other supranational.[39] When the Euro crisis exploded, an intergovernmental constitution to frame the policies for dealing with it was already in place, although mitigated by the existence of a powerful supranational (but technocratic) institution like the ECB. Although the Euro crisis opened a critical juncture where it was possible to redefine the institutional and policy features of the EU, its dramatic and

---

[38] G Bruzzone, M Cassella and S Micossi, 'The EU Regulatory Framework for Bank Resolution' (2015) *Working Paper* 8-2015, School of European Political Economy, LUISS Guido Carli, Rome.
[39] S Fabbrini, *Which European Union? Europe After the Euro Crisis* (Cambridge, Cambridge University Press, 2015).

accelerated impact has ended up reinforcing the path-dependent logic generated by the previous constitutional settlement.

Indeed, the Lisbon Treaty's allocation of economic policy responsibility favoured institutional and policy answers to the crisis that have increased the decision-making power of national governments coordinating within the inter-governmental institutions (the European Council and the Council of the EU), to the detriment of the Union's actors operating in the supranational institutions (such as the Commission and the EP). The BU epitomises the outcome of the struggle between the two logics and the configuration of interests and institutions backing each of them.[40] Indeed, this chapter has tried to show that the supranational logic has been preeminent in the setting up of the SSM, whereas the intergovernmental interests were able to impose their own view in the setting up of the SRM. Indeed, the struggle between the two logics has continued to be persistent to the point of causing a stalemate in the establishment of the third pillar of BU, the EDIS. Without the EDIS, not only the BU will be incomplete, but the 'bank crises/sovereign debt crisis' loop will not be interrupted.[41] After all, the EMU, and more generally the EU, are based on the attempt to compound the interests of national governments and the European citizens, an attempt that is destined to achieve inevitable sub-optimal equilibria because of the contradictory forces that generate them.

---

[40] A Ubide, 'How to Form a More Perfect European banking Union' (October 2013) *Policy brief* No PB13-23, Peterson Institute for International Economics, Washington D.C.

[41] D Schoenmaker, 'Firmer Foundations for a Stronger European Banking Union' (2015) *Bruegel Working Paper* no 2015/13.

10

Prudential Supervision and the European Central Bank Credit Data Registry (AnaCredit)

Legal Basis and Democratic Accountability

I. Introduction

This chapter discusses the centralisation of credit-risk data in the hands of the European Central Bank (ECB) within the set of new competences assigned to it under the Banking Union (BU). The ECB is creating the largest central registry or database of this kind, containing granular deposit and loan-by-loan data of borrowers from Euro-area banks (under the name of Analytical Credit and Credit Risk Dataset, or the acronym of 'AnaCredit'). It is meant to become a tool to perform the ECB's new function as the new macro-prudential supervisor of the Eurozone.

To establish this new reporting system, the ECB has issued a draft regulation which sets the details and the rules of its operation.

The goal of this chapter is to discuss the AnaCredit project and the ECB draft regulation in the context of the role and function of credit data sharing among lenders and the organisations currently operating in the Member States that collect a variety of financial data about transactions between borrowers and lenders.

The complexity of discussing this topic arises from the fact that credit reporting activities and functions in the economy differ significantly within the European Union (EU), depending largely on national cultures and traditions, institutional arrangements and the economic and regulatory environment. Macro-prudential supervision is only one of the possible functions of credit data which occurs in some Member States only, and which has to be proportionate to achieve the objectives that it aims to reach. Therefore, the ultimate question is to what extent the ECB is legitimately using the regulatory powers conferred to it by the Treaties to perform its designated tasks. The answer to this question may have far reaching consequences in terms of the democratic accountability of the EU as redesigned by the BU.

To address the questions that it asks, this chapter is organised as follows.

Section II presents AnaCredit and the ensuing ECB draft regulation in the framework of the BU with the aim of setting the background and context for further discussion.

The economic theories, purposes and traditional uses of credit data are analysed in section III. These include: the reduction of information asymmetries between lenders and borrowers; the use of information in credit-risk management and decision-making in the interest of creditors; the prevention of moral hazard of borrowers and information sharing as reputation collateral; the implementation by creditors of cost-efficient mechanisms for screening applications and managing customer accounts; and data pooling and sharing to enhance competition by lenders in credit markets.

Section IV focuses specifically on the use of credit data for prudential supervision purposes in some Member States.

The variety of information used in the Member States is reported in section V, which contains comparative Tables of the type of data in each national jurisdiction of the EU, outlining the considerable differences in the activities of credit registers and how the EU market for data is jeopardised in national markets. All these differences are reflected in the diverse legal forms and functions of credit registries across the EU. This section explains the private and/or commercial character of credit registries (also known as credit bureaus) in a number of Member States vis-à-vis their public nature and function in prudential supervision in other Member States, all having in common the centralisation and sharing of information but under different rules of participation and legal framework. Once more, comparative Tables will illustrate the fragmented picture across the EU.

Thus, section VI brings together the results of the analyses of the previous sections vis-à-vis AnaCredit, its draft regulation, and the legal basis used for its establishment. It is in response to an analysis of the legal basis of AnaCredit that the issue of democratic accountability becomes dominant.

The concluding remarks of section VI draw together the analysis of the previous section and cast doubts on the legitimacy of AnaCredit in its current form.

II. The Banking Union and the Credit-Risk Reporting of the European Central Bank ('AnaCredit')

A major Euro-area response to the 2008 financial and economic crisis has been the deeper integration – or ever closer union – of its banking system, which culminated in the formation of the BU.[1] In the rhetoric of the EU, this is an important

---

[1] Non-euro-area countries are entitled to join.

step towards a genuine Economic and Monetary Union which could allow for the consistent application of EU banking rules in the participating Member States, and which could be equipped to tackle those problems caused by the crises and the close relationship between public finances and the banking sector.[2]

One important goal of the BU is the pursuit of a number of initiatives to create a safer and sounder financial sector for the single market. One of such initiatives includes a common stronger prudential framework for financial institutions through the establishment of a Single Supervisory Mechanism (SSM) for banks.

The ECB is the European institution in charge of Europe's single currency, monetary policy, and price stability alongside the European System of Central Banks (ESCB).[3] In addition to these tasks, the SSM places the ECB as the new central prudential supervisor. On the basis of Article 127(6) of the Treaty on the Functioning of the European Union (TFEU) and of the Council Regulation (EC) No 1023/2013 ('SSM Regulation'),[4] the ECB is the institution responsible for specific tasks concerning the prudential supervision of credit institutions established in participating Member States. It carries out these tasks alongside the national competent authorities, where the ECB directly supervises the largest banks while national supervisors continue to oversee the remaining smaller financial institutions. As supervisors, the main task of the ECB and the national authorities is to work closely together within an integrated system to make sure that banks comply with the rules of the EU and to intervene early if problems are detected.

To achieve their goals in the framework of the SSM, supervisors need the tools to perform their newly assigned task. Among these tools, the ECB is promoting the setting up of a centralised infrastructure for the collection and sharing of granular credit-risk data within the banking sector on an EU-wide scale, called the Analytical Credit Dataset ('AnaCredit').

The idea of centralising credit-risk data for risk management and/or supervisory purposes is not new, and it already existed in a number of Member States in the form of national credit registries, that is, information systems providing central banks or other regulatory bodies and banks with data on the indebtedness of firms and individuals vis-à-vis the whole banking system.[5] However, not all Member States share the same regulatory and institutional experience of having national credit registries. In some countries such registries do not exist, and instead

---

[2] As indicated on the SSM's official website: https://www.bankingsupervision.europa.eu/about/thessm/html/index.en.html.

[3] Arts 127 and 282 TFEU.

[4] Council Regulation (EU) No 1024/2013 of 15 October 2013 conferring specific tasks on the European Central Bank concerning policies relating to the prudential supervision of credit institutions [2013] OJ L 287/63, pp.63–89.

[5] Reportedly, Germany established the first National Credit Registry in 1934, followed by France in 1946, Italy and Spain in 1962, and Belgium in 1967. See MJ Miller, 'Credit Reporting Systems around the Globe: The State of the Art in Public Credit Registry and Private Credit Reporting Firms' in MJ Miller (ed), *Reporting Systems and the International Economy* (Cambridge MA, MIT Press, 2003) 25.

data centralisation systems have been set up for different credit management purposes in the interests of the credit industry (ie credit bureaus or credit reference agencies – see section V below).

Yet, for coordination at EU level, the ESCB has long been exploring the potential statistical use of the data contained in national credit registries for macroeconomic and financial stability purposes. Even before the start of the crisis, national authorities had finalised a plan for a pan-European data exchange among the registries of Belgium, Germany, France, Italy, Austria, Portugal and Spain, as well as representatives of the ECB (later extended to Bulgaria, Czech Republic, Latvia, Lithuania, Romania, Slovenia and Slovakia). The plan consisted in the creation of a reporting system allowing data exchange on a regular basis on borrowers who also have debt in other European countries. The envisaged cross-border exchange was not intended for the consumer sector but, rather, to provide information to financial institutions across Europe about the indebtedness of their corporate customers. Also, the information exchange could provide supervisory authorities with useful additional information on credit concentration. For supervisory purposes, the growing internationalisation of lending to companies within the European Union, as well as the introduction of the single currency, required an exchange of information among national authorities in order to maintain the value of information contained in their databases.[6]

Reporting to central national credit registries has proved its analytical usefulness but it has also outlined the absence of homogeneity and the differences at national level of the data in terms of coverage, attributes and content. This lack of standardisation and comparable measurements has pointed to the need for harmonisation in concepts and definitions, as well as for convergence in the time, coverage and content of the data.[7]

However, the recent financial crisis and the impact of defaults of both business and personal loans on the banking system have increased the desirability for more credit-risk data in order to allow the ECB and the ESCB to perform their responsibilities with respect to monetary policy, price stability and the development and production of analyses and statistics, and also – last but not least – for micro-prudential supervisory purposes.

---

[6] As explicitly documented by the Deutsche Bundesbank (the Central Bank chairing the Working Group on Credit Registries), in fact, 'data on the total amount of loans taken up will be available for each of the participating countries as well as on an aggregated basis. The data will also provide a breakdown into asset items and off balance-sheet transactions. *There will be no cross-border exchange of information on loans to individuals*' (emphasis added). See Deutsche Bundesbank, 'EU central banks open their credit registers for the cross-border exchange of information on loans to enterprises', press release, 7 June 2005, available at www.bundesbank.de/Redaktion/EN/Downloads/Press/Pressenotizen/2005/2005_06_07_credit_registers.pdf?__blob=publicationFile. See also European Central Bank, 'Memorandum of Understanding on the Exchange of Information Among National Central Credit Registers for the Purpose of Passing It on to Reporting Institutions' (April 2010).

[7] AM De Almeida and V Damia, 'Challenges and prospects for setting-up a European Union shared system on credit' (January 2014) *IFC Bulletin* No 37.

Hence, the ECB and ESCB have accelerated the exploration of the potentials of credit-risk data and they are working towards collection and standardisation of such data in order to be able to have common grounds to engage in EU-wide credit analysis, and measure levels of indebtedness and over-indebtedness in the financial system.

In a nutshell, with the ultimate goal of addressing both micro- and macro-prudential issues in the supervision of the EU banking system alongside monetary policy, the ECB and ESCB have launched the 'AnaCredit' project with the mandate of:

(1) identifying a core set of data to meet the main users' needs and elaborate on their scope;
(2) further analysing and considering harmonised concepts and definitions, and methodological enhancements of the data;
(3) estimating the costs to be incurred by the ESCB to set up a sharing system and that of the reporting agents; and
(4) considering the governance issues, as well as the legal and confidentiality issues, for a centralised data-sharing system, and preparing the appropriate legal instrument.[8]

It is with the view of setting up such a dataset containing detailed information on individual bank loans harmonised across the Member States that the ECB has issued a draft Regulation on the collection of granular credit and credit-risk data (the 'Draft Regulation')[9] regarding the issue of technical rules, procedures and reporting thresholds. The expectation is of implementing a practical application of 'AnaCredit' by 2018 and have in place a 'Eurosystem' database of standardised deposit and loan-by-loan data on credit granted of €25,000 or above to legal entities, including small and medium-sized enterprises (SMEs) and sole traders/proprietors. The prospect is that of extending it also to credit to consumers, in particular mortgage loans and the evolution of indebtedness and defaults rates at national level.[10] Even more, it is proposed by the European Commission to broaden the scope of AnaCredit by including data on consumer credits, potentially provided by all lenders, not only banks, to enable it to monitor the performance of the consumer credit market and fulfil the obligations set by the Consumer Credit Directive 2008/48/EC[11] covering overdrafts, credit cards, credit lines and other consumer credits.[12]

---

[8] V Damia and JM Israel, 'Standardised granular credit and credit risk data', paper presented at the Seventh IFC Conference on 'Indicators to support Monetary and Financial Stability Analysis: Data Sources and Statistical Methodologies', Basel, 4 and 5 September 2014.

[9] European Central Bank, 'Draft Regulation on the collection of granular credit and credit risk data' (2015) available at www.ecb.europa.eu/stats/money/aggregates/anacredit/shared/pdf/draft_regulation_granular_and_credit_risk_data.en.pdf.

[10] See above.

[11] Directive 2008/48/EC of the European Parliament and of the Council of 23 April 2008 on credit agreements for consumers and repealing Council Directive 87/102/EEC, [2008] OJ L 133/66.

[12] See European Commission, Opinion of 7 August 2015 on the Draft Regulation of the ECB concerning the collection of granular credit and credit risk data (2015/C 261/01).

In essence, this means that the ECB is enacting legislation outside the prerogatives assigned under the ordinary EU law-making process of Article 294 TFEU on
the grounds of regulating mere technical standards in accordance with the regulatory powers conferred to it by the TFEU to implement its designated tasks.[13]

If the centralisation and sharing of granular credit-risk data are a matter of
mere technical standards for the stated purposes, not much could be said about
the process and the prerogatives of the ECB.

However, AnaCredit is likely to result in one of the most extensive databases
ever existed, containing not only financial information of a sensitive or personal
nature but also having the potential to interfere with the existing activities of other
organisations in the marketplace and the lives of persons.

As such, the technical nature or else of AnaCredit needs to be discussed in
more depth vis-à-vis the choice of the legal basis adopted, with further key consequences on the law-making process of its establishment and operation, as well as
possible misapplication of EU law – hence, broader ramifications on the broader
EU legal order.

To address this issue, it is important to first understand the theoretical
framework of credit data sharing, the institutional framework in place, and the
organisations currently serving the market alongside the type of data involved.
Only then it can be ascertained to what extent the legal basis used by the ECB falls
inside or outside the already weak democratic accountability of the EU.[14]

III. Theoretical Framework of Credit-Risk Data

A. The Reduction of Information Asymmetry and Risk Management

Credit data have become the instrument most extensively used by the credit industry to assess the creditworthiness of its customers and underwrite decisions on
borrowings or the supply of goods and services. As such, it is used for credit-risk
management in the interest of lenders as a practice of creditworthiness assessment.
Classical economic theory views the sharing of credit data in the financial system
as a tool to meet the problem of asymmetrical information between borrowers

---

[13] Art 132 TFEU and Art 34 of the Statute of the European System of Central Banks and of the European Central Bank. The legal acts of the ECB have the same status as the norms adopted by the other
EU organs.

[14] Debates over the democratic deficit of the EU are dated and well documented in the literature. For
all, see P Craig and G De Bùrca, *EU Law: Text, Cases and Materials* (Oxford, Oxford University Press,
2015) 151–59 and the literature there cited. On the democratic accountability of the BU and the ECB
see specifically K Alexander, 'The ECB and Banking Supervision: Building Effective Prudential Supervision?' (2014) 33 *Yearbook of European Law* 417.

and lenders, as well as problems of bad selection of customers, and the risk which arises from the characteristics of prospective borrowers that may increase the possibility of an economic loss.

Economists have identified the problem of 'asymmetrical information' as the situation when one party does not have the same information that is available to the other party in relation to the risks relating to the performance of the contract by such other party. In a nutshell, one party knows less than the other, a situation which is different from the one where a party has less information than the ideal, known as 'imperfect information'.

In finance, this may be seen as the different knowledge or level of information that the demand side, ie customers, has either on financial products or the market behaviour of providers. By the same token, from the perspective of the supply side of the relationship, ie the credit industry, this difference of knowledge or information relates to the payment behaviour of customers. In a credit relationship, lenders want to avoid lending money that will not be repaid. If they do not have the same information as borrowers have on their ability or willingness to repay a debt, they will incur in a higher risk of making bad business. This risk, in turn, poses problems of bad debts and adverse selection, ie the selection of the wrong customers. This explains why economic theory has traditionally emphasised the importance of information in credit markets.[15]

From the supply side, the reduction of asymmetric information and adverse selection of customers also encompass several elements relating to the market structure and marketing activities of the participants, especially in the retail finance marketplace.

The theory suggests that the lack of information on borrowers can prevent the efficient allocation of credit in a market, and that one way that lenders can improve their knowledge of borrowers is through their observation of clients over time.[16]

In turn, the reduction of asymmetric information affects many aspects of the lending business: risk management and pricing through the assessment of uncertainties about the ability and/or willingness of a debtor to repay, market entry and competition, customers' creditworthiness, application processing and screening, customers' segmentation and product specialisation, and improvement of the credit portfolio.[17]

---

[15] JE Stiglitz and A Weiss, 'Credit Rationing in Markets with Imperfect Information' (1981) 71(3) *American Economic Review* 393; AN Berger and GF Udell, 'Relationship Lending and Lines of Credit in Small Firm Finance' (1995) 68 *Journal of Business* 351; G Akelof, 'The Market for "Lemons": Quality Uncertainty and the Market Mechanism' (1970) 28 *Quarterly Journal of Economics* 523; DW Diamond, 'Monitoring and Reputation: The Choice Between Bank Loans and Directly Placed Debt' (1991) 99 *Journal of Political Economy* 689; AA Admati and PC Pfleiderer, 'Forcing Firms to Talk: Financial Disclosure Regulation and Externalities' (2000) 13 *Review of Financial Studies* 479.

[16] See above.

[17] See above.

B. Moral Hazard and Reputation Collateral

All financial transactions in general, and credit transactions in particular, involve risks or uncertainties. As anticipated above, among these an important risk concerns the ability and/or the willingness of the debtor to repay the debt. At the time of contracting, lenders want to assess whether borrowers are creditworthy, ie whether they have the ability to pay when the repayment is due, and/or that they have the willingness and incentive to pay back their debt. These are two different types of risk, because some people may be able to pay but unwilling to do it or, vice versa, they may want to pay but due to unexpected changes in their circumstances they may be unable to make repayment when this becomes due.

The unwillingness to repay is known as 'moral hazard'. It refers to the risk which arises from personal, as distinguished from physical, characteristics of a borrower that increase the possibility of an economic loss. It is a phenomenon normally associated with business credit: it occurs when entrepreneurs have incentives to invest in riskier projects and a larger proportion of the cost is financed by a lender. If the project is successful, they have much to gain from any excess return, but if the project fails their losses will be limited by bankruptcy. Hence, in this circumstance, as lenders will suffer much of the actual economic losses, borrowers do not have sufficient incentive to act prudently and take excessive risks in the attempt to maximise returns. Investments, by contrast, are deemed to become safer if entrepreneurs have more to lose, in particular if they are forced to bear a portion of the risk.[18]

But moral hazard is now considered directly relevant also for the behaviour of consumers in the use of mortgage or consumptive credit where a repayment reflects the willingness, not the ability, to honour one's debts. In the situation of consumer credit, individuals typically do not make risky investments but they use credit to consume or buy a property.[19] As the theory explains, when deciding to repay, a rational agent weighs the gain of failing to repay vis-à-vis the punishment for default. Since recovery of small debts may not be cost-effective for lenders, and debtors who default may receive no or little punishment by the law, a number of consumers may become prone to moral hazard, ie they may willingly decide not to repay their debts.[20] Likewise, homeowners in negative equity may decide to

---

[18] G Bertola, R Disney and C Grant, 'The Economics of Consumer Credit Demand and Supply' in G Bertola, R Disney and C Grant (eds), *The Economics of Consumer Credit* (Cambridge MA, MIT Press, 2006) 1.

[19] Of course, high levels of indebtedness are risky for consumers who may be exposed to economic shocks and over-indebtedness. For example, this is why Sweden is proposing new legislation forcing amortisation requirements which demands mortgage holders to repay more than they currently do, especially if they have borrowed high percentages of the purchase price of their home. See the official website of the Swedish central administrative body in charge of monitoring and analysing the trends in the financial market (*Finansinspektionen*) at http://www.fi.se/contentassets/90131a719cd243a9aec2e3f4e74cde67/measures-household-indebtedness-eng.pdf.

[20] Bertola, Disney and Grant, *The Economics of Consumer Credit* (n 18).

stop repaying a mortgage that is more expensive than the value of the property, as happened at the start of the 2008 financial crisis in the US.[21]

Similarly, economic theory also explains that information exchanges among lenders play a pivotal role as a discipline device for borrowers, as they may be aware that a delay or a default in repayment compromise their reputation with all the other potential lenders on the market, resulting in them being offered credit only on more costly terms or being cut off from credit entirely.[22] Therefore, information exchanges among lenders would strengthen borrower discipline and reduce moral hazard, since late payment or failure to repay a debt with one institution would result in sanctions by all or many others. According to Miller, a borrower's 'good name', ie his or her reputation collateral, should provide 'an incentive to meet commitments much the same way as does a pledge of physical collateral, thus reducing moral hazard'.[23]

From this perspective, some have gone as far as suggesting that information exchanges maintain accountability and honesty in society.[24]

C. Cost-efficiency in Retail Finance

Typically, the process of granting credit begins when a prospective customer approaches a credit provider and applies for credit or services/goods to be paid at a later stage. In the event that the latter agrees to enter the financing or credit agreement, then such a relationship ends when the last statement of the credit line is paid back in accordance with the same agreement or, in the worst case scenario, when the credit is unrecoverable and/or disregarded following debt-recovery proceedings and a judicial procedure, or in some jurisdictions the judicial declaration of insolvency of the borrower. The recourse to debt-collection procedures and legal actions, however, does not guarantee to lenders the recovery of the debt and, in any event, they are considered an instrument of last resort as they are perceived to be both costly and time-consuming.[25]

---

[21] KC Engel and PA McCoy, *The Subprime Virus: Reckless Credit, Regulatory Failure, and Next Steps* (Oxford, Oxford University Press, 2011).

[22] T Jappelli and M Pagano, 'Information Sharing, Lending and Defaults: Cross-Country Evidence' (2002) 26 *Journal of Banking and Finance* 2017; Diamond, 'Monitoring and Reputation' (n 15); Admati and Pfleiderer, 'Forcing Firms' (n 15). See also T Jappelli and M Pagano, 'The Role and Effects of Credit Information Sharing' in Bertola, Disney and Grant, *The Economics of Consumer Credit* (n 18) 347.

[23] MJ Miller, 'Introduction' in MJ Miller (ed), *Reporting Systems and the International Economy* (Cambridge MA, MIT Press, 2003) 1, 2. See also Miller, 'Credit Reporting Systems' (n 5).

[24] DB Klein, 'Promise Keeping in Great Society: a Model of Credit Information Sharing' (1992) 4 *Economics and Politics* 117; DB Klein, 'Promise Keeping in the Great Society: A Model of Credit Information Sharing' in DB Klein (ed), *Reputation: Studies in the Voluntary Elicitation of Good Conduct* (Ann Arbor, University of Michigan Press, 1997) 267.

[25] ASJ Riestra, 'Credit bureaus in today's credit markets' (September 2002) *ECRI Research Report* No 4, European Credit Research Institute, Brussels, 4; Bertola, Disney and Grant, *The Economics of Consumer Credit* (n 18).

Thus, risk-assessment and applicant screening have become particularly important also for the consumer credit industry which has to deal with a large number of small-sum (often unsecured) credit lines. It is widely agreed, in fact, that in this sector profitability is only achieved by minimising risk while ensuring that a sizeable volume of credit lines is granted. Hence, credit grantors consider information about borrowers vital for their risk-assessment purposes. Along these lines, one of the best predictors of future behaviour is considered to be past behaviour. Therefore, information on how a potential borrower has met obligations in the past enables lenders to more accurately evaluate credit risk, easing adverse selection problems.[26]

Moreover, the small or medium size of loans to consumers means that it is not cost-efficient to assess consumers on a case-by-case basis. Traditionally, when lenders evaluate borrowers to determine their creditworthiness for credit-risk assessment and management, they interview the applicants and ask them directly for personal information. together with the relevant supporting documents. At the same time, they seek and gather information from their own databases developed through years of experience and business practice in the credit market. Such a source of information, however, is incomplete as it covers a lender's own past and present customers, but it does not contain data about the same customers' past and/or present relationship with other financial institutions nor, from a competition perspective, information about new or prospective customers and their past and/or present relationship with other providers. Thus, it is with the view to supplement comprehensive information about these customers that information exchanges among lenders and sophisticated centralised databases have emerged and developed in the past few decades.[27]

D. Competition

As far as competition is concerned, the exchange of information on customer relationships or applicants reduces the information monopoly of individual lenders and the competitive advantage of large financial institutions. Although lenders lose the exclusivity of data in terms of competition against eachother, they would ultimately gain by sharing information as this additional accumulation of data enables them to distinguish the good borrowers from the bad ones. Information sharing would serve as a tool to predict the future payment behaviour of applicants allowing lenders to attract creditworthy borrowers and offering them better terms and conditions, thus promoting market competition that could ultimately result in

---

[26] Miller, 'Introduction' (n 23) 2. See also Miller, 'Credit Reporting Systems' (n 5).

[27] Bertola, Disney and Grant, *The Economics of Consumer Credit* (n 18); Riestra, 'Credit bureaus' (n 25). However, note that in some countries (eg Germany) credit bureaus have been in existence for a longer time (see sections V.A and V.B below).

benefits to those 'good customers'.[28] Hence, the adverse selection problem identi-fied by the economic literature indicates that should lenders fail to distinguish the good borrowers from the bad ones, all accepted borrowers would be charged at a higher rate an average interest rate that mirrors their pooled experience.[29] There-fore, the distinction between good borrowers from the bad ones allows lenders on the one hand to offer more advantageous prices to lower-risk borrowers while, on the other hand, higher risk borrowers are offered higher interest rates or can be rationed out of the market because of the lenders' unwillingness to offer these borrowers accommodating rates or any credit at all.[30]

The problem of asymmetric information and adverse selection becomes greater for new market entrants, particularly foreign lenders. This is particularly the case in the context of the creation of the EU single market and cross-border entry or cross-border provision of financial services. In addition to competitive disadvantages in relation to incurring greater risks of incorrectly estimating a borrower's credit risk, without relevant information on borrowers new market entrants would be likely to attract precisely those who were rejected by exist-ing lenders in the market.[31] This circumstance has induced recent literature to conclude that information sharing, market structure and competitive conduct are intrinsically intertwined in the financial services market and, from the stand-point of industrial organisation, the availability of information shared by the sector can affect foreign lenders' choice not only of whether to entry another jurisdiction but also the mode of doing it, ie whether through the cross-border provision of services, the setting up of branches or subsidiaries, or through mergers and acquisitions.[32]

Therefore, on the one hand such strategies may well have the potential to influence the intensity of competition in national markets and among national providers. On the other hand, however, this is an indication that the behaviour of one or few market players – particularly existing lenders – influences and drives the behaviour of others, especially new entrants, which will decide their strategies on the experience, or market intelligence, of existing lenders.

Prima facie, considerations of this type may have the effect of casting doubts as to whether or to what extent this may constitute a concerted practice or simply a reduction of market uncertainty.[33]

---

[28] European Commission, *Report of the Expert Group on Credit Histories* (Brussels, May 2009).

[29] D Alary and C Gollier, 'Strategic Default and Penalties on the Credit Market with Potential Judg-ment Errors' (2001) *EUI Working Paper*, European University Institute.

[30] M Barron and S Staten, 'The Value of Comprehensive Credit Reports: Lesson from the US Experi-ence' (2000) *Research Paper* – Credit Research Centre, Georgetown University; M Barron and S Staten, 'The Value of Comprehensive Credit Reports: Lesson from the US Experience' in MJ Miller (ed), *Reporting Systems and the International Economy* (Cambridge MA, MIT Press, 2003) 273.

[31] C Giannetti, N Jentzsch and G Spagnolo, 'Information-Sharing and Cross-Border Entry in Euro-pean Banking' (February 2010) *ECRI Research Report* No 11, Brussels.

[32] ibid.

[33] F Ferretti, *EU Competition Law, the Consumer Interest and Data Protection* (Cham, Springer, 2014).

Also, to the extent that information monopoly of individual lenders is reduced, this is transferred to those third-party subjects who become the providers of information and manage the corresponding databases, ie the credit bureaus.

This, in turn, may raise further debates over market competition and power which are beyond the scope of this work.[34]

IV. Credit-Risk Data and Prudential Supervision

Information exchanges among lenders can be justified and used for the supervision of the financial system as a whole and to assist in preserving financial stability. Under certain national systems, credit data are part of a broader information centralisation system managed by national central banks for the purpose of oversight of the financial system as a whole, ie they are an instrument for the macro-prudential supervision of the banking system. But credit-risk data may also become a tool for the micro-prudential supervision if used to oversee and safeguard individual financial institutions from excessive risk-taking.[35]

Financial prudential supervision encompasses a number of complex issues and elements that are beyond the scope of this work. But, among the tools to achieve it, there is the need for the authorities in charge of this public function to have adequate and timely information about the behaviour, leverage and condition of banks vis-à-vis the whole system. Among the many types of information needed by the authorities – such as asset quality, capital adequacy, liquidity, internal systems of control and security, income and dividends, foreign operations, and so on – is included the regular reporting on past due loans and non-performing loans. This not only allows supervisors to be in control and have the information on credit exposure concentrations, distribution of loans across sectors (consumer, mortgage, commercial) and the condition and performance of the supervisees in order to intervene promptly if there are problems, but it also constitutes an instrument to promote transparency in order to favour greater reliance on market discipline.[36]

---

[34] These issues have been addressed in Ferretti, *EU Competition Law* (n 33).

[35] For the institutional arrangements in the various EU Member States see section V and the Tables provided.

[36] T Jappelli and M Pagano, 'Information Sharing in Credit Markets: The European Experience' (2000) *Working Paper* No 35, Centre for Studies in Economics and Finance, University of Salerno, T Jappelli and M Pagano, 'Public Credit Information: A European Perspective' in MJ Miller (ed), *Reporting Systems and the International Economy* (Cambridge MA, MIT Press, 2003) 81; Jappelli and Pagano, 'The Role and Effects' (n 22); RA Brealey, A Clark, C Goodhart, J Healy, G Hoggarth, DT Llewellyn, C Shu, P Sinclair and F Soussa, *Financial Stability and Central Banks: A Global Perspective* (London, Routledge, 2001) Ch 2; P Cartwright, *Banks, Consumers and Regulation* (Oxford, Hart Publishing, 2004) 31–34; RM Lastra, *Central Banking and Banking Regulation* (London, Financial Markets Group LSE, 1996); RM Lastra and H Shams, 'Public Accountability in the Financial Sector' in E Ferran and C Goodhart (eds), *Regulating Financial Services and Markets in the Twenty First Century* (Oxford, Hart Publishing, 2001) 165.

The information available to financial supervisors also allows them to produce macro statistics and perform a number of analyses. For example, in Spain credit-risk data are used for the stress testing of banks.[37]

In turn, under a limited number of mechanisms supervisors provide feedback loops to the banks that provide the data. Banks benefit from supervision in that they are provided with the instruments to control the quality of their loans in their daily operations. To favour this, in a number of Member States centralised databases managed by public authorities provide banks and supervisors with aggregate or granular information (depending on national regulation) about the level of indebtedness of borrowers vis-à-vis the whole system, including natural persons. In these jurisdictions, information sharing by supervised banks is mandated by law, usually in a national banking act.[38]

This mechanism relies on information exchanges among financial institutions where the public authority acts as the third party for pooling, aggregating, and elaborating the information exchanged, and is the organisation setting the rules of the information exchanges.

It is anticipated that AnaCredit will collect information on a loan-by-loan basis, first from credit registers operated by national central banks of the European System of Central Banks (where such registers exist) or from other granular data sources. Thus, the exchange of financial information in this context may become clearer in the discussion below of the current organisations serving the market and their roles which, in turn, will later be helpful when considering matters concerned with the role of the ECB, the prospective function of AnaCredit, and possible problems.

V. Credit Registries in the EU

Credit registries (or credit bureaus or credit reference agencies) are the major data channels for a number of different purposes in the Member States. Credit registries now exist in all EU Member States with the exception of Luxembourg, but their legal form or institutional structure varies depending on different local policy or other objectives, and the function that they perform in the local economy and society. The way in which the databases are organised and the types of information provided will depend on the particular objectives or interests that they are meant to address. The different roles of credit information providers reveal a key distinction between public and private or commercial organisations. While the former is normally a part of a national central bank or supervisory authority, and institutionally and legally designed to address the stability of the financial system and

---

[37] See eg European Banking Authority, Results of the 2014 EU-wide Stress Test (26 October 2014).
[38] F Ferretti, *The Law and Consumer Credit Reporting Systems in the EC* (London, Routledge-Cavendish, 2008).

the monitoring of the indebtedness of legal persons and consumer households, the latter offer risk-management and market intelligence tools aiming to enhance economic efficiency and the profitability of financial institutions, irrespective of whether these are banks lending depositors' money or any other entity doing business involving the provision of credit in return for profit.[39]

A. Private or Commercial Credit Registries

These are fully fledged privately owned companies working for profit (see eg commercial companies in the UK, Germany or Italy) or for the benefit of banks (see eg not-for-profit entities designed to make the interest of commercial ventures such as banks in Slovenia, Poland or the Netherlands) that are no more controlled, monitored or influenced by State-controlled organisations or other public bodies than any other privately owned organisation or business. Nor are they accountable to central banks or other financial service regulators. They are subject to the same rules and regulations as every other business in the marketplace. Their job is to provide services to the financial services industry by compiling databases. Even looking at the websites of these companies, they clearly state that they provide decision-making tools or marketing intelligence to the credit industry. They do not claim to be carrying out public tasks and they do not hold themselves accountable for the decisions taken by the credit industry.

They can have a broad range of client members depending on the jurisdiction where they operate, including banks and non-bank lenders. In addition to traditional financing firms that are not banks, other less obvious examples may include telecommunication companies, utility companies, mail order companies, and/or any other business advancing goods or services to consumers who will pay for them at a later stage. Consultation of their databases is not mandatory by law prior to the underwriting of credit and is carried out on a voluntary basis (the exception is Slovenia where banks have to use a bank-owned database, but other non-bank lenders are not obliged to subscribe to it). As participation by lenders in a privately owned consumer credit information system is not compulsory, the rules relating to the functioning of the system are not imposed by statute or regulation but are governed by contract law.[40]

In some jurisdictions, these databases are supplemented with non-credit data collected from other sources. Thus, financial and non-financial entities may have access to information gathered across different economic segments. As commercial ventures, moreover, they integrate their services with other added value services for their customers such as risk scoring (which includes both behavioural

---

[39] Jappelli and Pagano, 'Information Sharing' (n 36); Jappelli and Pagano, 'Public Credit Information' (n 36); Jappelli and Pagano, 'The Role and Effects' (n 22); Ferretti, *The Law* (n 38).
[40] Ferretti, *The Law* (n 38).

and sociological customer scoring), loan or mortgage rating, risk screening, monitoring, propensity modelling, debtor tracking and support for debt collection.

B. National Credit Registries

National (or public) credit registries are institutions typical of continental Europe where they first originated. They developed with the objective of providing an information system for supervisors to use in order to analyse banks' portfolios and monitor the health and soundness of the overall financial system of a country, as well as the level of indebtedness of borrowers, both legal and natural persons.

Generally, they exercise a public function linked to prudential supervision by furthering the general stability of the banking and payment system. This requires the monitoring of the safety and soundness of banks, which includes the monitoring of the amount of exposure of each bank towards legal persons and individuals who, consequently, undergo checks over their levels of indebtedness.

Only banks participate in the system and are subject to its underlying rules, unlike private registries that are conceived as open systems with the incentive of bringing an increasing number of subscribers and information into play.[41]

Another key difference is that financial institutions that are under the supervision of a country's central bank or supervisory authority are required to report certain credit data on a regular basis by law or other regulation. As participation in the system is compulsory, its rules are imposed by law or regulation and not under contract. This compulsory nature also means that national credit registries have complete coverage of the financial institutions of a country, and no bank lenders are left out, as may happen when parties are free to negotiate whether to take part in a system or not, or which system to be part of if more than one exists.[42]

Equally, public authorities have a legal basis for demanding that reporting lenders remedy possible inaccuracies or make available missing data. Failure to comply can result in sanctions that may be imposed by law, such as penalty fees followed by supervisory actions.[43]

It appears undisputable from all the features discussed above that private or commercial credit bureaus on the one side, and public credit bureaus on the other side, cannot be substituted for each other to the extent that the latter exercise functions in the public interest that the former are not entitled to perform and do not perform. Public providers, however, can substitute for private/commercial ventures to the extent that the lenders' debt provisioning remains tightly controlled and the amount of overdue or defaulted debt is controlled.

---

[41] Jappelli and Pagano, 'Public Credit Information' (n 36); Ferretti, *The Law* (n 38).
[42] ibid.
[43] Miller, 'Credit Reporting Systems' (n 5).

In the end, as Tables 10.1 and 10.2 show, the current picture in the EU is fragmented. There are profound differences in the legal form and structure in the various Member States, the different roles of credit registries, and the various types of data exchanged. The Tables summarise the above discussion of the legal form of credit registries in terms of private versus public ownership and function. In the case of private or commercial registries, the self-interest pursued by the credit industry emerges clearly. In contrast, the goals, role and function of databases controlled by public authorities show the pursuit of public policy goals.

Table 10.1 Legal form and structure of credit bureaus in the Member States of the EU

Country	Public credit register	no. of private Credit Bureaus			Ownership structure		
		For profit	Not for profit	Not ownership by creditors	≤ 50% Ownership by creditors	> 50% Ownership by creditors	Other
Austria	Yes		1				1
Belgium	Yes						
Bulgaria	Yes	1		1			
Cyprus	No	1				1	
Czech Rep.	Yes	1			1		
Denmark	No	2		2			
Estonia	No	1		1			
Finland	No	1		1			
France	Yes						
Germany	Yes	1			1		
Greece	No	1			1		
Hungary	No	1			1		
Ireland	No	1			1		
Italy	Yes	2	1	1		1	1
Latvia	Yes						
Lithuania	Yes	1				1	
Luxembourg	No						
Malta	No	1				1	
Netherlands	No	1	1	1			1
Poland	No	1		–	1	–	

Country	Public credit register	no. of private Credit Bureaus			Ownership structure		
		For profit	Not for profit	Not ownership by creditors	≤ 50% Ownership by creditors	> 50% Ownership by creditors	Other
Portugal	Yes	2				1	
Romania	Yes	2		1	1		
Slovakia	Yes	2		1	1		
Slovenia	Yes		1				1
Spain	Yes	2		1		1	
Sweden	No	6		5	1		
United Kingdom	No	3		3			

Note: The Table below should be corrected as regards Romania. The number of private Credit Bureaus is 1 (instead of 2), and the ownership structure is >50% ownership by creditors (instead of <50% ownership by creditors – in fact it is 100% ownership by creditors).

Ireland is currently establishing a National Credit Registry but it is outsourcing the service under precise rules to a private sector credit registry after an open procurement competition.

Source: European Commission, Report of the Expert Group on Credit Histories (Brussels, May 2009); European Parliament, 'Responsible Lending – Barriers to Competition', DG For Internal Policies, Economic and Monetary Affairs, IP/A/ECON/ST/2011-05, Brussels, June 2011.

Table 10.2 Role and structure of private/commercial and public credit registries

	Credit Bureau	Public Credit Register
Ownership structure	Private/commercial entity	Central Bank or Supervisory Authority
Clients structure	Mainly creditors but sometimes also other services providers	Financial institutions authorised to grant credit
Scope	Credit assessment and monitoring	• Banking supervision, building statistics, financial stability studies • Monitoring and preventing over-indebtedness • Credit assessment • Fostering credit institutions prudent management
Creditors' participation	Generally voluntary	Mandatory by law

(continued)

Table 10.2 *(Continued)*

	Credit Bureau	Public Credit Register
Principle of reciprocity/ Non discriminatory access	Yes	Yes
Type of data stored	• Full credit data (positive and negative data) • Often also non-credit data	• Credit data from financial institutions authorised to grant credit (including both positive and negative data in a majority of cases) • Data on bankruptcy of natural and legal persons
Additional services provided to creditors	Mainly: • Credit scoring based on the whole CB dataset • Software applications • Portfolio management services • Fraud prevention systems • Authentication products …	None
Use of thresholds	Yes, but generally low	Yes
Degree of detail of the information provided	Detailed information on each individual loan. In some countries, credit information merged with other data (e.g. from public sources).	Information sometimes in a consolidated form (giving the total loan exposure of each borrower). In some PCRs, (Belgium, Italy, Portugal or Spain), the information is also given in a detailed form.
Coverage	Depends on the legislation, length of service provided, financial culture, etc.	Universal coverage

Source: European Commission, Report of the Expert Group on Credit Histories (Brussels, May 2009).

C. Type of Data Used

The detail of the source and type of information collected and disseminated by credit registries varies from country to country. In general terms, however, it may be synthesised that they store, process and disseminate customers' files containing data on their previous and existing accounts, which normally include detailed information about credit lines, mortgages, bank accounts, store cards, charge cards, credit cards, loan accounts, and in many jurisdictions even mail order accounts as well as telecom and other utilities accounts.

An important distinction to be drawn when referring to the type of data collected and distributed by credit registries is between the so-called 'negative' information and 'positive' information. 'Negative' information usually refers to negative data about defaults on payments, delays, delinquencies, bankruptcies etc.). That is, information with a negative connotation on the payment history and the financial behaviour of the borrower. 'Positive' information, by contrast, refers to positive data about the financial standing, payments and other details which do not indicate a default or a late payment.

Attempts have also been made to classify semi-negative or semi-positive information, which would refer to data on accounts which demonstrate some signs of problems but have not yet proceeded to the state of being 'negative', ie accounts which are in acceptable time arrears with no warning to the customer having yet been issued by the lender.[44]

At EU level, there is no commonly accepted use of this type of information. Some countries make use of both positive and negative information, while others prescribe that only negative information can be used. In extreme cases, in some countries non-credit data are also used (eg the UK), while on the other extreme in some countries the use of positive data is unconstitutional (eg France).[45] See Table 10.3.

Table 10.3 shows that there is no uniformity or common understanding regarding the depth and breadth of information, as well as the terminologies used.

The depth of data makes reference to the amount of information about a credit agreement that is available.[46] The breadth of data, in turn, refers to the level of product coverage (eg data related to consumer credit, to mortgage credit, to not-credit related debt such as telecom or utility bills, etc). In addition, the definitions used to assess which data should be entered into the databases also differ from a country to another. Moreover, the terminologies, meanings and significance of the data used may have diverse meanings from Member State to Member State.

---

[44] G Howells, 'Data Protection, Confidentiality, Unfair Contract Terms, Consumer Protection and Credit Reference Agencies' (1995) 4 *Journal of Business Law* 343, 344.

[45] See Conseil Constitutionnel, Décision no 2014-690 DC du 13 mars 2014. In 2010 France proposed legislation implementing the EU Consumer Credit Directive 2008 recommending a positive credit reporting system operated by the Bank of France. It was included within the *loi Hamon* which introduced a number of consumer protections. However, the relevant provisions on the establishment of a positive credit database were referred to the Constitutional Court (*Conseil Constitutionnel*) which declared them unconstitutional as a disproportionate intrusion on the constitutional right of privacy which was not outweighed by possible benefits related to credit decision-making.

[46] For instance, some Member States follow a comprehensive positive data reporting approach (every single credit is reported upon, independently as to whether the consumer is in arrears or not), while credit registers in other countries only engage in negative reporting (credits are only reported upon if the consumer does not meet his/her payment obligations).

Table 10.3 Depth and Breadth of Credit Data by Country

Country	Data structure PCR positive & negative	PCR negative only	CB positive & negative	CB negative only	Threshold (€) PCR	CB	CBs operations For creditors only	For creditors + other service providers	For credit assessment only	For other purposes
Austria	•		•		35000		•		•	•
Belgium	•				200					
Bulgaria	•		•				•		•	•
Cyprus			•						•	
Czech Rep.	•		•				•		•	
Denmark				•					•	
Estonia			•				•			
Finland				•				•	•	•
France		•			500					
Germany	•*		•		1,5 ML	100		•	•	•
Greece			•				•		•	
Hungary			•				•		•	
Ireland			•				•		•	
Italy	•		•		30000**		•		•	

Latvia	•	•				150					•
Lithuania	•	•			•						
Luxembourg											
Malta					•						
Netherlands	•	•				•	•				•
Poland	•	•				125	•				•
Portugal	•	•				50	•	•			•
Romania	•	•				•	•	•			•
Slovakia	•	•				•	•				•
Slovenia	•	•				•	•				•
Spain	•	•				6000	•	•			•
Sweden		•				•	•	•		•	•
United Kingdom		•				•	•	•		•	•

Note: *Does not cover consumer, **No threshold applies to bad debts.

Note: The name and website of the credit registries in each country is available from the credit information trade association 'Association of Consumer Credit Information Suppliers' (ACCIS) at https://accis.eu/about-us/.

Source: European Commission, Report of the Expert Group on Credit Histories (Brussels, May 2009); European Parliament, 'Responsible Lending – Barriers to Competition', DG For Internal Policies, Economic and Monetary Affairs, IP/A/ECON/ST/2011-05, Brussels, June 2011.

This exposes a limited cross-border exchange of credit-risk data[47] and an absence of interoperability among credit registries in the EU, which makes reference to the inability of making systems and organisations work together (inter-operate). Currently, credit registries are not interoperable for a number of reasons, but mostly for reasons of competition (where commercial organisations are involved); the different legal forms (public authorities vis-à-vis commercial organisations); the different data and systems used; the different criteria employed; and national regulations.

At the proposal stage of the Mortgage Credit Directive[48] the European Commission had included provisions that would have allowed the harmonisation of at least some key terms used in credit databases (terms such as 'defaults', 'arrears') and the definition of uniform credit registration criteria, as well as data processing conditions to be applied to credit databases (eg the registration thresholds), in order to increase reliability of information contained in databases, facilitate creditworthiness assessments and in the long-run promote cross-border supply of credit. But these provisions were not retained during negotiations and do not appear in the final text of the directive.[49]

The result is a fragmented and significantly diverse picture across the EU, as summarised by Tables 10.1, 10.2 and 10.3. Overall, they show profound differences in the legal form and structure in the various Member States, the different roles of credit registries, and the various types of data exchanged.

Arguably, the traditional absence of European market integration in consumer finance, coupled with differences in cultures, traditions, organisation, institutions and laws have contributed markedly to the uneven development and multi-layered segmentation of information exchange systems within the EU. But this picture is corroborated by the different legal forms, functions and role of credit registries in the various Member States, as well as the different type or nature of information that are exchanged nationally.

---

[47] According to the Association of Consumer Credit Information Suppliers (ACCIS), in 2015 only 38 per cent of its members participated in cross-border data exchanges. See ACCIS, 'ACCIS 2015 Survey of Members: An analysis of Credit Reporting in Europe' (November 2015).

[48] Directive 2014/17/EU of the European Parliament and of the Council of 4 February 2014 on credit agreements for consumers relating to residential immovable property and amending Directives 2008/48/EC and 2013/36/EU and Regulation (EU) No 1093/2010, L 60/34.

[49] Commission adoption of a proposal for a Directive on credit agreements relating to residential property, COM(2011)142. The following provisions were deleted during the negotiations between the Council and the European Parliament:

> Article 14(5) – 'Powers are delegated to the Commission ... to specify and amend the criteria to be considered in the conduct of a creditworthiness assessment as laid down in paragraph 1 of this Article and in ensuring that credit products are not unsuitable for the consumer as laid down in paragraph 4 of this Article.'

> Article 16(2) – 'Powers are delegated to the Commission ... to define uniform credit registration criteria and data processing conditions to be applied to the databases referred to in paragraph 1 of this Article. In particular, such delegated acts shall define the registration thresholds to be applied to such databases and shall provide for agreed definitions for key terms used by such databases.'

The type of information exchanged represents, however, a very important feature in the design of an information exchange system, and it may carry with it both an explanation and implications for the ECB initiative of AnaCredit.

VI. The Legal Basis of AnaCredit: A Democratic Gap?

AnaCredit is designed to address the need of the ECB and ESCB to have a central-ised European source of harmonised statistical data on credit and exposures to perform their institutional tasks of monetary policy analysis and research, systemic risk management and supervision, and statistics for policy purposes. Highly sophisticated analytical techniques have the potential to allow financial sector authorities to enhance the depth of the analyses they perform under their prudential supervisory tasks. Appropriate information tools may allow them to have a better grasp on potential problems of systemic nature in the EU financial system (Euro-area and possibly beyond).

As shown above, credit-risk databases are tools already in place in a number of Member States to monitor and manage credit risk and provide an overview of the level of credit exposures. In the single market, it could be maintained that the centralisation in the hands of the ECB satisfies the need to monitor cross-border credit flows and the levels of indebtedness not only of resident but also non-resident borrowers vis-à-vis national banks. This work has also shown how credit registries may provide an opportunity to improve credit management by banks. An EU-level information flow may facilitate the granting of appropriate credit lines in the thrust envisaged by the EU under the Capital Market Union[50] and the integration of retail financial services.[51]

At the same time, AnaCredit will become one of the largest databases ever created, comprising of the combination of datasets already existing at national level with the addition of new ones where Member States currently experience different arrangements. These datasets contain granular data of sensitive or quasi-sensitive nature as well as personal nature. As seen above in this chapter, credit-risk data serve different functions, where prudential supervision may be one of them. There are a number of different actors involved in the organisation and supply of credit-risk data for different purposes, each Member State having its own experi-ence and arrangements. AnaCredit, which is due to collect at least 94 different data attributes and become the most comprehensive dataset of the like,[52] will inevita-bly result in overlaps, duplications and redundancies with other existing reporting

---

[50] European Commission, *Green Paper – Building a Capital Market Union*, COM(2015) 63 final.

[51] European Commission, *Green Paper on Financial Services and Insurance. Better products, more choice, and greater opportunities for consumers and businesses*, COM(2015) 630 final.

[52] European Central Bank, 'Explanatory note on the draft ECB Regulation on the collection of granular credit and credit risk data' (November 2015).

systems regardless of the purposes. Moreover, the standardisation of credit-risk data means a change in the current rules or practices regarding the data necessary to assess credit risk, creditworthiness and to measure levels of indebtedness. As seen above, each Member State operates differently, so any change brought by the ECB standardisation is likely supersede national methods and the attribution of current values.

The rules governing the setting up and governance of AnaCredit – including details regarding the granularity, standardisation and operation of the system – are laid down in the Draft Regulation of the ECB.

Therefore, the first legitimate question that arises is to what extent the Draft Regulation contains mere technical standards that justify the ECB regulatory powers, or whether it contains rules likely to affect the rights or interests of individuals and/or third-party businesses beyond statistical, monetary and supervisory purposes. The answer to this question is critical because it determines the legitimacy of the setting up of AnaCredit by the ECB and, thus, the democratic accountability of the system. Ultimately, it turns into the broader issue of application of EU law and the trade-off between efficient economic problem-solving vis-à-vis democratic legitimation.

The whole legal process has commenced with Decision of the ECB no 6/2014,[53] which was taken having regard of Article 5 of the Statute of the European System of Central Banks and the European Central Bank[54] on the collection of statistical information. The Statute of the ESCB and of the ECB is laid down in a Protocol annexed to the EU Treaties, as provided for in the second paragraph of Article 129 TFEU. Article 5.1 of the Statute provides that in order to undertake the tasks of the ESCB, the ECB with the assistance of the national central banks has to collect the necessary statistical information either from the competent national authorities or directly from economic agents. To do so, it has to cooperate with the Union institutions and other agencies, as well as with the competent authorities of the Member States or third countries (in addition to the relevant international organisations). In turn, Article 5.2 states that the national central banks shall carry out, to the extent possible, the tasks of Article 5.1.

Of particular importance is Article 5.3, according to which 'the ECB shall contribute to the harmonisation, where necessary, of the rules and practices governing the collection, compilation and distribution of statistics in the areas within its fields of competence'.

The SSM Regulation confers prudential supervisory powers to the ECB. To carry out the supervisory activities required by Article 4 of the SSM Regulation, the ECB shall adopt guidelines and recommendations, and take decisions subject to and in compliance with the relevant Union law. The ECB may also adopt

[53] Decision of the European Central Bank of 24 February 2014 on the organisation of preparatory measures for the collection of granular credit data by the European System of Central Banks (ECB/2014/6) (2014/192/EU), [2014] OJ L 104/72.
[54] [2012] OJ C 326/230.

regulations only to the extent necessary to organise or specify the arrangements for the carrying out of the tasks conferred on it by the SSM Regulation itself.[55]

The Decision of the ECB defines the preparatory measures which are deemed necessary to establish in the long term a framework for the collection of the data based on harmonised ECB statistical reporting requirements.[56] It is addressed to the national Central Banks and the controllers of other credit registers or databases.[57]

In the end, the Draft Regulation setting up AnaCredit claims as its legal basis Council Regulation 2533/98[58] concerning the collection of statistical information by the ECB, which in its Article 5 allows it to adopt regulations for the definition and imposition of its statistical reporting requirements. Moreover, statistics requirements are defined in the ESCB Public Commitment on European Statistics[59] in consistency with the statistical principles laid down in Regulation 223/2009[60] of the European Parliament and the Council on European statistics. In addition, being concerned with technical standards, they do not require a public consultation process.

The European Ombudsman has found that the choice of the legal basis of the ECB does not appear *prima facie* wrong. The Ombudsman does not substantiate its decision but it limits itself in requesting measures to make sure that stakeholders and the wider public make their views known.[61] The choice to file a complaint to the European Ombudsman appears peculiar, for its mandate is to handle cases of maladministration in the institutions and bodies of the European Union (Article 228 TFEU) but not to decide over the legitimacy of the law-making process which is a prerogative of the Court of Justice of the European Union under Article 263 TFEU. In any event, the end result appears contradictory, with the Ombudsman sanctioning the legal basis used but requesting the ECB to adopt measures for a consultation with stakeholders.[62]

As shown in this work, however, the uses of credit-risk data go well beyond statistical purposes. They also serve micro-prudential purposes as well as creditworthiness assessment. Ultimately, their use supports decision-making, access to and cost of credit, and competition.

The Draft Regulation, therefore, seems to exceed the collection of statistical information and its requirements appear larger than the current scope of reporting. For example, the granularity and type of data collected, alongside the rules on the

---

[55] See Art 4.3 of the SSM Regulation.

[56] Art 1 of ECB Decision (n 53).

[57] Arts 3 and 4 of ECB Decision (n 53).

[58] [1998] OJ L 318/8.

[59] Public commitment on European statistics by the ESCB at www.ecb.europa.eu/stats/html/pcstats.en.html.

[60] [2009] OJ L 87/164.

[61] Case 1693/2015/PD opened on 20 November 2015, decision on 20 November 2015.

[62] Following to the Ombudsman decision, the ECB has offered the possibility of submitting informal observations to a dedicated email address. See European Central Bank, 'Draft Regulation' (n 9).

provision of feedback loops, do not seem to have a statistical justification.[63] These features raise questions of proportionality, especially if emanating from legislation of the ECB. Article 5(4) TEU requires that the content and form of Union action must not exceed what is necessary to achieve the objectives of the Treaties. Thus, it is not fully clear to what extent the type of data and feedback loops adopted in the Draft Regulation are proportionate with its objectives. Instead, to a large extent they overlap with the business of credit registries, in particular the private or commercial credit bureaus which have no prudential bearing. Indeed, 'AnaCredit' may have an important impact on the functions and activities of the private or commercial registries. On a purely speculative basis, it may be conceived that the standardisation of the measurement of levels of indebtedness, over-indebtedness, and the way to conduct creditworthiness assessment represent a back-door interference to the way credit bureaus conduct their business and the type of data they supply. Arguably, it will force them to adapt or rebuild their databases in order to remain up-to-date with regulatory requirements and/or competitive in the market. An extreme argument may consider them redundant to the extent that their role and functions may be substituted by the public authorities. A lighter scenario is that of damaging the competitive positioning of the credit bureaus. The bottom line is that the ECB intervention, if and when implemented, has the potential to make a major impact on the way existing commercial organisations operate to the point of forcing them to evolve, or risk their own continued existence. In that sense, further considerations should be given against possible interference with Article 16 of the Charter of Fundamental Rights of the EU which recognises the freedom to conduct a business. This is not to say that the Draft Regulation violates the Charter but that possible interferences with it should not be treated as mere technical standards.

Likewise, to same extent AnaCredit involves the processing of personal data. The ECB has obtained a favourable informal opinion of the European Data Protection Supervisor (EDPS)[64] and the Draft Regulation recalls the application of the Data Protection Directive 95/46/EC.[65] Yet again, though it may well comply with data protection law, it is not expected that the possible interference of the Draft Regulation with another right protected under the Charter (Article 8 Protection of Personal Data) may fall within the definition of technical standards justifying the legislative power of a technocratic body such as the ECB.

Moreover, as this work has shown, many Member States operate with different arrangements and principles regarding the use of credit-risk data which do not seem to align with AnaCredit. However, no impact assessment on the individual Member States has been undertaken.

---

[63] Article 11 of the Draft Regulation.
[64] EDPS Informal Comments on the Draft Regulation of the European Central Bank on the Collection of Granular Credit and Credit Risk Data, 24 June 2015, available at www.asktheeu.org/en/request/2400/response/8387/attach/7/EDPS%20Informal%20Comments%20on%20E CB%20regulation.pdf.
[65] Article 13 of the Draft Regulation.

All in all, these are examples that, coupled with an analysis of the role and function of credit-risk data as carried out in this chapter, show how the Draft Regulation is capable of affecting the Member States, their citizens, and their entrepreneurs (banks that undergo micro-prudential regulation, credit bureaus and businesses seeking credit lines).

Regulations on matters that are broader than the collection of statistical information, especially if interfering with existing legal rights or interests of the citizens or their businesses, should be adopted by EU institutions under the ordinary legislative procedure and prerogatives of Article 294 TFEU and the direct involvement of the European Commission, European Parliament, and the Council. Moreover, such legislative acts should be preceded by a formal open public consultation.[66] Arguably, therefore, the Draft Regulation may be using an incorrect legal basis and the ECB may be exceeding its competence.

This does not seem to be a legal technicality but a matter of democratic accountability worthy of further discussion. If, on the contrary, the Draft Regulation is passed in its current substance, it should become material for a decision of the Court of Justice of the EU.

VII. Concluding Remarks

This chapter has concentrated on a specific aspect of the new competences that the BU assigned to the ECB. It looked at the centralisation of credit-risk data reporting as one of the new powers and responsibilities of the ECB as the new bank supervisor of the Euro-area. With this unprecedented transfer of sovereignty from the Member States to the EU, the creation of the largest credit-risk database ever existed under AnaCredit raises questions over generally accepted accountability standards in the law-making process. AnaCredit claims the need to collect and share a vast amount of granular credit data with feedback loops to banks in the name of an effective banking supervision. In so doing, the ECB is using its regulatory powers assigned to it by the Treaty for the setting of technical standards, using the collection of statistical information as the legal basis for its actions.

However, this chapter has shown how credit data bear objectives beyond statistical macro-prudential supervisory purposes.

Across the EU there is still a great variety in the type of data used for different purposes. The three main identified functions of credit data that this chapter has identified are the supply of information for the credit-risk management of

---

[66] Under Article 11 TEU: '1. The institutions shall, by appropriate means, give citizens and representative associations the opportunity to make known and publicly exchange their views in all areas of Union action. 2. The institutions shall maintain an open, transparent and regular dialogue with representative associations and civil society. 3. The European Commission shall carry out broad consultations with parties concerned in order to ensure that the Union's actions are coherent and transparent. 4. ...'

financial institutions, the creditworthiness assessment of consumers, and the prudential supervision of banks. These different functions usually result in different legal forms of credit registries and their fragmentation into public and private or commercial credit bureaus.

Each function presents separate policy and legal issues which need to be addressed separately. In many ways, the use of credit data interferes with the personal and economic lives of both natural and legal persons. Information may become the gateway of the economic life of natural and legal persons (and social life also for natural persons) determining, *inter alia*, access conditions to services, and consequently they may play a role in inclusion or exclusion in the economy and society in a broad sense. Also, Member States avail themselves of a number of diverse institutional arrangements and type of data that do not align with AnaCredit. They all seem to have in place diverse systems but with no uniquely accepted criteria or standards. Top-down standardisation from the ECB to the Member States may have implications which go beyond a mere exercise of setting technical rules. Moreover, existing infrastructures managed by the private sector risk duplication and redundancies, and credit data reporting has strong bearings with micro-prudential regulation and the business conduct of financial institutions. The idea of standardising data is still in its infancy and it may be positive in stimulating debates over standardised data across the EU or cross-border data sharing to achieve common policy objectives, which ultimately may have the potential of transforming the way in which credit registries operate in the EU. However, as discussed in this work, AnaCredit seems to be taking directions well beyond the statutory goals of the ECB.

All in all, this is not to say that AnaCredit may not be beneficial and economically efficient, but that in the way that it has been conceived, it creates tensions between technocracy and economic problem-solving, on the one hand, and, on the other hand, the democratic accountability and legitimation of an unelected, independent and technocratic institution making legislation on matters exceeding the mere setting of technical standards and affecting many aspects of life.

11

The Internal Market
and the Banking Union

HANS-W. MICKLITZ*

I. Introduction

A. Purpose and Disclaimer

I will try to show the move from the technical and de-centralised Internal Market programme to the technocratic and centralised Banking Union. To understand the suggested move to technocracy and centralisation in the Banking Union, I will use the Internal Market programme as a yardstick, the ideas behind it and the manner in which it was implemented. I am aware that the Internal Market programme and the policy behind has developed over time and led to crucial changes.[1] Nevertheless, it might serve as a benchmark for understanding the regulatory design of the Banking Union (BU). I am equally aware that the Maastricht Treaty constitutes the bridge between the Internal Market and the BU. Much has already been written about the Economic and Monetary Union (EMU) and its relationship with the Internal Market. Therefore, the focus is on the BU and how the BU could be understood as a furtherance of the Internal Market.

The perspective of the Internal Market and how it then can be compared with the now implemented BU is highly illuminating, despite all the simplification that such an exercise entails. I will use nine parameters, which are listed in Table 11.1. I will then analyse them under three further categories, as shown in Table 11.2. Throughout the text I will compare the Internal Market programme with the design of the emerging BU. To avoid misunderstandings: I do not insinuate that the BU is disconnected from the Internal Market. It will be shown that there are

* I would like to thank A Busca, E Sedano and A Smolenska for their critique and their comments. The responsibility remains mine alone.
[1] S Weatherill, *The Internal Market as a Legal Concept* (Oxford, OUP, 2017).

deep connections. If I need to use examples, I will choose those which are closest to the BU. I understand 'banking' as a regulated market. That is why it does not seem far-fetched to refer to the regulated markets on telecom, energy, transport and of course to 'finance'.[2]

B. Parameters of Comparison

Table 11.1 Parameters of Comparison

	Internal Market 1986 **Technical and Decentralised**	**Banking Union 2018** **Technocratic and Centralised**
Crisis	Political crisis	Economic and financial crisis
Actor	The European Commission Jacques Delors	The European Central Bank Mario Draghi
Means	The White Paper on the Completion of the Internal Market	Draghi's declaration 'whatever it takes'
Ex ante / ex post	*Ex ante* programme to be implemented	*Ex post* legislative means (SSM, SRM, DGS) to legitimise
Regulatory **technique**	Harmonisation through directives and co-regulation	Harmonisation through regula- tion and institution building
Substance vs **procedure**	Making of rules Procedure *follows* substance	Making (EBA) Art 114 *and* enforcing rules (ECB), Art 127(6) Substance *follows* procedure
Accountability **and liability**	Making (EU), enforcement Member States	Making (EBA) enforcement (ESAs)
Legal culture	Legal cultures (are (not?) converging)	Enforcement culture (have to converge through centralisation)
External/Internal	Fortress Europe – the Brussels effect	External – ECB/EBA a global player via non-binding agree- ments (Basle Committee), Art 8 SSM

---

[2] M Cantero Gamito, 'The private law dimension of the EU regulatory framework for electronic communications: evidence of the self-sufficiency of European regulatory private law', (2015) PhD thesis, European University Institute; L de Almeida, 'Integration through self-standing European private law: insights from the internal point of view to harmonization in energy market' (2017) PhD thesis, European University Institute; F della Negra, 'Private Law and Private Enforcement in the post-crisis EU retail financial regulation' (2017) PhD thesis, European University Institute.

C. Analysis

Table 11.2 Analysis

Decision-making	Decentralised, but co-ordinated	Centralised through Single Rulebook by EBA, influenced by ECB
Paradigm	Technicality – Technocracy Standards bodies (CEN/ CENELEC) – non-binding, but compliance	Technocracy – Financialisation EBA – Binding Regulatory (Art 290) and Implementing Technical Standards (Art 291)
Law	Integration through law and governance	Enforcement through governance without law SSM, SRM

II. Crisis

In the early 1980s, the European Union, as it is called today, was in a deadlock – politically through the French policy of the empty chair; economically through the still incomplete Internal Market. There was a crisis, but the crisis was much nearer to agony than to emergency. The crisis was in essence a political one. There was political disagreement about the future of Europe and the future of European integration. There was no economic crisis. If anything, there was the ever more obvious 'crisis' of the welfare state, which triggered and accelerated the need for reform. The Internal Market programme was developed by a French President of the European Commission in an Anglo-Saxon spirit. This might have enhanced its acceptability.[3]

The Outright Monetary Transactions (OMT) decision of the European Central Bank Governing Council has enabled the BU to be concluded politically, although the objectives of the two are distinct, and the BU in particular extends beyond purely economic/monetary considerations. The background to the OMT decision and the interplay between the OMT decision and the BU has been neatly documented by Alessandro Busca.[4] The underlying crisis is both economic and financial. These dimensions of the crisis required immediate action. There was a situation of 'emergency'[5] the financial stability of the whole Eurozone and possibly, even beyond the Eurozone, the European Project was in jeopardy.

---

[3] H-W Micklitz, 'The Visible Hand of European Regulatory Private Law – The Transformation of European Private Law from Autonomy to Functionalism in Competition and Regulation' (2009) 28 *Yearbook of European Law* 3.

[4] A Busca, 'The Thin Red Line Between the OMT Decision and the Banking Union', Chapter 3 in this volume.

[5] C Kilpatrick, 'On the Rule of Law and Economic Emergency: The Degradation of Basic Legal Values in Europe's Bailouts' (2015) 35 *Oxford Journal of Legal Studies*, 325.

The European Central Bank (ECB), as an integral part of the European System of Central Banks (ESCB), under Article 127(5) of the Treaty on the Functioning of the European Union (TFEU) is to contribute to the stability of the financial system. The financial markets required immediate action. It suffices to recall that the market reacted immediately after the 'Draghi declaration' in July 2012.[6] The euro was stabilised. How and where can the Draghi declaration be located – an Italian President who took a French position with silent support from Germany and made it public in London? Would the decision have looked different if the UK had been a member of the Eurozone? Was English pragmatism missing in the way in which the EU (ie the ECB) handled the whole crisis? Would English pragmatism have avoided long-term discussions about whether the OMT was a bail out, about whether it is covered by the Treaty, and about whether a new Treaty was required? In the end, this discussion was all the more futile as the OMT was never actually implemented in the form initially announced.

III. Actor

The Internal Market initiative came from the Delors Commission. There were many brains behind it – the Sutherland Report[7] played a particularly crucial role. But the European Commission was in the driver's seat. The European Commission initiated the debate and launched the famous White Paper on the Completion of the Internal Market[8] (1985), which largely influenced the Single European Act (1986).

The OMT decision was announced by the President of the European Central Bank. A careful reconstruction[9] shows that there was political support from the key Member States – both in the Executive Board and in the Governing Council. This was not democratic support, but support from the Heads of State. The national central banks were not unanimous. One may ask how such political backing fits into the institutional independence of the ECB. What matters in our context is that Draghi took complete responsibility by arguing constantly that the ECB was always acting within its mandate – a reading, which was later by and large confirmed by the Court of Justice of the European Union (CJEU) and the German Constitutional Court.[10]

---

[6] https://www.youtube.com/watch?v=VWd9kQCMBIk.

[7] P Sutherland, 'The Internal Market after 1992: Meeting the Challenge. Report Presented to the Commission by the High Level Group on the Functioning of the Internal Market', (1992) European Parliament, SEC 92-final 2277.

[8] European Commission, 'White Paper on the Completion of the Internal Market', COM (85) 310 final, 14.6.1985.

[9] Busca, Chapter 3 in this volume.

[10] Case C-62/14 *Peter Gauweiler and Others v Deutscher Bundestag*, EU:C:2015:7.

IV. Means

The European Commission had started the debate with the White Paper on the Completion of the Internal Market. This chapter sets out the basic substantive issues which were later realised in the Single European Act (not the institutional issues such as the shift to majority decision-making and its implications). What matters in our context is the introduction of a pick-a-pack procedure for social issues (health and safety for citizens, health and safety at work, industrial relations, environmental protection, consumer protection – to name just some key areas). The shift from the Common Market to the Internal Market implied the need to integrate relevant social issues into European integration. However, they were not recognised as self-standing issues. Social policy issues were anchored in economic policies and had to be made compatible with the four economic freedoms and competition. The programme covered roughly 300 pieces of secondary EU law that had to be elaborated and adopted under the EU legislative procedure. The programme was addressed to politics and to politicians. The responsible EU institutions were required to take action to implement the programme.

The Draghi declaration looks very different: 'Within our mandate, the ECB is ready to do whatever it takes to preserve the euro'.[11] A single institution, the ECB, accepts responsibility for re-establishing financial stability and beyond for saving the political project of a Monetary Union. The content of the declaration is extremely vague. 'Whatever it takes' means all measures that are necessary. The declaration of 26 July 2012 does not tell us what 'it takes' means. On 6 September 2012, after the meeting of the Governing Council, the President of the ECB presented the main features of the OMT programme.[12] First, he explained the name of the programme ('Outright Monetary Transactions (OMTs)'), its aim of 'safeguarding an appropriate monetary policy transmission and the singleness of the monetary policy' and its scope of 'Euro system's outright transactions in secondary sovereign bond markets'. The programme is divided into six pillars: 'conditionality, coverage, creditor treatment, sterilization, transparency, security markets program'.[13] The technicality of the language is evident. Ordinary citizens might understand the 'what it takes', but they may not understand what is behind the six pillars. The declaration and the programme were addressed to the 'markets', not to the public or the people of Europe.

---

[11] Mario Draghi, 'Verbatim of the remarks made by Mario Draghi', 26 July 2012, available at http://www.ecb.europa.eu/press/key/date/2012/html/sp120726.en.html.
[12] ECB, 'Technical features of Outright Monetary Transactions', Press Release 6 September 2012.
[13] Busca, Chapter 3 in this volume.

V. *Ex Ante* vs *Ex Post*

The White Paper on the Completion of the Internal Market outlined the future of what the EU should look like. It was for the EU institutions to give shape to the programme, to adopt the necessary secondary EU law and to provide the necessary 'legitimacy' under the 'democratic' procedures foreseen in the Treaty.[14] The White Paper provided the basics – the ground level from which to start. One might argue that the European Commission was implementing and developing the *Dassonville*[15] and *Cassis de Dijon*[16] doctrine of the CJEU. There is some truth to this argument.[17] However, the White Paper went far beyond these judgments. EU Court judgments in which the 'compatibility' of a national legislative measure with the EU legal order is challenged can only lead to the annulment of national measures or the approval of their legality by the competent national authorities (courts or parliaments).[18] The White Paper meanwhile designed a target and an objective which had to be achieved through a whole set of regulatory measures. Within that broad direction, there was leeway for the EU institutions to influence the substance of the 300 measures.

There is a direct line of argument from the OMT decision, via the OMT programme to the BU. In that respect I rely on the reconstruction of the history of the BU by Alessandro Busca,[19] who quotes H Van Rompuy, the former President of the European Council:[20]

> The Central Bank was only able to take this decision because of the preliminary political decision, by the EU's Heads of State and Government to build a banking union. This was the famous European Council of June 2012, so just weeks before Draghi's statement; he himself said to me, during that Council, that this was exactly the game-changer he needed.

This statement challenges the position of President Draghi, who had argued that the ECB acted within its own mandate. The legitimacy of the ECB and the establishment of a BU lacking the necessary anchoring in democratic procedures is the subject of a different debate.[21] What matters is the link between the OMT

---

[14] There is no need to discuss either the reach of the EU legitimacy nor EU democracy. My point is that the Internal Market programme yielded effects for the future not for the past.

[15] Case 8/74 *Procureur du Roi v Benoît and Gustave Dassonville*, EU:C:1974:82.

[16] Case 120/78 *Rewe-Zentral AG v Bundesmonopolverwaltung für Branntwein* EU:C:1979:42.

[17] SK Schmidt, *The European Court of Justice and the Policy Process: The Shadow of Case Law* (Oxford, OUP, 2018).

[18] I set aside the fact that the CJEU can strictly speaking not decide over the compatibility itself, but can only give its own reading of EU Treaties and then leave it for the Member States' courts or legislators to take the appropriate steps, at least within the preliminary reference procedure.

[19] Chapter 3 in this volume.

[20] H Van Rompuy, Speech at the Brussels Economic Forum 2014 – 4th Annual Tommaso Padoa-Schioppa Lecture, Brussels, 10 June 2014, available at www.consilium.europa.eu/uedocs/cms_Data/docs/pressdata/en/ec/143160.pdf.

[21] See C Möllers, 'Some Reflections on the State of European Democracy with Regard to Banking Union and ECB' Chapter 8 in this volume.

decision and the building of the BU. The realisation of the BU through the Single Supervisory Mechanism (SSM), the Single Resolution Mechanism (SRM) and the still incomplete deposit guarantee scheme (DGS),[22] could be understood as political legitimisation for the bond purchase programme, with respect to national governments.

This bond purchase programme is indeed different than previous programs because it addresses only specific countries under financial stress. It involves full risk-sharing and it is carried out according to an *ex ante* undisclosed unlimited purchase. The German Federal Constitutional Court understood it as 'functionally equivalent' to the European Stability Mechanism (ESM).[23] It follows that, as the ESM was legitimated by the reform on the EMU economic governance, the same is true with respect to the OMT, which is justified by the reform of banking supervision and resolution, as this allowed restoration of financial stability to the Eurozone financial system and therefore unclogged the channels of monetary policy transmission. In other words, Member States politically approved such an extensive bond purchase programme precisely because the Single Resolution Fund and the Single European Supervisor potentially avoid future bail out and recapitalisation of the banking sector.

There is not only a political link between the two measures but also a significant economic connection. Both measures complement each other, as both are meant to strengthen financial stability and financial market integration. The BU allows the vicious circle between banking crises and sovereign crisis to be broken down, by tackling the issues related to banking mismanagement and insolvency; the OMT tackles the short-term banking liquidity problems so as to restore the broken transmission channels of ECB monetary policies. The integration of financial markets represents an essential goal of the BU and at the same time, a pre-requisite for the monetary policy of the ECB, as imperfect financial integration may significantly impair the transmission of monetary policy. Banks represent the building block for the entire financial architecture. They play a crucial role in both government bonds market and money markets.

Therefore the ground-breaking decision in favour of establishing the BU cannot be separated from the OMT declaration and the circumstances under which it was made. Even if Van Rompuy is right, even if the decision was taken at the European Council in June 2012[24] – prior to the OMT declaration – the overall argument still holds true. The establishment of the BU was meant to provide legitimacy *post factum* to a decision that had already been taken – whether by

---

[22] K Lannoo, 'ECB Banking Supervision and beyond' (2014), Report, CEPS Task Force, available at https://www.ceps.eu/publications/ecb-banking-supervision-and-beyond.

[23] BVerfG, Order of the Second Senate of 14 January 2014 – 2 BvR 2728/13 – paras (1–24). English translation available at https://www.bundesverfassungsgericht.de/SharedDocs/Entscheidungen/EN/2014/01/rs20140114_2bvr272813en.html.

[24] Van Rompuy (n 20).

the Heads of State, or by the ECB as the lonesome rider. Whether such measures meet the standards of democratic legitimacy is subject to debate.[25]

VI. Regulatory Technique

The White Paper on the Internal Market promoted the idea of mutual recognition along the line of the CJEU's judgment in *Cassis de Dijon*. The majority of the Member States resisted such a radical solution in the negotiations of the Single European Act. The outcome was Article 100a (now Article 114 TFEU) that relied (politically) on harmonisation as the primary means to realise the Internal Market. However, the core issues of the Internal Market – the famous technical barriers to trade – are no longer abolished by way of legislative means alone, which lay down all the technical details in directives, but by way of framework directives under the 1985 'New Approach to Technical Harmonization and Standards'.[26] These framework directives define binding mandatory requirements, which are then made concrete through technical standards elaborated by the European Standard Bodies, the Comité Européen de Normalisation / European Committee for Standardization (CEN) and the Comité Européen de Normalisation Électrotechnique / European Committee for Electrotechnical Standardization (CENELEC), and adopted by consensus. The cooperation between the European Standard Bodies and the European Commission was laid down in a Memorandum of Understanding. The Memorandum enables the European Commission to mandate the development of a particular technical standard, and in exchange the European Commission has to cover the costs. This is different for non-mandated standards, where the industry interested in the standards provides the necessary funds. The technical standards themselves are legally non-binding. Compliance is voluntary but guarantees access to the Internal Market. This mechanism and the shared responsibilities between the EU, the Member States and the European Standards bodies are the key to the success of the Internal Market programme – at least this is the official 'EU speak'. However, it seems as if the CJEU is ready to take a harder look at the *de facto* binding character of technical standards.[27] Overall, the CJEU has confirmed its jurisdiction over technical standards where they are approved by the European Commission.[28] This might lead in the long run to a judicial review of the cooperation procedure as laid down in the New Approach.

The New Approach-type directives are united in the overall objective to lift market access barriers through binding secondary EU law. Right from the

---

[25] C Möllers, 'Some Reflections on the State of European Democracy with Regard to Banking Union and ECB', Chapter 8 in this volume.

[26] Council Resolution 85/C 136/01 of 7 May 1985 on a new approach to technical harmonization and standards, [1985] OJ C 136/1.

[27] CJEU, Case C-171/11 *Fra.bo v DGWG*, EU:C:2012:453.

[28] CJEU, Case C-613/14 *James Elliott Construction*, EU:C:2012:453.

beginning there was a political debate on the potential need to introduce safeguards via EU law to prevent harmful products entering the EU market. Initially, the European Commission thought that the Directive 85/574 on Product Liability adopted in 1985, the year of the New Approach, would suffice as a safety net.[29] However, it turned out that an EU-wide post market control mechanism was required.[30] The mechanism took shape in Directive 92/59 on Product Safety, later amended into Directive 2001/95. The first asset test, the PIP scandal regarding silicone gel breast implants, revealed the deficiencies of the EU model.[31] Outside technical barriers to trade, the EU developed a broad variety of harmonisation techniques, which come close to be denoted as a new regulatory discipline: the 'art of harmonisation'.[32]

Again, there is a difference between the Internal Market 'Project' and the BU 'project', although it seems as if the difference is losing importance. The substantive law, the Bank Recovery and Resolution Directive (BRRD) for SRM and the Capital Requirements Directive IV (CRD IV) for SSM (with the exception of the Capital Requirements Regulation (CRR)) are directives with harmonisation taking precedence as the method of integration. The SSM and the SRM are using regulations to lay down the institutional design of these two pillars of the BU. This is different with regard to the third pillar, the deposit guarantee scheme. It is common ground that the BU remains incomplete without harmonisation of the organisation and management of the deposit guarantee schemes. The language is telling. In both regulations two of three key words are identical: 'single' and 'mechanism'. 'Single' sends a clear message. There should be no room for competition between legal orders. There should be no horizontality or heterarchy – just a simple and straightforward hierarchy within the reach of the ECB's competence. This is confirmed by the residual responsibility of the Single Supervisory Board (ECB) for the overall operation. 'Mechanism', quite to the contrary, is opaque. It reflects the dynamic interaction between the centre and the periphery, and the constantly changing number of supervised banks. One way of interpretation would be to suggest that vague language hides what is politically at stake: the aim to establish a new self-standing architecture for the supervision of banks in Europe through one single responsible body.

While the ECB is the coordinator and guarantor of consistency of the SSM, the ECB remains subject to national law when Member States have margin of discretion to transpose EU law or where the ECB has to rely on national competent authorities (NCAs) due to lack of competences under the SSM. The NCAs remain the

---

[29] Ch Joerges, J Falke, H-W Micklitz and G Brüggemeier, 'Sicherheit von Konsumgütern und die Entwicklung der Europäischen Gemeinschaft' ('European Product Safety, Internal Market Policy and the New Approach to Technical Harmonisation and Standards') (2016) *Hanse Law Review*.

[30] H-W Micklitz (ed), 'Post Market Control of Consumer Goods' (1990) *ZERP Schriftenreihe*, Band 11.

[31] CJEU, Case C-219/15 *Schmitt v TÜV Rheinland*, EU:C:2017:128.

[32] L Azoulai, 'The Complex Weave of Harmonisation' in D Chalmers and A Arnull (eds), *The Oxford Handbook of EU Law* (Oxford, OUP, 2015).

competent supervisors for less significant banks.[33] However, there is a grey zone, which leaves space for soft-law techniques – guidelines and recommendations – to influence the supervisory techniques and supervisory decisions of NCAs. That might be one of the reasons why a number of Member States adopted quite a hostile attitude towards the bundling of supervisory competences in the hands of the ECB.[34] At the moment, the former competent national authorities suffer from some disorientation as to how the interplay between the ECB and the national banking supervision authorities can and should work in practice.[35] However, this is also due to differences in substantive law as implemented via the directives.

VII. Substance vs Procedure

The Internal Market programme of 1985 focused on technical barriers to trade. Once customs charges had been abolished it turned out that barriers to trade cannot be abolished via single directives but that a new mechanism was needed. Barriers to trade reach far and wide. They range from merely technical issues such as differences in pressure equipment[36] to more sensitive issues like health and safety regulation. The 300 measures envisaged were united by a common denominator – the *substantive* dimension of the barriers to trade and how to overcome the differences by way of harmonisation and co-regulation. This was the famous New Approach. When the EU institutions started to implement the programme, it became clearer and clearer that procedural rules were also required to guarantee the effective and uniform application of EU law. Procedural rules should be understood broadly: rights, remedies, procedures and institutions.[37]

The adoption of the above mentioned Directive 92/59 on Product Safety constituted the turning point in the EU move towards institution building. The EU used Article 100(a) EC (now Article 114 TFEU) to oblige Member States to ensure that they had institutions in place which were competent and sufficiently equipped to enforce EU product safety regulation through warnings, the withdrawal of unsafe products from the market and/or their recall from consumers. A rapid alert system between the Member States' authorities, managed through the Commission, aims to coordinate national enforcement strategies.

---

[33] EIOPA declined its competence under Article 60 of EIOPA Regulation in favour of the Italian Authority, Case C-559/15 *Onix Asigurări SA v Istituto per la Vigilanza Sulle Assicurazioni (IVASS)*, EU:C:2017:316.

[34] L Wissink, 'Challenges to an Efficient European Centralised Banking Supervision (SSM): Single Rulebook, Joint Supervisory Teams and Split Supervisory Tasks' (2017) 18 *European Business Organization Law Review* 3, 431.

[35] Personal communication of a national supervisory body to the author.

[36] Directive 2014/68/EU of the European Parliament and of the Council of 15 May 2014 on the harmonisation of the laws of the Member States relating to the making available on the market of pressure equipment [2014] OJ L 189/164.

[37] See seminal article of W v Gerven, 'Of Rights, Remedies and Procedures' (2000) 37 *Common Market Law Review* 501, where the institutional dimension is missing.

The monitoring, the surveillance of the market and regulatory actions remained in the hands of the national enforcement agencies. However, the comitology procedure, adopted as a complementary legislative measure to the New Approach, left room for the European Commission to take emergency type measures with a rather restricted legal framework.[38] Gradually, the EU went further. Member States were required to establish supervisory agencies in regulated markets (telecom, energy, transport, financial services) with enhanced regulatory powers. European agencies, mainly conceived as coordinating bodies, complemented the institutional design. The CJEU meanwhile strengthened the European Commission's use of Article 114 TFEU as a competence base for building a genuine European enforcement infrastructure.[39] Characteristic for EU policy in this area was its incremental and uneven development. The Europeanisation of procedural rules broadly understood is a necessary consequence of the harmonisation of the substantive rules on lifting barriers to trade.[40] Just as in the BU, the regulatory tool has changed, from directives to regulations.[41]

The SSM Regulation changed the picture dramatically. The BU logic starts from the need to establish a single European supervisory mechanism to prevent a repetition of deficient crisis management in the aftermath of the crisis triggered by the collapse of Lehman Brothers. The Treaty basis is no longer Article 114 (in synergy with Article 53 TFEU, Article 62 TFEU),[42] but Article 127(6) TFEU (introduced in the Maastricht Treaty in 1991),[43] which explicitly enables the EU

---

[38] A dedicated website for comitology is available at https://ec.europa.eu/info/implementing-and-delegated-acts/comitology_en.

[39] First in product safety Case C-359/92 *Federal Republic of Germany v Council of the European Union*, EU:C:1994:306; later in financial services; Case C-270/12 *United Kingdom of Great Britain and Northern Ireland v European Parliament, Council of the European Union*, EU:C:2014:18. H Marjosola, 'Bridging the Constitutional Gap in EU Executive Rule-Making: The Court of Justice Approves Legislative Conferral of Intervention Powers to European Securities Markets Authority: Court of Justice of the European Union (Grand Chamber) Judgment of 22 January 2014, Case C-270/12, *UK v. Parliament and Council*' (2014) 10 *European Constitutional Law Review* 50.

[40] Denoted with the concept of *Sachzwanglogik*, which has no English language equivalent. Inherent logic comes close, in theoretical terms functional integrationist concepts to explain European integration.

[41] Telecom: National Regulatory ONP Directive 98/10. Nowadays, their obligations are set by the Framework Directive (latest consolidated version). The Body of European Regulators for Electronic Communications (BEREC) was created in 2009, the BEREC Regulation (2009): Art 114 TFEU. The pending Regulation Proposal calls for BEREC to be turned into an EU agency. Energy: National Regulatory Authority (Electricity Directive 2009/72/EC and Gas Directive 2009/73/EC): Art 53 TFEU, Art 62 TFEU, Art 114 TFEU; European Agency – ACER (Regulation 713/2009): Art 114 TFEU; ENTSO-e and ENTSO-g (Regulation 714/2009): Art 114 TFEU; NEMO (Nominated electricity market operator) (Commission Regulation 2015/1222): Art 114 TFEU. Finance: EBA, ESMA, EIOPA (and for the Single Resolution Mechanism and for the European Systemic Risk Board), the legal basis was Art 114 TFEU.

[42] On the difficulties which result from the different legal basis, see A Smoleńska, 'Single Resolution Board – Lost and Found in the Thicket of EU Bank Regulation', Chapter 7 in this volume.

[43] Art 127(6) TFEU. The Council, acting by means of regulations in accordance with a special legislative procedure, may unanimously, and after consulting the European Parliament and the European Central Bank, confer specific tasks upon the European Central Bank concerning policies relating to

to delegate certain prudential supervision powers to the ECB. The message is that banking is different from all other regulated markets – from telecom, energy, transport, but also from other financial services and insurance. Special competence rules are necessary for European institution building replacing national banking supervisory institutions. However, there is an important restriction. Article 127(6) TFEU does not provide for the establishment of a new – not previously existing – institution, which is to be entrusted with banking supervision. This is different from Article 114 TFEU, which enabled the creation of all kinds of agencies in the field of regulated markets, *including* the establishment of the European Banking Authority (EBA), the European Securities and Market Authority (ESMA) and the European Insurance and Occupational Pensions Authority (EIOPA) – as well as the Single Resolution Board for the second pillar of the BU – the SRM. In the case of SSM, the decision on institution building has been taken at Treaty level on a shaky competence basis and not (as in regulated markets) via secondary EU law. In direct reversal of the Internal Market programme the BU is built around the supervisory authority – the Single Supervisory Board – rather than substantive provisions, which remain embedded (for the most part, and notwithstanding the significance of administrative rule-making within SSM) within the Internal Market logic. The CRD IV precedes the SSM (June and October 2013 respectively), and the BRRD and SRM were voted on the same day in April 2014. The sequence matters because it demonstrates the link between the Internal Market and the BU.

Once the institution-building decision was taken and had passed the EU and national democratic procedures, the EU could start to develop the set of rules that were required. This is where the Single Rulebook comes in, which consists of three main legislative acts: the Capital Requirements IV Package (a regulation and a directive), which implements the Basel III capital requirements for banks,[44] the Deposit Guarantee Scheme Directive which regulates deposit insurance in the case of a bank's inability to pay its debts,[45] and the Bank Recovery and Resolution Directive,[46] which establishes a framework for the recovery and resolution of credit institutions and investment firms. The 'rules', which are integrated into the Single Rulebook are elaborated by the EBA.[47] The role and function of binding technical standards (BTS) will be discussed later.

---

the prudential supervision of credit institutions and other financial institutions with the exception of insurance undertakings.

[44] Directive 2013/36/EU [2013] OJ L176/338 and Regulation EU No 575/2013 [2013] OJ L 176/1.

[45] Directive 2014/49/EU of the European Parliament and of the Council of 16 April 2014 on deposit guarantee schemes [2014] OJ L 173/149.

[46] Directive 2014/59/EU of the European Parliament and of the Council of 15 May 2014 establishing a framework for the recovery and resolution of credit institutions and investment firms and amending Council Directive 82/891/EEC, and Directives 2001/24/EC, 2002/47/EC, 2004/25/EC, 2005/56/EC, 2007/36/EC, 2011/35/EU, 2012/30/EU and 2013/36/EU, and Regulations (EU) No 1093/2010 and (EU) No 648/2012, of the European Parliament and of the Council [2014] OJ L 173/190 ('BRRD').

[47] A helpful EBA website on the Single Rulebook is available at http://www.eba.europa.eu/regulation-and-policy/single-rulebook.

VIII. Accountability and Responsibility

The Internal Market programme started from the concept of decentralised enforcement enshrined in the Treaty. Apart from Article 127(6) TFEU, the division of competences in the enforcement of EU law has never been amended. The overall distinction between law-making at the EU level within the scope of enumerated powers and law-enforcement through the Member States remained intact. Such a clear-cut division implies an equally clear-cut distinction between accountability and responsibility. The EU is accountable and responsible for the making of EU law, the Member States for its enforcement. The European Commission has stretched the scope of Article 114 TFEU quite successfully to combine substantive law with procedural and even institutional requirements – largely supported and even promoted by the CJEU. This has led scholars to compare the principle of procedural autonomy to a Swiss cheese full of holes.[48] The gradual intervention of the EU into institution building outside the Treaty raises questions about its accountability and about the liability of the new national institutions created under EU law requirements and the EU agencies which have emerged out of the former committees. The parties affected by a regulatory decision may face the dilemma that the national authority which has taken the regulatory action is not 'responsible' for the rules on which it based its decision. These rules are frequently the result of a European coordination, if not harmonisation, process. However, the party concerned might find it difficult to identify the EU institution in charge. Even if this is possible, it might not have standing as it is not 'directly and individually' affected, as required by Article 263(4) TFEU.[49] Despite all uncertainty, the responsibility and liability of national agencies for wrongful actions taken under EU law has never been challenged.[50] The *Francovich* doctrine has strengthened State liability claims against the Member States. EU institutions are and remain liable under Article 340 TFEU.[51]

By and large, the same thinking applies to the banking sector. This covers the three European Supervisory Authorities (ESAs) – EBA, ESMA and EIPOA – and the ECB, which is entrusted with the direct supervision of 118[52] systemically

---

[48] M Bobek, 'Why There Is No Principle of "Procedural Autonomy" of the Member States', in H-W Micklitz and B Witte (eds.), *The European Court of Justice and the autonomy of the Member States* (Antwerp, Intersentia, 2012) 305.

[49] The new version amended under the Lisbon Treaty has not led to a change of the very restricted interpretation of Art 263(4) TFEU by the CJEU.

[50] R Condon and B van Leeuwen, 'Bottom Up or Rock Bottom Harmonization? Francovich State Liability in National Courts' (2016) 35 *Yearbook of European Law* 229.

[51] There are a number of judgments of the CJEU on the liability of the EU. Most of these judgments concern the potential liability for the EU for actions taken in the field of the common agricultural policy, see eg K Gutman, 'Liability for Breach of EU Law by the Union, Member States and Individuals: Damages, Enforcement and Effective Judicial Protection' in A Lazowski and S Blockmans, Research Handbook on EU Institutional Law (Cheltenham, Edward Elgar Publishing, 2016).

[52] The current list of supervised banks is available at https://www.bankingsupervision.europa.eu/banking/list/who/html/index.en.html.

relevant banks within the SSM on the basis of the SSM Regulation. Whenever the CJEU confirms the decision-taking power of EU regulatory agencies, as it did in the case of ESMA,[53] the question arises whether the EU will be liable for wrongful actions under Article 340 TFEU. Although it remained largely unnoticed, there was much political debate in the background whether or not rules should be introduced into secondary EU legislation adopted to exempt the competent EU supervisory bodies from liability claims. These attempts failed. The EU measures, which were finally adopted, do not exclude the accountability and liability of EU supervisory authorities in banking and finance. The battlefield to come, if there is a hard conflict between the EU supervisory authorities and the banking sector about compensation claims for wrongful supervisory action, is how Article 340 TFEU, in particular paras (2) and (3), should be read:

> In the case of non-contractual liability, the Union shall, in accordance with the general principles common to the laws of the Member States, make good any damage caused by its institutions or by its servants in the performance of their duties.
>
> Notwithstanding the second paragraph, the European Central Bank shall, in accordance with the general principles common to the laws of the Member States, make good any damage caused by it or by its servants in the performance of their duties.

The argument put forward by the banking sector is that the general principles common to the laws of the Member States should be read so as to more or less exempt the ECB from liability.[54] There is no room to embark on an exploration of these arguments, however doubtful they might be. What matters is the unprecedented attempt of the banking sector to gain a special status. The shift from substance to procedure (here towards institution building) goes hand in hand with a request for exemption from liability. Even if these attempts failed, it remains to be seen whether liability exists on paper only. In *Ledra*, the CJEU rejected the liability of the Troika.[55]

IX. Culture

The Internal Market programme has produced an enormous volume of EU rules in all areas of the law. In total, EU law is often claimed to cover 80,000 pages.[56] A huge part of these 80,000 pages has to be attributed to the Internal

---

[53] See n 39.

[54] R D'Ambrosio, 'The ECB and NCA Liability Within the Single Supervisory Mechanism' (2015) *Quaderni di Ricerca Giuridica della Consulenza Legale*, available at http://www.bancaditalia.it/pubblicazioni/quaderni-giuridici/2015-0078/QRG-78.pdf. The most recent publication of the ECB's Legal Conference 2017, 'Shaping a new legal order for Europe: a tale of crises and opportunities', covers questions of accountability and transparency, but liability issues were not discussed.

[55] Joined Cases C-8/15 P to C-10/15 P *Ledra Advertising Ltd and Others v European Commission and European Central Bank (ECB)*, EU:C:2016:701.

[56] This is the figure constantly referred to in the negotiations with candidate Member States.

Market programme. The ever stronger involvement of the EU – not only via the interpretation of the Treaty by the CJEU, but in particular through secondary law-making – has enhanced the debate about whether there is or could ever be something like a 'European legal culture'. Roman lawyers claim that the EU is united in a common legal culture (personalism, legalism, intellectualism) that dates back to Roman times.[57] The 'integration through law' paradigm dominated the European integration process until the new millennium and to some respect until today.[58] Integration through law insinuates foreign elements into an existing legal order. The debate around transplantability is legendary, and so is the debate about the emergence or non-emergence of a European legal culture. In 1996 Pierre Legrand published his influential article entitled 'European legal systems are not converging'.[59] Kaarlo Tuori recognised the potential for cultural convergence in Europe – at least in the deeper sediments of legal orders.[60] My own position is that there are areas of law where the systems are *not* converging – where the different legal cultures are clashing and are simply standing side-by-side. However, there are also areas of law (in society) where there is room for the gradual emergence of a genuine European legal culture as well as for the convergence of different legal cultures.[61] Regulated markets are providing a promising (?) example for a possible merging. The academic debate is very much focused on substantive legislation – on whether legal concepts such as *reasonableness* or *good faith* could converge or not. The proof of the pudding is the law in action – the way in which the courts handle these controversial concepts.

The BU is shifting the focus from the making of the law – its substance – to institution building and enforcement. The new institutions are all administrative. A new layer is introduced which strengthens administrative enforcement and while subject to judicial review, replace enforcement through the judiciary in practice. This is even true for core areas of the judiciary, for example in private law. The three ESAs – in particular ESMA and its national counterparts – use public administrative law to influence the existing contracts or future contract making in B2B and B2C relations.[62] There is a general shift from the judiciary to administrative bodies, which is stimulated by the Internal Market programme. The BU – and in particular the SSM pillar – constitutes the preliminary peak of this overall trend.

---

[57] F Wieacker, 'Foundations of European Legal Culture' (1990) 38 *The American Journal of Comparative Law*, 1.

[58] M Maduro and M Wind (eds), *The Transformation of Europe, Twenty-Five Years On* (Cambridge, CUP, 2017).

[59] P Legrand, 'European Legal Systems Are Not Converging' (1996) 45 *ICLQ* 52.

[60] K Tuori, 'Transnational Law: On Legal Hybrids and Legal Perspectivism' in M Maduro, K Tuori and S Sankari (eds), *Transnational Law, Rethinking European Law and Legal Thinking* (Cambridge, CUP, 2014) 11–58.

[61] H-W Micklitz, 'The (Un)-Systematics of (Private) Law as an Element of European Legal Culture' in G Helleringer and K Purnhagen (eds), *Towards a European Legal Culture* (München/Oxford/Baden-Baden, Beck/Hart/Nomos, 2014) 81–115.

[62] A Ottow and Y Svetiev, 'Financial Supervision in the Interstices Between Private and Public Law' (2014) 10 *European Review of Contract Law* 496.

What about administrative culture in administrative practice? Administrative practice largely occurs outside formal decisions. Getting to know the practices and the differences between institutions and countries poses particular challenges. Multi-cultural, multi-lingual and multi-national inspection committees will have to travel around Europe and inspect banks. Similar entities already exist at the international level – within the International Monetary Fund (IMF) – but they are not decision makers and they are not – within the limits referred to above – accountable and liable. Whether the result of the overall exercise is a genuinely European enforcement culture cannot be assessed on the basis of written and publicly accessible documents. What really happens within the institutions can only be discovered through empirical research.

X. External/Internal

The Internal Market programme was by and large an inward-looking exercise. The EU, the EU institutions and the EU Member States were focusing on removing barriers to trade between the EU Member States. The White Paper on the Completion of the Internal Market or even the political discussions that accompanied the adoption of the Single European Act, seem to tell a different message. The EU had no political intention to build a 'fortress Europe' by barring non-EU companies from gaining access to the Internal Market. However, the 300 measures adopted under the Internal Market programme were not based on a consistent policy. So far, a comprehensive analysis of the external effects of the EU Internal Market programme is missing.[63] What has been investigated is the so-called *Brussels effect*[64] in competition law, data protection and food safety. Available evidence beyond the *Brussels effect* demonstrates that the rules and procedures which connect the EU to the external world are mainly subject-related and subject-dependent.[65] In regulated markets, such as telecom, energy and transport, the rules are intended to enhance cooperation with non-EU countries (and their agencies) and to give third countries an observer status within EU bodies (such as agencies, supervisory colleges) where appropriate. However, a deeper analysis is needed to find out to what extent the EU Internal Market legislation differentiates between categories of non-EU countries.

---

[63] Brexit does trigger this kind of a review. N von Ondarza and C Borrett, 'Brexit and EU agencies. What the agencies' existing third country relations can teach us about the future EU–UK relationship' (2018), SWP Working Paper No 2, available at https://www.swp-berlin.org/fileadmin/contents/products/arbeitspapiere/Brexit_and_EU_agencies.pdf.

[64] A Bradford, 'The Brussels Effect' (2012) 107 *Northwestern University Law Review* 1.

[65] M Cremona and H-W Micklitz (eds), *The External Dimension of European Private Law* (Oxford, OUP, 2015). The book covers traditional private law issues such as the external reach of the EU international private law, and also European regulatory private law in banking and finance, company law, pharmaceuticals, energy and consumer protection.

The BU changes the picture radically. It suffices to compare MIFID I (Directive 2004/39) – with MIFID II (Directive 2014/65).[66] MIFID I was adopted before the Lehman Brothers collapse, MIFID II thereafter, but also after the SSM and SRM Regulations. The tone for shaping external relations in banking and finance is set by the SSM Regulation 1024/13. The SSM Regulation has to be read in light of the EU measures to establish the European Banking Authority (Regulation 1093/2010) and the rules on the mandate of EBA (Directive 2013/36). The cooperation model is much more specific, but also much more complex than for other regulated markets. The EU legislature had to further coordinate the rule-making competence of the EBA with the supervisory competence of the ECB. The EBA and ECB are expected to act in harmony. What is really striking is that the EBA and ECB are given the explicit power to engage in non-binding administrative arrangements with third countries.

Article 8 of the SSM Regulation reads as follows:

> Without prejudice to the respective competences of the Member States and institutions and bodies of the Union, other than the ECB, including EBA, in relation to the tasks conferred on the ECB by this Regulation, *the ECB may develop contacts and enter into administrative arrangements* with supervisory authorities, international organisations and the administrations of third countries, *subject to appropriate coordination with EBA*. Those arrangements shall *not create legal obligations* in respect of the Union and its Member States [emphasis added].

The addressee is clearly the Basle Committee (banking), but might also include IOSCO (finance). There are many questions: what are 'non-binding administrative arrangements'? What happens if the non-binding administrative arrangements are integrated into a piece of EU legislation, but this legislation is not supported by parliaments? Are the administrative arrangements meant to be the technical standards developed by EBA and ECB in the framework of the Single Rulebook? Does the status of membership matter in the discussions, the negotiations and the deliberations in international fora? The EBA and ECB have an observer status in the Basle Committee only, whereas the nine Member States are full members. Non-European countries are constantly challenging the over-representation of EU countries. The EU institutions and the nine Member States are regarded as representing 'Europe'. In practice, the formal status does not really matter, as the decisions within the committee are taken by consensus.[67] Consensus could enhance the position of the ECB and possibly also that of the EBA. There is external pressure on the EU institutions and the nine Member States to speak with one voice. Does this mean that the EBA and/or ECB have *de facto* taken over the

---

[66] Art 50(2): 'ESMA shall develop draft regulatory technical standards to specify the level of accuracy to which clocks are to be synchronised in accordance with international standards'. This is much weaker than the formula in the SSM with regard to international cooperation on administrative arrangements.

[67] Statement of the EBA Director at the State of the Union in 2014.

negotiations on the standards to be laid down in the Single Rulebook? The answers to all these questions can hardly be found in the regulations, directives and internal guidelines. Without a comprehensive analysis of the practice, it is impossible to provide a solid account of how the external relations are shaped, managed and monitored.

XI. Interim Conclusion

The analysis of the nine parameters of comparison reveals nine shifts which could be condensed in the following way:

1.   Crisis: towards economic policy, which now takes precedence over politics.
2.   Actor: from the European Commission as an institution to a specialised body – the ECB – which takes precedence over the role and function of the European Commission as the supranational authority within the Internal Market project.
3.   Means: from a politically designed and approved programme to one catch-all formula – a full power of attorney.
4.   *Ex ante/ex post*: from a programme that *ex ante* defines what has to be done to legislative measures that serve to provide *ex post* legitimacy to what has been decided already.
5.   Regulatory technique: from (minimum?) harmonisation which leaves space for (national?) differences to regulation and supranational administrative rule-making that replaces and substitutes national institutions and legislation.
6.   Substance vs procedure: from agreements on substantive roles that govern the Internal Market to the establishment of institutions and procedures that go beyond substance.
7.   Accountability and liability: from Member States being accountable and responsible to EU agencies and EU institutions being responsible but trying to escape liability.
8.   External vs internal: from varieties of judicial legal cultures to uniformity of administrative top-down culture.
9.   From imposing European standards on the rest of the world to negotiating European standards at the international level and reintegrating them back into the EU legal system.

The following three parameters are meant to give better and clearer shape to the BU – in contrast to and in comparison with the Internal Market programme. The three parameters are: the type of decision; the design of the decision (technicality vs technocracy); and last, but not least, the legal nature – is it still law we are talking about?

A. Decision-making

Decentralised enforcement was the original model under the Internal Market programme. Member States were responsible for the implementation and enforcement of EU law. The only yardstick against which their activities were assessed was the principles of 'effectiveness' and 'equivalence', which the CJEU developed over time into a dense body of rules that restrict rather than enhance the procedural autonomy of the Member States.[68] These principles are meant to guarantee a uniform application of European law. The need to coordinate national regulatory decisions in the different regulated markets became increasingly important. The first and may be most important complementary measure to the White Paper on the Completion of the Internal Market was the adoption of the comitology procedure in 1987 – just two years after the White Paper. In terms of institution building there is a direct line from the comitology procedure to agencification.[69] How did this development affect the decision-making process? What role remained for the Member States to influence the political process within the committees and beyond in the public fora; what remained for the parliaments to supervise and control the inside dynamics in all these committees; and what about the participation of civil society? The comitology procedure turned into a separate branch of research and has even resulted in a special newsletter, which is run by PACT, a training and lobbying organisation.[70]

My hypothesis is that the decision-making procedure in the regulated markets has gradually but steadily been streamlined, depoliticised, bureaucratised and centralised. Even if the established agencies have no decision-making power under the relevant EU rules other than those falling within the scope of non-discretionary decisions, and even if the European Commission is only empowered to adopt recommendations to guide administrative surveillance in the Member States, the EU agencies tend to determine the procedure: either directly or with the support of the European Commission as the driver behind the scene. Oversimplified, the mechanism looks like this: decision-making moves in only one direction, away from coordination towards centralisation. National enforcement authorities turn into 'agents' of EU agencies and/or the European Commission – they have to implement the rules decided at the European level. I rely here in

---

[68] M Bobek, 'Why There Is No Principle of 'Procedural Autonomy' of the Member States' in H-W Micklitz and B Witte (eds), *The European Court of Justice and the autonomy of the Member States* (Cambridge, Intersentia, 2012) 305.

[69] M Scholten and MV Rijsbergen, 'The Limits of Agentification in the European Union' (2014) 15 *German Law Journal* 1123; H-W Micklitz, 'Regulatory Strategies on Services Contracts in EC Law' in F Cafaggi/H Muir Watt (eds), *The Regulatory Function of European Private Law* (Cheltenham, Elgar, 2009).

[70] Premium Newsletter, available at www.comitology.eu.

particular on empirical evidence in the field of telecommunications, energy and financial services.[71] This does not mean that there are no frictions and that there is no resistance in the Member States. In the *OPTA* case the CJEU rejected the binding nature of recommendations issued by the European Commission in the telecom sector.[72] The judgment might well also have an impact on the banking sector. The CJEU thus strengthens the national authorities against the power of the European Commission to guide and influence their enforcement strategies. The most important counter-move against centralisation can be observed in the recent tendency of Member States to merge institutions competent for different regulated markets.[73]

The SSM has entrusted an EU institution, the ECB, with centralised decision-making power. The political and constitutional dimension of the SSM cannot be overestimated. Previously, a similar centralised decision-making procedure only existed in the field of competition law. Based on Article 103 TFEU, the European Commission was originally entrusted with the competence to enforce EU law by Regulation 17/1962. Regulation 1/2003 decentralised the European Commission's powers. Member States' cartel authorities are now in charge to enforce minor infringements of EU law, with the European Commission focusing on cases relevant from an EU-wide perspective.

The structural parallels between competition and banking supervision are obvious. The ECB is competent and responsible for 118 systemically relevant banks in the participating Member States and also for the coordination of the overall system. Non-euro countries may join the SSM: Bulgaria, Denmark and Romania seem ready to go that way and might trigger a domino effect. In the end, the ECB might be responsible for the supervision of the banks in 27 countries. There are questions about what the decision-making process will look like in that case. One of the key issues concerns the rules against which the activities of the systemically relevant banks are measured. The ECB has to coordinate with EBA inside and outside the EU. But will there be two sets of rules? Will there be a double standard – one set of standards for the systemically relevant banks and another set of standards for the 'rest', and can the tensions between the two be balanced out by the proportionality requirement? The ECB is currently acquiescently complying with BTS and soft law adopted by the EBA and, where there is margin for interpretation, the ECB takes only a temporary position, meaning that as soon as the EBA expresses its stand through Q&A, the ECB observes it.[74] In the Board of

---

[71] H-W Micklitz, Y Svetiev and G Comparato (eds), 'European Regulatory Private Law – The Paradigm Tested', *EUI Working Paper LAW* 2014/04, see also references n 2 above to L de Almeida, M Cantero Gamito and F della Negra.

[72] CJEU, Case C-28/15 *Koninklijke KPN NV and Others v Autoriteit Consument en Markt (ACM)*, EU:C:2016:692.

[73] A Ottow, *Market and Competition Authorities, Good Agency Principles* (Oxford, OUP, 2015).

[74] Personal communication of E Sedano, PhD Researcher at the European University, at the time of writing undertaking a stage at the ECB.

Supervisors of EBA, the ECB is a non-voting member. This suggests that ECB and EBA are collaborating and that double standards are hard to imagine. Questions remain: is it imaginable that the EBA will resist possible attempts of the ECB to influence the standard-making process for non-systemically relevant banks? To what extent is the ECB able, competent, and to what extent does it have the resources available to implement its supervisory measures? To what extent does it have to rely on national authorities as agents of ECB enforcement strategies? There are even deeper questions about the interrelationship between the ECB and other democratic institutions. What would happen if parliaments resisted supervision standards that were internationally agreed in the Basle Committee and that turned out to be 'rationale' for effective supervision at grass-roots level? Are parliaments effectively circumvented – not on paper, but in practice – by the way in which the democratically approved technical standards are applied?

B. Paradigm Change

The Internal Market programme was designed to abolish the so-called *technical* barriers to trade. The emphasis has to be put on technical standards in the meaning of the 'New Approach' and the 'Memorandum of Understanding' between the EU and CEN/CENELEC. The key actors were the standard bodies, the national standard bodies, with AFNOR (France), BSI (UK) and DIN (Germany) taking a leading role. The committees, which develop the technical standards to which the directives under the New Approach refer, are composed of engineers, who are delegated to the committees by their firms. Technical knowledge lies at the heart of the standardisation process. Nongovernmental organisations from the civil society were granted an observer status. In the EU, ANEC (the European consumer voice)[75] turned into the key player, also being financed by the European Commission. Ever since its creation, ANEC has had to deal with a lack of technical competence in the various committees in which it is a member. The dominant rationality in Internal Market standard-making is technical expertise, not political engagement. Technical standards are meant to provide guidance. They are not binding law. Those who voluntarily comply with the standards receive an advantage in that they are presumed to comply with the mandatory requirements laid down in the relevant directives. Producers may, if they so decide, develop their own technical solutions which meet the mandatory requirements laid down in the directives adopted under the New Approach.

The BU follows the logic of the Internal Market programme, albeit in a much more sophisticated form and with important modifications. First, I will briefly explain the new mechanism and I will then comment on its technocratic character. Under Directive 2013/36, the EBA is given the mandate to develop

---

[75] See institutional website, available at http://www.anec.eu.

'technical standards'. These standards cover the whole field of banking and finance, as listed in Article 8. Contrary to the New Approach technical standards, the BU technical standards can be made binding. Two procedures have to be kept separate: the procedure under Article 290 TFEU – specified in Articles 10–14 Regulation 1093/2010 – and the procedure under Article 291 TFEU – specified in Article 15 Regulation 1093/2010. There is a thin line between the two procedures and the distinction between the two is subject to intense debate between the European Commission and the European Parliament. The draft regulatory technical standards (RTS)[76] as developed by the ESAs are sent to the European Commission. Where primary legislation provides for RTS – which should be the rule[77] – the European Parliament and the Council have one month to object to their adoption (cf Article 149 TFEU). Alternatively, primary legislation provides for the implementing technical standards (ITS), which remain within the scope of what was previously known as the 'comitology procedure', with due control by the Member States as under Article 291 TFEU.

These technical standards are based on banking and financial expertise. The recitals to the Directive and the Regulation constantly refer to the particular expertise needed. Expert knowledge should normally prevail over any political reservations. In crude language: where engineers play a key role in adopting technical standards under the New Approach, economists have to fulfil this function for technical standards adopted under the BU. Where is the move from technicality to technocracy? What has changed? Is it not just a different form of expertise – economic expertise instead of engineering expertise? Why speak of technocracy in the BU and of technicality in the Internal Market? The shift, this is the argument, results from the 'financialisation' of the economy, which disconnected banking and finance from the market for goods and services.[78] In German we have the wonderful world of '*Verselbständigung*', to be translated as 'a process of gaining independence' – independence not only from the market for services and goods, but also and in particular from politics. Engineering/natural science

---

[76] On the distinction between RTS and ITS see eg the single rulebook here: https://www.eba.europa.eu/regulation-and-policy/single-rulebook/interactive-single-rulebook/-/interactive-single-rulebook/toc/2/article-id/80.

[77] Recital 23 Regulation 1093/2010, 'The Commission should endorse those draft regulatory technical standards by means of delegated acts pursuant to Article 290 TFEU in order to give them binding legal effect. They should be subject to amendment only in very restricted and extraordinary circumstances, since the Authority is the actor in close contact with and knowing best the daily functioning of financial markets. Draft regulatory technical standards would be subject to amendment if they were incompatible with Union law, did not respect the principle of proportionality or ran counter to the fundamental principles of the internal market for financial services as reflected in the acquis of Union financial services legislation. The Commission should not change the content of the draft regulatory technical standards prepared by the Authority without prior coordination with the Authority. To ensure a smooth and expeditious adoption process for those standards, the Commission's decision to endorse draft regulatory technical standards should be subject to a time limit.'

[78] J Vogl, *The Spectre of the Capital* (Stanford, Stanford University Press, 2014).

leaves the decision on the correct level of product safety to politics. The presumption of compliance might grant access to the market but cannot shield against eventual liability claims. Financial technocracy claims supremacy over politics – it substitutes the political process. The visible difference is documented in the existing of BTS in the BU whereas technical standards are non-binding in the Internal Market.[79] However, in *Elliott*[80] the CJEU accepted jurisdiction to review non-binding technical standards. It remains to be seen whether the CJEU is ready to accept jurisdiction when it comes to reviewing the soft-law measures standing behind the legally binding BU standards.

C. Law

The Internal Market programme perpetuated the 'integration through law' dictum on which the European Community was built. However, the paradigm thereby undermined its own foundations. I will take for granted what is meant by 'integration through law'. I equally take for granted that the law-making machinery, which the Internal Market programme set into motion, led to ever more 'rules' and to ever lesser 'law'. Integration through law was gradually replaced by 'integration through governance'. One of the hotly debated issues in law and political science is the question whether and to what extent there is still law in governance and, if there is no more law, whether and to what extent law is necessary to shape and 'control' governance.[81] The institutional architecture of the Treaty, the distinction between law-making in the hands of the EU and law-enforcement in those of the Member States, facilitated and accelerated the demise of 'law' in the name of the 'integration through law'. Therefore, the Internal Market programme, which was meant to promote integration through law, might turn out to have been the 'gravedigger' of the philosophy which guided the EU relatively successfully through more than 30 years of troubled waters.

The BU and the way it has been implemented – *post factum* by a whole series of regulations and directives that are then specified through regulatory and implementing technical regulations (RTS and ITS) – is perfectly in line with a move from 'integration through law' to 'integration through governance'. The 'machinery is again set into motion'. The data are from November 2017.[82] They can be characterised by the following: (a) the sheer quantity of rules (already more than 1000); (b) the outstanding use of delegation powers in regulations and directives to

---

[79] Case C-171/11 *Fra.bo*, EU:C:2012:453.

[80] Case C-613/14 *James Elliott Construction Limited v Irish Asphalt Limited*, EU:C:2016:821.

[81] M Dawson, *New Governance and the Transformation of European Law. Coordinating EU Social Law and Policy* (Cambridge: Cambridge University Press, 2011).

[82] The data have been collected by A Busca and E Sedano, PhD Researchers at the EUI as per November 2017.

the EBA; (c) the technical standards shaped by EBA, needing approval from the European Commission, and quite often the subject of disagreement.[83]

–   On the supervisory mechanism there are: two Regulations of the Council and one Regulation of the European Parliament and of the Council; seven ECB Regulations, two rules of procedure and one code of conduct; one Interinstitutional Agreement between the European Parliament and the ECB; two MOU between the ECB and the Council; 21 ECB Decisions, two Recommendations and five ECB Guidelines (not including a number of ECB decision updating supervisory fees and dividends policies each year). This gives a total of 514 pages of rules and regulations directly affecting banks and interested parties.

–   On the resolution mechanism there are: one Regulation of the European Parliament and of the Council; one Regulation of the Council; three Delegated regulations of the Commission; two Intergovernmental Agreements; two MOU between the ECB and the SRM Board; and seven Decisions of the SRM Board. This gives a total of 383 pages of rules and regulations directly affecting banks and interested parties.

–   The Single Rulebook is made up of: one Regulation of the European Parliament and of the Council and two Directives of the European Parliament and of the Council, giving a total of 595 pages (in English) of rules and regulations directly affecting banks and interested parties. To these rules one has to add the BTS for the implementation of the CRD IV package and the CRR, issued by the Commission on the proposals of the EBA. Up to eight ITS decisions and 17 RTS decisions have been taken.[84] Additionally, we have to take into consideration the EBA Guidelines. These guidelines are not legally binding, but supervisory authorities and institutions must make every effort to comply with them. Supervisory authorities, in particular, are obliged to inform the EBA of their compliance or intention to comply with them and to also explain the reasons for an eventual non-compliance. In connection with the BRRD alone there exist 19 guidelines for a total of 676 pages.

Can these abundant rules be called 'law'? Who is able and competent to overlook and democratically monitor the process of rule production? In theory it should be the European Parliament and the CJEU? Is this a realistic perspective?

This is not yet all. The BU puts emphasis on institution building and on centralised enforcement via the ECB. Is the ECB, as the major enforcement authority, in a position to hold all these rules together and to make sure that they

---

[83] See EBA, EBA expresses dissent over the EU Commission proposed amendments to technical standards under the IFR, 16 February 2016, available at https://www.eba.europa.eu/-/eba-expresses-dissent-over-the-eu-commission-proposed-amendments-to-technical-standards-under-the-ifr.

[84] The number is steadily increasing: https://ec.europa.eu/info/sites/info/files/crr-level-2-measures-full_en.pdf.

reach the public officials in charge who have to apply them in practice, whether it is EU law or national law (Article 4(3) SSM)? How much leeway is left to the law enforcers at the bottom level of the hierarchy within the Member States? The BU looks like the culmination point of the ideology behind the Internal Market programme. The shift towards administrative enforcement is marginalising the role and function of law – and now not only in the making but also in the enforcement.

XII. Instead of Conclusion

What is the way out? Is there a way out? What is the role for law, or for the rule of law? I do not think that there is a way back to the good old times. I am not following Alexander Somek in his swan song on the nineteenth century nation state democracy.[85] I understand Europe as a laboratory in which the transformation of the state and the changing role of nation states and democracies can be studied.[86] The interplay between the Internal Market, the Banking Union and democracy is a wonderful example for such an exercise.

---

[85] A Somek, *The Cosmopolitan Constitution* (Oxford, OUP, 2014).
[86] H-W Micklitz, 'Review of Philosophical Foundations of European Union Law by Julie Dickson and Pavlos Eleftheriadis' (2013) *Yearbook of European Law* 538.

12

Should Non-participating Member States Join the Banking Union?

A Legal Perspective

DALVINDER SINGH

I. Introduction

The Single Supervisory Mechanism (SSM) opens the door for participation by non-Eurozone Member States, and for the European Central Bank (ECB) to supervise those credit institutions that fulfil the criteria based on significance within the Member State.[1] The ECB is required regardless to work closely with non-participating Member States.[2] The participating and non-participating Member States' authorities will be expected to allow the ECB to take the lead and/or to cooperate with the ECB, as the competent home supervisor, to ensure appropriate cooperation and coordination of supervision and information sharing to inform banking group supervisory decisions. This chapter asks: What does close cooperation look like from a legal perspective for a potential Member State? The literature appears to assume it is 'equivalent' rather than 'comparable' in terms of its outcomes.[3]

---

[1] Council Regulation (EU) No 1024/2013 of 15 October 2013 conferring specific tasks on the European Central Bank concerning policies relating to the prudential supervision of credit institutions, Art 7, http://eur-lex.europa.eu/legal-content/EN/TXT/PDF/?uri=CELEX:32013R1024&from=EN ('the SSM Regulation').

[2] P Hüttl and D Schoenmaker, 'Should The "Outs" Join the European Banking Union?', Issue 2016/03, February 2016, p 5, available at http://bruegel.org/wp-content/uploads/2016/02/pc_2016_03.pdf.

[3] A Belke, A Dobrzanska, D Gros and P Smaga, '(When) Should a Non-Euro Country Join the Banking Union?' (2016) 14 *Journal of Economic Asymmetries* 4; Z Kudrna, 'Governing the ins and outs of the EU's Banking Union' (2016) 17 *Journal of Banking Regulation* 119; M Katalin and D Piroska, 'Banking Union and Banking Nationalism – Explaining Opt-Out Choices of Hungary, Poland and the Czech Republic' (2016) 35 *Journal Policy and Society* 215; K Mitręga-Niestrój and B Puszer, 'The Threats of the Banking Union for the Polish Banking Sector', European Financial Systems 2015, Proceedings of the 12th International Scientific Conference, June 18–19, 2015, Brno, Czech Republic pp 400–07; U Vollmer, 'The Asymmetric Implementation of the European Banking Union (EBU): Consequences for Financial Stability' (2016) *International Journal of Management and Economics* 7.

This chapter focuses on the procedures outlining how a non-Eurozone Member State would enter a close cooperation agreement with the ECB, thus coming under the umbrella of the SSM. In this respect, it asks whether the close cooperation agreement emulates the current SSM internal arrangements between the ECB, National Competent Authorities (NCAs) and National Delegated Authorities (NDAs) and briefly the Single Resolution Mechanism (SRM) and the National Resolution Authority (NRA) for the purposes of microprudential supervision and resolution. To this end, this chapter will also compare the difference in treatment between those participating in the SSM and those designated in close cooperation in the SSM, and discuss the incentives for entering close cooperation. It specifically looks at the position of non-participating Eastern European Member States. Finally, it will review whether non-participating Member States should join the Banking Union in the 'pure agency' relationship that is offered in close cooperation.

The authority to undertake the functions of bank regulation and supervision is legislated. The European reforms have provided considerable flesh on the bones of those functions and added to the powers of NCAs to exercise bank supervision. The functions of supervision are complex and its tentacles spread to a variety of discrete areas where there are complex overlaps and indeed distinct mandates to safeguard national interests both public and private, such as national security, financial stability and market integrity, and shareholders' and employees' and even creditors' rights. The mandate of the competent authority and resolution authority to work with the ministry of finance and the deposit guarantee agency require legislative rights to cooperate and coordinate efforts to achieve macroprudential and microprudential aims and objectives. The mandate for supervision is multifaceted, as well spilling over into civil and criminal law matters. The move to confer the responsibility of part of regulation and supervision of banks to another external agency with its own distinct jurisdiction requires considerable reform at the public and administrative law levels. It is not a simple baton that can be passed from one administrative agency to another administrative agency devoid of questions of public legal debate. It requires, in the case of domestic significant banks and in some cases less significant banks (per non-domestic criteria) a transfer, subrogation or assignment of rights to the NCA to take action against individual firms and individuals working within those firms when wrong doing to another legal person is found. While a decision by a non-participating Member State in close cooperation is perceived to be one of transfer of sovereignty through a form of replacement of a local NCA with the ECB, it will be shown below that this is not the case.

The relationship between the ECB and Eurozone Member States is significantly different to that between the ECB and non-participating Member States. The Statute of the European System of Central Banks and of the European Central Bank[4]

---

[4] Consolidated version of the Treaty on the Functioning of the European Union Protocol (No 4), on the Statute of the European System of Central Banks and of the European Central Bank.

sets out the authority of the ECB and its responsibilities. According to the European System of Central Banks (ESCB) Statute, Article 25.2, 'the ECB may perform specific tasks concerning policies relating to the prudential supervision of credit institutions and other financial institutions except for insurance undertakings'.[5] According to Article 131 of the Treaty on the Functioning of the European Union (TFEU), national legislation is expected to be compatible with the Treaties of the ESCB and of the ECB. To execute the tasks conferred on the ESCB, the ECB can make regulations, recommendations and opinions, and impose fines and penalties on undertakings for failure to comply with obligations under its regulations and decisions. Article 132 TFEU and Article 9 of the Protocol (No 4) set out the scope of the authority of the ECB explaining:

> The ECB which, in accordance with Article 282(3) of the Treaty on the Functioning of the European Union, shall have legal personality, shall enjoy in each of the Member States the most extensive legal capacity accorded to legal persons under its law; it may, in particular, acquire or dispose of movable and immovable property and may be a party to legal proceedings.

The tasks conferred on the ESCB[6] are to be undertaken by the decision-making bodies of the ECB[7] relating to prudential supervision, which are further articulated in the SSM Regulation. In many respects, the SSM replicates the Treaty aspiration that the central banks of the ESCB and the ECB should work together, rather than the ECB taking complete control of direct supervision of the credit institutions within the respective Eurozone Member States.

---

[5] Art 127(6) TFEU: 'The Council, acting by means of regulations in accordance with a special legislative procedure, may unanimously, and after consulting the European Parliament and the European Central Bank, confer specific tasks upon the European Central Bank concerning policies relating to the prudential supervision of credit institutions and other financial institutions with the exception of insurance undertakings.'

[6] Protocol (No 4):

Article 3 – Tasks:

3.1. In accordance with Article 105(2) of this Treaty, the basic tasks to be carried out through the ESCB shall be· – to define and implement the monetary policy of the Community; – to conduct foreign-exchange operations consistent with the provisions of Article 111 of this Treaty; – to hold and manage the official foreign reserves of the Member States; – to promote the smooth operation of payment systems.

3.2. In accordance with Article 105(3) of this Treaty, the third indent of Article 3.1 shall be without prejudice to the holding and management by the governments of Member States of foreign-exchange working balances.

3.3. In accordance with Article 105(5) of this Treaty, the ESCB shall contribute to the smooth conduct of policies pursued by the competent authorities relating to the prudential supervision of credit institutions and the stability of the financial system.

[7] Art 9(2): 'The ECB shall ensure that the tasks conferred upon the ESCB under Article 105(2), (3) and (5) of this Treaty are implemented either by its own activities pursuant to this Statute or through the national central banks pursuant to Articles 12.1 and 14.'

The respective Member States that are the focus of this chapter are classed as Member States with a derogation.[8] It excludes them from the rights and obligations within the ESCB, and their respective voting rights of the Council are suspended when it comes to recommendations made to Eurozone Member States concerning surveillance, stability programmes and warnings; and measures relating to fiscal policy, namely excessive deficits (Article 139 TFEU). In respect of these Member States, the ECB (Article 141 TFEU) is expected to strengthen cooperation between central banks, coordination of monetary policies, and more specifically hold consultations with the respective central banks for the purposes of financial stability. The strengthening of the cooperation is formalised with the option for the non-participating Member States to enter close cooperation with the ECB in the SSM in accordance with the SSM Regulation which is further articulated in Regulation 468/2014 in terms of cooperation with the SSM and NCAs.

The SSM framework for cooperation between the ECB and NCAs and NDAs is set out in a further ECB Regulation which covers the relationship between the ECB with both participating and those seeking to became participating Member States once they enter close cooperation.[9] Regulation 468/2014 adds practical details regarding the respective competent authorities and designated authorities to Articles 4, 5 and 6 of the SSM Regulation. This more formalised arrangement needs to be distinguished from Memoranda of Understanding which non-Eurozone non-participating Member States are expected to enter into with the ECB to determine how they will cooperate and divide responsibilities with one another in terms of supervision.[10] More importantly, assessing this framework will determine whether it forms a level playing field between Eurozone and non-Eurozone Member States. In this respect, we ask here whether there is a sufficient degree of reciprocity in the way participating Member States interact with one another to the extent that Member States are aware of the unintended consequences of non-participating Member States in the SSM. The misalignment of reciprocity in the SSM, it is argued, gives rise to agency problems and, to a certain degree, the Eurozone acting in its own self-interest.

The SSM requires significant reliance on the cooperation of the ECB and the NCAs to achieve the aims and objectives of a single supervisory approach. The complexity of the mechanism means the different cogs in it need to be synchronised in a way that will achieve what can be broadly understood as a single supervisory decision-making mechanism. In the light of the granularity of the

---

[8] European Commission, Convergence Report 2016, 07 June 2016 (last update on: 7 June 2016), Institutional Paper 26, available at https://ec.europa.eu/info/publications/economy-finance/convergence-report-2016_en. Bulgaria; The Czech Republic; Croatia; Hungary; Poland; Romania.

[9] Regulation (EU) 468/2014 of the European Central Bank of 16 April 2014 establishing the framework for cooperation within the Single Supervisory Mechanism between the European Central Bank and national competent authorities and with national designated authorities (SSM Framework Regulation), available at http://eur-lex.europa.eu/legal-content/EN/TXT/PDF/?uri=CELEX:32014R0468&from=EN.

[10] SSM Regulation, Art 3(6).

macroprudential and microprudential requirements which must be implemented, for a decision to be formulated detailed cooperation and coordination are required at a variety of levels to maintain the financial stability and integrity of the market. One only needs to count the number of additional Decisions and Regulations wrapped around the core Regulations and Directives to see the sheer scale of the number of legal instruments required to ensure consistency of cooperation and coordination. It is useful in the context of assessing the relationship between ECB and participating Member States to describe the cooperation and coordination measures and assess the extent to which these minimise asymmetry of information problems between the national authorities of the home and host.

If it wishes to enter into close cooperation, a Member State is required to make a request to the ECB.[11] To this end, the requesting Member State is to set out how it expects to adhere to ECB instructions, guidelines and requests for information in relation to all the supervised entities established in its jurisdiction. This will be expected to be undertaken across the areas of responsibility that come within the umbrella of the ECB's tasks within the SSM.[12] With the request to enter into close cooperation the Member State must also submit draft legislation so that the ECB can satisfy itself that the Member State has all the necessary legal means in place to ensure that the competent authority can comply with ECB decisions. A significant part of this process is, therefore, to ascertain the quality of supervision and the crisis management arrangements in place to ensure that the requesting Member State can fulfil the standards of supervision of the SSM, so as not to have a detrimental impact on the SSM achieving its objectives and principles. In this respect, the principle of *mutatis mutandis* applies when it comes to the respective ECB responsibilities: the assessment of significance of credit institutions; macroprudential tools; administrative penalties; and investigatory powers. In this respect, the ECB needs to be satisfied that the directions it gives in the above matters can be executed by the NCA in accordance with its standards.

The ECB makes its decision on the basis of a comprehensive assessment of the Member State and its banking system in the widest sense. In this process (which is expected as a minimum to take approximately three months) the ECB can request further documentation to assist it when making the decision. Entry into close cooperation is therefore not a simple entry but rather an ongoing process of working towards close cooperation and then continuously complying with the decisions and instructions associated with supervision. However, the concept of close cooperation is not actually defined, so it is likely that what constitutes close cooperation for one requesting Member State will be different for another requesting Member State. Once the ECB has formed a view on the close cooperation, it will adopt a decision based on Article 7(2) of the SSM Regulation, addressed to

---

[11] Decision of the European Central Bank of 31 January 2014 on the close cooperation with the national competent authorities of the participating Member States whose currency is not the euro (ECB/2014/5).

[12] SSM Regulation, Art 4 and Art 5.

the Member State. Lack of compliance with this decision on close cooperation can lead to a situation where close cooperation is suspended or terminated by the ECB. The supervisory relationship will in all intents and purposes be wider than simply microprudential decisions and instructions since it will be also be applicable on the macroprudential level, so invariably encroaching, by necessity, on the wider issues associated with the financial system and the economy in light of the interdependence of the two strands of policy.

ECB's Regulation 468/2014 explains the role of the ECB and respective Member States within the SSM and how they are expected to cooperate more specifically as well as how non-participating Member States should request to enter into close cooperation, thus building on the SSM Regulation. It explains the criteria for and the implications of the ECB's decision to determine significant and less significant credit institutions and how the ECB directly supervises significant banks, and in some cases less significant banks. A request to an NCA from a significant bank to set up a branch or provide services in another Member State is expected to be communicated to the ECB immediately.[13] It also further explains how the ECB is to take on the role of Chair and Member of the supervisory college in the capacity of consolidated supervisor of the significant bank in a participating Member State, while the NCA reverts to a position of Observer for the same significant bank.[14] Regulation 468/2014 does not expressly refer to the ECB as the new competent authority, albeit it undertakes the role in a quasi competent authority role, akin to an agency relationship, by instructing the NCA in the way that significant banks are expected to be supervised.[15] In view of this, the Member State has to initiate legislative reforms to ensure the national competent authority can 'abide by any guidelines or requests by the ECB'.[16] In the context of close cooperation, however, the SSM Regulation refers only to the 'tasks' associated with Articles 4 and 5. To understand what form close cooperation in those tasks will take, it is important to refer to Regulation 468/2014, Article 107(2):

> If a close cooperation has been established pursuant to Article 7(2) of the SSM Regulation the ECB and the NCA in close cooperation shall, in respect of significant supervised entities and groups and less significant supervised entities and groups established in the participating Member State in close cooperation, be in a position comparable to significant supervised entities and groups and less significant supervised entities and groups established in euro area Member States, taking into account that the ECB does not have directly applicable powers over significant supervised entities and groups and less significant supervised entities and groups established in the participating Member State in close cooperation.

The wording of Article 107(2) therefore suggests the ECB in close cooperation with a Member State is not going to have the same or equivalent powers

---

[13] Regulation 468/2014, Arts 11–12.
[14] Regulation 468/2014, Arts 9–10.
[15] SSM Regulation, Art 7(1).
[16] SSM Regulation, Art 7(2)(b).

it has within SSM regarding a Eurozone Member State with significant banks and less significant banks. By contrast to the powers that are conferred on the ESCB and ECB in the respective Eurozone Member States, the ECB in close cooperation will rely on the NCA of the Member State more than it does with a Eurozone Member State. Regulation 468/2014 sets out in clear terms that the ECB does not have equivalent responsibility to the competent or designated authority (as it does in Article 9 of the SSM Regulation) since the SSM is not a monolithic regulatory and supervisory authority but one constituted of a relatively complex set of obligations and functions at multiple levels, ie national and regional central banks and the ECB. In this respect, the close cooperation arrangements give rise to different agency problems and uncertainty associated with the regional interests and national interests not being aligned in a formal sense – since it provides 'comparable' but not 'equivalent' supervision of significant entities. Therefore, where is it equivalent and where is it comparable, to ascertain the benefits of opting in or out? In the context of Article 4(1) and (2), in the Eurozone the ECB is given exclusive competence to exercise the tasks set therein. In accordance with Article 108 of Regulation 468/2014,[17] the ECB has the discretion to give 'instructions', 'make requests' and 'issue guidelines' which are primarily addressed to the Member State's NCA. In this respect, the NCAs remain the competent authority for supervision but the instructions will come from the ECB. For example, decisions normally addressed to a supervised entity or group are addressed to the NCA to implement for the purposes of assessment

---

[17] Article 108: Legal instruments related to supervision in connection with close cooperation

1. With respect to the tasks referred to in Article 4(1) and (2) and Article 5 of the SSM Regulation, the ECB may give instructions, make requests or issue guidelines.
2. If the ECB considers that a measure relating to the tasks referred to in Article 4(1) and (2) of the SSM Regulation should be adopted by the NCA in close cooperation in relation to a supervised entity or group, it shall address to that NCA:
   (a) in respect of a significant supervised entity or significant supervised group, a general or specific instruction, a request or a guideline requiring the issuance of a supervisory decision in relation to that significant supervised entity or significant supervised group in the participating Member State in close cooperation, or
   (b) in respect of a less significant supervised entity or less significant supervised group, a general instruction or a guideline.
3. If the ECB considers that a measure relating to the tasks referred to in Article 5 of the SSM Regulation should be adopted by the NCA or NDA in close cooperation, it may address to that NCA or NDA a general or specific instruction, a request or a guideline requiring the application of higher requirements for capital buffers or the application of more stringent measures aimed at addressing systemic or macroprudential risks.
4. The ECB shall specify in the instruction, request or guideline a relevant time limit for the adoption of the measure by the NCA in close cooperation, which shall be no less than 48 hours, unless earlier adoption is necessary to prevent irreparable damage. When determining the time limit, the ECB shall take into account the administrative and procedural law with which the relevant NCA in close cooperation has to comply.
5. An NCA in close cooperation shall take all necessary measures to comply with the ECB's instructions, requests or guidelines and it shall inform the ECB without undue delay of the measures it has taken.

of the significance of credit institutions, and decisions to apply administrative penalties.[18] Moreover, in terms of investigations relating to significant banks, the NCA is to undertake these following ECB instruments and then report the findings to the ECB.[19] In such investigations the ECB staff are present in the capacity of Observers.[20] Within the Eurozone, meanwhile, the ECB can conduct investigations itself, including by way of requesting documentation, obtaining evidence and conducting interviews.[21]

It is no surprise that the ECB is to act as the consolidated supervisor for significant banks and their group entities.[22] Since the focus of the ECB is significant banks, the responsibility for less significant banks – including in consolidated supervision – is left with the NCA. It is important to point out, however, that the role of consolidated supervisor and college of supervisors in the Banking Union is reconfigured. In the Eurozone, the ECB is the consolidated supervisor and the chair of supervisory colleges for significant banks, and the Member State NCA of the banking establishment acts in the capacity of Observer[23] – and therefore they are no longer 'members' of the colleges. In the Banking Union, therefore, for pure Eurozone banks the importance of supervisory colleges is less important since the ECB is both home and host and there would be limited asymmetry of information as in the previous model. However, if the consolidated supervisor is in a non-participating Member State, then the ECB and the NCA with respective interests are invited to participate:[24] for all significant banks the ECB is to participate as a member in the supervisory college and the NCA as an Observer. The status and membership in the supervisory college would change respectively in the case of less significant banks.

Similar rules apply to those Member States that enter in close cooperation.[25] Therefore when a Member State decides to enter in close cooperation, if the NCA of the Member State is the consolidated supervisor of a significant bank, it will lose the position of chair of the supervisory college and will be replaced by the ECB. The NCA of the newly participating Member State would meanwhile be relegated to the position of an Observer. Moreover, if the Member State in close cooperation has a significant branch or a subsidiary and is already a member of a supervisory college, then its position will also be changed to one of Observer. In its capacity as consolidated supervisor, the ECB as chair and competent authority has the discretion to give instructions to the NCA in close cooperation. The ECB is, however, reliant on the NCA in close cooperation to act on its instructions because the ECB does not have jurisdiction to act on its

---

[18] Regulation 468/2014, Art 113(1)–(3).
[19] Regulation 468/2014, Art 114(1)–(4).
[20] Regulation 468/2014, Art 114(4).
[21] SSM Regulation, Arts 9–11.
[22] Regulation 468/2014, Art 8.
[23] Regulation 468/2014, Art 9.
[24] Regulation 468/2014, Art 10.
[25] Regulation 468/2014, Art 115(5).

own initiative and directly liaise with the significant bank as it would within a Eurozone Member State.

A question that does need reflecting on is whether, in the Eurozone, the asymmetry of information between the home and host State is changed with the introduction of a single regulator for Eurozone Member State and close-cooperating Member States? A part of this is addressed with the adoption of Joint Supervisory Teams, which makes it possible for the competent authorities to enable the Joint Supervisory Teams to break down the obstacles they tended to face when seeking information and data from the home country responsible for consolidated supervision. With Joint Supervisory Teams composed of staff from the ECB and the competent authorities from the different parts of the banking group, the above becomes less of a challenge. Opting in would certainly address the concern of home bias and enable the Member State in close cooperation to better prepare at the macroprudential, microprudential and resolution levels for future crises. A recent review by the European Court of Auditors of the SSM has, nevertheless, found that a significant proportion of the JTS staff are from NCAs since the ECB simply does not have the volume of staff needed to improve the ratio between ECB and NCA staff making up the team.[26]

II. The Outcome of Entering Close Cooperation

The number of banks classed as significant by the ECB and so falling within the remit of the SSM is likely to be much lower from the Central and Eastern Europe (CEE) Member States.[27] The threshold of most significant banks is set relatively high, and is based on:

(1) asset size more than €30 billion;
(2) ratio of total assets and GDP is more than 20 per cent;
(3) one of the three largest banks;
(4) directly assisted by the European Stability Mechanism (ESM); or
(5) based on cross-border activities, the credit institution has total assets exceeding €5 billion and its cross-border activities in a participating Member State exceed 20 per cent of its total assets, or its liabilities in a participating Member State exceed 20 per cent of total liabilities.

The ECB can also consider a bank is significant if it has subsidiaries in two or more participating Member States; the bank is supported by the European Financial Stability Facility (EFSF) or ESM; or the ECB, in agreement with the local

---

[26] European Court of Auditors, Special Report Single Supervisory Mechanism – Good Start But Further Improvement Needed, No 29, 2016.

[27] List of supervised entities: https://www.bankingsupervision.europa.eu/ecb/pub/pdf/list_of_supervised_entities_201611.en.pdf?a9caa144fa232a75fb36cf1213edd990.

competent authority, decides that the institution should come under the umbrella of the SSM rather than remain under the helm of the local competent authority.

Figure 12.1 shows the current number of significant banks in the Eurozone CEE region: Estonia, Latvia, Lithuania, Slovenia and Slovakia. The respective Eurozone Member States have a banking system model which is similar to the rest of the CEE non-participating Member States. The ECB classification indicates that no bank would be classed as significant based on total assets or liabilities or indeed based on GDP criteria: the banks are classified as significant based on them being one of the three largest banks in the Member State. The figure illustrates the point made above, showing the different outcome between SSM significant banks and those listed as O-SIIs (Other Systemically Important Institutions) in the Euro-zone CEE region. These are identified as institutions that pose a potential risk to financial stability because they provide critical functions in the financial system and their business has a large market share, is not easily substitutable, is complex or is too interconnected in the market. Figure 12.1 indicates that the number of O-SIIs is higher than those which would have been designated as significant under the ECB criteria. While most of the banks which are less significant and classed as O-SIIs would remain under the supervision of NCAs, only two or three have moved under the umbrella of the SSM. The implications of this is that for the less significant institutions, albeit designated as O-SIIs, the NCA and the NRA will have responsibility for the decision whether the less significant institution is fail-ing and then to decide which resolution or insolvency options will best achieve the resolution objectives and principles.

Figure 12.1 Number of Significant and Less Significant Banks and the Number Classed as O-SIIs in CEE Eurozone Member States

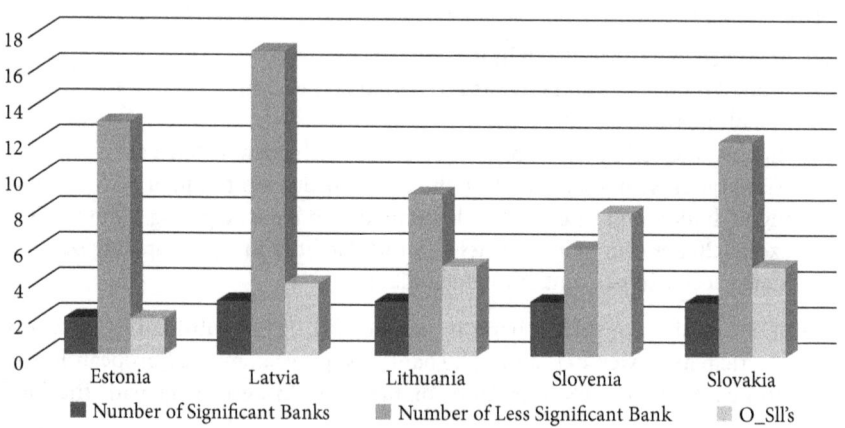

Source: Dalvinder Singh, Cross-Border Bank Supervision and Resolution: The Home-Host Dilemma for Significant-Material Subsidiaries from a 'Small' Host State Perspective, Financial Sector Advisory Center (FinSAC) Conference on EU Bank Resolution and Workshop on Bail-in, Vienna, Austria, December 12–13, 2016.

The Member State central bank decides which banks require additional capital buffers in view of their systemic significance of the entity to the local market.[28] This is decided by the central bank under its responsibility as the macroprudential authority for the Member State. The central bank has the discretion to set capital buffers, subject to notifying the ECB within the Banking Union. In this respect, Member States opting to enter into close cooperation with the Banking Union would not lose their discretion to classify banks as O-SIIs and set capital buffers for macroprudential purposes. The arrangements associated with macroprudential matters with the introduction of formal Capital Conversation Buffer Article 129, Systemic Risk Buffers with Article 133, and the Counter Cyclical Buffer with Article 136 set out in CRD IV leave room for national discretion when going about setting these three buffers in accordance with EBA guidelines.[29] The ESRB can recommend reciprocation of such decisions in view of their cross-border implications on banks in other Member States. For instance, the decision of the Central Bank of Estonia to apply a 1 per cent systemic risk buffer to all credit institutions authorised in Estonia on their domestic exposures is recommended to be met with an equivalent response by other Member States.[30] From this viewpoint, national central banks as macroprudential authorities are indicating that a larger number of banks are expected to comply with capital buffers in view of their importance in the financial system.

Some of the banks required to hold additional buffers from non-participating Member States are Raiffeisen (Austria), Unicredit (Italy), Société Générale SA (France), Alpha Bank (Greece) and Erste Group Bank AG (Austria). Since in these cases the ECB is already the consolidated supervisor, from a home Member State perspective, it would mean significant subsidiaries in those respective CEE Member States that do enter close cooperation would also come under its umbrella and benefit from the joined-up supervisory oversight offered by a single regulator. Since consolidated supervisory information under the Supervisory Review and

---

[28] EBA, Guidelines on the criteria to determine the conditions of application of Article 131(3) of Directive 2013/36/EU (CRD) in relation to the assessment of other systemically important institutions (O-SIIs), 16 December 2014, http://www.eba.europa.eu/documents/10180/930752/EBA-GL-2014-10+%28Guidelines+on+O-SIIs+Assessment%29.pdf/964fa8c7-6f7c-431a-8c34-82d42d112d91.

[29] EBA, Guidelines on the criteria to determine the conditions of application of Article 131(3) of Directive 2013/36/EU (CRD) in relation to the assessment of other systemically important institutions (O-SIIs) EBA/GL/2014/10, 16 December 2014, http://www.eba.europa.eu/documents/10180/930752/EBA-GL-2014-10+%28Guidelines+on+O-SIIs+Assessment%29.pdf/964fa8c7-6f7c-431a-8c34-82d42d112d91. EBA, Compliance Table – Guidelines. Based on information supplied by them, the following competent authorities comply or intend to comply with: EBA Guidelines EBA/GL/2014/10 on criteria for the assessment of O-SIIS, published on 16 December 2014. EBA/GL/2014/10 Appendix 1; 22 December 2014 – Updated 3; November 2015; EBA/GL/2014/10 Appendix 1, http://www.eba.europa.eu/documents/10180/930752/EBA+GL+2014+10-Compliance+Table-Guidelines+on+Criteria+for+the+assessment+of+O-SIIS.pdf/1f62d5db-043c-4a2a-a942-ca107d6b1a34.

[30] Recommendation of the European Systemic Risk Board of 24 June 2016 amending Recommendation ESRB/2015/2 on the assessment of cross-border effects of and voluntary reciprocity for macroprudential policy measures (ESRB/2016/4) (2016/C 290/01).

Evaluation Process (SREP) system would be available to the small host, this would minimise the potential problems of asymmetry of information between large and small Member States.

As already mentioned above, legal entities of banks located in the non-participating Member States would be unlikely to be significant, mostly because of asset size. They could be considered significant due to the other criteria used to designate a bank as significant, namely the size of the bank relative to other banks in the Member State or the level of cross-border presence in other participating Member States. For example, consider the exposure of Member States in the region to OTP Bank, a Hungarian bank present in Bulgaria, Croatia, Poland, Romania and Slovakia. In this case, the Hungarian authorities could in close cooperation surrender responsibility as the home supervisor to the ECB who would be the consolidated supervisor for the group, with an impact on cooperation with authorities of other non-participating Member States, given the bank's significant cross-border banking presence. However, if OTP's presence in those Member States was not considered material to the banking group as a whole then OTP could be supervised as a significant bank because it is one of Hungary's three largest banks. Moreover, in the case of Poland, the largest Member State in the non-participating Member State category (post Brexit[31]) is unlikely to experience a significant shift of banks to the SSM arrangement. At most it would see its top three largest banks move, according to recent figures regarding the size of assets of Polish banks.[32]

The CEE Member States provide another interesting dilemma for the Banking Union. While foreign banks are a crucial part of the banking system in their respective markets, they are unlikely to command the same commitment by the host authorities as would local domestic banks, since they are not the Member State's 'national champions'.[33] The experience from the global financial crisis is one of Member States and their central banks standing behind their respective national champions, meaning that in the CEE markets such political commitments may not be forthcoming.

The Banking Union is not proposing to rein in integration and jeopardise the benefits of cross-border banking. On the contrary, it is attempting to centralise supervision in order to better address the asymmetry of information problems of supervising and resolving cross-border banks in the different participating Member States.[34] In view of this centralisation, financial support is necessary in

---

[31] Ie after the withdrawal of the UK from the EU.

[32] Leading banks in Poland as of 4th quarter 2017, by total assets (in million Polish zloty): https://www.statista.com/statistics/765766/leading-banks-poland-assets.

[33] Nicolas Véron, Banking Nationalism and the European Crisis, "The Transformation of Europe's Financial Landscape" at the 30th Anniversary Symposium of the European Private Equity and Venture Capital Association (EVCA) in Istanbul, Turkey, on 27 June 27: https://piie.com/publications/papers/veron20130627.pdf.

[34] C Holthausen and T Rønde, Cooperation in International Banking Supervision, Working Paper Series, NO. 316 / MARCH 2004. https://www.ecb.europa.eu/pub/pdf/scpwps/ecbwp316.pdf?0bf69eb382026645f9754a6df187eee5.

order to develop the economies of scale for the financial arrangements to support resolution options. The move to pool resources should theoretically reduce conflicting incentives between the home and host Member States, and more specifically between large and small Member States, since the cost of resolution is likely to be different from the home and host perspective and since centralisation of supervision is not going to be enough to incentivise cooperation and coordination at the resolution level.

III. Wider Ramifications of Opting In or Out of the Banking Union

The Member States which do not participate in the Banking Union are varied and the benefits of opting in to the Banking Union need to be assessed on a case-by-case basis, since the move to close cooperation, as shown above, does not in practical terms create a level playing field between the Eurozone and those which may eventually decide to enter into close cooperation. Ultimately, the linchpins are those non-participating Member States which move to adopting the euro in place of national currencies once they meet the convergence criteria. It would be for the Council to decide whether those non-participating Member States have met the convergence criteria. This decision would ultimately be superseded by the political will of the Member State to adopt the euro. In this respect, the European Union consists of a number of subcategories of Member States, albeit there is sovereign equality in its legal foundations.

There are a number of considerations Member States should take into account before deciding on opting in. Since the criteria are not completely transparent, albeit having sound banks and be trusted to undertake supervision is a good starting point, opting in is not a matter of right since it is the ECB that ultimately decides on this. Moreover, the ability to formally showcase Member States entering into close cooperation is a signal of the ECB's movement in a relatively short period of time towards building the reputation of being a credible supervisory authority. The counterfactual is also evident, and the reluctance of Member States to enter close cooperation also signals a lack of confidence in the credibility of the ECB as a single supervisory authority, or doubts over its double role as also responsible for monetary policy for the Eurozone. This results in perhaps the most important obstacle to opting in, where the governance arrangements of the ECB, notably the Governing Council, do not allow for a seat for non-euro Member States. This is partly addressed by enabling Member States in close cooperation to attend Governing Council meetings relating to Supervisory Board decisions when the Governing Council is of the view that the Member State in question is likely to challenge the draft supervisory decision by the Supervisory Board. This is useful since it will enable the Member State to put forward its position before the Governing Council, which is generally not possible for a non-Eurozone Member

State. The leverage the ECB has, however, is the right to terminate the close cooperation, even if that right is shared with the opting in Member State as well. But it could also signal the need for the Member State to build up the capacity and resources to demonstrate it can put a credible case forward to the ECB to enter close cooperation. If one were to be elitist about the type of Member State entering close cooperation, the larger the non-participating Member State the better for the reputation of the ECB as a supervisor.

In view of the significant presence of EU foreign banks in the Eastern European banking market, the home and host relationship becomes very important. The relatively unique position of the ECB acting as the home and the host, will be a very important factor in considering close cooperation, as it is likely to mean fewer obstacles and challenges of cooperation and coordination within the Eurozone. A prospective participating Member State needs to reflect on the level of discretion it is likely to lose with the transfer of supervisory decision-making to the ECB. While it is assumed that competent authorities will cooperate with one another and share information on reciprocal basis, in practice this is not always forthcoming. This is a concern when it specifically relates to capital and liquidity levels.

It is important to consider how the underlying legal framework can propagate the home host challenges and home bias despite there being a single centralised supervisor. For example, if the ECB is acting as the consolidated supervisor for a significant bank within the Eurozone, the underlying model of consolidated supervision explicitly requires that the host State supply information and data to the ECB associated with a range of Capital Requirements Regulation, Regulation No 575/2013 (CRR) matters. However, the host State in this relationship is required to 'request' that information under the legal framework for its own purposes, ie to better supervise the subsidiary that is part of the group, especially where home State cooperation was not always forthcoming. Under the Banking Union, the ECB will also act for the host so there should be improvements in term of asymmetry of information. But the purpose of consolidated supervision is aimed at the interests of the group, which is likely to make the parent's position and indeed the leverage to influence matters that much greater on the whole, side-lining the views of the Member State where a subsidiary is located but that subsidiary being immaterial to the safety and soundness of the group. In the countries under consideration this is an acute problem, since the CRD IV and CRR frameworks and technical standards provide the consolidated supervisor significant discretion to act in the interests of the group rather than in a reciprocal manner. Finally, a dilemma exists with the transfer of decision making to the ECB and SRB when it comes to failing institutions and planning for resolution options and assessing the best options for the local circumstances. While a Single Point of Entry resolution strategy may be in place for the core part of the group, that does not negate the fact that the peripheral parts may be required to have a separate Multiple Point of Entry strategy in the form of insolvency. The benefits of centralised decision making in close cooperation would be a clear awareness of these decisions *ex ante* and the ability to prepare for such options. The decision as to whether the bank offers critical functions regardless of whether it is significant or less significant is another challenge at the heart of how banks need to be managed when they are experiencing problems. The NCA and NRA may be of the view that the bank is undertaking critical functions for the purpose of being classed an O-SII and it should equally be considered to be offering critical functions for the purposes of resolution as well. However, the SRB may decide otherwise when deciding on whether a bank should be dealt with in resolution or insolvency based on recent decisions,[35] see Table 12.1. However, again, the SRB would assess such options with the NRA in the resolution plans, so it is not as if the NRA would be in the dark on such matters.

Table 12.1 SRB Resolution Decisions

Name of bank	ECB significant bank	Other systemically important institution	Resolution – within public interest threshold	Liquidation – outside public interest threshold
Monte dei Pasche di Siena	✓	✓	✓	×
Banco Popular Español	✓	✓	✓	×
Banca Popolare di Vicenza SpA	✓	×	×	✓
Veneto Banca SpA	✓	×	×	✓
ABLV Bank Latvia (parent)	✓	✓	×	✓
ABLV Bank Luxembourg (subsidiary)	×	×	×	✓

The ECB relationship with a Member State in close cooperation as shown in Table 12.1 is akin to the agency relationship that the SRB exercises with Member States in the Banking Union. In view of this, those Member States in close cooperation will have transferred decision making for supervision and resolution to a centralised body but the NCA and the NRA retain responsibility for executing those decisions. The benefit of close cooperation, in many respects, is access to the single resolution fund and the proposed European single deposit guarantee fund (EDIS), once it is in place, as lines of defence during a crisis. Those should go some way to minimise the risks of home bias especially when the level of foreign

---

[35] See J-H Binder, M Krimminger, M Nieto and D Singh, 'The choice between judicial and administrative sanctioned procedures to manage liquidation of banks: A transatlantic perspective', unpublished manuscript, 2018.

bank presence in those markets give rise to a significant interconnection risk. They could also go a long way to minimise the risk of the host authority deciding *ex post* to ring-fence activities of the group operating in their jurisdiction to reduce local damage. In view of the importance of funding during a crisis, access to the SRF and EDIS go a long way towards minimise local bias in order to support orderly cross border resolution or payout and protect depositors in the interests of both the home and host State.

INDEX

NB – Page numbers in **bold** refer to information in tables and those in *italics* refer to information in figures

Ingram Content Group UK Ltd.
Milton Keynes UK
UKHW022309300323
419453UK00005B/107

9 781509 907540